D0604945

Imperial Gamble

Imperial Gamble

Putin, Ukraine, and the New Cold War

Marvin Kalb

BROOKINGS INSTITUTION PRESS
Washington, D.C.

Library of Congress Cataloging-in-Publication data is available.
ISBN 978-0-8157-2664-7 (cloth : alk. paper)
ISBN 978-0-8157-2665-4 (epub)
ISBN 978-0-8157-2744-6 (pdf)

9 8 7 6 5 4 3 2

Typeset in Minion

Composition by Elliott Beard

To Jon Sawyer

and the Pulitzer Center

for inspiring a new day of

informative and pioneering journalism

all over the world

Contents

Acknowledgments

THE IDEA FOR THIS BOOK came from Valentina Kalk, director of the Brookings Institution Press, and I am grateful to her and her colleagues for their encouragement and support. I enjoyed the project, which brought me back to an earlier time in my life when I covered Russia, Ukraine, and the rest of the Soviet Union for CBS News during the cold war. Most especially, I wish to thank Janet Walker, Bill Finan, Yelba Quinn, Rebecca Campany, and Carrie Engel; they were always there at the press when I needed them. John Felton, not for the first time, provided invaluable editorial advice and suggestions. He is a proven pro.

My friend Andrew Glass, a journalist of the highest quality, helped me, first, by listening to me and offering fresh ideas and, second, by carefully editing the whole manuscript. He again stretched the definition of friendship.

A small team of research assistants also pitched in and helped, none more so than Vassilis Coutifaris, whose technological wizardry continues to impress me and whose friendship I cherish. At the Pulitzer Center, where I currently hang my hat, Rebecca Gibian, Alyssa Howard, and Rachel Bolte each helped with research for a time, and Jin Ding displayed her technical artistry on an almost daily basis. Jon and Kem Sawyer, Nathalie Applewhite, Ann Peters, and Tom Huntley were more helpful than they probably realize. Thanks to them all.

As always, I am grateful to Michael Freedman, Heather Date, Robert Ludwig, and Lindsay Underwood for their advice and kindness, as well as to all other colleagues on the *Kalb Report*, a program I've hosted at the National Press Club for more than twenty years. Their friendship means so much to me.

Though they did not know it, I also benefited enormously from the work and guidance of the many scholars and officials associated with Brookings, Carnegie, the Peterson Institute, and the many centers of public policy inquiry in the Washington, D.C., area. They know their stuff, and, happily, they are ready to share it.

From day one of this project, no one has been a more constant source of encouragement and enlightenment than my brother, Bernard, a journalist of unparalleled honesty, dignity, and objectivity. His flaming curiosity has always inspired me; he ought to be a model for anyone calling himself or herself a reporter or, indeed, a citizen of a civilized world. He is the taller half of a twosome: his wife, Phyllis, is just as impressive and helpful.

Finally, in so many ways, I am a very lucky guy. I have a brilliant, sympathetic wife, Mady, my buddy for the past fifty-seven years; two exceptionally loving daughters, Deborah and Judith; their smart and responsible husbands, David and Alex; and their children—my grandson, Aaron, and granddaughter, Eloise, the lights of my life.

Shine on—you deserve a free and open world.

Preface

WHEN RUSSIAN PRESIDENT Vladimir Putin seized Crimea in late February 2014, in one stroke transforming the post–cold war diplomatic calculus, many Western statesmen and a good number of my colleagues, angry and disappointed, not only criticized him, bemoaning the return of a new harshness in East-West rhetoric; they also threatened economic sanctions and diplomatic isolation. Putin's gamble in Crimea (and it was a gamble) was reckless, even dangerous. Why had he acted so impulsively, so Russianly?

An international border was, after all, an international border, not to be violated by a powerful neighbor when it suited his interests. The Helsinki Accords of 1975, signed by Russian and Western leaders, specifically stated that Europe's borders would henceforth be regarded as "inviolable." More relevant, perhaps, ever since the Soviet Union and its creaky East European empire disintegrated in late 1991, Russia has signed a string of solemn agreements with the West guaranteeing the "territorial integrity" of all of the newly independent nations in Eastern Europe, those that were formerly component parts of Moscow's communist empire. Yet, despite these agreements, Putin gobbled up Crimea and, in short order, instigated a pro-Russian rebel insurrection in the southeast corner of Ukraine. One felt the chill of a new cold war.

For a time, with the demise of the Soviet empire, many of us, in a blush of naivete, hoped that a new dawn in international cooperation was rising, one in which Russia would play a positive role. From Western capitals came well-intentioned invitations to Moscow: opening doors and opportunities to this and that, even to the North Atlantic Treaty Organization (NATO), constructed, ironically, to repel Russia. But from the Russians, sadly, came only an occasional, and obviously reluctant, acceptance. Putin clearly had a different agenda in mind, framed by a deep distrust of Western intentions and an even deeper sense of national grievance: ever since the Soviet collapse in 1991, which he labeled "a major geopolitical disaster of the twentieth century," Russia had been wronged in many ways, he felt, and he was determined to right those wrongs.

Putin built a kleptomaniacal autocracy, which he has ruled like a modern mix of Stalin and Peter the Great. He cracked down on the media, narrowed the field of play for all foreign companies operating in Russia, and made it painfully clear that he would tolerate only gentle domestic criticism of his problematic policies. He pursued an ultra-nationalistic foreign policy. He basked in the glory of the 2014 Sochi Winter Olympics, and while strutting around the world like a spoiled Hollywood star, he yearned at the same time for Russia again to be recognized and respected as a global player. His brash diplomacy was often a convenient cover for Russia's traditional insecurities.

But in late 2013 things changed. Massive anti-Russian demonstrations began to rumble in Kiev's Maidan Square, threatening the position of Putin's client, Ukrainian president Viktor Yanukovych, and posing an appealing, democratic alternative to his autocratic rule. Putin worried not only about his own grip on power but also about Western encroachments into his backyard, his "sphere of influence," what Russians call the "near abroad." Then, in late February 2014, only a few months later, a frightened Yanukovych fled from Kiev, angry mobs barking at his heels. Putin blamed this dramatic turnaround on the West, on NATO, on the United States—all of them aligned, he charged, in an anti-Russian conspiracy and determined to stage a pro-Western "coup." In Putin's rear-view vision, Ukraine was losing its Slavic soul.

Chto delat'? "What's to be done?" as Lenin famously asked. Putin's answer was to seize Crimea, a low-hanging fruit that had been a part of the Russian empire since 1783, when Catherine the Great took it from the Turks. Actually, Crimea had been in and out of Russian hands for more than a thousand years; one of the out periods was from 1954 to 2014, when it officially was part of Ukraine. Putin's pretext was that the Russians who lived there, roughly 60 percent of the population, had to be protected from Ukrainian oppression. Far more likely, though, Putin imagined that the coup leaders in Kiev, whom he described as "fascists," were secretly plotting to occupy the Russian naval base at Sevastopol, Russia's only warm water port. And if the "fascists" did occupy Sevastopol, he feared, then NATO would not be far behind. Sevastopol was, for Putin, as for any Russian leader, a vital national interest, and, like the Russians living in Crimea, it too had to be protected.

Suddenly, as though on cue, "little green men" operating in uniforms without insignia appeared at Crimean airports, railroad stations, and radio and TV stations and, within a matter of days, took effective control of the entire peninsula. A short time later, the same "little green men," by this time identified as Russia's elite special forces, showed up in the Donbas region of eastern Ukraine, where many Russian-speaking Ukrainians lived. Again in uniforms without insignia, as in Crimea, they swiftly assumed administrative control of Donetsk and Luhansk and then, like throwbacks to the Soviet era, proclaimed their conquests as "People's Republics." The West pointed an accusing finger at the Kremlin, but Russian leaders pretended they had nothing to do with these rebel uprisings. This all happened with an unSlavic efficiency, as though the Russians had miraculously become Prussians. The world had turned a scary corner.

In diplomatic chanceries and think tanks, questions were raised, but not easily answered. After years of apparent indifference to events in Eastern Europe, many in the West, responsible for making or shaping policy for this neglected region, suddenly found themselves facing a spreading war in Ukraine and a geopolitical challenge unlike any since the early 1990s. What was Putin's strategy? What did he really want? Who was this chocolate king named Petro Poroshenko, who had emerged as an active supporter and financier of the Kiev coup? Before Ukraine could absorb Western military and financial support, was it even capable of reforming its corrupt politics and its crumbling economy? Who was behind the anti-Russian militia commanders, some of whom were seen unfurling Nazi-style banners? What, in fact, did the Western world know about Ukraine or, for that matter, contemporary Russia? In recent decades, not very much, as it turned out.

During the cold war, Western governments benefited from the advice of "Russian experts" who were consulted on policy choices. No longer, it seemed. Britain's House of Lords lamented in a special report that Europe had "sleep-walked" into the Ukraine crisis largely because of a "catastrophic misreading" of Russian policy and mood. Britain lacked, the report said, "a robust analytical capacity." One reason was that Western foreign ministries were described as ill-equipped to formulate an "authoritative response" to Putin's seizure of Crimea. There were too few Russian experts. In some cases, none. The ministries were caught flat-footed.

Now, post-Crimea, Western policy emerged more from a nostalgic, one-dimensional reading of Kremlin policy than from a realistic judgment, based on a sound reading of history. The unfortunate result was that many Western pundits and politicians painted Putin's seizure of Crimea in ahistorical blacks and whites, as if he were Hitler invading the Sudetenland as a prelude to World War II. Cartoonists labeled him "Putler." Statesmen thought he lived "on another planet." More damning, they based their Ukraine policy on uninformed and incomplete intelligence. They composed, for example, fanciful tales about Ukrainian "democracy," conveying the utterly misleading impression that it was a deeply ingrained political tradition in Ukraine and not a relatively new and fragile offshoot dating only to 1991, when Ukraine declared its independence from Soviet communism. Up to that point, but for a brief flickering moment during the 1917 Russian Revolution, Ukraine had never been independent or democratic.

By 2015 the Ukrainian crisis had gone from being a puzzling expression of Russian aggression to an unstoppable, devastating war. Cease-fires were painfully negotiated, and then quickly violated. The war was growing into a costly, complex cancer, raising doubts about European stability and fears of an even wider war. More than 6,000 people had already been killed, a million displaced, according to the United Nations. But before the war could be stopped, it had to be understood—a first step, one would have imagined, for diplomats, think tank experts, and journalists. But it was a first step rarely taken. Instead, the war provided rich fodder for the pundits and soon became a weapon in domestic politics: In Washington, the question was who was more strongly behind poor, struggling, "democratic" Ukraine, congressional Republicans or President Obama? In Moscow, was there anyone in or near the Kremlin with the courage to challenge Putin's problematic policy? And in Kiev, was Poroshenko tough enough, shrewd enough, to fight the Russian-supported rebels? The politicization of Ukraine frustrated diplomatic efforts to solve the conflict. It clearly was no time for cheap posturing, yet there was much of it on all sides. The longer the war continued, the more positions hardened. The more they hardened, the more difficult the search became for a political solution, the only sensible way out of the crisis.

How might one reach such a solution? Perhaps, I thought, in preparing this book, by dipping back into the history of the belligerents. What better way to appreciate their motivations, instincts, fears, and aspirations? One might then understand what was possible and realistic in a negotiation, and what was not. Indeed, it would not have been unreasonable for diplomats to dip all the way back to the tenth century, when there was a prosperous place in Eastern Europe called "Kievan Rus'." Responsible historians referred to this medieval empire not as "Ukraine" but as the "first Russia." This was a history, from Vladimir the Great to Vladimir Putin, that many in the West have tried over the years to study and understand, often with confusing results.

For example, recently in Kiev, Ukrainian legislators told a visiting American diplomat that they saw their war against the rebel insurgents in southeastern Ukraine in a broad historical context; they saw it as a "civil war" between Ukraine and Russia. The diplomat was momentarily stumped. How, he wanted to know, could they have reached such a conclusion? Ukraine and

Russia, the legislators explained, were both nations in an old, Slavic civilization that was now struggling to find its modern soul: Ukraine pulling in one direction, toward the West, and Russia holding fast in the East. Both knew that they shared a common history, a common culture, a common language base, a common faith. Their histories were intertwined. What affected one would inevitably affect the other as well.

If, for example, Ukraine were to win the current struggle, then Russia would in time have to bend to the West. That is the optimistic view, from the West's perspective. But if Ukraine were to lose, which is the more likely scenario, then it would have to bend to Russia's will, whether it liked to or not. Russia has always been the stronger, the more influential, of the two, the boyar as compared to the peasant, the mentor to the student. Still, stranger things have happened. Out of the current conflict may yet emerge a new alignment of Slavic powers. History may yet uncork a surprise.

Much of this might well have been in a corner of my mind when, on March 10, 2014, I had lunch at Washington's Cosmos Club with Valentina Kalk, the new director of the Brookings Institution Press, which had in recent years published two of my books, *Haunting Legacy*, co-authored with my daughter Deborah, and *The Road to War*. I was under contract with the press to write another book, focusing on my experiences as a journalist covering the cold war. Given my background, it seemed like a sensible subject. I had been involved with Russian affairs for most of my professional life.

In the early 1950s, I was a PhD candidate in Russian history at Harvard. As one of Professor Michael Karpovich's section men, I was privileged, on occasion, to substitute for him and teach a class on Kievan Rus' or the Cossacks. At the tail end of the Korean War, I joined the U.S. Army, where I studied North Korea's brutal treatment of American prisoners of war. Why this assignment and not another? We lived then in the "know your enemy" phase of the cold war. I spoke Russian and taught Russian history, which seemed to slot me for work in Army intelligence.

In 1956 a job opened at the U.S. Embassy in Moscow for a Russian-English translator. A Harvard colleague, knowing of my interest in Russia, recommended me, and I got the post. While there, I also worked as a very junior press officer and traveled throughout the Soviet Union, from Ukraine to Siberia. I returned to Harvard in early 1957. Four months later, after I wrote about Soviet youth for the *New York Times* and *The Reporter* magazine, the legendary broadcaster Edward R. Murrow offered me a job at CBS News as a writer and budding Moscow correspondent. I joyfully accepted. My PhD was shelved, but a career in journalism beckoned.

By the summer of 1959, I was back in Moscow, helping correspondent

Paul Niven cover Vice President Richard Nixon's visit to the Soviet Union. I was only a few feet from Nixon's memorable "kitchen debate" with Soviet leader Nikita Khrushchev. They argued, among other things, about which "system" of government would "bury" the other. Nixon won, but Khrushchev was more fun to watch. I returned to Moscow in May 1960, as CBS's bureau chief. It was an extraordinary time for a journalist: the shooting down of the American U-2 spy plane, the dangerous crisis in divided Berlin, and then the Cuban missile crisis, which brought the world to the brink of a nuclear war in October 1962.

While Americans were digging bomb shelters and ducking under desks for air raid alerts, I canvassed Russian attitudes toward war and the United States. The Russians did not expect war; many Americans did. On the fateful Sunday morning in late October when the crisis ended, I said in a broadcast that it appeared Khrushchev had "caved" to Kennedy's demand that he remove his nuclear-tipped missiles from Cuba. The president objected strongly to CBS over my use of the verb "caved." He did not want to "corner" Khrushchev, he explained, or to "humiliate" him. But in a later broadcast I again used the same verb. Thinking back, could I have used another verb to express the same thought? Probably.

Also in 1962 I joined a small group of reporters on a trip to Mongolia, a historic country locked in a crevice between China and Russia. I think we were the first Western reporters to crack the Iron Curtain there. Mongolia was at the time seeking both American recognition and admission to the United Nations. It was a study of communism in transition. But the trip almost led to my imprisonment in Ulan Bator, an unsettling end to an otherwise fascinating visit. CBS, a television network, obviously expected my cameraman, John Tiffin, to take pictures of what we saw, and Tiffin took pictures, many of them, always with a Mongolian minder at our side. His name was Lochin. Occasionally, he would warn us not to shoot an army truck passing by, or a policeman on duty, or a building, and we did not. I assumed we could shoot everything else. The question was, when we left, would I be allowed to take our exposed film with me? Mongolia had a law against shipping or carrying exposed film out of the country.

On the day of our departure, customs officials, spotting the exposed film in my suitcase, charged that I was breaking the law, and they took me into custody. Tiffin was let through. I was put in a small, dark room, where I waited for several hours. Finally, Lochin and a Mongolian military officer came and told me that I would be allowed to argue my case before a military jury. The jury consisted of three Mongolian officers. Behind them, in semi-darkness, sat a Russian colonel. His presence was somehow reassuring. The Mongolian officers asked a few pro-forma questions and then sent me back to my room. I waited another few hours, and then Lochin returned to escort me back to the jury room. The lead officer, with a dismissive wave of his hand, ordered me to leave Mongolia "immediately," even though, he stressed, I had violated the law. He said nothing about my exposed film, a deliberate omission, as it turned out, for it meant that I could take it with me. I was rushed back to the airport and through customs, and happily boarded a flight to Irkutsk, a bustling city on Lake Baikal in Siberia. At 18,000 feet, I finally took a deep breath. Mongolia down below looked calm and peaceful.

In February 1963 CBS named me its first diplomatic correspondent. I was transferred from Moscow to Washington. For many years thereafter, until the summer of 1980, operating primarily out of the State Department, I covered a wide range of stories from East-West summits to proxy wars, from Vietnam to the Middle East. In 1973–74 I accompanied Secretary of State Henry Kissinger on his famed "shuttle diplomacy" through the Middle East—from one Arab country to another, with frequent stops in Israel—in a ground-breaking attempt to find an acceptable formula for Arab-Israeli accommodation. It was a seminar in crisis management like no other, Russia always in the back of Kissinger's mind.

In 1980 I switched networks, largely because my boss at CBS, Bill Small, had left to become president of NBC News, and he asked me to join him. What I did at NBC was similar to what I had done at CBS, except I was given two additional responsibilities—anchoring its documentary series called "White Paper" and hosting its Sunday interview program "Meet the Press." In truth, though, no story absorbed me more than the plot to kill Pope John Paul II in May 1981, in which Russia played a suspicious role.

Then, in May 1987, came a job offer crafted in heaven: director of the new Shorenstein Center on the Press, Politics and Public Policy at Harvard's Kennedy School of Government. I accepted. I was also named Murrow Professor of Press and Public Policy. It was the highest compliment. When Murrow and I worked together at CBS, he often called me "Professor," possibly because I had left a career in teaching to join him.

Through all this time, from Moscow in the early 1950s to Cambridge in the late 1980s, no matter what I did on a day-to-day basis, I always found time to write books, most of them about Russia's role in the cold war. In all, I wrote or cowrote thirteen of them. I also wrote the introduction to Alexander Solzhenitsyn's *One Day in the Life of Ivan Denisovich*, the first of his books published in the West.

So, when Valentina and I spiced a good lunch with talk about Crimea and Putin, the natural topics of the day, she asked about my experiences in Russia. We spoke about Russian leaders from Khrushchev to Putin, and by dessert time she popped a question that took me totally by surprise. She asked if I might be interested in writing a book about the mushrooming crisis in Ukraine. I gulped. But what about my book on the cold war? I asked. She replied I could always pick up the threads of that book after finishing the Ukraine book. Off we went then, she back to the press and I to the Pulitzer Center, where I serve as senior adviser. No more than an hour after returning to the center, I shot her an e-mail gratefully accepting her offer. In a crowded year of researching, interviewing, writing, and editing, I learned a great deal: about Putin and Russia, about Poroshenko and Ukraine, about the United States and its West European allies. I learned, not for the first time, that East and West speak different languages, both literally and figuratively. Though they face a surprising number of common challenges, such as climate change and global terrorism, they often seem to live on different planets when considering solutions to these problems.

Ukraine is a prime example of a problem searching for a solution. Ideally, Western officials would like to see a Russian withdrawal from Crimea and an end to Russian support of the rebels in Donetsk and Luhansk. They would also like to see a free, independent and democratic Ukraine, tied however loosely to the West. They believe justice is on their side. Russia was undeniably the aggressor, and it must be made to pay a price. Unfortunately, judging by the balance of forces in the region, they are not likely to get their way.

Putin will not return Crimea to Ukraine, because Russians believe it never really belonged to Ukraine. They feel it always has been theirs. Nor will Putin abandon the rebels in southeastern Ukraine, because they have become his wards and because their realm gives him undeniable leverage over the future of all Ukraine. If there is a Putin doctrine, hidden somewhere in his rhetoric, it would be that people who consider themselves Russian, no matter where they live, cannot and will not be abandoned by Moscow. The Russians living in Estonia and Latvia may in time provide a pretext for a Russian move against these Baltic nations. Since both are NATO members, the United States would then be obliged by Article 5 of NATO's charter to come to their defense. If Putin, for whatever reason, were to leave the Ukrainian rebels on a slim limb, he would be inviting criticism from his own military-industrial complex, which depends on fat budget outlays and welcomes military adventures in Russia's "near abroad." More than anything, it seems, Putin wants to hold on to his job, and he cannot afford to risk losing the support of his old KGB buddies, especially at a time of punishing sanctions and economic woe. Putin may be an example of "impotent omnipotence"—philosopher Guillermo O'Donnell's apt description of an autocrat crowded by crushing problems.

There is another reason for Putin's infuriating intransigence, and it cuts to the heart of Russia's national policy. Here Putin is not the reckless, unorthodox, swaggering Kremlin chief usually depicted in the West, but rather one operating in the mainstream of Russian policy for the last 100 years and more. Like Yeltsin, Gorbachev, Brezhnev, Stalin, and Lenin before him, Putin believes that he cannot "lose" Ukraine to the West. With Ukraine under Moscow's thumb, these leaders have come to believe, Russia remains a major global power, exercising control (or, at a minimum, influence) over a vast Slavic empire running from the Polish border to the waters of the Pacific. Without Ukraine, Russia quickly becomes a vulnerable "regional power," to quote President Obama, subject to Islamic, possibly terrorist, pressures from the northern Caucasus and Central Asia.

In 1991 Yeltsin, deeply concerned about Islamic encroachments, all but begged Ukraine to join a Russian-led Slavic federation. He feared that without Ukraine, Islamic neighbors would quickly acquire too much power and force Russia, even in its own neighborhood, to slide into minority status. With Ukraine, he argued, not only Russia but the whole Slavic world, including Ukraine, would benefit, while holding Islamic forces in check. For a brief time, Ukraine listened to Russia's appeal and logic, but no longer.

History can explain Putin's policy, but only up to a point, and no one expects history to serve as an excuse for his policy. This book looks to history to help guide us toward a richer understanding of Russian and Ukrainian policy and politicians, hopefully even toward a possible approach to bringing the Ukraine war to an acceptable end. The rest, as a wise man once said, is only commentary.

Imperial Gamble

CHAPTER 1

Crimea: From Catherine the Great to Vladimir the Gambler

He is creating his own reality . . . his own sort of world.
JOHN KERRY

Putin is, in many ways, I think, delusional about this.
MADELEINE ALBRIGHT

IN CASE YOU MISSED IT, history is back, in a dizzying mix of Byzantine deception and Cossack adventurism. Some, with playful wit, have called it the "Soviet spring."

In late February 2014, shortly after the Sochi Winter Olympics, which succeeded in projecting the image of a sleek modern Russia, President Vladimir Putin suddenly sent his army, masked and minus insignia, into the Ukrainian peninsula of Crimea, which sits in the blue waters of the Black Sea. Save in the Kremlin, everyone, everywhere, seemed surprised, even shocked. In Western chanceries, protests were drafted and sanctions threatened. Within days, Crimea was occupied, and within weeks it was the Potemkin-like backdrop for a faux referendum, providing the legal pretext for its swift annexation by Russia. Barely a shot had been fired. For the first time in decades, a European border had been crossed, a nation's sovereignty violated, and diplomats and political leaders began to wonder whether they were witnessing the rebirth of the cold war.

This takeover immediately raised questions about Russian policy and intentions. Among the most pressing:

—Is Crimea just the beginning of a new expansionist policy for Russia?

—Will Russian-speaking eastern Ukraine be next, or will it be the odd sliver of Moldova called Transnistria?

—Or, worst of all, is it possible that Russia will test the cohesion of NATO by invading Latvia or Estonia on the Baltic?

It all came down to the decisions of one man: Putin, a one-time KGB lieutenant colonel—cunning, manipulative, and ultranationalistic—who was president of a severely vulnerable Russia and determined to right the wrongs he saw in post–cold war Europe. Another question quickly arose: Was Putin representative of Russia's rising political elite, or was he someone special? Put another way, had there been no Putin, would Russia still have annexed Crimea and triggered the subsequent crisis in eastern Ukraine? We shall never know for certain. Russian history does march to its own libretto, orchestrated in the Kremlin, where one person generally calls the tune. Crimea was juicy, available, low-hanging fruit. If it were not Putin, then another Russian leader might very well have swooped in and snapped it up, when he needed an easy victory. To make sense of the current Ukrainian crisis, one must first make sense of Putin and Russia's long and often troubled history.

Putin on a Couch

Searching for explanations, experts—Russian and non-Russian alike—have put Putin on the kind of couch often found in a psychiatrist's office. A number thought his adventure in Crimea proved he had lost his diplomatic marbles. German chancellor Angela Merkel confided to President Barack Obama that in her judgment, Putin was "in another world." Or, as Secretary of State John Kerry observed: "He's creating his own reality . . . his own sort of world." "It doesn't make any sense," former secretary of state Madeleine Albright confessed. "Putin is, in many ways, I think, delusional about this." And, if Putin was not "in another world," or "creating his own reality," or "delusional," he was, according to Brent Scowcroft, who served as national security adviser under President George H. W. Bush, "a person full of venom," suggesting he could not think rationally about Ukraine.[1]

Putin's seizure of Crimea was so startling, so disruptive of Western expectations, that many leaders seemed to forget that he had been the leader of Russia for the last decade and a half. He was not a new kid on the block. When stumped, unable to divine his next move, they would whisper behind a cupped hand that the newly assertive Russian leader was "nutty," "strange," and "unpredictable." Chess master Garry Kasparov described him as "evil, pure evil." Actually, as Henry Kissinger noted more accurately, "the demonization of Vladimir Putin is not a policy; it is an alibi for the absence of one."[2] But why "the absence of one?" One Putinologist (the modern-day equivalent of a

Soviet-era Kremlinologist) explained that "our ability to understand just what is driving him or what he actually wants to achieve is far weaker than it should be." So why this failure of insight and intelligence?

One possible explanation is the current shortage of Russia and Putin specialists. After the disintegration of the Soviet Union in 1991, Russian studies faded from academic curricula in the West, displaced by an emphasis on China, high technology, and the rise of radical Islam. The widespread feeling was that young scholars should be encouraged to go where the foundations distributed money and where universities cultivated job opportunities. Russia was considered passé, a legacy of an earlier era of East-West confrontation. Indeed, for a time after the cold war, Harvard, of all places, did not offer a course in Russian history. For several years, the university could not find a senior professor up to the task, and it seemed in no rush to find one. Likewise with the American media, which were in no rush to send reporters back to Russia after closing many of their Moscow bureaus.

Look further east, young scholar, to China, to Islam, to high tech, for that is where the promise of tenure and treasure burns most brightly.

Georgetown's accomplished Angela Stent summed up the problem. "Instead of embracing a deep understanding of the culture and history of Russia and its neighbors," she wrote, "political science has been taken over by number-crunching and abstract models that bear little relationship to real-world politics and foreign policy. Only a very brave or dedicated doctoral student would today become a Russia expert if he or she wants to find academic employment."[3]

Yet another explanation lies in the disillusionment felt by a string of American presidents, from Bill Clinton to Barack Obama, over their dealings with postcommunist Russian presidents—first Boris Yeltsin, who seemed unsteady in his gait and uncertain in his policies, and then Vladimir Putin, who seemed too frozen in old-fashioned grievances to appreciate the value of a number of opportunities that had been laid before him. In their exchanges, best described as minutes of optimism usually trailed by hours of gloom, these presidents hoped that Putin might flower into a pragmatic, pro-Western politician, sharing their vision of the post–cold war world. After all, it made sense, at least from Washington's perspective. And, for a brief time in late 2001, they thought they had found such a politician in Putin. He was, they noted, the first of major world leaders to express sympathy to President George W. Bush and the American people after the 9/11 terrorist attacks on the United States. Putin also allowed American warplanes to fly military supplies through Russian airspace to Afghanistan, a generous gesture few in

Washington had expected. The fight against terrorism was as high on Putin's list of worries as it was on Bush's, and for a time this common concern put the two leaders on the same path toward mutual cooperation and understanding.

But on two fundamental issues, namely, building democracy in Russia and encouraging independence in the former Soviet satellites, it soon became clear that the American presidents and Putin did not see eye to eye. Indeed, their relations suffered badly. And after the Crimean annexation, which violated the American sense of fair play and proper protocol in the twenty-first century, they began to see Putin as a resurgent, revanchist, old-school Russian bear. Reluctantly, wrote columnist Anne Applebaum, they concluded that Putin's Russia "is not a flawed western power," but an "anti-western power with a different, darker vision of global politics."[4]

Peter Baker, a reporter who covered the White House after completing an assignment in Moscow, wrote that the Russian leader did not speak the language of American presidents. Duplicitously, he "argued with them, lectured them, misled them, accused them, kept them waiting, kept them guessing, betrayed them and felt betrayed by them."[5] Putin was an exasperating adversary. What was he up to? For a time, when Russia after the cold war was seen as nothing more than a defeated, defanged, debilitated shadow of a country, no one seemed to know, and, moreover, no one seemed to care.

The Death of the Cold War

Much of this presidential disillusionment stemmed from an American failure to understand not only Putin, the KGB colonel who was now president, but also Russia, a once-proud nation that found itself in a deep pit of decay and disorientation. Imagine for a moment the earth-shattering changes that confronted a Russian leader—really that confronted any leader—at the end of the last century and the beginning of the new one:

—Demise of the cold war, which had framed decades of East-West confrontation from the late 1940s to the early 1990s;

—Unexpected disintegration of the Soviet Union, which led quickly to proclamations of independence by former Soviet satellites in Eastern Europe and, more significantly, by former Soviet republics from the Baltics to central Asia;

—Collapse of communism as a governing philosophy—everywhere, it seemed, except Cuba; and

—Smashing of the Berlin Wall and the amazingly peaceful reunification of Germany in the heart of Europe.

No state could be more concerned by these changes than the old Soviet Union, which was swiftly reduced to a shadow of its old self called Russia. But what was this Russia? Yesterday it was a nuclear-armed superpower; today is it a nuclear-armed wimp? How was Russia to deal with its reduced stature? How would its leading politicians explain this change to a puzzled populace, assuming they were willing to acknowledge the change? Would Russia need another Yeltsin, or another Stalin?

Perhaps it was inevitable that in this whirlwind of diplomatic uncertainty, a myth emerged, principally in the West, that undercut the chance for a better Russian-American relationship. The myth, at once understandable but still dangerously misleading, was that the United States had "won" the cold war. Much closer to the truth was that the United States had "survived" the cold war, while the Soviet Union had slumped into an embarrassing heap. It seemed as if Ronald Reagan had got it right when he wrote in his memoirs that it was the victory of one system of government over another—in other words, of capitalism over communism or, put another way, individual freedom over collective diktat.[6]

By suggesting that the United States had defeated the Soviet Union, like one nation over another in a hot war, the myth put Washington in the diplomatic catbird seat, thinking of itself as the capital of a victorious nation able to dictate terms to the vanquished—or, if not always to dictate, then surely get its way on just about anything it fancied. To be sure, it should have been expected that Russia, in this shriveled state, would angrily object and even come up with obstructionist alternatives. It could, much like Germany after World War I, wait for a charismatic hero to rise from the ashes of defeat to lead the nation to a new mountaintop of resurrection and—why not?—revanchism. Hitler was that leader for Germany. Would Putin be that leader for Russia?

A haughty arrogance defined Western and American attitudes toward Russia in the immediate post–cold war period. Questionable and controversial policies blossomed, like roses in springtime, none more important and consequential than the eastward expansion of the North Atlantic Treaty Organization (NATO), which the Russians, during the cold war and afterwards, always regarded as a direct threat to their basic national security interests. NATO expansion meant extending a Western military alliance, created originally as a bulwark against Soviet expansionism, to Russia's very borders. If you were a Russian president or strategist, how would you have reacted? Would you have seen it as a "provocation" or would you have accepted it as an essentially meaningless gesture?

Sergei Karaganov, a respected foreign policy analyst at Moscow's Higher

School of Economics, explained the current crisis in Russian-American relations by going back to this pivotal issue of NATO expansion. "The rupture is due to the West's refusal to end the Cold War de facto or de jure in the quarter century since the collapse of the Soviet Union," he has written. "In that time, the West has consistently sought to expand its zone of military, economic and political influence through NATO and the E.U. Russian interests and objections were flatly ignored. Russia was treated like a defeated power, though we did not see ourselves as defeated. A softer version of the Treaty of Versailles was imposed on the country. There was no outright annexation of territory or formal reparations like Germany faced after World War I, but Russia was told in no uncertain terms that it would play a modest role in the world. This policy was bound to engender a form of Weimar syndrome in a great nation whose dignity and interests had been trampled."[7]

Karaganov's argument, which seems to closely reflect Putin's own thinking, deserves a rebuttal. First, Russia's interests were recognized, though clearly not in the way Karaganov would have preferred. A NATO-Russia council was formed, specifically to ease Russian concerns about NATO's eastward expansion. Russia was invited to join a "Partnership for Peace" program, and Russia was recognized as one of the world's leading industrial powers, a bow more to its bruised ego than to its industrial might, for many did not really believe Russia deserved membership. Russia's formal admission to this elite society expanded the Group of Seven into the Group of Eight, and Russia remained a member until it annexed Crimea in March 2014. Then, as punishment, its membership was suspended.

Second, after the collapse of both communism and the Soviet Union, Russia was, in fact, "defeated." Only in a world of dreams, where nostalgia trumped reality, could Russia seriously be regarded as a "great power." Still, even though the cold war had ended, a number of key policymakers in Washington, who were fiercely anticommunist, remained distrustful even of a "defeated" Russia. For them, NATO expansion served as an insurance policy against the possibility of a resurgent Russia.

In 1949 NATO was a defense-oriented collection of twelve Western nations bound by an Article Five pledge that an attack on one would be regarded as an attack on all. For the next three decades, during the height of the cold war, NATO added only four new members—West Germany, Greece, Turkey, and Spain. But when the Soviet Union began to crumble and come apart in 1991, NATO looked covetously to the east. Taking advantage of Russia's relative weakness, it added twelve new members to its alliance, most of them former Warsaw Pact allies of the former Soviet Union, all seeking NATO protection against the prospect of a resurgent belligerent Russia. They are Albania, Bulgaria, Croatia, the Czech Republic, Estonia, Hungary, Latvia, Lithuania, Poland, Romania, Slovakia, and Slovenia.

Only a handful of Western analysts questioned the presumed wisdom of this military expansion. Realistically, Russia was no longer in a position to attack the West. It was too weak, and it was no longer the driving engine of an expansionist communist ideology. Indeed, the original raison d'être of NATO—a military alliance against the Soviet Union—could well have been challenged; but it was not challenged, and the expansion continued. Western leaders looked further east, even southeast. Georgia was considered for NATO membership. Russian strategists wondered why NATO needed an outpost in the Caucasus. Even Ukraine, until 2008, was considered for membership. The Kremlin bristled. Putin strongly objected to such a prospect. Everyone knew—or should have known—that, for the Kremlin, Ukraine was special. After all, it had been part of the Russian empire for hundreds of years. In Moscow's view, so it would remain! Putin told President George W. Bush in 2008: "You have to understand, George, that Ukraine is not even a country. Part of its territory is in Eastern Europe and the greater part was given to them by us."[8] The Kremlin's thinking seemed to be that if Ukraine wanted to play around with this Western notion of independence, fine, but Moscow made it clear that, independent or not, Ukraine would remain under Russia's firm influence and control. No Western leaders chose either to listen or to comprehend what Putin was signaling.

Even though the Russians complained bitterly, NATO's policy held, always on the assumption in Western capitals that the Kremlin was in no position to do anything more than bellow at the winds of expansion. The Russians had lost and we had won, American strategists argued. President George H. W. Bush bluntly told German chancellor Helmut Kohl, "We prevailed, and they didn't. We can't let the Soviets clutch victory from the jaws of defeat."[9] One day, William Safire, the *New York Times*'s sharp-tongued columnist, giddily praised NATO's continuing expansion. Afterward, over dinner, I told Safire I thought he might have gone too far. "No," he replied, always the happy warrior, "when your enemy is down, kick him." George Kennan, the American diplomat who penned the famous "X" article in 1947 spelling out the policy that came to be known as "containment" and that defined American policy throughout the cold war, disagreed with Safire; he denounced NATO expansion. "The Russians will react quite adversely," he told Thomas L. Friedman, another *Times* columnist. "I think it is a tragic mistake. . . . It shows so little understanding of Russian history and Soviet history." Friedman, inspired by

Kennan, wrote disparagingly of American policymakers, citing specifically President Bill Clinton and his top advisers. "We are in the age of midgets," he noted with barely disguised contempt. NATO expansion showed their "utter poverty of imagination."[10]

Enter Fukuyama

But interestingly it was not the likes of a Kennan or a Friedman who accurately reflected the mood of Washington's policymakers and pundits at that time. They were exiled to a narrow shelf in a corner of the room. It was rather the writings of Francis Fukuyama, a relatively unknown State Department official. The then 36-year-old scholar with a Harvard PhD was serving as deputy director of policy planning. More than anyone else, he best framed the argument of American triumphalism after the end of the cold war. In so doing, he became an overnight literary and political sensation as author of an article, "The End of History?" in 1989 and then a book entitled *The End of History and the Last Man*.

When the cold war finally sputtered to a close, many questions arose over the ideological conflict between East and West:

—Was the conflict really over?

—If it was, had the United States won? Yes, but . . .

—Would a successor ideology rise to replace communism? Possibly, but . . .

—Most important, what happens now?

Everyone wanted to know the answers to these questions. Fukuyama, with perfect timing, entered the klieg-lighted arena of Washington policy and punditry with the answers—or so it appeared to quite a few decisionmakers and pundits at the time. If Kennan, years before, had written the definitive "X" paper on America's cold war policy toward the Soviet Union, then Fukuyama now seemed to have drafted its legitimate, post–cold war successor thesis. In fact, newspaper commentators immediately speculated that Fukuyama's end-of-history would emerge as the intellectual backbone for President George H. W. Bush's policy toward postcommunist Russia.

So what precisely was the Fukuyama thesis? The soft-spoken scholar/ bureaucrat borrowed extensively from the German philosopher G. W. F. Hegel, who held that history reflected a protracted struggle between freedom and oppression; one day freedom would win the struggle and become the dominant political philosophy in global affairs. In the twentieth century, Fukuyama wrote, the forces of freedom, marshaled by the United States, had decisively defeated the forces of totalitarianism, controlled from Moscow. He saw this as the ultimate triumph of freedom—the long-awaited "end point of mankind's ideological evolution and the universalization of Western liberal democracy." That meant, in his view, that America's unique brand of "liberal democracy" would now be able to spread throughout the world, no longer facing any significant ideological competition. Thus, "history" would "end." Fukuyama sounded serious, awesomely so. But his thesis was, in fact, a shallow description of what was, in reality, a complex turn in history.[11]

Still, here at last was a story with a seemingly happy ending, and it quickly zoomed to the top of the best-seller lists. Its author was befuddled by his swift leap from policy planner to intellectual rock star. "I don't understand it myself," he modestly told a *New York Times* reporter. "I didn't write the article with any relevance to policy. It was just something I'd been thinking about."[12]

Everyone in and around government read Fukuyama, although, to be sure, not everyone bought into his thesis. Irving Kristol, a seminal neo-conservative writer, said, "I don't believe a word of it." The late Christopher Hitchens sneered, "At last, self-congratulations raised to the status of philosophy." Strobe Talbott, then *Time* magazine's principal correspondent on Soviet-American relations and now president of the Brookings Institution, brushed it away. "'The End of History?'" he asked; "more like 'The Beginning of Nonsense,'" he answered.

Political scientist Robert Kagan, a senior fellow at Brookings, also joined this dissident jury of Fukuyama critics. In an erudite essay in 2008, replete with historical analogies, entitled "The End of the End of History," Kagan acknowledged that if only one political philosophy had survived the cold war, and it was "liberal democracy," as Fukuyama asserted, then that would indeed be a most gratifying outcome. But unfortunately that was not the case. For centuries, ever since the Enlightenment, argued Kagan, liberalism had contended with autocracy for ideological supremacy. Even though the end of the cold war did introduce a "new era" in global relations, liberalism had failed to emerge as the unchallenged victor. In different guises, autocracy continued to wage a relentless war against liberalism. Kagan forecast "growing tensions and sometimes confrontation between the forces of democracy and the forces of autocracy" for decades to come. The twenty-first century, he wrote, far from it becoming an oasis of democratic values, would more likely resemble the struggles, wars, and conflicts of the nineteenth century.[13] Beijing's attempts to project its power into the East and South China Seas and Russia's irredentist threats against its "near abroad" neighbors, principally Ukraine, in addition to the upheavals rocking the Arab world, testify to the accuracy of Kagan's forecast and the fragility of Fukuyama's.

But still, even if Fukuyama thought that the dissolution of the Soviet Union and the demise of communism ended history (in fairness, he did put a question mark after the word "history" in his original 1989 essay), Putin put an end to this theoretical prattle when he boldly annexed Crimea on March 21, 2014. Suddenly, history was back—it had never left!—and political figures on both sides of the crisis in Ukraine sought to make their points through historical allusions. From each perspective, "history" added a patina of legitimacy to their policy pronouncements.

CHAPTER 2

The End, or the Beginning, of History

We are in the twenty-first century. We don't solve conflicts militarily.
ANGELA MERKEL

IN THIS RENEWED CONFRONTATION, the United States sought to pre-empt the twenty-first century, ascribing to it virtues and values as noble as democracy, individual liberty, and economic progress, while at the same time disparagingly tossing the nineteenth century to Russia, as if only in the nineteenth century could one have come upon war, aggression, corruption, and deception. Early in the Ukraine crisis, on March 2, 2014, Secretary of State John F. Kerry reached back into history to make his case against Russia. Appearing on a blizzard of Sunday morning interview programs, he denounced Russian aggression in Crimea. "It's really nineteenth century behavior in the twenty-first century," Kerry proclaimed. "You just don't invade another country on phony pretexts in order to assert your interests."[1] Time and again, Kerry would use this juxtaposing of centuries to criticize Russian behavior. Were Putin and his svelte foreign minister, Sergei Lavrov, to have listened to Kerry, they might have been heard to reply, "Really?"

During a visit to Western Europe in late March 2014, President Obama reinforced Kerry's nineteenth- and twenty-first-century juxtapositions, repeatedly suggesting that Russia's military absorption of Crimea was reminiscent of the barbaric nineteenth century and America's measured but firm response reflected a more enlightened twenty-first century. German chancellor Angela Merkel began echoing the same theme. "We are in the twenty-first century," she told reporters. "We don't solve conflicts militarily."[2]

The president stopped to visit the U.S. Flanders Fields cemetery in Belgium, just months before the 100th anniversary of the start of World War I. "Flanders Fields" is the catch-all title for an early twentieth-century killing field in a war-battered Europe. While there, Obama recited from "In Flanders

Fields," a poem written in 1915 by Lt. Col. John McCrae, a Canadian army physician, who was deeply moved by the indiscriminate slaughter of Allied soldiers. Obama was reminding everyone about the long record of American sacrifice on behalf of European security. He was also saying that there were times when wars were necessary tools of statecraft, a theme he had first struck when he delivered his Nobel Prize speech in Oslo, Norway, in December 2009, though this was a theme he now often soft-pedaled.[3]

> To you from falling hands we throw
> The torch, be yours to hold it high,
> If ye break faith with us who die
> We shall not sleep, though poppies grow
> In Flanders Fields.

A frequent Obama theme during the early days of the Ukraine crisis was that although relations between Russia and the West had soured abysmally since the Kremlin's annexation of Crimea, he did not believe that the world was returning to the cold war. Rather, Obama seemed to believe that there were no repeats in history, and observers, if possible, should try to keep things in perspective. "This is not another cold war that we're entering into," he said. "After all, unlike the Soviet Union, Russia leads no bloc of nations, no global ideology."[4] On other occasions, Obama would use a similar formulation to belittle Russia, no longer referring to it as a "superpower" but rather as a "regional power." Obama had to have known that such a dismissive putdown would infuriate Putin, but he didn't seem to care. Obama never liked, or particularly respected, Putin.

Normally the cool, unflappable negotiator, Obama allowed his dislike for Putin to influence his policy toward Russia. In the halls of diplomacy, it has often been said that nations have interests, and nations should not allow personalities to determine those interests. Apparently, Obama had permitted his displeasure with Putin to shape America's policy toward Russia. Whether it was Putin's KGB background or whether it was his policies, Obama seemed instinctively to pull back from any positive, long-term relationship with Putin.

Actually, when Putin assumed power in Russia on December 31, 1999, there were concerns in Moscow about his KGB background. "Be kind to Russia," Boris Yeltsin pleaded with Putin, as he handed the keys to the kingdom to his younger protégé. Yeltsin was apparently concerned not only about Russia's shattered economy and disorganized politics but also about Putin's predisposition to see the world through a KGB lens. And at the beginning of his tenure in the presidency, Putin did try to balance Russia's interests and even extend a hand of friendship toward the West. But as the years passed and problems, both domestic and foreign, mounted, his grip on power tightened, and he relied more and more on his veteran KGB allies. "They're back," moaned Naina Yeltsin, the former president's wife, referring to Putin's reliance on his onetime KGB buddies.

One of the first moves Obama made on the foreign policy front when he assumed the presidency in January 2009 was to "reset" U.S. policy toward Russia. He would try to pull it out of the rut left by the Bush administration and put it on a promising track. One way was for Obama to go around Putin, who had just accepted the lesser post of prime minister after finishing eight years as president, and instead embrace Dmitry Medvedev, the newly installed Russian president, whose early pronouncements suggested a willingness to open Russia to meaningful change. Before visiting Moscow in July 2009, Obama told the Associated Press that he was going to develop "a very good relationship" with Medvedev, in part because Putin displayed "cold war approaches" to East-West relations. "I think Putin has one foot in the old ways of doing business," said Obama, "and one foot in the new."[5] In Moscow, where such criticism predictably was not appreciated, Obama spent five hours negotiating with Medvedev (including a dinner) and only one hour (during breakfast) with a disgruntled Putin, who still remained the most powerful political figure in the country. Before their brief and uncomfortable talk, an unsmiling Putin, sitting beside Obama, said on Russian TV that "there were periods when our relations flourished quite a bit and there were also periods of, shall we say, grayish mood between our two countries and of stagnation." Putin clearly placed himself in the "grayish" zone.[6]

During the next two years, as Obama wooed Medvedev, relations between the United States and Russia bloomed, largely because both countries wisely focused on issues of common concern, such as the war in Afghanistan, terrorism, and nuclear arms reductions. However, whenever the focus shifted back to the question of democracy-building in Russia and NATO's eastward expansion, relations suffered, no more so than in late 2011, when disputed legislative elections in Russia triggered an extraordinary series of anti-Putin protests. Tens of thousands demonstrated holding inflammatory banners reading "Russia without Putin." Putin's antagonists charged voter fraud, probably with good reason. Putin's party, United Russia, won 52 percent of seats in the Russian Duma, a dramatic drop from the 70 percent it had won in the 2007 election. One protester in February 2012 bravely informed *The Guardian*: "Under Putin, many thieves have come to power. The authorities are totally closed. They don't talk to the people. We want to choose leaders who listen to us. And we don't want to worship a single person." He was not the only Russian who agreed to speak to foreign reporters.[7]

Obama's secretary of state, Hillary Clinton, expressed sympathy for the demonstrators. How could she not! Although she voiced her views with lawyer-like restraint, Putin nevertheless blew his top, accusing Clinton of funneling "hundreds of millions" of dollars to the demonstrators and encouraging "mercenaries" to disrupt public order. "She set the tone for some opposition activists," he charged, "gave them a signal, they heard this signal and started active work."[8] Even though Putin's popularity had dropped during his time as prime minister, he still won a third term as president, which was not really a surprise. When, shortly after his inauguration on May 7, 2012, another anti-Putin demonstration took place, he launched a sweeping crackdown on domestic dissent and opened a generally anti-Western, and specifically anti-American, campaign designed to appeal to the deeply conservative character of many in Russian society.

Putin created the image of the "good Russian," someone devoted to traditional family values, someone who was patriotic and religious, someone decidedly different from the "faceless, sexless mass" supposedly tolerated in the West. He had his obedient Duma pass antigay legislation, promptly approved by 88 percent of the Russian people.[9] He stripped to his waist, flexed his muscles, rode horseback across the Siberian steppes, shot wild animals—he did anything to strengthen the homophobia he wanted his followers to assume was rampant in Russia.

One reason for his movie star approach to domestic politics was the urgent need to reverse the nation's declining birth rate. In Soviet times, the population was about 240 million. Now it had fallen to 143 million and showed signs of a continuing drop.[10] For a time, Putin also halted American adoptions of Russian orphans.

In 2013 U.S.-Russian relations went into an even deeper tailspin when Putin granted temporary asylum to National Security Agency whistleblower Edward Snowden. Obama responded by canceling a planned Moscow summit with Putin, the first time in fifty years such a summit had been canceled.[11]

A sign of the chilly Russian-American relationship was a photo of Obama and Putin at a G-8 summit meeting in Scotland in 2013. It caught them in a pose of mutual disrespect. The photo reflected reality more accurately than a dozen briefings. Neither one wore a tie, and neither made an effort to smile or appear friendly. They sat on opposite sides of a small table, their hands folded, their faces showing sad acceptance of the fact that at this point they had little to say to each other. Obama pursed his lips and stared away; Putin looked dyspeptic. They were going through the motions of diplomatic proto-col but defeating its very purpose by failing to show even the slightest interest or pleasure in each other's company. Clearly, Obama had come to see Putin and Russia largely as dead-end projects, not as a person or a place where hard diplomatic work could possibly produce a happy outcome. Sadly, Obama and America had come to be seen by Putin in a much more unfavorable light.

Still, when the European Union offered a hand of friendship to Ukraine in late 2013, offering it EU membership and thereby an institutional link to the West, Obama quickly supported the initiative, suspecting Russia would object. Why then extend the offer? Probably for PR value. Possibly to annoy Putin. It was a way to show the world that the United States would go the extra mile to improve bilateral relations with Kiev. In concert with other West-ern leaders, Obama usually blamed Putin for most East-West problems. He personalized his Russia policy, apparently hoping Putin would fail and van-ish from the scene. Obama seemed to see the chance for cooperation in the future, but not now. Maybe Medvedev would return to power, maybe some-one else, but not Putin. This was short-sighted. "Putin is a reflection of Rus-sia," explained Matthew Rojansky, a Russia expert at Washington's Woodrow Wilson Center, a think tank. "This weird notion that Putin will go away and there will suddenly be a pliant Russia is false."[12]

In effect, the EU and Obama were trying to entice Ukraine to bond with the West. Wasn't Ukraine entitled to freedom and democracy? officials asked. Why must Ukraine be saddled with the dark legacy of East European autocracy and inefficiency? This made good sense in the White House, but not in the Kremlin, where Ukrainian acceptance of the EU's invitation could mean the effective end of Putin's cherished dream of a Eurasian economic union, one in which Ukraine would be a crucial player. It would also mean that a western-ized Ukraine would function, possibly even prosper, on the borders of Russia, one that might be dangerously attractive to the Russian people. For Putin, who needed no additional evidence of what he considered Western duplicity, this proved that the West was seeking once again, as it had done during the cold war, to surround Russia with hostile neighbors. "The real red line," said for-mer U.S. ambassador Jack Matlock, whose knowledge of Russia was deep, "has always been Ukraine. When you begin to poke them in the most sensitive area, unnecessarily, about their security, you are going to get a reaction that makes them a lot less cooperative."[13]

As Putin described it, the very existence of NATO was a "most sensitive area," a strategic challenge that has always bothered the Kremlin. Its actual expansion eastward toward Russia was one problem; its treaty language posed a different kind of problem, even though few leaders might have ever bothered to read the whole text. What most of them knew about the treaty was Article Five, which said, quite unmistakably, that an attack on one would be considered an attack on all, requiring, if necessary, a full military response, namely, war. As the Ukrainian crisis deepened, American leaders felt the need to underscore America's commitment to Article Five, using such words as "firm," "absolute," and "unshakable." Obama and Kerry wanted especially to reassure the three Baltic members of NATO—Lithuania, Latvia, and Estonia—plus Poland that if Russia attacked any one of them, or all of them, the United States would come to their immediate assistance. But how? That was the question—it had always been the question, when the subject of NATO commitments arose. With words, or air power, or naval intervention? Or with American boots on the ground? Or with a mix of modest military action backed by a major diplomatic demarche? What would it be? Words or action or perhaps "consultation," a word also in Article Five as a kind of escape hatch if one were needed?

Over the years, American diplomats and politicians have often spoken of a strong commitment to Article Five. In a TV interview after a NATO meeting in Ankara, Turkey, I once asked Defense Secretary Caspar Weinberger whether the United States would, without doubt or hesitation, defend Turkey with planes and troops were Turkey to be attacked by guerrilla bands from the neighboring Soviet Union or by Russian army units bursting across the border. Weinberger grimly replied: "Of course, Article Five says an attack on one would be regarded as an attack on all." He paused, before adding, "The language of the treaty is very clear." I pressed him further, but got nowhere.

Later that evening, on a flight from Ankara to Paris, Weinberger invited me to join him in his private quarters in the front of the plane.

"Why did you ask that question?" he wanted to know.

I told him I asked it because I had never believed the standard answer from him or any other U.S. official—that the United States adheres to Article Five, because . . . well, the United States says it adheres to Article Five. But just what does that mean? Under what circumstances? When there is an overwhelming attack? Or when a guerrilla force crosses an allied national border? Does the American response depend on the severity of the provocation? I was interested in a credible official explanation.

"Exactly," Weinberger interrupted me.

"Exactly what?" I wondered.

Weinberger wiggled in his seat. "We need the ambiguity," he said. "Then we'll decide. The bottom line is we have to give the president room to say 'yes,' 'no,' or 'maybe.' We have to consult."

"Then what's the value of Article Five, if nothing is automatic?"

"We need the implied ambiguity," he repeated and ended our conversation. Weinberger was not happy that I had asked the question, or that I had been left dissatisfied with his answer.

The point of Article Five has always been ambiguity, to leave the American president with a range of options, not to lock him into a rhetorical vise. And yet, in the Ukraine crisis, Obama and Kerry skipped no opportunity to stress that the United States remained committed to Article Five, and that NATO nations on the border of an agitated Russia could count on a firm, clear American military response if Russia moved against them. Obama insisted in neon-lighted language that if Russia crossed a NATO border, the United States would fight. "What we will do—always—is uphold our solemn obligation, our Article Five duty," he stressed, "to defend the sovereignty and territorial integrity of our allies." He continued, hitting every word with special emphasis: "And in that promise we will never waver; NATO nations never stand alone." The president clearly hoped Putin was listening. [14] Kerry used similar language, apparently with the Baltic NATO members in mind. "We have to make it absolutely clear to the Kremlin," echoed the secretary of state, "that NATO territory is inviolable. We will defend every single piece of it." Then, with an almost plaintive pitch to his voice, he added, interestingly: "Article Five of the NATO treaty must mean something, and our allies on the front lines need and deserve no less."[15] Was there any doubt in Kerry's mind about whether NATO's Article Five did "mean something," a doubt he was now trying to erase? Was he concerned that the United States was promising more than it could realistically deliver? That was the urgent question one heard in many Washington conversations.

From NATO's very inception, everyone understood that the key decision on the implementation of Article Five would rest with the American president, and he always needed to retain options. Obama could not have only the one option of going to war, in defense of an endangered NATO ally, without first going to Congress for approval, or taking account of public opinion polls, or making sure he had sufficient allied support. He could also change his mind. In 2013 Obama favored air attacks against Bashar al-Assad's forces in Syria, but running into stalwart congressional opposition, he risked political embarrassment and flip-flopped. From one day to the next, he dropped the strike option, explaining that in exchange he got Assad (with Putin's help, no doubt) to give up his chemical weapons. To be sure, Syria was hardly a NATO ally, but the episode demonstrated that presidents could indeed change their minds.

It must be obvious that, in the Ukraine crisis, too, the United States has stood firmly behind its commitment to Article Five, but it must be equally obvious, from public opinion polls and pundit commentary, that the American people lack any appetite for further military adventures. Indeed, they seem now to favor a foreign policy less risky, less costly, less draped in khaki. This was not a new form of isolationism, as many feared, but it was a powerful sentiment, as George Washington famously put it in his Farewell Address, to "avoid foreign entanglements," at least for the foreseeable future. After the Iraq and Afghanistan wars, following so closely on the heels of the Balkan engagements of the 1990s, the wisdom of continuing a policy of American military intervention here, there, and seemingly everywhere has come in for serious questioning, except when Obama decided in 2014 to bomb Islamic State strongholds in Iraq and Syria. Even though the president commands an all-volunteer force, he is not a medieval European monarch able to order his troops into battle without taking account of public opposition, especially if such a venture showed signs of coming up short. Presidents have been seared by America's Vietnam experience, when the nation's streets were crowded with angry antiwar protestors. Patriotism still retains its post-9/11 clout, but it no longer serves as a mindless lubricant for war.

Were Putin to choose to challenge Obama frontally, he needed only threaten a small NATO nation, such as Estonia, stir up latent pro-Russian sentiment there, move a few Russian battalions toward the border, and Estonia would likely invoke Article Five. What would Obama do? Would he go to war to defend Estonia? The question, asked, let us imagine, at a street corner rally, would ignite a chorus of doubts and second-guessing, out of which would quickly flow other questions about America's reliability as a NATO ally, Obama's toughness, or weakness, such as it may be, Putin's true strategic goals, and, in the final analysis, NATO's continued value as a military alliance. If Estonia could not depend on NATO at crunch time, could America, or France, or Germany? In other words, a Russian military move against a small Baltic country, such as Estonia, could result in the humiliation of an American president and the unraveling of NATO.

In his Ukraine quiver, Putin had many options, ranging from Crimea to the Baltic states and perhaps even to a diplomatic pause on his march to imperial glory. Again, no one at the White House, from Obama on down, could be sure.

CHAPTER 3

Putin's March 18 History Lesson

They are constantly trying to sweep us into a corner. But
there is a limit to everything. . . . If you compress the spring
all the way to its limits, it will snap back hard.
VLADIMIR PUTIN

ON MARCH 18, 2014, in a Kremlin speech explaining—and justify-
ing—the formal annexation of Crimea into Russia, Putin roamed through
his country's history to provide fascinating insights into his thinking and his
policies.[1] By seizing Crimea, Putin arbitrarily changed the ground rules of
modern international relations, throwing the rest of the world into a whirl of
diplomatic uncertainty. "Whither Putin?" became the question of the day. It
opened the door to the broader questions of "whither Russia?" and "whither
Ukraine?"

In Russia, where the news media, after a brief flirtation with freedom in
the 1990s, have once again become the tamed mouthpiece of the state, where
policy options are rarely if ever leaked in advance as a way of judging popular
appeal or acceptance, speeches have become the safest way for an autocrat
to advance policy. They are carefully crafted, even those aimed at making
routine announcements. Every now and then, though, one or another speech
bumps up against history. Thus, in February 1956 Nikita S. Khrushchev, then
Russia's supreme leader, delivered a speech that could be defined as historic.
He spoke for four hours. Not a word of what he said was broadcast "live":
secrecy still reigned in Soviet politics and society. Called the "secret speech"
(though published in the West within months, it was neither published nor
broadcast in Russia until 1989), it denounced Stalin's cruel, maniacal leadership and, exactly three years after his death, brought his reign of terror to a
close. De-Stalinization was its code name.[2]

When word of it first leaked out, Khrushchev's message touched off extraordinary meetings throughout the Soviet Union, many of them exploding into anticommunist tirades. At the time, I attended several of them at the Lenin Library in Moscow. While working at the U.S. Embassy as a translator and junior press officer, I was also doing research for a PhD and frequently in the evening visited this famous library. I remember the scene. The large, rectangular reading room was usually silent and solemn; now it was crowded and noisy. Students were arguing, many waving placards. Suddenly, as though playing a role in a Soviet play, a student would jump on a table and launch into a vicious anticommunist attack that could last for a half hour. No one in authority stopped the student. From the side, senior librarians listened, but didn't move. Other students would interrupt and question the speaker. Who said so? they wanted to know. Where did the information come from? If the answer was *Pravda*, the official Communist Party newspaper, everyone laughed. They thought *Pravda's* greatest value now lay in providing the paper for wrapping fish. Everyone seemed disrespectfully to be speaking at the same time. One had the sense of a nineteenth-century-style Russian intellectual brawl. Missing only was the vodka.

These eruptions were spontaneous and amazingly fearless. I learned later that similar scenes were taking place at libraries and lecture halls throughout the country—all prompted by Khrushchev's "secret speech." This was unforgettable stuff. Far more important, the speech also spawned anti-Russian and anticommunist uprisings in Hungary and Poland and contributed eventually to the dissolution of the Soviet empire in 1991. And it all started with a speech.

Mikhail Gorbachev, a student at the time, was so moved by Khrushchev's message that when he came to power in 1985—to become, as it happened, the last leader of the Soviet Union—he initiated two key domestic reforms that brought the communist empire to its knees, though that was not his intention.[3] One was called *glasnost*, or "openness," which had the effect of liberalizing Russian life by ending censorship and encouraging more candid exchanges with authority. The other was *perestroika*, or "transformation," which attempted to oil the creaky machinery of Soviet industry. Both *glasnost* and *perestroika* were aimed at reforming the communist system, not ending it. But once uncorked, they led to the demise of the system anyway. Gorbachev, though a product of the communist system, had monumentally underestimated the extent of its internal rot and decay.

We now know the full effect of Khrushchev's 1956 speech. It *was* truly historic. We do not yet know the effect of Putin's March 18, 2014, speech. It may ultimately come to be seen as offering little more than interesting insights into Putin's thinking. Or it may in time prove to be historic, too—an eye-opener on a newly aggressive Russian policy, designed to capture the world's attention by doing the impossible: conveying the impression of a global powerhouse, an Olympic winner, when everyone knew (perhaps, in a quiet moment, Putin did, too) that in fact Russia was experiencing severe economic and political weaknesses. Putin's explanation of the Crimean annexation confirmed what American diplomats had feared—that the diplomatic dynamic between East and West, between Russia and the rest of the world, had now dramatically shifted. The immediate and, as it turned out, naive post–cold war hope that we could all somehow entice Russia to be "more like us," to join the Western system of thought and business, slipped away, like a nostalgic wisp of smoke reminding everyone of a dream gone by.

The Putin speech set an authoritarian, nationalistic tone for Russian foreign and domestic policy that Kremlin old-timers seemed to have found totally congenial. Russians in the palace frequently interrupted their leader with "thunderous applause," according to a *New York Times* report.[4] The speech ran forty-five minutes. Many people wept. Putin had touched a deep emotional chord; his poll numbers spiked.

But as popular as the speech might have been inside Russia, it had a totally different effect outside of Russia. In fact, it sent an icy chill through the West, certainly through Eastern Europe, whose fortunes always seemed to hang on Russia's mood and actions. It inspired a rush of Western media commentary amazingly similar to what one read and heard during the cold war, namely, that Russia was an aggressive bully, engaged in a historic effort to recreate a modern variation of the imperial tsarist empire—minimally, a Slavic confederation consisting of Russia, Belarus, and Ukraine, which was Putin's definition of national nirvana. In this feverish vision, which unfortunately set the tone for media coverage of the "Ukraine crisis," one knowledgeable Russian writer wondered what's next in Putin's plans—and guessed Finland!

Even if one could ignore the media hype, which was impossible, what remained depressingly clear was that President George H. W. Bush's 1991 proclamation of a "new world order" had been upended.[5] Unprepared and wary, the West now faced a new Russian belligerence, shaped by a hungry, shrewd Putin, who had come to believe that he, and he alone, had a rendezvous with destiny: It was his mission in life to save Russia from a depraved and duplicitous West. But how?

In his speech, Putin never used the name of Sergei Semyonovich Uvarov, Tsar Nicholas I's minister of education, but he could have—and he should have. In recent years—perhaps because he wanted to be seen as a cool, very modern intellectual, not just as a powerful Russian leader—Putin began to sprinkle the names of three conservative, respected Russian scholars into his speeches. They were Nikolai Berdayev, Vladimir Solovyov, and Ivan Ilyin. Putin urged his regional governors to read three of their books: Berdayev's *The Philosophy of Inequality*, Solovyov's *Justification of the Good*, and Ilyin's *Our Tasks*. He wanted the governors to understand that *his* thinking was a reflection of *their* writings. If Putin tested the governors, he never released the results. The themes highlighted in these books were not necessarily inspired by Uvarov's mid-nineteenth-century work in Greek classics and Russian governance, but they could have been. They flow from many of the same intellectual currents of Russian philosophy. As minister of education, Uvarov dedicated himself to raising the standards of Russian education by stressing the values of the classics and placing them within the broader framework of Russia's history, heritage, and perceived destiny. During my research on Uvarov in Moscow and Leningrad (as St. Petersburg was then known), librarians and archivists would often express their surprise that a foreigner would want to know about Uvarov and do research about him. Why? they would ask; he was not a communist, not a revolutionary!

And, indeed, he was neither. But he achieved a degree of notoriety among Russian historians for one very important reason: he was the official, known only to a handful of St. Petersburg courtiers and scholars, who created the slogan that sparked the conservative movement in tsarist Russia—"Orthodoxy, Autocracy, Nationality." Uvarov's conservatism never seriously challenged revolutionary communism in late nineteenth- and early twentieth-century Russia. However, his three-headed emblem of tsarist power and legitimacy attracted the attention of many conservative politicians and intellectuals, among them, apparently, a number of Putin advisers. Nearly two centuries later, Putin saw in Uvarov's handy nineteenth-century conservatism a convenient formula for governing Russia in the twenty-first century. Putin loved being compared to the swashbuckling tsar, Peter the Great, who opened Russia to the Western world. In some ways he could also be compared to Nicholas I, who was so frightened by the brief 1825 rebellion known as the Decembrist Revolt that he resisted all attempts to reform Russia and found comfort only in those governing theories that glorified absolutism, nationalism, and orthodoxy. Liberating the serfs, for example, was a change that was desperately needed in Russia. But it had to wait for the next tsar.[6]

During the Soviet period, Russia's conservative philosophers, such as Uvarov, were deliberately ignored. Their viewpoints stood in rigid opposition to the prevailing ideology of the Communist Party. But now, under Putin, his three favorite philosophers have enjoyed a genuine rebirth of respect and relevance.

If conservatism, under Nicholas I, was a quiet wallflower, it now blossomed, under Putin, into an aggressive dynamo, driving other competing ideologies to the sidelines of Russian political thought.

Putin's March 18 speech was, in a way, his short course on Russian history, occasionally inaccurate, exaggerated, but always patriotic. From Vladimir the Great, the grand prince of Kiev who brought Orthodox Christianity to the Slavic peoples in the tenth century, to the courageous Russian soldiers who helped defeat Hitler's invading hordes during World War II, and finally to the annexation of Crimea, which he described as "historically Russian land," Putin repeatedly rang the bells of Russian nationalism. He considered Ukraine to be little more than an extension of Russia, never as an independent state, never deserving of national respect. He spoke with pride of the "aspiration of the Russians, of historical Russia," of Kiev as "the mother of Russian cities," and of "Ancient Rus," binding Russia and Ukraine into a common history, sharing a common destiny, already more than a thousand years old.

As he did on March 18, and again on May 9—when he celebrated Russia's victory over Nazi Germany, first in Moscow and later the same day on a warship off the Crimean coast—Putin reached back to World War II for examples of Russian strength, sacrifice, and courage that he could use to stimulate a fresh rush of national pride and patriotism. His PR advisers had but one goal in mind: to transform Putin into the patriotic symbol of a Russia reborn. When 11,000 troops marched through Red Square, red flags fluttering in the breeze—followed by T-90A tanks, sophisticated Triumf-S-400 anti-aircraft missile batteries, and Topol-M intercontinental missiles rumbling past the reviewing stand atop the Lenin Mausoleum—Putin, by positioning and rhetoric, was established as the leader of the new nationalist Russia, the red star sparkling from the Kremlin tower.

Putin knew that in Russia the new nationalism would be regarded as incomplete if Russians living from the Baltic to the Pacific across nine time zones were not also, at the same time, lighting millions of candles in celebration of their Orthodox faith. Not all Russians were religious, of course, but nearly all Russians seemed to appreciate the special power of their Orthodox faith to rally the nation during times of crisis. Stalin, who had earlier in his reign defined religion as "the opiate of the people," resurrected and embraced Orthodoxy during World War II, blending religion with nationalism in the fight against the invading Germans, and it helped inspire a bleeding nation in need of a patriarch's prayer. In this sense, Putin was different from Stalin. He always embraced Orthodoxy, wearing a cross at all times, proudly telling foreign visitors that his mother had given it to him when he was a child, and he'd worn it ever since. Putin tried to come through as a true believer, marching arm in arm with Orthodoxy from day one of his meteoric rise to political power.[7]

In his March 18 speech, Putin denounced the West, especially the United States, for encircling Russia during the cold war. Russians had tended to strike similar themes during the nineteenth century, seeing their religion as being encircled and infected by western atheism and nihilism. "An anti-Christian virus" has been infiltrated into Russia, wrote Ilyin, and it must be eliminated before it breaks "our bond with God and the Christian tradition."[8] Berdayev focused on Orthodoxy's unique mission. "The Russian messianic conception," he wrote, "always exalted Russia as a country that would help to solve the problems of humanity."[9] Ilyin added that the Russian people were the "core of everything European-Asian and, therefore, of universal equilibrium."[10] By the early twentieth century, Nikolai Bakhtin, an émigré Russian scholar, could write that "Russia appeared now as the only rightful heir of the European past, and it was on her that the duty devolved of taking over the torch from the weakening grasp of contemporary Europe."[11] Putin, like other Russian conservatives, raised Russia to a high pedestal of European responsibility. The rest of Europe was weak and demoralized. Only Russia, in their minds, could grasp the "torch" of right, might, and purity, and hold it aloft in all of Europe's name.

The third and final leg of Putinism was autocracy. But because Putin, like many other modern autocrats, used the language of democracy to describe his brand of autocracy, he needed to find another way of persuading the Russian people that his ayatollah autocracy was really in their interest. He found it in the distorted allegation that the West, led by the United States, was again pursuing the "infamous policy of containment," the same policy, he charged, it had pursued in "the eighteenth, nineteenth, and twentieth centuries." Putin was right about the twentieth century, during the cold war, but not about the previous two centuries, when containment as a doctrine was beyond the imagination of any U.S. president. When John Quincy Adams, a future president, went to Moscow as an American envoy in the early nineteenth century, he was not thinking about containment, a concept that did not exist. He was thinking of strengthening U.S.-Russian relations by means of an alliance against a Napoleonic France. Putin has always demonstrated a capacity to manipulate history. He was, after all, a product of the Soviet educational system, which prepared him to become a KGB officer. His grasp of Russian history was a narrow one, his understanding of world history narrower still and often inaccurate at that.

Therefore on March 18, as on many other occasions, Putin was not above conjuring up a foreign enemy to satisfy a pressing domestic need. The enemy was, as usual, the West, led, of course, by the United States, and the need was molding a Ukraine that would be acceptable to vital Russian interests. Such a Ukraine would not be allowed to follow "in [Stepan] Bandera's footsteps," meaning it could not install a profascist, ultranationalist regime, as Bandera had attempted in 1941. Nor could Ukraine reach for any sort of association with NATO, which, as a "military alliance," would not be permitted to "make itself at home right in our backyard or in our historic territory." By Putin's definition, Ukraine existed "right in our backyard" and "in our historic territory." Western leaders were not obliged to read Putin's March 18 speech. But if they entertained any questions about his policy, they could have found answers there. He could not have been clearer.

"They are constantly trying to sweep us into a corner," Putin said with a mix of anger and resignation. "But there is a limit to everything. And, with Ukraine, our Western partners have crossed the line, playing the bear and acting irresponsibly and unprofessionally."[12] Meaning what, exactly? He did not say. Pointing to a possible casus belli, Putin carefully noted that there were "millions of Russians living in Ukraine and Crimea," and if they were mistreated Russia would have to defend them. On this issue, national boundaries did not seem to faze Putin. He did not see them as obstacles to the implementation of his grandiose vision of Russian national interest. Furthermore, he emphasized that he "could not retreat" from this position, warning quite pointedly that "if you compress the spring all the way to its limit, it will snap back hard."[13] He did not threaten to invade Ukraine—such a threat would have been unnecessary: Putin already had 40,000 Russians troops maneuvering near Ukraine's borders.

Even though, he said, Russia favored a "strong, sovereign and self-sufficient" Ukraine, Putin nonetheless tried to make it clear that Russia and Ukraine, in his mind, historically have been and remained one country. "We are not simply close neighbors," he stressed, "but, as I have said many times already, we are one people. Kiev is the mother of Russian cities. Ancient Rus is our common source, and we cannot live without each other." This was a theme Putin was to repeat time and again. The West saw it differently, and so did, for that matter, many Ukrainians. But Putin emphasized that Russia's national security was directly affected by the Ukrainian crisis. Russia was a major player, it had core interests, and, if necessary, it was perfectly prepared to defend them.

In conclusion, Putin acknowledged that Russia would run into "external opposition," meaning "some western politicians" who would try to stir up "serious problems on the domestic front." He then asked the key question: "Are we ready to defend our national interests, or will we forever give in, retreat to who knows where?" Here Putin unveiled an old, very deep sense of Russian insecurity—that under foreign pressure, Russia would inevitably cave. But Putin wanted his countrymen to understand that, under his leadership, Russia would no longer cave. From now on Russia would stand tall, a nation once again strong and determined, no matter the degree of foreign pressure brought against the *rodina*, the motherland.

Putin wondered aloud precisely how these "Western politicians" planned to attack Russia—if not militarily, as they had vowed, then how? Economic sanctions, of course, but Putin and his advisers had already dismissed sanctions as a form of toothless provocation. "They badly want to bite us," Putin said, "but their opportunities are limited." So, what else? He answered, "Action by a fifth column, this disparate bunch of 'national traitors,'" operating on behalf of foreign powers. Then he asked, "Are they hoping to put us in a worsening social and economic situation so as to provoke public discontent?"[14] Putin was alluding here to the unusually widespread antigovernment demonstrations in late 2011 that greeted his plan to return to the presidency, initially spawned by a new generation of postcommunist Muscovites. A number of foreign pundits had hoped these demonstrations would spread through the country and topple the Putin regime. Spread they did. But they did not topple the regime.

No Kremlin ruler could tolerate such open defiance of his rule, and, within a few months, Putin smashed his political opposition by instituting a series of strict regulations limiting such public demonstrations. He imposed heavy financial penalties, arrested many of the ringleaders and closed media outlets critical of his regime. By threatening "national traitors," by raising the shadow of an internal "fifth column," he intimidated many critics, opening the door to a still-wider crackdown on his political opponents by an increasingly powerful secret police. In Putin's mind, there was little difference between a critic and a "national traitor." He seemed to be saying that if a Russian still insisted on being a critic, he could be a critic so long as his criticism never left the confines of his kitchen. The effect was to contain the criticism, but not to end it. Russians could still travel, invest abroad, and go on to the Internet. But their loyalty to Putin's Russia had to trump all else. Uvarov's mid-nineteenth-century slogan of Nationalism, Orthodoxy, and Autocracy had morphed into Putin's dream formula for governing his vast, vulnerable nine-time-zone land. And so devoted was Putin to this conservative formula that he personally arranged for the remains of philosopher Ivan Ilyin, who had died in Switzerland in 1954, to be returned to Moscow in 2005. Putin paid a well-publicized visit to the Ilyin grave site in 2009.[15]

The broad message enunciated on March 18 then spread through Russia, affecting everything from policy to propaganda. First, policy. After the annexation of Crimea, the immediate question was, what's next? The answer lay in a map of the region. Crimea was largely dependent on southern and eastern Ukraine for supplies as basic as water and fuel. Once Crimea again became part of Russia, the purchase and transport of these basic supplies could no longer be taken for granted. Prices spiked and supply lines were jeopardized. How to ensure supplies? One way was for Russia to control the parts of southern and eastern Ukraine where these supplies originated.

Within days of the Crimean annexation, pro-Russian insurgents seized government buildings in Ukrainian cities from Donetsk, Kharkiv, and Slaviansk to Mariupol and Odessa, and many more. Thousands of "insurgents"— many with Russian accents, wearing masks, armed with Kalashnikov rifles, and employing guerrilla tactics last seen during the Crimean takeover— swaggered into power, proclaiming the birth of the Donetsk People's Republic, the Luhansk People's Republic, and even the Odessa People's Republic. They appealed to President Putin to send troops into Ukraine, as he had done in Crimea, and come to the rescue of Russian-speaking friends and family who wanted nothing more now than to become an integral part of the Russian Federation.[16]

Insurgent leaders announced a referendum for May 11. The options were: stay in Ukraine, join Russia, or be independent. Putin moved roughly 40,000 troops to the Ukrainian border, but they were not ordered to cross it; and though Putin spoke sympathetically of the pro-Russian cause and denounced the Kiev regime as "fascist" and "ultra-nationalist," he carefully kept his options open. He could invade, he could negotiate, he could strike a different pose entirely. Interestingly, in mid- to late May, as the West was preparing stronger sanctions on Russia, warning Putin not to interfere with Ukraine's national presidential elections set for May 25, Putin suddenly switched tactics. He spoke approvingly of the Kiev regime, expressed support for the Kiev-sponsored elections, and thrice ordered his troops to pull back from the Ukrainian border and return to their barracks. Perhaps most significant, he struck a major gas deal with China that tilted Russia's economic future eastward, thereby freeing Russia from major dependence on Western buyers.[17]

None of this changed the essence of the Ukraine crisis, which remained dangerous and uncertain. Putin had created international disorder, thereby pushing the world back toward the cold war. How far was he prepared to go? Again, no one was really sure.

CHAPTER 4

Kievan Rus': The "First Russia"

To Kiev, your tongue will find the way.
OLD UKRAINIAN PROVERB

UKRAINE IS A STRANGE PLACE. It has existed as a political entity for more than a thousand years—first, as a jumble of city states along interconnecting rivers, then as an empire called Kievan Rus', and then, for many centuries, as a Cossack-dominated borderland that was eventually, under Peter the Great, folded into the Russian empire. Except for a few years after the Russian Revolution, Ukraine remained under Russian rule until 1991, when, after the dissolution of the Soviet Union, it finally declared its independence. But it has been an independence severely constrained by political corruption, guerrilla war, and the omnipresent shadow of Russia. In this sense, Ukraine has not yet fully enjoyed the fruits, and responsibilities, of independence, even though it is, by any acceptable international standard, an independent nation. One reason is that its history is so tightly intertwined with Russia's that it cannot meet the day-to-day challenges of national independence until it has reached a workable modus vivendi with its powerful neighbor. That is the key. Peace may remain elusive, war a constant threat, economic and political progress a teasing dream. Nothing of positive and sustaining value is likely to emerge until Ukraine and Russia settle their differences, through negotiations, and create a sensible space for mutual cooperation and coexistence. For Ukraine, Russia holds the key to its successful survival, even though Ukraine is struggling to break away from Russia. For Russia, Ukraine is an essential component of its image of a successful Slavic world.

For some Russians, such as Putin, Ukraine has never really been a country, only a collection of Russian-owned or -administered lands acquired by Ukraine as it grew into statehood. For other Russian leaders, such as Foreign Minister Sergei Lavrov, Ukraine has always been an inseparable part of

Russian history and, implicitly, so it shall remain. "Kiev is the mother of Russian cities," he told Bloomberg TV in May 2014, echoing Putin's line during his March 18 speech. "Russian language, Russian religion, Orthodox Christianity, [were] born on the territory of Ukraine, as it stands now. We have been one nation for more than 300 years, even before that. The Slavs brought their religion there more than 1,000 years ago. It's absolutely impossible to miss the psychological, historical, family feeling, if you will."[1]

And, for a very long time, "family" is what it was. That corner of Europe now defined as "Ukraine" was at the time of the first millennium an exciting, dangerous place. National borders were for a later era. If one prince happened to conquer the town of another, then the town fell under his control. His personal domain became his "national" borders, usually reflecting the results of military conquest. There was no Ukraine, as such, and certainly no Russia. Byzantium ruled in the south, and warriors from the north—Swedes who came to be called Rus'—fought their way south, occupying trading posts along the way, razing villages, and terrorizing people. The ultimate prize was always Kiev, the jewel of the lower Dnieper River, a bustling marketplace near an extraordinary intersection of river-based transportation networks, and Kiev became the heart of this emerging Slavic empire. In many ways, it was, to quote historian Bernard Pares, "the first Russia," and it flourished for more than 300 years.[2]

In retrospect, this empire, called Kievan Rus', had all the ingredients of a great historical tale, even though its origins were lost in the mist of time. Were the so-called Swedes, for example, really the Vikings, or the Varangers, and were they the people we today call Slavs? Was there really a Viking leader named Rurik, who was invited by irreconcilable Slavic factions in Novgorod to rule over them in 862? Did he finally agree, but only after hesitating "because of the savage habits of the people"?[3] Did he, once there, quickly dispatch two of his relatives to outlying trading posts, in this way connecting one to another in a primitive system of governance? Was Rurik the first Russian tsar? Or was he, as some have argued, but a legend?

To this day, neither Russian nor Ukrainian historians are certain about the answers to these questions. Convincing evidence is scarce and spotty. Much depends on the so-called "Russian Chronicle," a monumental collection of foreign records and writings, mostly from Byzantine and Arab traders and travelers, of archeological and linguistic data, and, perhaps most important, of popular songs and folklore. One traveler from Baghdad, Mas Octi, noted in the eleventh century that "the Rus are many nations, divided into different groups. They separate and travel far and wide."[4] The work of a number of history scholars—Bernard Pares, George Vernadsky, Michael T. Florinsky, and Hugh Seton-Watson, among them—informs this part of the book.

No doubt, legends and myths have also informed our understanding of early Ukrainian/Russian history. Unfortunately, as Florinsky noted, it was not until the nineteenth century that the Russian Chronicle was seriously analyzed by scholars.[5] They found much that was valuable and intriguing. But, Florinsky wrote, scholars were also troubled by errors and, worse, by a "definite and pronounced theological point of view." These problems raised questions about the Chronicle, which was, after all, the work of poorly educated monks who rarely ventured beyond the church's simplistic view that Russian history was, more than anything else, a struggle between good and evil.

But there was much more: rich stories of feuding princes, wars to the death, fierce commercial competition, and collapsing empires. These were the stories of the first Russia, Kievan Rus', from the ninth through the thirteen centuries. The Viking named Rurik had founded a dynasty, and his sons and grandsons fought among themselves for control of the expanding empire. In their wars, nothing was more important than control of Kiev, the capital, though the empire had spread as far east as the Urals and as far west as the Danube. Trade dominated everything, even politics—silver and horses from faraway Bohemia and Hungary; gold, wine, fruits, and silks from Greece; and honey, furs, wax, and slaves from the Slavic lands. Among Kiev's upper class—comprised of Slavic and Scandinavian boyars and merchants, wealthy and ambitious—arguments erupted about religion, whether it was better to believe in a single God or in many gods, and about the pros and cons of war as a preferred way of expanding the boundaries of trade.

Svyatoslav I, the first of the Kievan princes to adopt a Slavic name, reigned from 964 to 972, a relatively brief time. True to his Scandinavian roots, he was blond and blue-eyed, and he was a valiant warrior. Shortly after assuming power, he expanded Kievan authority to the northeast, conquered the Volga steppes, drove south into the Caucasus, made a special point of occupying the province of Ossetia, and then moved into Crimea, where he destroyed the Khazar kingdom. One visitor to the capital city of Atil reported that "the Ros [sic] attacked, and no grape or raisin remained, not a leaf on a branch."[6] Their sword was their pride. In 903 an Arab writer noted, "When a son is born, the father throws a naked sword before him, and says: 'I leave you no inheritance. All you possess is what you can gain with this sword.' "[7]

Svyatoslav, known for his effectiveness as a warrior, then turned west. He had been invited to join Byzantium in a war against Bulgaria; as an inducement, a rather sweet one, he was paid more than 1,500 pounds in gold. An alliance with Byzantium had one other major advantage: It tied Kiev to the region's dominant power. According to historians Florinsky and Pares, in 968 Svyatoslav attacked Bulgaria and quickly vanquished his adversary. Then, instead of returning as a triumphant hero to Kiev, where his sons desperately needed their father to contain their fratricidal warfare, he permitted his ego to ride roughshod over his strategic judgment and foolishly turned on his new Byzantine ally. He ordered his 60,000-man army to march on Constantinople, where he ran into rugged resistance by a Pecheneg (Turkic) army, and he was defeated.

Svyatoslav, not accustomed to military setbacks, retreated to the shores of the Black Sea, where he hoped to rest his troops before returning to Kiev. But he ran into another Pecheneg force, apparently determined this time not only to defeat Svyatoslav but also to humiliate him. And they did—with stunning effectiveness and brutality. In the climactic battle, they killed Svyatoslav and decapitated him, converting his skull into a drinking cup for his Pecheneg conqueror.

It was 972, a crucially important year in the early history of Kievan Rus'. Svyatoslav, so obsessively absorbed with war, had never bothered to arrange a proper succession, and Kiev fell into a period of decline.

Enter Vladimir the Great, the bastard son of Svyatoslav. If there had been television in his time, he would have had a show of his own. He was a star, a natural leader, who proved to be the finest fighter and wisest ruler of Kievan Rus'. Before assuming power, Vladimir traveled first to Scandinavia, where he conferred with one of his relatives, Ladejarl Hakon Sigurdsson, who happened to be the King of Norway. The king's advice was typically Viking in character: organize an army of Varangian mercenaries, invade the northern regions of Kievan Rus', reconquer Novgorod, be tough, even cruel if necessary, and only then, with a full complement of troops, move on Kiev, arriving for your accession to the throne as the undisputed leader of the country.

Nearly all of Vladimir's subjects were heathens. Playing to this raucous gallery, he opened his reign with what historian Pares described as "an orgy of paganism." Vladimir made a show of enjoying the company of hundreds of concubines; he even married a few dozen of them. He worshiped old Slavonic gods and placed their figures in front of his palace: Svarog, the father of gods; Dazhd-Bog, his son; Veles, the patron of cattle; Stribog, the god of wind; and Perun, the god of thunder, who was, for Vladimir, the most appealing god of all, for he was always pictured with a huge silver head and mustaches of gold. He was loud, boisterous and cruel—so Vladimir thought. Before these mythical gods, there was no caste of priests, no regular public worship, but there was still public sacrifice. Soon after Vladimir defeated the Viking prince Rogvolod, who had governed Poland, he celebrated by sacrificing close to a thousand people, ostensibly to satisfy the gods. One boyar who had become a Christian objected when his son was sacrificed. "Yours is not a god," the boyar cried, "but a piece of wood." A furious crowd killed both the boyar and his son. For reasons murky and mysterious, their deaths had a profound impact on Vladimir. After an uncharacteristic period of reflection, he decided to end the practice of human sacrifice and went one big step further—he wondered whether Kiev should choose another form of worship.

Here the Russian Chronicle recites a story of religious conversion so remarkable that one can only surmise that it is the stuff of legend. Vladimir, living in a bubbly capital filled with tradesmen and travelers, must have heard about other religions from nearby communities. The chronicler Nestor, whose "Tale of Bygone Years" might be seen as a fragmented history of the time, tells a fascinating story about Vladimir's search for a new religion. According to Nestor's Tale, Vladimir sent a team of envoys to research the religions of nearby communities. One team went to the remnants of the Crimean Khazars, who were Jews. The khan made a pitch for Vladimir's conversion. He explained Judaism and reviewed Jewish history. Vladimir apparently listened intently, but decided against Judaism. Why? Because the Jews were scattered everywhere, and they had lost Jerusalem—a clear sign, Vladimir believed, that they had lost God's favor.

Another team of Kievan envoys went to a Muslim tribe living along the Volga. But when the envoys learned that Muslims did not drink alcohol nor eat pork, they quickly rejected the Muslim faith. "Drinking is the joy of all Rus'," said Vladimir. "We cannot exist without that pleasure."

Other Kievan emissaries visited Rome and Constantinople. They were impressed by Catholicism except for one overriding factor: The Pope considered himself to be superior to all secular leaders, and that belief was totally repugnant to Vladimir. That was the end of his brief flirtation with Roman Catholicism. Next was the Christian Orthodoxy of Constantinople, where the conversion of Vladimir's Kievan Rus' to Orthodoxy would have been considered a prize worthy of a journey to heaven. Byzantium pulled out all stops. To impress Vladimir's envoys, the leaders of Byzantium hosted an extraordinary festival in the Hagia Sophia, the splendid Orthodox church in Constantinople, which profoundly impressed Kiev's envoys. "We no longer knew whether we were in heaven or on earth," they reported to Vladimir, "nor such beauty, and we know not how to tell of it." They were speechless in adoration of church and faith.

Vladimir accepted their judgment: Henceforth, Kievan Rus' would be converted to Orthodox Christianity. This was a decision of historic importance; not only would Kievan Rus', the first Russia, become Orthodox Christian, but so too would the second Russia, Moscow's Russia. In time, the entire Slavic world would become Orthodox.

Always operating on several levels, Vladimir believed that the conversion might also open the door to a diplomatic alliance with Byzantium. What his father, Svyatoslav, had failed to achieve, he would achieve, and he would do it through marriage.

First, in a show of strength, he conquered the Greek colony of Kherson in Crimea, and then he boldly proposed marriage to Anna, the 27-year-old sister of Emperor Basil II. She was an imperial princess, Vladimir still regarded as a pagan ruler, and Basil II balked at the proposal. He would not sanction his sister's marriage to a non-Christian. Vladimir, having already accepted Christianity for all of Kievan Rus', decided on the spot that he, personally, would also accept Christianity. In great pomp and ceremony, Vladimir, the Prince of Kiev, was baptized. This time, as a Christian ruler, he again proposed marriage to Anna. This time her brother agreed, not only to the marriage but to the alliance. Anna and Vladimir were married in Kherson in 989, and Kievan Rus' and Byzantium were united in marriage, faith, and military control of the Black Sea region.

Vladimir took Christianity seriously. He set up schools to train young men from good families to enter the priesthood. It did not take long before the top position of metropolitan went to a Russian named Hilarion. Vladimir also employed the priests as his close political advisers. Indeed, he formed a great council of priests and boyars to help him govern his empire. The priests were his only literate aides, and they eased his path from pagan savagery to temperate civil rule. They kept his records and ran his court. They also established a crude form of civil justice. Instead of killing highway robbers, as had been the custom, Vladimir henceforth ordered them into slavery, by any standard a more benign punishment.

Vladimir also sought to civilize himself and his kingdom. It was no easy task. His troops were rough and tough, his people no less so. An Arab diplomat, Ibm Fadlan, obviously of a delicate nature, after visiting Kiev wrote: "They are the filthiest of God's creatures. They do not clean themselves after urinating or defecating, nor do they wash their hands after having sex. They do not wash their hands after meals. They are like wandering asses."[8] In the later years of his long rule, Vladimir engaged in benign and uplifting endeavors. Instead of riding off to war, which, consistent with his Viking tradition, he had done for decades, he changed course and struck peace agreements with many of his neighbors while encouraging the construction of Orthodox churches. Among them, the largest in the capital, was St. Vladimir's Cathedral, as well as a college, which blossomed eventually into the University of Kiev, also named after Vladimir. To this day, folk songs and legends still intone St. Vladimir, who has become a symbol of Ukrainian nationalism even at a time when Ukraine's identity is still being debated.

When Vladimir died in 1015, he left twelve sons born to different mothers. One of them, Yaroslav, ruled from 1019 to 1054. During his long reign, Kiev flourished. Yaroslav cut all ties to the fighting Pechenegs, allies on occasion, adversaries often, challengers always. With no security threat looming on the near horizon, Yaroslav devoted himself to Kievan culture. He had always been interested in Byzantine books and law. He was, for a prince of his time, a learned man. Pares used the word "scholar," which might have been a bit of a stretch. Yaroslav did beautify Kiev, prompting a true scholar, Adam of Bremen, to describe it as "the glory of Greece," an interesting choice of words in that Adam obviously thought of Kiev as part of Byzantium, not as the capital of a separate and independent people.[9] Yaroslav built many churches, including a replica of St. Sophia, and he founded the impressive Monastery of the Caves, which evolved into the first center of Orthodox study in Kievan Rus'. It also became the official home of the Russian Chronicle, which, among many other things, recorded the history of local communities, occasionally adding colorful descriptions of the major cities, such as Kiev as "radiant and many-colored," Novgorod as "short and drastic," and Suzdal as "dry and plain." From his palace to his church, he constructed a passageway painted, as in Constantinople, with scenes of hunting, music-making, love, and dancing.

Most important, perhaps, Yaroslav imported Greek law, in this way establishing for the first time in Kievan Rus' a legal system tested over centuries in ancient Greece and challenging how the church in Kiev determined what was right and wrong. This became the basis of "Russkaya Pravda," or true Russian law. Civil jurisdiction, originating in the Byzantine secular tradition, covered commerce and trade, loans and commissions, differences between malicious or accidental bankruptcy, and an acceptable definition of credit.

His diplomacy was eye-catching, sparking stories that he was one of the greatest European sovereigns of his time. He formed many alliances. He married his sister Mary to Poland's King Kazimir I, his daughter Elizabeth to Norway's King Harald Hardrada, his daughter Anastasia to Hungary's King Andrew I, his daughter Anne to France's Henry I, and his son Vsevolod to a daughter of the Greek emperor Constantine Monomachus. Through these marriages he strengthened Kiev's ties to potential friends and allies and spread the word of Kievan Rus' throughout the civilized world.

So impressive, in fact, in so many different ways was Yaroslav's governance that Metropolitan Hilarion extolled him as a "Solomon following in the footsteps of a David." A Kievan prince was expected to honor the church, to be good to the poor, to keep the royal family in a harmonious relationship, and to fight the heathens. Yaroslav fulfilled all his obligations to church and state. Finally, what his father and grandfather had been unable or unwilling to do, Yaroslav did—he broke the destructive habit of fratricidal warfare and established a system of princely succession that was, on the whole, observed from his time until the Mongol hordes leveled Kiev in 1240.

Vsevolod, Yaroslav's son, followed his father as grand prince of Kiev, and then, remarkably, six sons from six successive generations, one after another, rose to the throne and ruled in Kiev. None was more impressive or single-minded in pursuit of policy goals than Vladimir Monomakh, who ruled from 1113 to 1125. Inspired perhaps by the Vatican-sponsored "first crusade," which had sought with brutal vengeance to liberate Jerusalem from Muslim control in 1096, Vladimir Monomakh was determined, more than anything, to unite all Kievan princes and boyars in his own crusade against the heathens. In 1101 and again in 1103, even before he became grand prince, he brought the full might of Kiev against the Polovtsy, a nomadic Turkic tribe that wandered through the southern corners of his empire selling its soldiers to the highest bidder, engaging in battles against a number of Kievan princes, and thereby involving itself in deadly fraternal politics. Vladimir Monomakh won, destroying much of the Polovtsy nation. Proclaiming "this is the day which the Lord has made; let us be glad and rejoice in it," he settled down for a decade of nation-building, as U.S. presidents would say today. But in 1111, again feeling the itch for battle, he launched still one more crusade against the depleted forces of the Polovtsy, and again won the day. "He had been in constant travel," Pares wrote, "he reckons eighty-three 'long journeys', often sleeping in the open. . . . He had been thrown by a bull, butted by a stag, trampled by an elk, bitten by a bear, borne to the ground by a wolf." Vladimir Monomakh often cautioned his sons to shed no blood except in battle. "Children, fear neither battle, nor beast," he told them. "Play the man! Nothing can hurt you unless God wills it. God's care is better than man's."[10] The reign of Vladimir Monomakh was, in many ways, the last of the great periods of Kievan Rus' history. From 1125, when he died, until the Mongol onslaught in 1240, Kiev was still the prize desired by any regional prince with drive and ambition. But it was losing its luster, in part because its major trading partner, Constantinople, was fading as the commercial hub of the region, and in part because princes saw new economic and political opportunities in the northeast towns of Suzdal, Vladimir, and Moscow, first mentioned in the Russian Chronicle in 1147. Still, Kiev, even in decline, was an attractive jewel of Slavic civilization. "To Kiev, your tongue will find the way," said one proverb. Its river roads ensured a vibrant trade. Its architecture, inspired by Constantinople, exuded a distinctive character of its own. Its Orthodox faith infused the Slavic soul with an original religiosity distinctive even today in any Russian or Ukrainian church. Its legal system, originating in Byzantium, became the basis of Slavic jurisprudence.

Kiev was thus the symbol of Kievan Rus'. It was the soil in which the first sprouts of Russian nationalism arose. It was, in fact, the first capital of Russia. But it could also be argued that it was the first capital of what came to be called Ukraine. In this way, both Russian and Ukrainian history shared the same common root, namely, the capital city of Kiev. Over the next several centuries, they were to share a lot more.

CHAPTER 5

The Mongol Legacy:
The Fall of Kiev and the Rise of Moscow

Two Romes have fallen, but the Third [in Moscow]
stands, and a Fourth shall not be.
IVAN III

OUT OF NOWHERE, IT SEEMED, the Mongols came and conquered, emerging out of what Henry Kissinger called "the hard school of the steppe" to crush Kievan Rus; and to help create the "second Russia," the one that today sends ripples of anxiety through Eastern Europe.[1] The date, according to historian Pares, was June 16, 1228. (Other historians, including Michael Florinsky, put the date at 1223.) Whichever date is used, every Russian historian thrills to the researching and writing of the Mongol chapter of Russian history. The story of the Mongols—their rise, impact, and demise—represents an unforgettable adventure. Their impact on Russia was huge.

An unimaginable force of more than 300,000 Mongol troops stormed out of the Siberian steppes and, in a remarkably brief period of time, changed the political, military, and cultural landscape of an emerging Slavic empire in the northern bend of the mighty Volga River. Who were these Tartars from Mongolia? No one knew. What did they want? No one knew that either.

For the next eight years, Orthodox bishops begged the princes to unite for the defense of Russia and Christendom, but the princes, preoccupied with their own petty squabbles, did little to nothing. Toward the end of 1236, the Mongol warrior Batu, grandson of the great Genghiz Khan, suddenly appeared on the eastern shores of the Volga with hundreds of thousands of troops—an army so large, so well-disciplined that no opponent wished to engage them in battle. This time they were accompanied by their wives and children, implying they had come not just to conquer but to stay. Batu's first target was the Volga Bulgar kingdom, which he destroyed in days. Then, in early 1237, he crossed the Volga, entered Russian territory, and directed his troops toward the town of Vladimir, which had become the unofficial capital of post-Kievan Rus'.

The principality of Ryazan was in their way. The Mongols, as was their custom, first surrounded the town before attacking and demanded one-tenth of the population and property—or else. Ryazan's princes replied bluntly but foolishly: "When there is none of us left, then all will be yours." And soon no Russians were left. The Mongols resumed their advance on Vladimir, razing villages on route and killing every Russian in sight. Soon Vladimir was surrounded, and the Mongols demanded one-tenth of its population and property. Grand Prince Yury rejected the Mongol demand; but instead of leading a fight against the Mongols, he fled. Vladimir was then demolished, its people slaughtered, its major cathedral burned to the ground.

Batu, scanning the western horizons, then opened a brutal, two-year-long scorched-earth offensive that took his warriors to Novgorod in the north and, on December 6, 1240, to Kiev in the south. The once beautiful capital of Kievan Rus' was leveled. Again, as elsewhere along the Mongol path, the people were killed and their cathedral burned.

His mission to conquer the world still unfulfilled, Batu pressed on. He occupied and demolished Galicia, scaled the Carpathians to rout the Hungarians, laid waste to Poland, and finally reached the Adriatic—a military feat only matched, possibly, by Alexander the Great's victorious march from Greece to modern-day Pakistan. Everywhere, according to Plano Carpini, a Franciscan monk who visited the Mongols, skulls and bones scarred the landscape. Russia looked like a graveyard.[2]

For reasons relating to problems of succession and family, Batu abruptly called off his mind-boggling offensive and retreated to the lower Volga, where he established a base of operations for his Golden Hordes that lasted for many decades. The base was the city of Sarai, 100 miles north of modern day Astrakhan. Of the Russians, the Mongols demanded tribute, honor, and obedience. When they wished, Mongol envoys, with large entourages, would surprise a town, occupy the palace, and demand total subservience. During wars among Russian princes, of which there were many, the Mongols would determine the victor, and thereby win his allegiance, by throwing their troops into the fight. This system worked so long as the taxes flowed and the khans were gratified.

Until the late fifteenth century, a period of more than 250 years, Russia lived under the Mongol yoke. Most historians believe that Russia paid a terrible price. While the Italians, French, Germans, Belgians, and English—all of western Europe, in fact—threw off the shackles of the Middle Ages, benefiting greatly from the Renaissance and the Reformation, Russia slumbered in darkness, cut off from the breezes of change sweeping through the rest of Europe. Its culture, which had blossomed during the Kievan Rus' period, lay still, virtually extinguished under the Mongol yoke. The way ahead to personal edification and enterprise was barred. Life along the Volga proved to be painfully parochial, uninspiring, often bloody.

Historian Florinsky, after studying the Mongol impact on Russia, concluded that "the effects of the Tartar domination in Russian history were felt long after the Golden Horde had ceased to exist." The Mongols had left a legacy of "semi-oriental absolutism," which defined Moscow's politics for hundreds of years, from the tsars to the commissars and now to Putin.[3] The small number of Kievan Slavs who had survived the Mongol occupation suffered the same political fate as did the Russians in Moscow. They too lived in political darkness.

The Rise of Moscow

As the sun set over Batu's Mongol hordes, the sun rose over the northeast principality of Moscow. A second Russia was now in its ascendency, the first in Kiev having been destroyed by the Mongols. Moscow rose to be the capital of the new Russia after showing proper obeisance to Mongol authority. Its princes always bowed before Sarai, sharing military objectives, checking local appointments, and even, when absolutely necessary, paying their taxes. Often in a bloody contest for power, one prince would out-bow another and win not only Mongol approval but also Mongol troops—a blessing in bodies from a crafty khan always happy to shed blood in pursuit of Mongol mastery of its yoke.

So it was with Ivan I, known as Ivan Kalita, or "moneybag," the first in a dynasty of Ivans, who, employing a flexible alliance with the Mongols, the Orthodox church, and wealthy boyars, laid the foundation for the rule of tsarist absolutism—a reign that lasted until the Russian Revolution of 1917. Year after year, Ivan I seemed always to be in conflict with the princes of neighboring Vladimir and Tver, east and north of Moscow, respectively. In 1327 he sensed a golden opportunity. Chol Khan, a high-level Mongol emissary, heading a large, pushy entourage, had arrived in Tver, expecting service and demanding an exorbitant tribute, but this time the people of Tver rose in angry revolt and, much to everyone's amazement, slaughtered every intruding Mongol. Ivan, a shrewd prince, decided the moment had come to outmaneuver his princely competitors. He rushed to Mongol headquarters in Sarai, expressed his outrage, more feigned than real, and asked the khan's permission to lead a 50,000-man Mongol expedition against Tver. "Yes" was the khan's response, and, under Ivan's command, the Mongols savagely leveled Tver, killing many of its inhabitants and extracting maximum tribute from the others. Grand Duke Alexander of Tver, a key Ivan rival, fled for his life—first to nearby Pskov and then to hostile Lithuania. Ivan had clearly won the day; much more, he had won the khan's favor. From then on, it was no longer the Mongols who collected the taxes; it was Ivan himself, who, as collector-in-chief, became the most powerful Russian leader of his day, earning the "moneybag" title. Apparently Ivan never objected to serving the khan so long as the khan bestowed additional favors on Ivan. The two worked as one. The result: Ivan's Moscow was confirmed by the Mongols as the leading center of Russian power, wealth, and influence. In this way, the Mongols laid the foundation for a new Russia.

When it came time in 1340 for Ivan's son, Simeon, to ascend the throne, the khan supported Simeon and "brought all princes under his will."[4] Simeon would become known as "Simeon the Proud." The khan ruled that the grand prince of Moscow would be the grand prince of all of Russia. Interestingly, the descendants of Batu had determined who would be the ultimate victor of Russia. "Rus was only strong and glorious," Simeon said, "when the princes obeyed the eldest without contradiction." He demanded "unqualified obedience," and for the most part he got it. Simeon's was a successful reign.

Once his Moscow rose to absolute power, the succession, from one tsar to the next, became the most reliable staircase to power. With increasing confidence, the tsars expanded their grip over nearby Russian lands, including Pskov, Tver, Vladimir, and Novgorod. In 1480 Ivan III took a risky step, rupturing all administrative ties with the Mongol empire, which, like an embryo, was splitting along regional lines and losing its power.

In all of these new territories, Ivan III demanded—and got—absolute authority. "The sovereignty is to be the same in Novgorod as in Moscow," he said. "There is to be no town bell in Novgorod . . . all the sovereignty is to be ours." Ivan III took the title "Sovereign of all Russia," meaning in post-Mongol Russia that he was the tsar, or the caesar, and no one could question his power.[5]

Ivan III, like many other Russian leaders, down to Putin today, used the church to strengthen his political clout. Metropolitan Peter, after leaving a devastated Kiev, was looking for another "permanent" home for the Russian Orthodox Church. He paused briefly in Vladimir, but soon realized that booming Moscow, expanding exponentially through a flood of tens of thousands of former inhabitants of Kiev, was a better, more secure place for the church. In timely fashion, Ivan beckoned to Peter, offering vast tracts of land and the promise of increased church power. Peter, a very practical priest, accepted the offer. He brought the dignity and authority of Orthodox Christianity to Moscow, where it remains to this day.

At different times, especially after 1453, when Constantinople fell to the Muslim Turks, Russian leaders have presumed that they, and they alone, were the "great and sole champions of the true faith." Rome had fallen, and now Constantinople; only Moscow remained. This sequence, more political than theological, gave rise to the powerful nationalistic/religious "doctrine of the Third Rome." It was ascribed in the early sixteenth century to Filofei, the abbot of a monastery near Pskov, and it has been echoed ever since by a succession of Russian tsars. There is every reason to believe that Putin, like the tsars, is a loyal adherent of the "Third Rome" concept. The doctrine held that Moscow was the third and final home for Christianity. "Two Romes have fallen," Ivan III proclaimed, "but the Third [that is, Moscow] stands, and a Fourth shall not be." So described and so blessed, Moscow had come to acquire a unique responsibility: It was the capital, and Russia the country, both the self-proclaimed guardians of Christianity against all heathen encroachment.

In this context, it was not hard for Ivan III to believe that he derived his power from the Almighty and that his power was absolute. So when Emperor Frederick III of the Holy Roman Empire offered to crown him "King," a royal gesture most other rulers might not only have accepted but also desired, Ivan III dismissively crowed: "We have no need of [your] recognition."

"We, by God's grace," he pronounced, "are sovereigns in our land from the beginning, from our first forefathers, and our appointment we hold from God." When, in 1501, the king of Poland, an annoying adversary with budding power, complained that Ivan III was seizing his (Poland's) patrimony, Ivan III shot back that, in fact, Poland was seizing Russia's lands, and Russia had a right to retake them. "The land of Russia is often from our ancestors of old our patrimony. . . . And do I not regret my patrimony, the Russian land which is in the hands of Lithuania—Kiev, Smolensk and the other towns? . . . . Why, not only that is our patrimony, the towns and the districts which we now have, but all Russian land of old from our forefathers, too." Ivan III's vision included Russian control over Kiev and other Slavic cities, which were bending to the West for inspiration and investment. Had Putin read Ivan III's reply before he delivered his March 18, 2014, speech to the

Russian Duma? Could there ever be peace with an enemy such as Poland? No, Ivan III replied, "only truces in order to draw a breath."

"All Russian land of old," including Kievan Rus', was considered by Moscow to belong to Russia since time immemorial. In good times and bad, Moscow has always had a very expansive view of "Russian" territory. It has held that view since Ivan III articulated his governing philosophy, rooted in a very firm religious and national conviction. The territory to Ivan III's southwest, known today as the nation of Ukraine, fit into his broad understanding of what constituted Russia.

CHAPTER 6

The Star Tsars: Peter and Catherine

I will rescue the whole Russian people from Polish slavery.
BOGDAN KHMELNITSKY, COSSACK HETMAN

HISTORIANS, SUCH AS Bernard Pares and his mentor V. O. Klyuchevsky, have often referred to Ivan III as "Ivan the Great," because he was the tsar who first acquired the awesome title "Sovereign of all Russia." And he meant "all Russia," including all lands once owned, conquered, or occupied by the armies of Moscow. "All Russian land of old" was his designation. Succeeding tsars used the same designation, assuming others would accept the legitimacy of their patrimony, which many did until the early eighteenth century. Then, Russia's two star tsars, Peter and Catherine, thought they had to be more precise, especially about "Ukraine," the space to their southwest, to the "rim" or "border" of Moscow's empire—the original home of Kievan Rus' and the "Little Russians," as its inhabitants were called in official documents.

The name "Ukraine," given to a vast tract of land on both sides of the Dnieper, first appeared in 1187 in church records, although it was not used much until centuries later. Prince Vladimir Monomakh had just died, and a monk wrote: "The Ukraina groaned for him," probably meaning in the context of the time that all the lands, even those along the borders of Kievan Rus', mourned the prince's death.[1]

Peter the Great

It was actually Peter's preoccupation with war that led him to think about Ukraine and the Cossacks, the Slavic word for the Turkic tribe called Kazakhs, which meant "outlaw" or "adventurer." Peter, tall and exceptionally energetic, governed from the saddle. Except for the year 1724, Russia was always at war during his reign, usually at Peter's instigation. Tsar of Russia from 1694 to

1725, Peter was not the beneficiary of a formal education. But from an early age he loved to tinker with military gadgets (building warships was a childhood passion). Moreover, he was convinced that a backward Russia desperately needed Western expertise—not in absorbing the ideas and philosophy of the West but rather in acquiring the basic instruments of warfare.

For reasons relating to Kremlin politics, Peter was reared in a Moscow suburb, where two of his closest friends were West Europeans. One day, still as a young man, he abruptly broke protocol and traveled to Western Europe. No tsar had ever left Russia. He visited Berlin, Amsterdam, London, and other capitals, and he returned eighteen months later with a cornucopia of architects, engineers, designers, and craftsmen. He wanted to remake Russia—not the monarchy, not the church—just its ability to wage an effective war.

His impetuous curiosity led to a number of extraordinary decisions. He was determined to open a "window on the west." Without much forethought, he decided to move the Russian capital from Moscow, which he detested, to his vision of St. Petersburg, which he had not yet even begun to plan. And then, also with little forethought, he fixed his sights on building a "warm water port," even though Russia did not yet have a navy. One initiative led him to look northwest to lands occupied by Sweden and Lithuania, and the other to the southwest, to the rich black soil of "the Ukraine," in part controlled by the Zaparog Cossacks, and then further south to the Black Sea, dominated by Muslim Turks, where Peter envisaged building his "warm water port." Wherever he looked, up or down, he saw war, and the prospect of engaging in actual battle enthralled him. He soon learned, however, that war is costly in life and treasure, that it is filled with surprise, that he could no longer take "the Ukraine" for granted, and that, in one battle after another, he could not depend solely on Russian manpower to ensure his victory. He also needed Cossack muscle, and to acquire Cossack muscle, he had to strike deals with often unscrupulous Cossack leaders, known as *hetmen*. He was also soon to learn, much to his satisfaction, that he was up to the challenge.

Just who were these Cossacks? The answer, as always, is to be found in history. When Kievan Rus' collapsed after the Mongol assault, many of its inhabitants fled to the northeast, to the principalities surrounding Moscow. Still others fled westward, to Galicia, which soon fell under Polish rule. They lived there as peasants, sometimes as slaves. Left as squatters in the lower Dnieper valley were other former residents of Kievan Rus', who lived a tough frontier life, not unlike their cowboy equivalents in the American West years later. Also in this region—working the fields, stealing, hunting, and trading—were the descendants of the Siberian tribes, who had invaded Russia centuries before. They might best be described as entrepreneurial brigands and warriors. When not tilling the fields, they would sell their military skills to the highest bidder. These were the early Cossacks, living their day-to-day adventures in the uncharted, borderless land we now call Ukraine.

In the immediate west, Poland and Catholicism ruled, in the east, Russia and Orthodoxy. The Ukraine was split down the middle, not by executive fiat but by migrations propelled by war, creating a bifurcated personality, a polarized people pulled at one and the same time in opposite directions. It is, sadly, a condition that has survived to the present day. In the south, running from the Carpathians in the west to the Urals in the east, including the Donets basin, lay a banana-shaped land, *Malorossiya*, or Little Russia. (Putin used this terminology in his March 18 speech.) One large Cossack community lived on the Don River, another on the Dnieper. Because they owed their allegiance to no one government, enjoying a measure of independence rare for its time, they were feared by everyone, ready at any time to join a challenge that held out the promise of adventure, plunder, and profit.

By the middle of the seventeenth century, the Cossacks, led by Bogdan Khmelnitsky, a prominent *hetman*, exploded into widespread revolt and conflict. There was no one cause, but Poland's brutal oppression of Russian orthodox peasants served to touch off a Polish-Cossack war that rocked the countryside. Jan Kazimir II, the Polish king, had given aristocrats enormous tracts of land in the western half of Ukraine in an effort to ensure their loyalty and Catholicize the country. That did not happen, but they did become wealthy landowners, taking full advantage of the fertility of the soil and cheap peasant labor. In time, though, it became clear that many did not want to live in western Ukraine, and they returned to Poland. They became, in effect, absentee landlords, often hiring local Jewish businessmen to manage the estates, the fields, even the churches, according to the same rigid rules of management practiced in Poland. Wittingly or not, this approach stoked an undercurrent of anti-Semitism that was already deeply entrenched in Ukrainian culture. Clearly, the Polish landowners believed that they could trust the Jews more than they could the Cossacks to run their profitable farming enterprises. The peasants objected strenuously to their Polish Catholic overlords and to their Jewish managers, and their objections led to open revolt.

Few novelists felt the pulse of the Ukrainian peasant better than Nikolai Gogol. Though born a Ukrainian, endowed with a special sensitivity to all things Ukrainian, he regarded himself a Russian writer. In his classic *Taras Bulba*, which critic V. G. Belinsky called "an episode from the epic life of the whole people of the Ukraine," Gogol at one point describes a boatman arriving at a Cossack port and reporting on a meeting of hetmen leaders.

> The boatman says: ". . . even our holy churches are not our own."
>
> "How not our own?"
>
> "They have been leased to the Jews. If a Jew is not paid in advance, there can be no service."
>
> "The man must be raving!"
>
> "And if the damned dog of a Jew does not put his mark on our holy Easter bread with his unclean hands, it cannot be consecrated."
>
> "He lies, gentlemen brothers. It cannot be that an unclean Jew puts his mark upon the holy Easter bread."
>
> . . . The whole crowd came to life. At first a hush fell over the shore, as before a fierce storm; then all at once voices were raised and all the shore burst into speech.
>
> "What! Jews renting Christian churches! Roman priests harnessing Orthodox Christians to their gigs!"
>
> "Hang all Jewry!" a cry sounded in the crowd. "Teach them not to make petticoats for their Jewesses out of priests' vestments! Teach them not to put their mark on our holy Easter bread! Drown all the heathens in the Dnieper!" [2]

Gogol was an avid reader of sixteenth- and seventeenth-century Ukrainian chronicles. "Songs are my joy, my life," he wrote after completing *Taras Bulba* in 1842. "Every song is a piece of folk history, living, vivid, full of color, truth, revealing the whole life of a people."[3] Though he translated "folk history" into a raw and exciting novel about a Cossack warrior named Taras Bulba, he was really describing the life and mood of Ukraine during the Khmelnitsky uprisings of the mid-seventeenth century.

Peasant riots broke out in one Ukrainian town after another—peasants killing Poles and Jews. Sometimes Polish mercenaries fought back, slaughtering the peasants. Khmelnitsky, with a keen sense of *hetman* responsibility, joined the struggle, which quickly spread and degenerated into an anti-Catholic, anti-Polish, anti-Semitic bloodbath.

Khmelnitsky soon realized that, on his own, he could not defeat the Poles; but if he won the support of the khan who ruled in the Crimea, he could. In 1647 Khmelnitsky, acting like the tsars of old, went to the khan, conveying a false image of personal obsequiousness, seeking both his advice and, more important, his Tartar army for a war against Polish rule in western Ukraine. The khan, seeing Tartar glory in a victory over Polish Catholicism, gave his approval, and within months, by April 1648, a Khmelnitsky-led Tartar army defeated the Poles. King Jan Kazimir sued for peace, but Khmelnitsky smelled a victory with far-reaching rewards. "The time has gone by for that," he replied. "I will rescue the whole Russian people from Polish slavery." Here was a Cossack leader speaking with pride about his ability to "rescue the whole Russian people." He then offered what historian Bernard Pares has termed "the allegiance of Little Russia" to Tsar Alexis. Khmelnitsky was actually prepared to give up his freedom of action for the security he found in an association with the Russian empire.[4]

On January 8, 1654, seeking support for his controversial decision, Khmelnitsky convened a special session of his Rada, or parliament. He asked only one question: which would the Rada prefer—to live under Polish, Crimean, Turkish, or Russian sovereignty? It was an important question, for it cut to the core of a chronic Cossack dilemma. Russian protection offered physical security but at the high price of losing their autonomy.

The Rada's answer came swiftly, and it was historic: a unanimous vote for Russian association and protection. The tsar, in exchange, did for the Cossacks what he would not do for any other people: He agreed that the Cossacks could maintain an army of 60,000 troops, elect their own *hetman*, administer their lands, and collect their own taxes. They could even retain their own foreign policy, save for one thing: when it came to communicating with Poland or Turkey, at the time the Ottoman Empire, Russia's two principal adversaries, they had first to check with the tsar. This deal was written into the historic Treaty of Pereyaslav, which codified Ukrainian subservience to Russian rule.

Peter's first target, on assuming power, was Azov, a warm water port on the Black Sea, then controlled by the Turks. It proved to be a valuable experience for the young tsar. Encouraged by Franz Lefort, a Swiss friend of enviable charm and intelligence but little experience with actual warfare, Peter, with a small flotilla, sailed down the Volga in 1695, swung his forces over to the Don, and advanced on the Turkish fortress. Two regiments of the Russian Guard, recently formed and barely trained, buttressed by a major Cossack force, attacked the Turks. Peter, assigning himself the title "Bombardier," was in the vanguard, enjoying the spectacle of actual warfare for the first time. A bloody battle followed, in which the Turks prevailed.

Peter, undaunted, studied the battle with Lefort, who held the titles of "General" and "Admiral." They concluded that they could win the day only if they were able to break the Turkish lines of communication. Peter ordered new ships to be built and new troops to be trained, and the following year he led a fresh assault on Azov. This time, having promoted himself to "Captain of the Navy," Peter commanded a sizeable force that succeeded in overwhelming the Turkish-held fortress, snapping their lines of communication, and forcing the emperor to sue for peace.

Peter was overjoyed. Almost immediately, he launched a gigantic program to construct other ports along the Black Sea coastline and to set up a national competition on which of his provinces could build the most ships. He also pressed his struggle against the Ottoman Empire, enlisting European support. In 1700, as the new century was about to dawn, Peter realized that he was unable at the time to defeat the Ottomans, so he signed a peace treaty with Constantinople, which proved in time to be nothing more than a pause in the fighting.

Peter had attracted the attention of European leaders as a power in the east to be recognized and respected. Even so, he understood that Sweden, to his northwest, already in command of the entire Baltic region, was the nation he had to confront before he could dream of pushing Russia's borders to the Baltic and building his "window on the west"—his capital city of St. Petersburg on the Gulf of Finland. This confrontation was to grow into an all-consuming war that lasted from 1700 to 1721. It resulted in a historic Russian victory, although it began with a cataclysmic Russian defeat. Peter formed a secret anti-Sweden coalition with Poland and Denmark in 1699 and moved 40,000 troops to Narva, a city near the Gulf of Finland, the following year, a not insignificant military accomplishment. However, he still could not win the opening round with Sweden's young King, Charles XII, an 18-year-old soldier of fortune, courageous and brilliant. Charles XII inspired his comparatively small but well-trained and disciplined army of 8,000 to sneak up on the Russians and inflict a punishing defeat. The Swedes captured Russian generals, artillery, and supplies.

For Peter, the battle at Narva was a moment of truth. When he spotted the Swedes, instead of rallying his troops, he fled, in fear for his life. The hero of Azov had become the coward of Narva. The tsar was actually seen crying, and he contemplated suing for peace with Sweden. In time, though, he took a deep breath and reemerged as a tsar of determination and discipline. Peter was never a theorist, often an opportunist. He decided, Narva notwithstanding, that this was his time. With a surprising burst of energy, he set about reorganizing his army, rebuilding his artillery and armor, and expanding his fleet.

In May 1703 Peter took advantage of a momentary lull in his war against Sweden—Charles XII was absorbed elsewhere—and sent his reequipped army back to the Gulf of Finland, where he conquered Ingria and Livonia, two provinces held by Sweden, and there founded St. Petersburg. He was thrilled;

his "window on the west" finally opening. But, in fact, his war against Charles XII had entered a new and critical phase.

In 1707 Charles XII had a choice: He could recapture what Peter had won in small skirmishes along the Baltic coast (there was little doubt he could), or he could invade Russia and head toward Moscow, still the heart of the country. After long deliberations, he decided to attack Moscow, but his military calculations, usually so reliable, came upon totally unexpected obstacles. One of his key generals, whose army was equipped with fresh supplies and troops, ran into a much larger Russian force blocking his planned rendezvous with the main Swedish army. The general tried to outmaneuver the Russians but failed to do so. A major battle ensued, and the Russians emerged triumphant.

Charles XII, having fewer options now, changed his plans and marched into the Ukraine, where he was hoping to meet up with a secret ally, Ivan Mazepa, an Orthodox *hetman* who had opposed the Cossack alliance with Russia. Even more, Mazepa opposed Peter's constant demands for more Cossack soldiers to fight and die in Russia's nonstop wars. It could be argued that Mazepa, by joining up with Sweden, was only trying to protect the comparative autonomy of the Cossack nation, but Russians have portrayed him as a traitor. Their proof lay in his duplicitous negotiations with Poland, Russia's chronic enemy, and in his secret dealings with Charles XII, which, when disclosed, so disillusioned his Cossack followers that only a modest force of 2,000 fighters joined him in Sweden's war against Russia. Peter, furious at Mazepa's deception and defection, instantly encouraged the Russian church to excommunicate Mazepa and arranged for another Cossack leader to replace him as *hetman*.

The Russian winter of 1709 was especially harsh, even for a rugged Swedish king, deprived of adequate supplies and numbers of troops. With a splash of pathetic humor, the joke among the Swedes that winter was that they had but three doctors to treat Charles XII's shivering army and spreading epidemics: vodka, garlic, and death. On June 27, 1709, Swedish and Russian armies met on a field of battle at Poltava in central Ukraine. The Russians won a convincing victory. It was a victory for the ages, recalled by Russian nationalists to this day. Not only did it vindicate the Russian defeat at Narva; it also brought Russia into the European limelight—Russia's Peter and Russia's power.[5]

While more Russian-Swedish battles took place over the next several years, they proved to be of lesser consequence. Sweden was on the decline, and Russia on the rise. When Charles XII was killed in December 1718, the die was cast. Russian troops landed in Sweden in July 1719, ransacked the coastline; a Cossack corps, raping and pillaging, raced to within two miles of Stockholm.

Finally, in August 1721, Russia and Sweden negotiated a peace treaty in the Finnish town of Nystadt. The treaty transferred much of the Baltic coast to Russia "for all time to come" (a coast that now incorporates Latvia, Lithuania, and Estonia), and Russia returned Finland to Sweden, seen at the time as a generous gesture.

Militarily, economically, and diplomatically—thanks to Peter's determination and vision—Russia had arrived on the European stage.

Catherine the Great

If Peter opened his "window on the west," Catherine opened her front door, and, when she wished, shut it, too, suggesting that she was having trouble figuring out whether Russia ought to be part of the West or remain anchored in the East.[6]

Catherine, ruling from 1762 to 1796, was an impresario of style and power. Plots and pretenders, insurrections and uprisings, wars and intrigues marked her extraordinary tenure as leader of a Russia on the rise. She was an empress, a tsarina, exceptional in almost every way. She was, to begin with, not a Russian but a German—born Sophie Frederika Augusta von Anhalt-Zerbst and reared as an impecunious provincial princess, bright and manipulative, but with no right whatever to the Russian throne. She happened, however, to be in the right place at the right time: unmarried, unattached, primed for an arranged marriage so common at the time among European royalty. In 1742, Empress Elizabeth, Peter's reigning daughter, also unmarried and unattached, was looking for a reliable heir, and she settled on her nephew, the duke of Holstein-Gottorp, her sister Anna's son. Elizabeth invited this unimpressive young man to St. Petersburg, where, as grand prince, he took the name Peter III, though he was not even a shadow of his grandfather, Peter the Great. He spoke German better than Russian, and his idol was Prussia's Frederick the Great. Three years later, looking for a marriage to improve Russia's relations with Prussia, Elizabeth decided that the grand prince would marry young Sophie of Anhalt-Zerbst. He did as he was told, and the new bride was thrilled at the opportunity.

Within months after the marriage, though, it became clear that Peter III took little interest in Catherine, and she almost none in him. Each developed a private life totally independent of the other. Moreover, Peter III was pathetically ill-equipped for the job of heir apparent, and once he became tsar, Catherine quietly and quickly helped arrange a coup d'état. Peter III had been in office less than six months. Shortly after he was arrested, he was murdered.

Alexis Orlov, charged with protecting the former tsar, when asked how he died, replied: "We cannot ourselves remember what we did."

Catherine, a Lutheran who had converted to Orthodoxy and spoke Russian with a German accent, wasted no time ascending the vacant throne. She had already paved the way by organizing army brigades loyal only to her and by seeding the top of the Russian bureaucracy with her people. She was tough and shrewd, playing one general off against another, sensitive to any political challenge, and merciless when dealing with an adversary. She opened a chapter of dramatic change in Russian domestic and foreign policy so successful that when she died, at age sixty-seven, a plump but still authoritative figure after thirty-four years on the throne, she left behind a Russian empire strong and cohesive enough to survive until the 1917 communist revolution.

Catherine led a double life. One was being a consummate diplomat. The other was a carryover from Elizabeth's emphasis on expanding Russia's cultural connections with Western Europe. Elizabeth had put vast sums into constructing museums and universities and establishing contacts with writers and scholars, inviting them to St. Petersburg and encouraging Russian nobility to speak French and German and travel to the West. Catherine warmly embraced Elizabeth's policy. Indeed, once in power, she pushed it with a passion that shook the intellectual foundations of the Russian capital.

Unlike Elizabeth, who was an empress of limited intellectual rigor, Catherine was attuned to the highest cultural rhythms of her time. She maintained a personal correspondence with philosophers, such as Voltaire and d'Alembert; with statesmen such as Prussia's Frederick the Great and Austria's Joseph II; and with the encyclopedist Friedrich Melchior Grimm, who once said she was so dazzlingly brilliant that after talking with her for an hour, exploring issues as diverse as philosophy and economics, he would retire to his room, stimulated but exhausted, and pace the floor for hours unable to sleep. Catherine boasted that she read Blackstone's *Commentaries on the Law* for pleasure and Buffon's study of *Natural History* for relaxation. She invited a procession of poets to her court, the classicist Gavrila Derzhavin among them, and she would listen as they read their latest works. She also sculpted and painted. Late in life, she even attempted to write a history of Russia, which she never finished.

But if you asked her what challenged her the most, she would reply: diplomacy. Nothing thrilled her more than adjusting policy to a changing situation, manipulating foreign leaders, working closely with her generals during wars—of which there were many during her tenure—and playing with power. When she looked at the map of Russia, she saw a nation ready to burst out of its borders. First, Russia could turn east—to the promise and mystery of Siberia. To the south was Little Russia, or the Ukraine, ready, she felt, to be bound to Mother Russia, the Black Sea, and the Caucasus. Finally to the west, the challenge was to complete the job begun by Peter the Great—to finish off Sweden; subjugate Poland, Lithuania, and Galicia; and generally to join the grand game of European diplomacy. These were tasks as far-reaching as Catherine's own dreams for her adopted country, and she never doubted for a moment that she could lead Russia to its deserved place in the sun.

Siberia: An Empty, Tempting Target

Catherine's first goal was to conquer Siberia. It had always inspired dark memories of tribes invading from the east, the Mongols and others, spilling across the Urals and glaring down at Russia. For a time, the endless steppes stretching from the Urals to the Pacific remained largely uninhabited, a intriguing attraction for those who prized hunting, commerce, and adventure. Large Cossack communities and small Russian garrisons, mixing with runaway serfs, Bashkirs and Kalmucks and other discontented tribes—these were the people of a Siberia stretching over what today would be nine time zones, then essentially empty, its arms open to a Russia on the move.

Of all the Siberians, it's fair to say that the Cossacks played the most prominent role, founding towns and supporting military colonies. Though they chafed under Russian control, ironically by their presence and drive they advanced Russian interests. When the Cossacks stumbled occasionally upon scattered groups blocking their expansion, they dealt with them with characteristic toughness, brushing them aside or killing them. The Cossacks were used to life on the frontier. They had experienced it in the Ukraine, in the lower Volga, and now, on the other side of the Urals, in Siberia.

In this sense, the conquest of Siberia was not the result of government programs and planning, though there were some; it just happened, a natural extension of Russian power and ambition in the absence of any serious opposition.

In the early 1620s the Russians had already moved halfway across Siberia. By the 1640s they had reached the Lena River and offered land to settlers. By 1689 they had reached the Pacific and signed the Treaty of Nerchinsk, their first treaty with the Chinese, which effectively divided the territory of northern China into Russian and Chinese spheres. The treaty was China's idea. Russia, under Peter's rule, was engaged in frequent warfare with Sweden,

Poland, and Turkey. He did not have time to think about Siberia, and China was a challenge for a later time.

Even Catherine was so absorbed with the literary excitement of the Enlightenment and the potential threats of the American and French Revolutions that she too ignored the problems and promise of the Siberian expanse. And as a result she was the tsar who paid a heavy price.

The Pugachev Rebellion

In 1773–74, an illiterate Don Cossack named Emelyan Pugachev, pretending that he was Catherine's murdered husband, Peter III, rose from the relative obscurity of the southern Urals to demand Catherine's attention, and he got it—but only after leading a stormy, year-long revolt that briefly menaced Catherine's throne.

At first , Pugachev commanded a modest force of no more than 300 men, but soon, as he raced from one village to another, defeating Russian garrisons and raising hell, his force grew to thousands, and his message of rebellion spread like wildfire through dry sagebrush. To Catherine, the rebellion seemed at first to be a local affair, not a spreading revolution. She wrote a letter to Voltaire, describing Pugachev as "impudent" and a "common highway robber."

Pugachev's rebellion spread north on the Volga to the old Mongol capital of Kazan, a few hundred miles east of Moscow. With a force now of more than 20,000 troops, he captured Kazan and burned it to the ground. This finally caught Catherine's attention. She sent a large army to Kazan with orders not just to contain the rebellion but to destroy it. On July 15, 1774, the Russian army finally trapped and defeated Pugachev's troops and, shortly thereafter, captured and killed Pugachev. "No one since Tamerlane has [anyone] done more harm than he," Catherine admitted to Voltaire.

Ukraine, Always Ukraine

For Catherine, far more pressing and emotional was Ukraine, Little Russia, plus the contested crescent of black soil from Galicia to the Urals, which she envisaged as her gateway to the warm waters of the Black Sea. Blocking her path was the Ottoman Empire, which, ever since its conquest of Constantinople in 1453, sat stubbornly like an imperial bulldog atop many of the same territories claimed by Russia since the days of Kievan Rus'. Turkish control was motivated by imperial ambition; Russia's claim was rooted in blood and history—plus imperial ambition.

of "Russification." In 1764, pointing to Ukraine, Finland, and the Baltic provinces, she told her advisers that "to call them foreign and to treat them as such would be more than a mistake; it would be, indeed, plain stupidity. These provinces," she continued, "should be easily reduced to a condition where they can be Russified and no longer, like wolves, look for the woods. This can be achieved without effort if reasonable men are put in charge."

By "reasonable men," Catherine of course meant Catherine (and those she appointed), and she knew that phrases, such as "without effort," were for fairy tales, not hard-headed policy, which could and probably would include the use of military power. The Ottoman empire was Russia's enduring enemy. Twelve times, since 1676, they had fought, and Catherine was certain they would fight again—and they did in 1768, when Turkey, locked into an awkward alliance with Poland, demanded that Russia stop meddling in Poland's domestic politics, a demand that Catherine found impossible to obey. It would be like asking a Russian to stop drinking vodka.

A Cossack uprising and slaughter of Poles and Jews in the Turkish frontier town of Balta provided a convenient pretext for igniting yet another war with the Turks. There was no particular reason for the Cossack bloodletting; like so many others before and after, it was what Cossacks did every now and then, with or without a reason. Only this time the Poles amplified the Turkish demand by telling Catherine that she also had to force the Cossacks to withdraw from Balta. Catherine had been aching for a war with the Ottoman empire (Poland would come later), and she responded by ordering an attack on Turkish troops near a town called Galta on the other side of the border. She put Prince Golitsyn, another one of her favorites, in charge of the attack. The Turks were defeated, but they were still capable of mischievous doings. One was to tell their Crimean Tartar allies to invade southern Russia, thus opening another front in the war. In this way, attack and counterattack, another Turkish-Russian slugfest began. European strategists, judging the two adversaries, would have bet that Russia, as one of Europe's rising powerhouses, would emerge the ultimate winner, and it did.

On July 21, 1774, in Kuchuk Kainarji, a town in today's Bulgaria, the two sides signed a treaty that confirmed the Ottoman Empire's slide into imperial decline and extended Russian influence. Crimea, which had been under Turkish control, was declared independent, and Russia obtained sovereign authority over Azov, Kuban, and Terek, which meant effective access to the Black Sea, one of Russia's principal objectives, and to the northern Caucasus. As significant, Russia was also given all land from the Dnieper to the Bug rivers, extending her reach into central Europe. And on the religious front, Russia got the right to protect the Christian populations of Moldavia and Turkey and to build a church in Constantinople, which, for the sultan, was a concession as consequential as abandoning Crimea.

But the "independence" of Crimea, while for Russia a step in the right direction, did not really satisfy Catherine. Her "emperor" for southern Russia, Gregory Potemkin, whose authority over this region was second only to hers, kept urging Catherine to annex Crimea. "Now, just imagine that the Crimea is yours," he wrote, stroking her vanity. "Believe me, you will acquire immortal fame such as no other sovereign of Russia ever had. This glory will open the way to still further and greater glory." Finally, in July 1783, setting the stage for what Putin did a few centuries later, Catherine followed Potemkin's advice, making the strategic peninsula of Crimea an integral part of Imperial Russia.

Potemkin also urged Catherine to visit southern Russia. He had more than PR in mind; he wanted formally to incorporate southern Russia into Catherine's empire. The Ukraine had always been considered part of Russia, ever since Kievan Rus'; it had never been a foreign country. For Potemkin, who had worked for more than nine years to transform Ukraine into a prosperous part of her empire, a journey by Catherine would seal the deal.

Finally, in 1787, Catherine agreed—she would make the trip. It turned into the longest of her life, lasting six months and covering more than 4,000 miles by land and water with sledges, river galleys, and carriages. It started in St. Petersburg with stops in Smolensk, Kiev, Kherson, Poltava, Bakhchysarai, and Sevastopol in the Crimea. It was, without doubt, one of the most spectacular journeys any tsar or monarch could ever imagine. In political terms, it fixed Catherine's seal of approval on Potemkin's impressive though controversial achievements in the south. And, in diplomatic terms, it confirmed the strength and audacity of the new empire rising on the northern shore of the Black Sea in the rich soil of the Russian heartland, in a place now called Ukraine.

Potemkin realized that Catherine's journey had to be flawless. He planned everything: the route, the stops, the food, the distractions. How would an empress be carried down the Dnieper? In large and luxurious galleys, of course. He had them built. Where would Catherine and her entourage stay along the way? In borrowed houses, palaces, and mansions, many of them constructed precisely for this purpose. When Catherine and her entourage left Kiev after a break lasting six weeks, they journeyed down the Dnieper in seven large galleys, followed by eighty smaller vessels and 3,000 servants. Along the river, they passed villages where every roof seemed freshly painted, every street freshly paved, giving rise to the legend of "Potemkin villages," or false fronts to cover a gloomy reality.

Dreams of a Russian Constantinople

But if Catherine thought that her journey through southern Russia and Crimea would be seen primarily as her personal tribute to Potemkin, a spectacular way of saying "thanks," she changed her mind shortly after returning to St. Petersburg. Turkey provided the reason. The sultan saw her trip as a hostile, deliberately provocative challenge, and, offended, he again declared war on Russia.

The sultan's declaration fired Catherine's imagination and stoked her ambition. In recent years, she had been toying with the notion of creating a "Greek eastern empire," which she believed her grandson, Constantine, named after Constantinople, should govern. With Potemkin, always bursting with ideas, she concocted the "Greek Plan," according to which Russia, allied with Austria, would encourage a general uprising of Balkan Christians and a holy war against Islam. More than anything, she dreamed of driving the Turks out of Europe and planting a Russian flag over Constantinople. A smashing Russian victory over the Ottoman Empire would achieve that end—of that she was certain!

The sultan's call to arms was accompanied by demands he knew Catherine could not accept. He wanted her, in effect, to scrap the Treaty of Kuchuk Kainarji—to abandon Crimea, retreat from the Black Sea, and give up her newly acquired territory between the Dniester and the Bug rivers. Adding insult to injury, the sultan had the Russian ambassador imprisoned.

Neither Russia nor the Ottoman Empire was really ready for another war, but both fought gallantly. Losses were heavy, and alliances were fragile: Russia's with Austria collapsed, as did the Ottoman Empire's with Sweden. But by 1789, thanks to General Aleksandr Suvorov's unorthodox tactics, the Russian army began to score impressive victories, perhaps none more so than its conquest of the Ottoman fortress of Ochakov near the Black Sea. Potemkin surrounded the fortress with a 50,000-man army, but he did not order an attack. For reasons unclear, he waited, and waited, and waited. Suvorov wondered why. "You cannot capture a fortress," he kibitzed Potemkin, "merely by looking at it." Potemkin hesitated no longer; he gave Suvorov the green light. The general organized his attacking force into six columns of 5,000 troops each, and at dawn on December 6, 1788, they attacked. The battle lasted only four hours, but it proved to be one of the bloodiest in Russian history. Twenty-thousand Russians and 30,000 Turks were killed.

Then the battle scene shifted to the Danube, where again Suvorov won one victory after another. The Russians reached the lower Danube. Ahead was Izmail, a massive Turkish fortress of towers and ramparts, guarded by 35,000 troops and 265 cannon. A Russian force of 30,000 troops, equipped with 600 cannon, surrounded the fortress. Suvorov warned the Turks: "If Izmail resists, no one will be spared." When the Russians attacked, the Turks defended every rampart, cannon, and street—but they lost. Russian troops were then given three days to loot and rape, and they obliged. "Mother," Suvorov wrote to a jubilant Catherine, "Izmail is at your feet."

The Russians won the Balkans but could not yet declare victory, for a major naval battle was still under way in the Black Sea. The outcome would determine the winner. Russia's top admiral, Fyodor Fyodorovich Ushakov, was in charge of the Russian fleet, which, for a relatively new navy, did remarkably well. In a series of engagements, Ushakov outmaneuvered the Turks, scored a decisive victory, and headed toward Constantinople, no more than a two-day victory lap away. The sultan, in a sudden panic, sued for peace. As dramatically as he had started the war, he ended it. It was late December 1791. All of the sultan's demands were withdrawn. The Treaty of Kuchuk Kainarji stood unchanged. Crimea remained part of Russia, and Sevastopol was still a Russian port.

Possibly, if Catherine had not needed to worry about another war with Sweden, she might have made the time to push her "Greek plan," but it had to be shelved since Gustavus III—"such a feeble instrument as the king of Sweden," to use Catherine's dismissive description—decided to take advantage of Catherine's preoccupation with Turkey to attack Russia. He wanted to retake the Baltic states—and he had more in mind. He demanded that Catherine accept Swedish mediation in the Russian-Turkish war and that Russia return all Turkish lands conquered since 1768, including Crimea. It was a delusional demand, and Catherine ignored it. In July 1789, Gustavus III sent his fleet into the Gulf of Finland, but he could not destroy the Russian fleet, nor dislodge the Russian army. On August 3, unable to score a victory, he sued for peace. Catherine, otherwise absorbed, agreed to a peace treaty that left everything as it was. Catherine wrote to Potemkin: "We have pulled one paw out of the mud [Baltic]. As soon as we pull out the other [Turkey], we'll sing alleluia."

By the summer of 1791, the Russians again proved they were Turkey's master. In one battle after another, Suvorov's experienced army defeated the sultan's tattered forces. By December 1791, the Ottoman Empire had had enough and finally surrendered. The two sides met in Jassy, Moldavia, and concluded an historic peace agreement. Although Catherine had hoped to plant a Russian flag over Constantinople (in this respect, she failed), she did manage to advance Russian interests in a number of ways:

—The Ottoman Empire gave up its historic claim to Crimea, whose annexation by Russia was now confirmed by international agreement;

—The empire accepted Russian control of Sevastopol and therefore acceptance of a Russian naval presence in the Black Sea;

—Russia gained control of Ochakov, opening the Dniester to further exploitation; and

—Russia confirmed, by treaty, its possession of the land between the Bug and Dniester rivers.

The Partitions of Poland

Now Catherine turned her full attention to Poland, for centuries a Russian adversary. Earlier, in August 1772, while still absorbed in a war with the Ottoman Empire, she joined forces with Prussia and Austria to begin the partitioning of Poland; it was an outlandish idea, but each nation, for its own reasons, adopted it. Austria had already invaded Galicia, crossed the Carpathians, and occupied southern Poland. "It seems that in Poland," a Prussian diplomat observed, not in wonder, "one only has to stoop and help oneself." Catherine replied: "Why shouldn't we both take our share?"[7] At the time, Poland was in a pathetically weak state, its independence totally dependent on Catherine's whims. She had appointed its king, Stanislaw August Poniatowski, one of her former lovers. She controlled its economy and politics. She could at any time have turned Poland into a Russian satellite. Alarmed at the prospect, King Frederick II of Prussia, though an ally of Russia, proposed a three-way partition of Poland as a way of heading off such a move. In this way, he thought, Prussia and Austria could at least control parts of Poland. Catherine, absorbed with other problems, both domestic and foreign, accepted Frederick's proposal. On August 5, 1772, the unholy troika of Russia, Prussia, and Austria, operating as the cynical overlords of a neighbor's sovereignty, started to slice up Poland, an independent country. It was to be the first slice; years later, two other slices were to follow. The result was that the Polish-Lithuanian Commonwealth, founded in 1569 as a Catholic counterweight to Orthodox Russia, simply ceased to exist. Poland lost a third of its territory and more than a third of its population. What was left was a crumbling shadow of its former self.

Sixteen years later, with Russia distracted by another war with Turkey, the Polish parliament, the *Sejm,* bestirred itself into a modest revolt against Russian domination. It voted for majority rule, replacing a system that left most decisions to a group of Polish noblemen loyal to Catherine. Anti-Russian demonstrations took place, and in 1791 the *Sejm* approved a new constitution. When Catherine heard that Prussia and Austria had accepted the constitution, she decided that Russia would act on its own. She believed that a democratic Poland would set a dangerous precedent for Russia, and she was determined, she wrote Grimm, to "exterminate that nest of Jacobins in Warsaw."[8]

On May 7, 1792, Catherine sent 65,000 Russian troops across the frayed Polish border; a few weeks later, another 35,000 troops. Poland's position was hopeless, and King Stanislaw August instantly surrendered. His *Sejm*, though, continued to rumble with dissatisfaction, split down the middle into pro- and anti-Russian factions. Catherine decided, in December 1792, that it was time for another partition of Poland, and, a month later, Russia and Prussia—this time without Austria—signed a secret treaty sanctioning yet another partition of Poland. Russia got another large slice of eastern Poland, including Minsk and the rest of what is now Belarus; another slice of Lithuania, including Vilnius; and all of western Ukraine. Prussia acquired Danzig and Thorn, both long coveted, and much of northwestern Poland.

As her biographer, Robert K. Massie, wrote: "Catherine told herself that not only had she fended off the revolutionary virus spreading from France, but she was simply reoccupying lands that had once belonged to the great sixteenth-century [sic] principality of Kiev, 'lands still inhabited by people of the Russian faith and race.'"[9] Earlier Russian rulers might have considered these moves, but Catherine was the first to cite "Russian faith and race" as a reason or pretext for occupying a foreign land. In this way, Catherine set a precedent for Putin.

It is likely that Catherine would have found another reason to complete the partitioning of Poland, but one was unintentionally presented to her in April 1794, by Thaddeus Kosciuszko, a dashing Polish officer trained in France who had fought alongside Washington and Lafayette during the American Revolution. Angry at Catherine and disappointed in Poland's abject surrender to Russian power, he rallied an army of 4,000 troops and 2,000 peasants and on March 24 defeated a 7,000-man Russian army near Krakow. This victory sparked a rush of Polish patriotism through much of the country. Indeed, Kosciuszko's revolt spread so rapidly that when his rebel forces suddenly appeared before Warsaw, they surprised and overwhelmed the Russian occupation garrison. Three thousand Russian soldiers were killed, their bodies stripped and left naked in the streets. A portrait of Catherine, ripped from the Russian Embassy, was torn to pieces in front of a cheering Polish crowd.

Catherine, the empress who had corresponded with Voltaire and brushed shoulders with the European enlightenment, decided it was time to "extinguish the last spark of the Jacobin fire in Poland."[10] Unable any longer to depend on Prussian fortitude or Austrian guile, she sent the ever-ready Suvorov to Poland with orders to capture or kill Kosciuszko. On October 10, a Russian force of 13,000 troops decisively defeated a ragtag Polish regiment of 7,000 troops. Kosciuszko was wounded and captured in the battle and sent in chains to St. Petersburg.

Next in Suvorov's path to Warsaw was Praga, a fortified suburb across the Vistula from the capital. Before ordering an attack on Praga, Suvorov reminded his troops of the Polish slaughter of Russian troops in Warsaw in the spring. The Russian troops were primed for a slaughter of their own—and that is what happened. Three hours after the attack started, "the whole of Praga," Suvorov later reported, "was strewn with bodies, and blood was flowing in streams."[11] As many as 20,000 Poles were killed—not just troops, but women, children, and priests as well. Suvorov then warned Warsaw to surrender—or else. Warsaw surrendered.

Catherine was not in a forgiving mood. She believed that the dangers of revolutionary Jacobinism continued to smolder in the wreckage of Poland, and Poland itself had to be smothered to death. This once proud country was to be partitioned yet again, this time until nothing would be left. Alexander Bezborodko, a Ukrainian on Catherine's staff, confided to the empress that, in his judgment, Poland had proven over many centuries that it could not be trusted. Therefore it should be treated as a conquered land, meaning all Polish regalia, banners, and state insignia, along with archives and libraries, should be packed up and sent to Russia. Poland as a nation should simply cease to exist.

On January 3, 1795, an agreement among Russia, Prussia, and Austria ordered the final partition of Poland. Nothing was left. Catherine later explained that she had not annexed "a single Pole"—that all she had done was take back ancient Russian and Lithuanian lands with Orthodox people who were "now reunited with the Russian motherland." Russians thought Catherine made a great deal of sense. She was praised. That she was manipulating history for her own ends was of no importance to them.

Poles and many others had a different view. They knew that the third partition meant the extinction of a nation. For the next 126 years, until the Versailles Treaty ending World War I called for Poland to be reborn, Poland was not a nation. It was a memory, a culture, a tradition, a language entombed within the Russian empire.

CHAPTER 7

A Ukrainian Volk Emerges, on Paper

I myself do not know whether my soul is Ukrainian or Russian. I know
only that on no account would I give priority to the Little Russian
before the Russian, or to the Russian before the Little Russian.
NIKOLAI GOGOL

FIRST PETER AND THEN CATHERINE spent most of their tsardoms
expanding the Russian empire, and then consolidating it. By the time of
Catherine's death in 1796, the empire stretched from the Baltic Sea in the
northwest to Vladivostok in the east, embracing all of Siberia along the way.
An empire so vast could not all be controlled with Prussian-like efficiency,
every part marching to a single drummer, but both tsars sought to tighten
the screws of empire, making certain that St. Petersburg would be the only
postmark of the Slavic universe. Their goals were identical: to exercise absolute authority, to crush political opponents at home and abroad, and to
advance Russia's national interests, usually through military strength. These
approaches worked well through much of the nineteenth century, indeed until
1917 when the Russian Revolution changed the calculus of world politics.

Interestingly, the end of their rule coincided with the birth of European
nationalism, which elevated the *volk*, the "people," into being the social and
political force that defined a nation. The eighteenth-century German philosopher Johann Gottfried Herder, a student of Immanuel Kant, helped spark
the creation of a new romantic nationalism that fed the sophisticated chatter
of the European salon. "There is only one class in the state," he wrote, "the
volk, and the king belongs to this class as well as the peasant." Of course, there
was a world of difference between the king and the peasant, but Herder was
an idealist, ushering in a new age of nationalism, and he was reaching for
the stars. "Do not nationalities differ in everything," he asked, "in poetry, in
appearance, in taste, in usages, customs and languages?" One day he looked

at a map of Europe and, for a German, drew the remarkable conclusion that "the Slavic nation will one day be the real power in Europe."

Ukraine was only a small corner of the Slavic nation. In fact, Ukraine was part of Russia, formally and fully. For most Ukrainians, the tsar was their unchallenged leader, and Russia their home. The sparsely settled *Novorossiya* regions of southern Ukraine were absorbed into the ever-expanding Russian empire, and Russians from other parts of Ukraine, the Balkans, and Germany settled there. The Black Sea port of Odessa blossomed into a cosmopolitan metropolis, home for Russians, Ukrainians, Jews, and many other peoples. The Donbas emerged as an industrial boomland, attracting Russian workers from all over the country.

Ukrainian nationalism, to the degree that it existed at all in the nineteenth century, lived in the seminar rooms of the newly created universities, which the modestly reformist tsar Alexander I allowed to emerge in Ukraine. The first was built in Kharkov in 1805. A second was founded in Kiev in 1834, and another in Odessa in 1865. Though they were administratively part of the Russian educational system, they served nonetheless as places where the study of local language, literature, culture, and ethnography was encouraged—and enjoyed. Indirectly, this stimulated the rise not of nationalism, as such, but rather an appreciation of Ukrainian history, which eventually nourished a feeling of nationalism.

During the nineteenth century, in a part of Europe where national boundaries were always hazy, changing with disturbing regularity, Ukraine was more a culture than a country. Only among a small number of Ukrainian intellectuals was there the flickering of nationalism, and here too it was more the stuff of poetry than politics.

In this spirit, scholar Andrew Wilson focused on two Ukrainian writers as examples of the differences in the budding nationalism. One was Mykola Hohol, known to the world as Nikolai Gogol, his Russified name. Gogol was born in Ukraine. He used Ukrainian folk themes and humor. He lampooned corruption and petty bureaucracy, common to both Ukraine and Russia. But he wrote in Russian, because he believed, according to some experts, that "great literature in the Ukraine could be written only in Russian." For literary glory, he looked to St. Petersburg; for inspiration, he looked to "the Ukraine."[1]

"I myself do not know," Gogol mused, "whether my soul is Ukrainian or Russian. I know only that on no account would I give priority to the Little Russian before the Russian, or to the Russian before the Little Russian. Both natures are too richly endowed by God, and, as if by design, each of them separately contains within itself what the other lacks—a sure sign that they complement one another."[2] For proof, read *Taras Bulba*. If still not convinced, read *The Inspector General*.

In his writing, Gogol battled with both the Russian and the Little Russian components of his life and career; in the end, though, he was content with both. Not so Taras Shevchenko. Though born a serf in an impoverished village, he evolved into Ukraine's national bard, largely because he joyfully raised the Cossack banner and drew sharp distinctions between Russia and Ukraine. To this day, he is hailed by Ukrainian patriots as a national hero, the George Washington of his country. (A statue of a defiant Shevchenko stands proudly at the intersection of 22nd, 23rd, and P streets in Washington, D.C., a gift of Ukrainian émigrés to the United States.) To Shevchenko, the Cossack tradition reminded him of Herder's *volk*, the heart and soul of a new, rising Ukraine. He too could have written in Russian, but he purposely chose Ukrainian, and his poetry exuded an unmistakable pride in all things Ukrainian and a deep dislike, distrust, and suspicion of all things Russian and, to lesser degrees, Polish, Jewish, and German.

In his poem "The Dream," written in 1844, Shevchenko mocks Pushkin's poem "The Bronze Horseman," lambasting the horseman's inspiration, Peter the Great, with enough venom to earn the outspoken poet a trip to Siberia that could have lasted ten years.

> Thou evil tsar!
> Accursed Tsar, insatiate,
> Perfidious serpent, what
> Have you done, then, with the Cossacks?
> You have filled the swamps
> With their noble bones! And then
> Built the capital (St. Petersburg)
> On their tortured corpses.

He continued, shooting barbs at both Peter and Catherine:

> It was (Peter) the First who crucified
> Unfortunate Ukraine,
> And (Catherine) the second—she who finished off
> Whatever yet remained.[3]

While Gogol saved all of his energies for satire, Shevchenko expanded his reach, plunging into politics when the opportunity arose. And it did in 1846, when a small group of Ukrainian intellectuals, mostly teachers and writers, formed the secret "Brotherhood of Cyril and Methodius" in Kiev. The name recalled the two ninth-century monks who alphabetized the Slavic language and began the Christianization of Eastern Europe. Shevchenko happily joined the Brotherhood. It was for him a lifelong dream: a political organization with an exciting platform promising political independence and the abolition of serfdom. It was also a platform that terrified Tsar Nicholas I, who promptly shut down the Brotherhood and arrested and exiled its leaders.[4] The Brotherhood existed for all of fourteen months. According to Mikhaelo Hrushevsky, a Ukrainian historian and political leader in the early twentieth century, "this practical activity (of the Brotherhood) was killed at birth. . . . This repression put a stop to any development of political thought in the Ukraine."[5] But Hrushevsky, despite his training as an "objective" historian, might prematurely have buried Ukrainian political thought, perhaps as a deliberate counterpoint to the modest success he enjoyed during the Russian Revolution. While political debate in mid-nineteenth-century Ukraine was not open and robust, it still existed. For a limited number of Ukrainian intellectuals and teachers, it was their cause. They argued, they debated, they wrote, all with the hope they were breathing life into Ukrainian nationalism. Some even linked their "nativist" narrative to the Slavophile movement then absorbing many Russian intellectuals. The Ukrainians folded their own literature, language, and Cossack traditions into a distinctive file, labeled "Ukraine," thereby in their romantic dreams elevating Ukraine to the status of a nation, the same as Russia, Prussia, or Austria.

Some writers even went one step further—advocating a union of Slavic nations, led by Ukraine and deliberately excluding Russia. In one formulation, the union consisted of "Ukraine, including the Black Sea, Galicia and Crimea; Poland with Poznan and Lithuania; Bessarabia with Moldavia; and Wallachia, the Eastern Sea, Serbia, Bulgaria and the Don." By excluding Russia, the Ukrainian nationalist writer Heorhii Andruzkyi could have it both ways: he could place Ukraine at the head of a Putin-type Eurasian coalition, following a goal sacred to the Slavophile tradition, but he could at the same time exclude Russia, which would have satisfied his fellow nationalists.[6]

The pro-Russian writer A. I. Savenko, on the other hand, stressed the importance of a continuing bond between Russia and Ukraine, almost as though defending an old love. "The Polish, Armenian, Finnish and other problems are peripheral, secondary problems," he wrote, "but the Mazepist injures Russia at the origins of its existence as a great power. . . . Poland, Finland and other borderlands did not give Russia her greatness. Ukraine did."[7]

For Russian nationalists, such as Savenko, Ukraine was an essential part of the Russian empire—and always had been. (A "Mazepist" refers to followers of the anti-Russian Cossack *hetman* Ivan Mazepa, who took up arms against the Russians in the eighteenth century.) Indeed, the concept of Ukraine as a nation was beyond their imagination, much less comprehension. In their minds, since it had always been a part of Russia, its origins and Russia's were spun from the same cloth.

Therefore, those few Ukrainian intellectuals who were inspired by Western theories of national independence and personal freedom had to be put in their place. So believed a succession of Russian tsars, starting with Nicholas I, whose first decision as tsar was to crush what became known as the Decembrist Uprising of 1825. A small group of Russian officers and aristocrats had taken the unprecedented position, in public, of opposing Nicholas's accession to the throne. They preferred his more liberal brother, Constantine. Unafraid, they demonstrated, and thousands joined them. Nicholas, shocked, ordered his army commanders mercilessly to suppress the uprising, which they did with stunning swiftness and brutality. Five leaders were hanged, and others sent into Siberian exile.

For this reason and others, Nicholas I came to distrust even the smallest rumbling of political reform at home, and he wanted no part of the liberal thinking then sweeping through Western Europe. In 1828 he abolished the tender autonomy enjoyed by Bessarabia; same in 1830 in Poland. When Sergei S. Uvarov, his scholarly minister of education, provided him in 1833 with a doctrinal underpinning for his rule, Nicholas I enthusiastically embraced its three-sided formula of "Orthodoxy, Autocracy, and Nationalism." It won many adherents and quickly became the banner of Russian conservatism, raised aloft even to this day by fans of Putinism.

What followed was increased political oppression; deeper censorship of books, magazines, and newspapers; and tighter control over provinces, such as Ukraine. In 1863 the tsar banned virtually all publications in the Ukrainian language, with the exception of belles lettres, and in 1876 this ban was extended to include even them. Books published abroad in Ukrainian could no longer be imported into Russia, nor would public readings or theater presentations in Ukrainian be allowed in Russia. Worse still, these bans had a major negative impact on Ukrainian education, accounting in part for the low literacy rate among Ukrainians toward the end of the nineteenth century. In 1897, 87 percent were illiterate.

Interestingly, writers living in those parts of Ukraine run by Russia chose to publish their works in Austrian Galicia, which was home to many other

Ukrainians. Thus, it was in Galicia at this time that there were the early stir-rings of a Western-oriented Ukrainian national movement. A similar move-ment, though Russia-oriented, was formed secretly in *hromadas*, or "com-munities," throughout Russian-ruled Ukraine. They promoted Ukrainian culture and education and illegally published brochures and magazines. Mykhailo Petrovych Drahomanov, a leading Ukrainian nationalist, chal-lenged the St. Petersburg salon by openly advocating the transformation of the Russian empire into a federal republic, in which Ukrainian national rights would be assured. The proposal got nowhere, of course, but it created a stir among both Russian and Ukrainian intellectuals, who began to think about an alternative to Uvarov's concept of imperial Russian power.

In 1900, for the first time, Ukrainian nationalists in Kharkov formed a political party, called the Revolutionary Ukrainian Party, and boldly pro-posed the goal of "one single, indivisible, free, independent Ukraine." They were proud nationalists, but their proposal was, for its time, totally unreal-istic. Few of their countrymen were seriously engaged in politics; most were still focused on more modest goals, such as loosening Russian constraints on the Ukrainian language and literature.

CHAPTER 8

In Revolution, the Birth of Modern Ukraine

It is a pity that pogroms take place, but they uphold the discipline of the army.
SYMON PETLYURA, UKRAINIAN POLITICIAN

REVOLUTIONS USUALLY ARE MESSY THINGS, and the ones in the Russian empire in the early years of the twentieth century were messy, indeed. And bloody, too. The first revolution, in 1905, quickly spread from St. Petersburg to Kiev and other provincial capitals. Worker strikes erupted in the Donbas, and peasant unrest swept the countryside. The 1905 revolution shook the tsar's absolute control of his empire. Reform was in the air. In April 1906, when the pressure to upend his old, rickety political system seemed overwhelming, Tsar Nicholas II reluctantly yielded to the creation of a Duma, or elected assembly, the first of its kind in Russian history. It was a new, exciting place for political dialogue. Ukraine won its share of the prize, electing enough delegates to form its own caucus. Though debate was raucous, it was also misleading, for, in fact, the tsar still had enough clout to influence the flow of legislation. Russians controlled the agenda, and national minorities were encouraged to wait their turn.

That is, until World War I. It was an unnecessary war, one of the bloodiest in European history. More than 9 million combatants were killed, along with an estimated 7 million civilians. When it finally ended, four empires had collapsed into history: the Russian, German, Austrian, and Ottoman. The nationalities that had survived in the grip of those empires now sprung to life. A new dictatorship, under a fiery, dedicated band of communists, took power in what was left of Russia. Chaos, rather than a new world, reigned in postwar Europe. Perhaps in no place more than in Ukraine—which never had firm borders and which quickly found itself divided into two parts—was that chaos more evident. One part of the land looked for its destiny in the West, the other hooked into its historic dependency on Russia.

For the first time in its turbulent history, between 1917 and 1921, Ukraine experienced a quick immersion in national independence. In this fleeting four-year hiatus, Ukraine was trapped in the crosshairs of a world war, a revolution, a counter-revolution, and a nationalist crusade pulling in two opposite directions—the Bolsheviks determined to keep Ukraine in Moscow's grip, the Poles aligned with anti-Russian nationalists fixed on tying the new Ukraine to the West. The tides of war and revolution, unsettling to both sides, shifted dramatically. By 1921 most of Ukraine was again under Moscow's control, though it was a Moscow under new management.

Adieu to Nicholas II, Salut to Lenin

Nicholas II's pathetically poor leadership of the Russian army and "mad monk" Rasputin's maniacal manipulation of the tsar's wife finally precipitated the Russian Revolution in February 1917. A provisional government was established. Freedom of speech and assembly was proclaimed. The Russian monarchy was doomed. As the tsar's power diminished, Ukraine, along with other parts of the former empire, fell into a political void. In March Ukrainian nationalists formed the Central Rada, or council, and in April the All-Ukrainian National Congress selected the esteemed historian Mykhaelo Hrushevsky to head the Rada.

Uncertain about the dimensions of his power, yet determined to make a difference, Hrushevsky called first for the transformation of Russia into a democratic, federal republic and then for the territorial autonomy of Ukraine—stopping short of calling for the independence of Ukraine. Still, within weeks, differences arose between the Rada and the provisional government in Russia over territorial jurisdiction and political power. Worse, deeper differences arose between the Rada and local workers' and soldiers' soviets, or legislative assemblies, dominated by socialists and communists, about the true purpose of the revolution: Was it to ignite a global communist revolution, with Moscow as the guiding ideological force, or was it simply a gaudy way of sponsoring a national liberation movement?

The answer came on November 7, 1917, when the Bolsheviks, led by Vladimir Lenin, seized power in St. Petersburg—which had been renamed Petrograd at the beginning of World War I—and proclaimed its dominion over the many splintering parts of the old tsarist empire, including Ukraine. Less than two weeks later, on November 20, Hrushevsky formally objected to

Russia's land grab. With the authority of the Rada behind him, he took a big step toward national independence, solemnly announcing the creation of the Ukrainian National Republic.

This exchange might have had the appearance of ping-pong politics, but it was deadly serious. The argument was about whether Ukraine would remain part of a new Russian empire or whether it would become an independent nation. A month later, in December 1917, the Bolsheviks, meeting in Kharkov, declared that, so far as they were concerned, Ukraine was to be a soviet republic, part of a larger union of soviet republics. A month later, the Bolsheviks opened a military offensive against Kiev, soon overwhelming the ancient capital. The Rada, seeing its options limited, made two quick, eye-catching decisions: It proclaimed Ukraine's total independence and opened negotiations with the so-called Central Powers, hoping to align Ukraine with Austria and Prussia against Russia, an arrangement historians would find quite familiar. The new alignment paid an immediate dividend. Prussia and Austria, attacking from the north and west, dislodged the Bolshevik hold on Kiev, forcing a broad Russian retreat. For a time, anyway. The Bolsheviks were to return twice more.

What then followed was a bewildering mix of war, revolution, and counterrevolution. The Germans unceremoniously overthrew the Rada in April 1918 and set up a new regime, run by General Pavlo Petrovych Skoropadskyi, an obedient *hetman* claiming direct lineage to the eighteenth-century Cossacks. His dream was an independent Ukraine, but one that looked and acted as though it hadn't emerged from Mazepa's time two centuries earlier. Skoropadskyi and his German supporters had an initial run of good luck and extended their writ deep into Ukraine, absorbing Kiev and other major cities. He established an old-fashioned, conservative regime, abrogated all Rada decrees, and battled the Bolsheviks with a measure of success—that is, until his backers, Prussia and Austria, capitulated to the Entente powers in November 1918, ending the war. Skoropadsky was then finished, and he knew it. He abdicated in December 1918, and a newly formed Directory of the Ukrainian Republic, based in Kiev, devoted to a modern Ukraine and led by Symon Petlyura, took power.

Except, at the time, it was not the only Ukrainian Republic, a circumstance that should not have surprised anyone. The other Ukraine, called the Western Ukrainian National Republic, had been created in October 1918. It embraced Galicia, Northern Bukovina, and Transcarpathia, home for millions of Catholic Ukrainians, who saw Moscow not as a savior but as an oppressor. This Ukraine was backed by a resurgent Poland, recently liberated from a long stretch of Russian domination dating back to the three partitions of the late eighteenth century. The eastern Ukrainians, eager to assert their authority over their western brethren, marched into Lvov, the cultural capital of the western Ukrainians, on November 1, 1918. It hit a nerve end so sensitive to the Poles that they declared war on the Moscow-backed Ukrainians. Three weeks later, after bitter battles, the Poles reoccupied Lvov. But, at that moment, both Ukraines, distressed by the shifting military and political landscape, came on their own to roughly the same conclusion—let's unite! And unite they did on January 22, 1919. Though it was unity more in name than fact, they did manage to establish Ukrainian as the official language of the state and to proclaim the independence of the Ukrainian Orthodox Church, up to that time a subordinate branch of the Russian Orthodox Church.[1]

Complicating Ukraine's problems still further, the French then moved 60,000 troops into the Black Sea port of Odessa to support the Russian "Whites," who, led by General Anton Denikin, were in a counter-revolution against the Bolsheviks, the "Reds." The Whites wanted to destroy the Reds and restore a united anticommunist Russia. Ukraine suddenly found itself caught in another war, a civil war between Reds and Whites, supported by foreign armies.

Things got tense, and unpredictable. The Bolsheviks again fought their way back into Kiev. More than anything, they wanted this time to reimpose Russian control over all of Ukraine. Totally heedless of Ukrainian needs and sensitivities, the Bolsheviks launched a terror campaign against "counter-revolutionaries" and "alien class" reactionaries. Thousands of Ukrainians were rounded up and killed. The Bolsheviks dispatched armed Russian detachments into the countryside, where they seized grain for their own use, leaving none to the peasants, and confiscated large estates, sloppily transforming them into inefficient state farms. The impact was widespread and horrific. Local peasant chieftains, called *otamany*, organized armies of desperate peasants, who went on a Cossack-like rampage through the countryside, killing Bolsheviks one day, socialists the next, as well as one another. One of these armies drove the French out of Odessa. Another, under anarchist Nestor Makhno, wanted to set up a peasant republic but never did. He fought against Denikin's Whites and Lenin's Reds and settled for skirmishes against other peasant armies, when he had no other convenient enemy.

In this wild civil war in 1919, perhaps no group suffered more than Ukrainian Jews, always a convenient target in Ukrainian history. In a brief period of time, more than 30,000 were slaughtered. Everyone joined in this exuberant anti-Semitic pogrom—the Reds, the Whites, the autonomous *otamany*, even the governing Directory, which was accused in some accounts of being responsible for 40 percent of the killing. It was reminiscent of earlier Cossack pogroms, when Jew-killing was an acceptable form of mass murder. Petlyura, the commander-in-chief of the Directory, was a charismatic politician and, judging by his troops' slaughter of the Jews, an anti-Semite by instinct and action. "It is a pity that pogroms take place," he said, "but they uphold the discipline of the army." If the quote accurately reflected his sentiments, Petlyura seemed to be saying that killing Jews helped keep Ukrainian soldiers in line. It was their way of letting off steam. Petlyura's Directory did condemn the pogroms, but they continued anyway, as marauding bands of undisciplined soldiers and peasants, aligned with the Ukrainian, Russian, Red, and White armies, moved randomly from village to village killing Jews, gypsies—anyone who happened to be in their way.[2]

Caught in the middle of the civil war, Ukraine became an impossible place to govern. The Bolsheviks could not impose their "dictatorship of the people," in part because it was at the time an untested policy, and in part because the Whites, bolstered by the Western powers (the Entente), and Petlyura's forces, equipped by the Ukrainian Galician Army, were advancing on the Bolsheviks, defeating them in battle and forcing them to retreat to the eastern rim of Ukraine, where many Russian speakers lived. This might have been a turning point in the civil war, except for a tragic typhus epidemic that swept through western Ukraine. For some reason, the Entente blocked medical supplies from reaching the front, and by October an estimated 70 percent of the Directory's army fell to the disease, and more than 90 percent of the Galician army. Thus, laid low by a cruel typhus bug, Petlyura's forces could no longer fight, and he struck a deal with Poland, Galicia's historic enemy. Poland would get parts of Volhynia and Podolia, both in western Ukraine. The deal brought Petlyura's alliance with the Ukrainian Galician Army to an abrupt end. On November 15 Petlyura named himself dictator of the Directory and fled to Warsaw.

As a force in Ukrainian politics, he was now finished, his legacy a spotty one of lofty Ukrainian nationalism besmirched by anti-Semitism, but he still hoped to persuade the Poles to join him in one final offensive against the Bolsheviks. The Poles agreed after winning territorial concessions in eastern Galicia and western Volhynia—not because they thought they could defeat the Bolsheviks but because they wanted to establish a Ukrainian buffer state between themselves and the Russians. In April 1920 Polish and Ukrainian troops attacked the Russians and recaptured Kiev. But it was to be a Pyrrhic victory. By June the Russians were back, the vanguard of a massive offensive that actually brought the Red Army to the gates of Warsaw. The Poles, backs against the wall, decided that an armistice made more sense than a buffer. The Treaty of Riga, signed in March 1921, sealed the status quo: The Poles recognized a country called Soviet Ukraine, thereby abandoning Petlyura's "western" Ukrainians, and they retained control of eastern Galicia and western Volhynia. Peasant uprisings, popping up all over Ukraine, continued to trouble the Bolsheviks, but they no longer threatened Moscow's domination of Ukraine.

The Ukrainian revolution was over, but it changed Eastern European history in two ways: The idea of an independent Ukraine, while unsuccessful, was now credible, and the Bolsheviks had to establish and recognize a Ukrainian state within the newly formed Soviet Union. For the first time in its history, Ukraine had "national" borders. It had a "parliament," and it had a cabinet of ministers. It also had a flag. In other words, it had the framework of national independence, all unintended byproducts of Lenin's decision to address the nationality problem in revolutionary Russia.

CHAPTER 9

Lenin and the "National Minorities" Conundrum

Enemy number one for Stalin and his circle was not the Ukrainian peasant,
nor the Ukrainian intelligentsia. The enemy was Ukraine itself.
JAMES MACE, HISTORIAN

LENIN WAS NO FOOL. As he plotted his revolution, he was always mindful of the fact that Russia was composed of many national minorities. According to the 1926 census—the first since the Russian Revolution—the number, carefully delineated, was 176. The question was, how could he win their support? Better still, their loyalty?

At a Bolshevik gathering in Kharkov in 1913, Lenin turned to a devoted, young revolutionary, a Georgian named Josef (Djugashvili) Stalin, and asked him to write a paper on Marxism and the nationality question. At the time, Lenin was worried that Otto Bauer, a leader of Austria's Socialist Party, was successfully propagating the view that "cultural autonomy" was the key to understanding the essence of nationalism. No, argued Lenin. "Cultural autonomy" suggested that the worker and the capitalist shared the same underlying beliefs. Lenin was certain that was not true. In his interpretation of Marxism, the worker was engaged in a class struggle, the capitalist was his enemy, his oppressor, and in no way did they share the same "cultural" foundation. Lenin wanted Stalin to prove Bauer was wrong.[1]

Stalin was not a theoretician. He was a party organizer, a talented *apparatchik* who had proven his devotion to the Marxist cause by getting himself arrested five times. Lenin had given him an assignment, and Stalin quickly produced a pamphlet innocuously titled "Marxism and the Nationality Question." Given Stalin's subsequent stature and power, it was not surprising that it became a best seller in communist kiosks around the world, the starting point for any serious discussion of the nationality problem, no matter how theoretical. There was at the time speculation that Lenin had in fact authored the pamphlet, but chose, for political and PR reasons, as a Russian nationalist, to allow a national minority (a Georgian, in this case) to state the party's position on the nationalities issue.

Regardless of whether it was penned by Lenin or Stalin, the pamphlet clearly reflected Lenin's views. It defined a nationality as a "historically constituted, stable community of peoples, formed on the basis of a common language, territory, economic life and psychological make-up manifested in a common culture." Each and every nationality, Stalin wrote, had an inherent right to "national self-determination," even to the point of creating an independent nation.[2] This was heady stuff, considering the potential danger of 176 nationalities rising and demanding their independence. It could be that at the time Stalin and Lenin actually believed in "national self-determination," but only within the context of a worldwide communist revolution. If India was to demand its independence from Great Britain, if Indochina was to demand its independence from France, that was consistent with another slogan in their rhetorical arsenal—namely, anti-imperialism. Oppressed peoples were merely "overthrowing the shackles of colonialism."

Lenin was then in the revolutionary phase of his career. His enemies were the obvious ones: the Romanov monarchy, capitalism, imperialism, colonialism. To win the allegiance of the many nationalities that made up the country, he was ready to say and support just about anything that would advance his revolutionary goals. Both Lenin and Stalin said, with apparent conviction, that "no people oppressing other peoples can be free." They also echoed the popular theme of "national self-determination"—the right of all "peoples" to national independence. Why not? They were practical Marxists, hungry for power and impatient, indeed eager, to shatter the status quo and happy to use theoretical slogans as down-to-earth tools of revolutionary warfare. What they were to do with that power, once in office, was for another time.

When, finally, on November 7, 1917, the Bolsheviks seized power in a collapsing Russia, they were "dizzy with success," as Stalin was later to say in another context. They wanted quickly to establish their bona fides, especially on the nationality question. Within eight days, in one of their first state proclamations, they laid out their official position on the nationality question— the validity of which was to be tested in the roiling collision of theory and practice. It was called "The Declaration of Rights of the Peoples of Russia." It recognized the "equality" and "sovereignty" of all peoples, and, in defining "national self-determination," the newly minted communist government stressed that all national minorities could, if they wished, secede from the Russian Federation and create their own independent states. There was, however, one crucially important caveat, not noted in the Declaration but dear to Lenin's heart: Each nationality would have its own communist party, and it would, naturally, be subservient to the Russian Communist Party. If the Russian party did not agree with the idea—or the timing—of the secession, then it would not happen. After all, Lenin might actually have believed that no sensible, rational, intelligent national minority would wish to secede from Russia, which was carrying the banner of a global revolution.

Ukraine, for one, had more mundane matters at hand. It was again being divided into two parts. Dreams of unity and independence had to be shaken back to the reality of the day: the violent, borderless confusion resulting from the Russian Revolution and World War I. In the west, those Ukrainians living in Bukovina (on the eastern slopes of the Carpathian Mountains) became subjects of an enlarged Romania. Those living in Transcarpathia (south and west of the mountains) were folded into the new country of Czechoslovakia, and those in Galicia and western Volhynia again became citizens of Poland. And those living east of the new Polish border were incorporated into what became Soviet Ukraine. Again, essentially, there were two Ukraines: one tilting toward the West, the other toward the east, meaning Russia.

The Soviet Union Rises

Once in power, the revolution behind them, the responsibility of governing before them, the Bolsheviks showed their colors. The Union of Soviet Socialist Republics (USSR) rose from the ashes of civil war; it was proclaimed a country on December 30, 1922. Vast and messy, the USSR initially consisted of Russia, Ukraine, Byelorussia, and Transcaucasia—the very same Slavic heartland that had been forged over the centuries by the tsars. The first Soviet constitution, ratified in January 1924, confirmed the theoretical right of secession (as outlined in Stalin's pamphlet) but vested all true power (military, economic, political, diplomatic) in the Soviet Communist Party, based in Moscow. After Lenin's death in 1924, the party soon fell under Stalin's control.

The party was hailed as the "dictatorship of the proletariat." It would brook no opposition. It set the line for the national minority parties. From its beginning in 1918, the Ukrainian Communist Party, most of whose members were Russian (only 20 percent were Ukrainian), situated itself under the reigning wisdom and authority of the umbrella all-union Soviet Communist Party. It did what it was told to do. When a few party leaders objected, as they did in the early 1920s, they were purged, disgraced, and killed.

The Bolsheviks had two immediate problems: the economy, which was in shambles, and the restless nationalities.

First, the economy. The Bolsheviks, true to their ideology, tried nationalizing industrial production and then forcibly requisitioning food. As an introduction to the communist "experiment," as it was once put, the policy was catastrophic. A major drought hit Ukraine in 1921–22, resulting in a widespread famine; more than 1 million people died. To ease the crisis, Lenin, pragmatic when necessary, shelved his ideological approach to governing and inaugurated his New Economic Policy in 1921. The NEP reintroduced private enterprise, replacing grain requisitions with a flexible tax policy plus permission to sell surplus grain on the open market. The NEP worked. In a few years, the economy more or less recovered.

Second, the nationalities problem. In 1923 the Bolsheviks launched a misguided program, called "indigenization," hoping to win the support and allegiance of the USSR's many nationalities. Here, as elsewhere in these early years, the Bolsheviks sought to balance theory and practice. However, in the end, practice invariably prevailed. Theory would have pointed them once again toward national self-determination and even secession, practice toward imposing centralized control over the nationalities. The Soviet leaders nearly always chose practice. Moscow's control was a central precept of the way they chose to govern, trumping nationality theory.

This was especially clear in Ukraine, where frequent outbursts of nationalism infuriated the Russians. In 1925 Stalin appointed Lazar Kaganovich, one of his most trusted henchmen, to run the Ukrainian Communist Party. Kaganovich unceremoniously rid the party of so-called "deviants," replacing them with "national communists" loyal to Moscow. By 1929 Ukrainian membership in the Ukrainian Communist Party rose to more than 50 percent. But the Russians still controlled the agenda and the decisions.

Ironically, Kaganovich also oversaw the promotion of the Ukrainian language in education and culture, in government and at the workplace. A decade romantics would later call the "Ukrainian Renaissance" followed. Enrollment in Ukrainian-language schools and the publication of Ukrainian books skyrocketed. Lively debates appeared in newspapers and magazines. Independence was not the theme of the day, but it too was discussed, softly, as though behind a cupped hand.

One writer, Mykola Khvylovy, a devout communist, once a security agent, went to the outer limits of acceptable criticism in those days by pushing the slogan "Away from Moscow!" arguing that Ukrainian culture ought to open its doors to "living individual[s] with thoughts, will and aptitudes." He yearned for a Ukraine of the West, not a Ukraine of Shevchenko's romanticized Kievan Rus' world of Cossacks.[3] But such criticism, even during a period of Ukrainization, could go only so far. In the early 1930s, as a sign of the times, Khvylovy committed suicide, while still proclaiming his love of Marxism.

Ukrainization had an interesting twist, unimagined by Moscow's leaders. It was intended to stimulate a loyal, communist bonding of Ukraine to Russia, and to an extent it succeeded. Many Ukrainians and Russians shared and enjoyed a common history and culture, many Ukrainians joining the Communist Party, supporting Soviet policy at home and abroad, and, during World War II, fighting gallantly with their Russian brethren against the Nazis. But, in the process, Ukrainization also laid the foundation for a later blossoming of Ukrainian nationalism, seen and appreciated most demonstrably after the dissolution of the Soviet Union in 1991, with the founding of a new Ukrainian nation.

Along the way, many nationalities, including Stalin's Georgians, revolted against Moscow's rule. Islamic Basmachi radicals, living in what became Soviet Central Asia, rose against communism and Russia in the early 1920s, maintaining hit-and-run guerrilla attacks until the late 1930s, when the Russians finally crushed their uprising. Though they were proud of Stalin, Georgians objected to Russian rule, and in 1924 the Soviet KGB executed 4,000 of them. The Yakuts people, in Siberia, revolted in 1928, and the Buryats a year later. In 1930 a Kazakh revolt was crushed, with an unknown number killed. And so it continued: After World War II, in the Baltic area, "forest brotherhoods" sprang up and fought a guerrilla war against the Russians until 1952; in western Ukraine, right-wing militias battled the Russians until 1952; anti-Soviet riots erupted in Georgia in 1956, in Kazakhstan in 1958, and in the southern city of Novocherkassk in 1962. None of these nationalist uprisings, some quite bloody, were reported in the Soviet press, where there were only stories about the success of the nationality program.[4]

In Stalin's Shadow

Stalin was no Lenin. Shortly after he solidified his control over the party apparatus—by 1928 he was already master of the Marxist universe—he arbitrarily closed down any semblance of the New Economic Policy and opened his "revolution from above." Moderation gave way to ideological extremism.

He introduced a totally new economic policy: a five-year plan for industrial-ization, to be conducted at a breakneck pace. Stalin also began an agricultural program of dekulakization, meaning dispossessing and deporting hundreds of thousands of so-called wealthy peasants, or *kulaks*. Stalin's revolution was not tidy, and his industrialization drive steamrolled millions of workers into becoming sullen servants of the state. Disgruntlement was deep, but that was of little concern to Moscow. Stalin was convinced that capitalism was out to suffocate socialism, and he had to strengthen the Soviet state before it was too late. By 1939, his spokesmen boasted, industrial output had quadrupled, the number of workers had tripled, and the urban population had zoomed from 19 percent to 34 percent of the national total. Interestingly, Moscow focused on industrial development in the Donbas region and the central Dnieper val-ley, though both were in Ukraine. At the time, no one in Moscow seriously considered the Donbas and the Dnieper to be in another country. Ukraine was a Soviet republic, an integral part of the Soviet Union. So it was, and so it would remain!

Dekulakization resulted in a twisted transformation of the countryside. Wholesale collectivization of agriculture began in 1929, when only 9 percent of farms were organized as collectives. Within a year, the number shot up to 65 percent, and within five years to 90 percent. Ukrainian peasants angrily resisted collectivization. The Communist Party, just as angrily, uprooted rebellious families and sent more than 100,000 of them to Siberia. Still, many peasants, refusing to play by the newly imposed rules, slaughtered their cat-tle, destroyed state-owned equipment, and revolted against their communist overlords, who responded by increasing quotas and confiscating foodstuffs. After a few years, the countryside was transformed into a burning hulk, with the peasants and their communist overlords locked in a bloody standoff.[5]

By 1932–33 a second Great Famine swept through Ukraine, later affecting all of the Soviet Union. It was a man-made crisis, no doubt, and it caused the deaths of an estimated 7 million Ukrainians. Moscow sold Ukrainian wheat for foreign exchange, knowing that it should more properly have been used to feed hungry people. The 1932 harvest produced enough grain to feed the people and even provide for limited exports. But Moscow then mindlessly set even higher quotas for 1933. When the peasants objected, they were either killed or sent to Siberia.

Scholar Andrew Wilson wrote: "Whole villages were wiped out, people ate domestic pets, grass, even next year's corn, and cannibalism was widespread." A number of Ukrainian nationalists, including poet and politician Ivan Drach, said that the 1932 famine was "one stage in the planned eradication of the Ukrainian nation." Historian James Mace believed that "enemy number one for Stalin and his circle was not the Ukrainian peasant, nor the Ukrainian intelligentsia. The enemy was Ukraine itself."[6]

If it was possible at the time to convert a horrible situation into something even worse, the Bolsheviks then announced that the theft of "socialist property" would henceforth be considered a "capital crime." Meaning, if a hungry peasant was caught stealing even a small amount of wheat from a state store, he would be brought before a firing squad and shot. By the spring of 1933 starvation was a daily curse for millions of Ukrainians, but the state still managed to export more than a million tons of grain to the West. The explanation was that Moscow needed foreign currency.

The upshot was that the traditional Ukrainian village—the breadbasket of the tsarist empire—was destroyed, and Russians were called upon to repopulate the countryside.

Moscow, in the meantime, denied that a famine had occurred, knowing all the while that, in the animal world alone, the number of horses had fallen from 35 million to 17 million, the number of cattle from 70 million to 38 million, the number of pigs from 26 million to 12 million, and the number of sheep and goats from 147 million to 50 million.[7] Perhaps it was inevitable that along with forced industrialization and collectivization would come Russification. Enough of Ukrainization, Moscow decided; it was time for a new, sweeping program of Russification, the weeding out of "national deviationists" from Ukrainian politics, culture, and religion. This process started, not by coincidence, in 1929 when a fictitious organization, called the Union for the Liberation of Ukraine, was "uncovered" by the Russian secret police. Its leaders, including the foremost Ukrainian literary critic of his time, Serhii Yefremov, were arrested and sentenced to hard labor in a Siberian camp. There were many show trials in the 1930s, top communists forced to "confess," and others sentenced to death. More arrests followed a year later, decimating the ranks of intellectuals, writers, and artists. Ukrainian politicians, all of them party members, were purged from the Ukrainian Communist Party. Even old Bolsheviks, such as Mykola Skrypnyk, were kicked out of the party. Things only got worse: By 1936 half of the membership of the Ukrainian Communist Party had been purged, and 990 out of 1,002 members of the Ukrainian Central Committee were shot.[8]

In 1938 Nikita Khrushchev picked up where Lazar Kaganovich left off. Another Stalin favorite, he was picked to head the Ukrainian Communist Party. He arrived in Kiev with a substantial contingent of Russian communists. Khrushchev, a Russian, was born in Ukraine and started his party career there. His immediate responsibility was to fill all the empty party chairs with reliable pro-Moscow communists. Though he might have had a soft spot in his heart for Ukraine, he showed little heart for those Ukrainians he considered "enemies of the people." He authorized the arrests of tens of thousands of Ukrainians and showed no hesitation about ordering them to a Siberian gulag.[9]

Another Khrushchev responsibility was to return Ukraine to a semblance of normality, including the gradual lifting of food rationing in the cities and a cut in the number of arbitrary arrests. For the majority of Ukrainians, though, the 1930s were horrendous, and World War II was to prove to be even worse.

CHAPTER 10

World War II: A Ukrainian Horror

With the Germans, we run the risk of losing our
liberty. With the Russians, we lose our soul.
EDWARD RYDZ-SMIGLY, POLISH ARMY MARSHALL

WORLD WAR II STARTED, officially, on September 1, 1939, when Nazi Germany invaded Poland, but it was foreshadowed by a political upheaval in Transcarpathia in April involving Ukrainian nationalists, followed by a stunning announcement in August of a nonaggression pact between Germany and Russia.

At the Munich conference in September 1938, Great Britain's Neville Chamberlain had submissively agreed to the German seizure of the Sudetenland on the northwestern rim of Czechoslovakia—a shameful step later described, perhaps generously, as "appeasement." Adolf Hitler had argued that many Germans living there were unhappy, and he felt a responsibility to help them. Nothing more. "I am simply demanding," he pronounced, "that the oppression of the three-and-a-half million Germans cease and that the inalienable rights to self-determination take its place."[1] Hitler could not know it, of course, but years later Putin was to use the same rationale for occupying Crimea and stirring up trouble in eastern Ukraine.

Once Hitler had Chamberlain's acquiescence, he marched into the Sudetenland; it was an easy first step to war. He then proceeded to dismember Czechoslovakia. On March 14, 1939, with Hitler's blessing, the eastern half of the country, Slovakia, declared its independence. On March 15, the Nazis moved into Prague, then quickly fanned out and dismembered the rest of what remained of Czechoslovakia. Also on March 15, Ukrainian nationalists living in Transcarpathia, taking advantage of the noisy Nazi blitzkrieg, decided to proclaim the establishment of the Republic of Carpatho-Ukraine. For the first time since the revolutionary struggles of 1917 to 1921, a Ukrainian state was proclaimed, thanks to Nazi sponsorship. The "Republic" was not really a republic, nor was it independent. It was a province of Hungary, a Nazi ally, but for western Ukrainian nationalists it was good enough, a modest piece of the Ukrainian dream of national independence. For eastern Ukrainians, it earned little more than a passing thought, if that. They were not at the time thinking about national independence.

On August 23, 1939, during Europe's march to war, the sun stopped when Nazi Germany and Communist Russia announced the signing of a nonaggression pact. After years of nonstop propaganda warfare, each side accusing the other of duplicity and double-dealing, Moscow and Berlin stunned the world. Their foreign ministers shook hands in public while in private they divided up Eastern Europe: for Germany, as a prelude to war; for Russia, as a bloodless way of acquiring still more territory. Poor Poland was to be partitioned yet again, all of its eastern lands to fall under Soviet control in an enlarged Ukraine. When Polish marshall Edward Rydz-Smigly was asked which was worse—German or Russian control?—he reportedly answered with sad insight: "With the Germans, we run the risk of losing our liberty. With the Russians, we will lose our soul."

With Stalin's approval now in his hip pocket, Hitler invaded Poland on September 1, 1939, formally setting off World War II. Polish military resistance cracked within two weeks. As the Nazis moved east, the Russians moved west. Under Soviet general Semen Tymoshenko, a Ukrainian by birth, the Russians invaded western Ukraine, the general boasting along the way that his invasion was "the historic reunification of the great Ukrainian people."[2] He then drove into eastern Galicia, which had been under Polish control since the early 1920s. Stalin announced that both western Ukraine and eastern Galicia would become provinces in Soviet Ukraine.

There was more to come. In June 1940 the Red Army slipped a khaki noose around Estonia, Latvia, and Lithuania, reminding the Russian people that Peter the Great had won much of the Baltic from Sweden in the early eighteenth century. Soviet propagandists pictured the acquisition as nothing more than the return of the Baltic to Russia.

With Germany's approval, the Red Army then took northern Bukovina and all of Bessarabia from Romania. For Moscow, the next step was consistent with an earlier step: incorporating Bukovina and southern Bessarabia, where many Ukrainians lived, into Soviet Ukraine. The rest of Bessarabia and a nearby Moldovan province were united into a new Moldovan Soviet republic. It was a confusing time of territorial claims, shifting borders, and cynical diplomacy.

But one key fact concerning Ukraine emerged that was to be of crucial importance in 1991. Never before in history had so many Ukrainians been brought together in a single national state, but it was a state within the USSR. It enjoyed no international recognition. Though Ukraine now had numerical strength (outside of Russia, it was the most heavily populated "republic" in the USSR), it lacked political authority. Like all of the other Soviet republics, it was subordinate to Russia, and both Ukraine and Russia knew it.

Although many Ukrainian nationalists, thinking they could profitably collaborate with the Nazis, fled to the German-occupied zone in Poland, those nationalists who remained were quickly swept up by the Russians— and shipped off to labor camps deep in the USSR. For many in Moscow, these Ukrainians were "foreigners," in their view probably Nazi collaborators, and they were distrusted. According to reliable estimates, for the brief period from 1939 to 1940, about 312,000 families, or roughly 1,250,000 people, were deported from western Ukraine to Siberia, the Arctic Circle, and Soviet central Asia.[3] Twenty percent of them were ethnic Ukrainians; many others were Poles and Jews.

Stalin, in a mad moment, also considered the wholesale deportation of *all* Ukrainians. But in February 1956, in his "secret" speech at the Twentieth Party Congress, Nikita Khrushchev, a surprise critic of the leader he had once revered, disclosed that Stalin could not give the order, "because there were too many of them and there was no place to which to deport them. Otherwise he would have deported them too." An official footnote said there was "laughter and animation in the hall."[4] Chekhov's phrase "laughter through tears" would have been more appropriate, and perhaps was even recalled by some of the delegates attending the Congress.

Though Stalin refused to believe a steady flow of intelligence that unmistakably pointed to an impending Nazi betrayal, including an outright invasion of the Soviet Union, he was shocked, truly shocked, when on June 22, 1941, German panzer divisions smashed across the Soviet border. It was the start of what Moscow would call the "Great Patriotic War." The Germans moved swiftly through lands that only recently had been incorporated into the Soviet Union—western Ukraine, Byelorussia, the Baltic republics—and then they struck more deeply into Russia itself. The Red Army, forced into a hasty retreat, shot political prisoners, blew up buildings and bridges, burned crops and food reserves, and flooded mines. It was called a "scorched earth policy."

By the end of November, the Nazis had occupied most of Ukraine. But, in a fascinating turn of history, rather than being feared, they were welcomed by many Ukrainians, who believed that Germany was their liberator—their natural ally against Poland and Russia. Join up with the Germans, they seemed to feel, and together we can destroy the Soviets.[5]

Enter OUN, the Organization of Ukrainian Nationalists, which, formed in 1929, provided the ideological backbone of Ukrainian nationalism for many years, especially during World War II. The OUN was founded on Johann Gottfried Herder's vision of *volk*, or "people," banded together in "social volunteerism" and led by a single *vozhd*, or "leader." Its chief ideologist was Dmytro Donstov, who, surveying the European landscape, saw a deep conflict developing between Europe and Russia, between "two civilizations, two political, social and cultural-religious ideals." Russia's leaders, he said, were "absolutist," determined to "destroy" Europe, and Ukraine's mission was to save Europe from Russia. [6] But how?

Donstov believed fiercely in "the fire of fanatical commitment" and "the iron force of enthusiasm." His ideal was "the rule of one ethnic group over a territory"—the ethnic Ukrainians over historic Ukraine. He acknowledged mournfully that "Ukraine does not yet exist," but "the organization of a new violence" could create a nation "on the initiative of the minority" and driven by a "strong man."

Donstov set the political and ideological tone for the OUN.[7] At its Krakow congress in 1941, perhaps only as a hate-filled overture to the Nazis, it promised to "vanquish" the Jews from Ukraine, because, OUN said, they were "the most loyal prop of the ruling Bolshevik regime and the avant-garde of Muscovite imperialism in Ukraine."[8] In this way, the OUN harbored many of the same views as the Ustashe in Croatia, the Fascist People's Party in Slovakia, the Legion of the Archangel Michael in Romania, and the Iron Wolves in Lithuania—all far-right political movements noted for their hyped nationalism and lamentable anti-Semitism.

The OUN clearly tied the Jews to Ukraine's traditional enemies, Poles and Russians, believing that, if necessary, they were all to be "exterminated" in the Ukrainian struggle for independence. Jews, especially, were to be "isolated" and "excluded from government positions."

Opportunities for the OUN opened in the early years of World War II. In the period from 1939 to 1941, the map of Eastern Europe was being radically redrawn. Holding aloft the banner of fascism, the Nazis struck. In the name of nationalism, the Ukrainians marched. It was a time for war.

Enter Bandera

Under the leadership of a dynamic *vozhd*, Stepan Bandera, a political leader from western Ukraine, the OUN urged tens of thousands of young Ukrainians to seize the moment to battle the Bolsheviks and fight for national independence. They raced excitedly to Lvov and, on June 30, 1941, proclaimed the founding of an independent Ukraine. They spoke primarily for western Ukrainians; the easterners had more immediate priorities, such as fighting the Germans. "The Ukrainian National Revolutionary Army," it declared, "will henceforth fight along with the Allied German Army against Muscovite occupation for a Sovereign United Ukrainian State and a new order in the whole world." It made no effort to conceal its pro-German sympathies.[9]

Another such pro-German operation was called the Russian Liberation Movement, formed in 1942 by General Andrei Vlasov. He was a headline hero, decorated by Stalin himself for his courageous leadership of Russian army detachments defending Kiev and Moscow. But in June 1942 his army division was decisively defeated by the Germans, and they arrested him. During his time in prison, he bafflingly switched sides and agreed to join the Germans and set up a liberation army consisting of Russian prisoners of war—all in an effort to defeat Stalin. That never happened, of course, and Vlasov went down in Russian history as a "traitor" who "betrayed his Homeland."[10]

Bandera, for his part, believed that a Ukrainian army, representing an independent Ukraine, could help the Nazis overthrow the Bolsheviks. In theory, he might have been right. A number of Nazi leaders, including Alfred Rosenberg, actually agreed with Bandera. But Hitler disagreed, and of course his racist policies prevailed. The Nazis decisively rejected both Bandera's offer and the warm Ukrainian welcome. Hitler considered the Ukrainians to be *untermenschen*, good for nothing more than slave labor. Two million Ukrainians were sent to Germany to work as slave laborers, or *ostarbeiter*. Hitler thought even less of Ukrainian Jews. During the war, his troops, aided by Ukrainians, killed an estimated 1.5 million Jews in Ukraine. One place for mass murder was the Kiev suburb of Baby Yar, in September 1941.

President George H. W. Bush, during a visit there fifty years later, "choked up" when describing the scene: "The Nazis had lined up their naked victims in front of a trench, their clothes saved for reuse by the SS for people back in Germany, and systematically shot more than thirty-three thousand over thirty-six hours," he later wrote. "The Germans had played dance music over loudspeakers to drown out the screams."[11]

The Russian poet Yevgeny Yevtushenko, ashamed of his country's complicit anti-Semitism, condemned "the rabble of pogrom" in a memorial to the many whose blood soaked the soil of this Kiev suburb.

> No monument stands over Baby Yar,
> A steep cliff only, like the rudest headstone.
> I am afraid.
> Today I am as old as the entire Jewish race itself.[12]

For the remainder of the war, the OUN functioned underground, accomplishing little but surviving as an organization. Though Bandera was ready to sell his soul to the Nazis, they were not ready to buy it. In fact, the Germans arrested and imprisoned Bandera. His ideas and plans were put on hold.

Only in September 1944, when the Germans were thrown on the defensive by a hardened Red Army, was Bandera released, apparently on the assumption that only he could rally the Ukrainian Insurgent Army, formed the year before, to help the Nazis hold off the advancing Russians. Bandera did try. Working out of his Berlin headquarters, where he received arms and money from the Nazis, he did for a time lead his troops in battle against the Russians, but it was too late. Bandera's mission failed. The UPA, as it was called, had 90,000 men, a formidable force, but it functioned mostly in western Ukraine and could not help the Germans in the east, where they were in hasty retreat. An undeclared war between the Soviets and the OUN-UPA lasted until the early 1950s. It was a bloody one, fought most intensively in those parts of western Ukraine that Moscow had acquired in the wrap-up of the war. The United States and Britain, seizing a chance to help the UPA in order to hurt Stalin's Russia, began supplying arms and intelligence to the Ukrainian insurgents. When the Russians learned of these western supply operations in parts of Eastern Europe they considered to be theirs by international agreement, they angrily denounced the West. This proved to be yet another small step on the road to the cold war.

Western Ukraine was a chronic migraine for Moscow. While Stalin and Khrushchev were again pushing collectivization, this time forcing existing collectives into "agro-cities," they met with modest success only in the eastern half of Ukraine, the largely pro-Russian half. In the western half, new to Soviet domination, Ukrainian nationalists resisted Russification. They stuck to the use of the Ukrainian language in schools and media and boasted of very low membership in the Ukrainian Communist Party. Historian Roman Szporluk said that western Ukraine was "the least Russian and least Russified" area in the entire Soviet Union.[13] It was indigestible.

Bandera, in the Russian mind, represented western Ukraine, and Moscow distrusted him—indeed, hated him. The Russians had never forgotten, or forgiven, his anti-Soviet, Nazi-inspired activities. Khrushchev, reflecting the views of the communist aristocracy, bristled with anger when he described Bandera in his memoirs. Bandera was an "outright agent of German fascism," Khrushchev wrote, "a Ukrainian nationalist [with] a pathological hatred of the Soviet regime."[14] A disillusioned nationalist at war's end, Bandera turned on the OUN, denouncing its flimsy efforts at accommodation with eastern Ukrainians. He left behind a controversial legacy of passionate Ukrainian nationalism polluted by a continuing association with fascist ideology, German aggression, and anti-Semitism. In 1959 the KGB, which had a long list of enemies, assassinated Bandera in Munich, Germany. After Ukrainian independence in 1991, statues of Bandera began to appear in villages throughout the western half of the country. He was a hero, modern Ukraine's version of the seventeenth-century Cossack leader Bogdan Khmelnitsky. But in villages in the east, Bandera was nowhere to be seen. There, the statues were of Lenin, a Russian; they were omnipresent, constant reminders of the Soviet era. A pro-Russian activist told a visiting friend in Donetsk: "Lenin and Bandera would never meet in a Ukrainian park."

The Early Flickering of Nationalism

"Ukrainians gave us more trouble than anyone else," wrote Khrushchev, who, as head of the Ukrainian Communist Party for ten tumultuous years, from 1938 to 1947, should have known. He had "indisputable documentary proof," he said, that "they were receiving instructions and money from the Germans."[15] He was apparently writing about those Ukrainians who collaborated with the Nazis.

In his memoirs, Khrushchev also wrote about Ukrainian nationalism and courage, especially during the Great Patriotic War, with a surprising degree of understanding, while at the same time emphasizing Stalin's cruelty and indifference to Ukrainian suffering. In this sense, Khrushchev agreed with many Ukrainian scholars, such as Ivan L. Rudnytsky, who bitterly criticized Stalin's wartime policy toward Ukraine. Rudnytsky labeled Stalin "the perpetrator of unspeakable crimes against the Ukrainian people."[16] He was thinking about Stalin's policies of forced collectivization and industrialization, plus the Moscow-arranged famine of 1932.

From his early days in power, in the 1920s, Stalin had been absorbed with the problem of Russia's national minorities, hounded by the question of whether, as leader of the Soviet Union, he could ever trust them. By war's end, he had his answer: no. Bandera's collaboration with the Nazis had persuaded him that Ukrainians would never be loyal to Moscow. He did not draw a distinction between western or eastern Ukrainians.

Stalin the politician was often at war with Stalin the ideologue when the question arose about Ukraine and the other national minorities. On the one hand, as a Georgian Marxist and revolutionary, he seemed truly to believe that national minorities had to have the "right" of self-determination, including secession. In each Soviet republic, he built the framework of governance, meaning each had to have a president, a parliament, and a cabinet of ministers. It was nothing more than an empty framework. It enjoyed no independent standing. And yet it sparked and nourished the idea of national independence, even for such anti-Russian nationalist leaders as Mazepa and Bandera. On the other hand, as a brutal dictator, Stalin had no intention—ever—of allowing a Soviet republic to proclaim its independence from Russia. That was not an option. Stalin intended to exercise absolute control over the affairs of every Soviet republic, and he did.

The result was an obvious collision between theory and practice. By war's end, when Stalin looked out of his Kremlin window to survey his empire, two disturbing visions must have snapped into focus: Ukraine had grown into a large republic, larger than ever in its history, and Stalin had allowed theory to come close to trumping practice. He had underestimated the growth and potential of national institutions, a profound blunder. The idea of Ukrainian self-determination was sprouting wings, though it was not yet flying. The western Ukrainians were marching to their own drummer, and Stalin and his henchmen chose to hear the wrong beat. Before their eyes, Ukrainian national independence had mushroomed into a major problem during the war, but they did not see it. More than any other Soviet leader, Stalin had breathed life into the shell of a Ukrainian state. He did not have to incorporate all the western Ukrainian lands he got from Germany into the Ukrainian Soviet Republic, in this way short-sightedly opening the eastern half of the country to the nationalist appeal and tumult agitating the west. Stalin was greedy, thinking of territory and glory, not long-term strategy.

Rudnytsky observed: "It was in the name of Ukraine, and not of Russia, that Stalin successfully claimed vast territories west of then pre-1939 frontier, thus extending the USSR into central Europe and the Danubian valley."[17] This was a prized moment when almost all ethnic Ukrainians lived in one state. Unwittingly, Stalin had fulfilled a Ukrainian dream—all Ukrainians living in a land called Ukraine. In this way, the war defined Ukraine as a political and cultural entity, not yet truly a state, but an entity moving in the direction of statehood.

Harvard's Roman Szporluk put this result in a historical context. The year 1991, when Ukraine declared its independence from Russia, he wrote, "would have been impossible without 1939–1945."[18]

CHAPTER 11

Between 1945 and 1991

You know, Americans don't really understand what is Ukraine.
SERGEI KHRUSHCHEV

WITH THE WAR OVER, Josef Stalin insisted in October 1945 that Ukraine (and Belarus) be treated as independent nations, not just as parts of the Soviet Union. As such, they would be entitled to seats at the United Nations, the same as France, Japan, or any other sovereign nation. In this way, the Soviet Union would have three votes in the assembly and not merely one. Every delegation understood that Moscow was playing diplomatic games, but in an attempt to win its cooperation, the other war-time allies agreed to give Ukraine and Belarus the same privileges (a seat and a vote at the UN General Assembly and an embassy in New York) as any other member state.

Drought and Purge

Ukraine, land of recurring famines, experienced another painful one shortly after World War II, caused, Nikita Khrushchev said, by the "worst drought in history." It was, in fact, so devastating in 1946–47 that Khrushchev, still the party chief in Ukraine, pleaded with Stalin for relief. Furious, Stalin fired Khrushchev and once again sent Lazar Kaganovich to Kiev, hoping that this veteran party troubleshooter could reenergize the Ukrainian countryside. He could not, the drought defying his best efforts, but he could come up with another acceptable chore: spotting and uprooting "nationalist deviants" in Ukrainian culture, education, and politics. At the time, another of Stalin's favorite hard-liners, Andrei Zhdanov, was launching a drive for ideological purity throughout the country. Kaganovich's cleansing of the Ukrainian party fit perfectly into *Zhdanovschina*, as it was called, and many in Moscow applauded his effort, believing that Ukraine was crowded with "political deviants," who were guilty of many "mistakes."

This purge ended in late 1947 after Khrushchev had regained Stalin's favor and returned to his job as Ukrainian party secretary. Under his direction, the Communist Party attracted more members, its ranks swelling by 1949 to its prewar strength of 680,000. Seventy percent were ethnic Ukrainians. But in the early 1950s, in Stalin's final years in office (he died in March 1953), Kremlin policy turned ugly. "Deviationists" were again fingered and arrested by the KGB. A strange anti-Semitic campaign against "rootless cosmopolitans," another way of describing Jews, took root in late 1949. A "doctors' plot" was uncovered a few years later, according to which Jewish doctors were supposedly engaged in a plot to kill party leaders. It was fantasy, but fear quickly resurfaced, especially among party officials who wondered whether they would soon hear a knock on their door at two in the morning. Was another purge only a day or two away?

Crimea Gift-Wrapped for Ukraine

The date was February 27, 1954. It was a small, seemingly inconsequential, one-sentence news item in *Pravda*, the Communist Party newspaper. But years later it kicked up a global storm. The news item read:

> "Decree of the Presidium of the USSR Supreme Soviet transferring Crimea province from the Russian Republic to the Ukraine Republic, taking into account the integral character of the economy, the territorial proximity and the close economic ties between Crimea province and the Ukraine Republic, and approving the joint presentation of the Presidium of the Russian Republic Supreme Soviet and the Presidium of the Ukraine Republic Supreme Soviet on the transfer of Crimea Province from the Russian Republic to the Ukraine Republic."

Translation from the original Bolshevikese: Khrushchev, now in charge, had decided to give Crimea to Ukraine. Why? First, because, as he saw it, the Soviet economy was one united, national economy. A hydroelectric power dam in Russia or in Ukraine—it made little economic difference to the state. Second, Ukraine was geographically close to Russia, indeed bordered on Russia. It would save money. And, finally, Crimea and Ukraine already enjoyed "close economic ties." This would make them even closer. Not in the official account, nor in the unofficial translation, were the true underlying reasons disclosed, which, at the time, were of no political or economic significance. What was known was that Khrushchev had made his decision, the party presidium had rubber-stamped it, and Crimea had slipped quietly, without objection, into Ukraine's administrative embrace. Deal done.

Why then the global storm 60 years later? In late February 2014, Russian soldiers, described curiously in news reports as "little green men," occupied Crimea, and a month later Russia ripped Crimea from Ukraine and annexed this strategic peninsula, home, by treaty, of the Russian Black Sea fleet.[1] It was a surprise move that shook up global diplomacy and fired up visions of a new cold war. Diplomats and commentators had to fashion new formulas for dealing with a suddenly expansionist Russia. For the first time in decades, European borders were violated, and the international order, established with care after World War II, was being threatened.

Khrushchev's Explanation?

The way Sergei Khrushchev, Nikita Khrushchev's son, explained it on March 20, 2014, in his suburban home a few miles from Brown University in Providence, Rhode Island, Stalin had given his father an order in 1946: "You will be [held] personally responsible for the restoration of the Crimea and Sevastopol." Both places had been the scene of ferocious fighting during World War II, Germans pitted against Russians. Crimea, especially the naval base in Sevastopol, had been left in ruins. At the time of Stalin's order, Crimea was an *oblast*, or province, in the Russian republic, reduced from its former status as an autonomous republic, and Sevastopol—though in Crimea—was considered an independent, "closed" city, largely because it housed a military base.

In 1950 Soviet planners were thinking of building a hydroelectric dam along the Dnieper River in Ukraine. Power from the dam would flow along two canals, one through Ukrainian territory to the Donetsk basin and the other through Russian territory to Crimea. In other words, the governments of two republics in the Soviet Union would be jointly responsible for administering the canals. That, Sergei Khrushchev said, would have "create[d] a complete mess." Arguments would have erupted between Russian and Ukrainian technicians. "Who was right? Who was wrong?" Khrushchev mimicked a presumed dispute from that time. After Stalin died and Nikita Khrushchev replaced him as supreme leader, he sent one of his aides to Crimea and Sevastopol to look for better ways of running the canals. What the aide found was embarrassing confusion. No one seemed to know who was in charge: a Russian or a Ukrainian?

When Khrushchev got the aide's report, he decided on the spot to give full responsibility to the Ukrainians. In practical terms, as an administrative matter, that meant turning Crimea over to Ukraine. At the time, there was speculation that Khrushchev was either drunk or had a soft spot for things Ukrainian. Although a Russian, he had, after all, been reared in Ukraine, his wife was Ukrainian, and his career as a party leader was launched in Ukraine. And, for these reasons, as a "gift," he gave Crimea to Ukraine. When I asked son Sergei whether his father had a "romantic attachment" to Ukraine, accounting for the "gift," he answered firmly: "Absolutely not." Then repeated, more resolutely, "Absolutely not." Sergei joked: "Why not give everything to Ukraine, huh?" Turning serious, Sergei continued: "No. You know, Americans don't really understand what is Ukraine. In Russian language, Ukraine means 'border.' " He then explained how, after World Wars I and II, Ukraine's borders had often been changed by German and Russian generals, as if to suggest that changing a Ukrainian border should not be seen as a startling, or disturbing, event, and that when his father gave Crimea to Ukraine, he was not doing something all that remarkable—at least, as seen at the time.

Explaining the transfer to Andre de Nesnera of VOANews on March 6, 2014, Sergei Khrushchev said: "As the Dnieper and the hydroelectric dam [are] on Ukrainian territory, let's transfer the rest of the territory of Crimea under Ukrainian supervision so they will be responsible for everything. And they did it. It was not a political move. It was not an ideological move. It was just business." It made sense, he argued, that the dam and the canals be under a single administration. "We have this speculation that my father wanted to satisfy Ukrainian democracy, that he even made a gift to his wife, my mother, because she was Ukrainian—all this have nothing with reality [sic]."[2]

According to a February 19, 2009, report on *Pravda*'s website, Khrushchev dealt with the question of when to transfer Crimea to Ukraine by recalling that Moscow would soon be celebrating the 300th anniversary of Ukraine's absorption into the Russian empire. Why not then, on the 300th anniversary? On his way to lunch one day, Khrushchev turned to a few of his colleagues and casually mentioned, "Yes, comrades, there is an opinion to deliver Crimea to Ukraine." Everyone understood that the "opinion" was Khrushchev's, and no one raised an objection. He was, after all, the head of the party. On January 25, 1954, Khrushchev sought the official blessing of the Presidium of the Central Committee of the Soviet Communist Party. After only fifteen minutes of discussion, the Presidium unanimously endorsed Khrushchev's "opinion." In theory, there should also have been discussion by the Supreme Council of the Russian Republic; there should also have been a referendum in the Russian and Ukrainian republics. There was little discussion and no referendum.[3]

On February 19, 1954, a scant eight days before the official transfer, thirteen of twenty-seven members of the Presidium of the Russian Supreme Council met and voted unanimously for the transfer of Crimea to Ukraine.[4] No one raised a fuss, or an objection, or a question. In the mindset of the time, this was no big deal. After all, Russia and Ukraine were both republics in the Soviet Union. They were, theoretically, equal partners in the supposedly glorious building of communism. What difference did it make whether Crimea was considered a Russian oblast or a Ukrainian one? No difference, at least not then.

The Khrushchev-Brezhnev Thaw

Khrushchev ruled the Soviet Union from 1954 to 1964. During this time, in foreign affairs, he boasted constantly about the ultimate triumph of communism over capitalism, but he ran into serious trouble in Berlin and Cuba. He had to build a wall through the heart of the German capital for one purpose only—to stop East Germans from fleeing to the west. He had to pull his nuclear-tipped missiles out of Cuba to head off an American invasion of a communist ally. In domestic policy, he achieved a measure of success, giving Ukrainians a brief period of post-Stalin normality. As industrial and agricultural production increased, reaching all-time Soviet highs, according to Ukrainian scholars, Ukrainians moved into a new world of consumer goods, buying new apartments, their first refrigerators and TV sets, and even a car.

Khrushchev's "thaw"—his relaxation of Stalin's dictatorship—filled Ukrainians with reborn hopes and opportunities. The Ukrainian language returned to the schools and the newsrooms. The Ukrainian Writers' Union protected pamphleteers and poets. Oles Honchar wrote *The Cathedral*, a popular novel pleading for the restoration of historical monuments and glorifying Ukraine's Cossack traditions. Modest flickers of dissent shimmered across the Ukrainian landscape; there was some self-publishing, there were some demonstrations and some strikes, but they were never widespread, never united into a force strong enough to spark a political awakening. For a time, the generation of the 1960s, the children of the thaw, the *shistdesiatnyky*, as they were called, dreamed about a future of meaningful change, but it was, for its time, unrealistic. It did not happen, not then.

In the annals of Soviet history, Khrushchev was a notable figure. When he was dismissed from office in mid-October 1964—accused of "hare-brained scheming" for sneaking missiles into Cuba only to have to withdraw them under U.S. pressure—rather than being killed, as might have been expected during Stalin's time, he was paid a measure of respect for his contributions to the Soviet state: given a retirement dacha and a chauffeur-driven limousine. He was even permitted to write his memoirs. That decision was made by his successor, Leonid Brezhnev, an ethnic Russian who also was born in Ukraine and, like Khrushchev, also was raised and began his party career there. Indeed, when as a young man Brezhnev applied for membership in the Communist Party and was asked his nationality, he answered: "Ukrainian."

Brezhnev ruled for eighteen long years, his time in the Kremlin so undistinguished that many in Mikhail Gorbachev's subsequent regime, looking back, called it "the era of stagnation." That might have been too harsh a judgment. Though not much happened in domestic policy (indeed, Khrushchev's liberal reforms underwent a broad retreat), in foreign policy much did happen. For example, Brezhnev fathered a controversial "doctrine," later labeled the "Brezhnev Doctrine," that, when implemented, brought the cold war to a hot boil. Its central tenet was that "socialist gains, once realized, could never be erased." In practice, the doctrine meant that once a country had turned communist, it had to remain communist, even if that required the Soviet Union to send in troops to keep it communist, as it had done in Hungary in 1956 and proceeded to do again in Czechoslovakia in 1968 and Afghanistan in 1979. Also, Brezhnev exchanged summit meetings with President Richard Nixon and in May 1972 signed two arms control treaties, even while the United States was bombing North Vietnam, a communist ally of Moscow.

More significant for Ukrainian nationalists, Brezhnev agreed in August 1975 to the Helsinki "Final Act," under which the thirty-five signatories formally recognized the postwar political boundaries in Europe as permanently fixed—an important breakthrough for the Soviet Union. He also accepted the concept of "human rights" as a condition of proper national and international behavior, a highly problematic matter in Moscow.[5] It set in motion the establishment of Helsinki monitoring groups in the Soviet Union. With little effort, they found evidence of widespread violations. In late 1975, the Ukrainian Helsinki Group submitted sixty reports of human rights violations to Moscow. Unsurprisingly, Moscow not only did nothing about them, it arrested and imprisoned twenty-four of the Ukrainian Helsinki Group's thirty-nine leading members. Still, the Helsinki "Final Act" played an important role in the development of a political opposition in Ukraine. It provided a theoretical framework for a discussion of human rights, which in time awakened a serious commitment to national independence.

Gerontocracy to Disintegration

It was, in many ways, an odd period in Ukrainian history. A gerontocracy ruled in Moscow, and although it was not widely evident at the time, the sclerotic Soviet state was suffering from terminal incompetence. In the early 1980s, "stagnation" would have been too kind a word to describe the aging mess in Moscow. After Brezhnev's death in November 1982, Yuri Andropov moved his office from the KGB to the Kremlin. A frail man, he governed for only two years. In 1984, after Andropov died, Konstantin Chernenko, another old man, took charge, so to speak, but only for one year. He died in March 1985. The next ruler was Mikhail Gorbachev, a relatively young man, propelled into power by Politburo colleagues desperate for a colleague who could survive the rigors of office. Little did they realize at the time that Gorbachev would be the last leader of the Soviet Union. Communism died six years later, and the USSR dissolved into history. It was a moment to remember. What happened?

Gorbachev, when he assumed power, did not have to be persuaded that the Soviet Union was in urgent need of reform. He was smart and ambitious, but not always very practical, often allowing a personal grudge to distract him from a primary objective. He quickly reached out to the United States, promising a fresh start to nuclear arms reductions, and he launched two domestic programs, nicknamed *perestroika* and *glasnost*, designed to renovate Soviet industry and to relax Stalinist strictures on what citizens could write and say. In this way, Gorbachev hoped to salvage communism in the Soviet Union, but he lived in a world of illusion. The system could not be reformed, as he had hoped. It had to be revamped, thoroughly, which he was not yet ready to do or even to acknowledge as necessary.

Still, his efforts were admirable and important. In industry, they pointed to a desperate need for radical change; and in politics they uncorked a torrent of criticism of the corruption and malfeasance in the communist system. Rebellion was in the air. Things would never be the same again.

Deepening the general dissatisfaction were the events at Chernobyl, a Ukrainian town where one of the worst nuclear accidents in history occurred. On April 26, 1986, one of the four reactors at Chernobyl's nuclear power plant was destroyed during a steam explosion, filling the air with poisonous radioactive dust ninety times more deadly than the dust kicked up during the Hiroshima bombing in 1945. Winds carried the dust to other parts of Ukraine, including Kiev, to Scandinavia, but mostly to neighboring Belarus, poisoning a fifth of the arable land there.[6] For three days, there was no official acknowledgment of the disaster, which was typical of Soviet times. Only when Swedish meteorologists reported the radioactive dust over their country did Moscow acknowledge what had happened. In this crisis, Gorbachev looked and acted like an old-fashioned communist bureaucrat. Even though he knew the dust had reached Kiev, he still insisted that the May Day parade take place there, oblivious to the obvious dangers to public health. Ukrainians were furious and disappointed. They demonstrated against Gorbachev and the Ukrainian Communist Party, not knowing that party leaders had sensibly advised Gorbachev to cancel the parade.

After Chernobyl, popular respect for communism, the decrepit Soviet system, and the party dropped to all-time lows. More than 130,000 people had to be evacuated from a thirty-kilometer zone around the Chernobyl power plant.[7] One estimate put the figure of Ukrainians exposed to the poisonous radioactivity at 2.4 million. Although the accident exposed millions of people to excessive radiation, a later report by the U.S. Nuclear Regulatory Commission claimed that the long-term health consequences turned out to be less severe than initially thought.

In Eastern Europe, Chernobyl proved to be political poison. Communism had long since lost its appeal to many people. Chernobyl only further revealed how rickety the Soviet system had become. It was clearly a time for change. In the early 1980s, Poland's Solidarity movement started the unraveling of communism in the Soviet satellites. By 1989 Gorbachev's *perestroika* and *glasnost* reforms crashed against the walls of old party shibboleths in such East European capitals as Warsaw, East Berlin, Prague, and Budapest. Almost overnight, people who lived in the so-called Soviet satellites awoke to new realities. Anticommunist demonstrations spread like wildfire from one East European capital to another. Thousands of people, no longer acting like frightened gray globs, took to the streets, giving speeches, waving banners, demanding freedom and independence. The communist police looked on, helpless and possibly frightened, yet fascinated.

Nothing more articulately symbolized the failure of communism than the forbidding Berlin Wall that had divided the German capital since 1961. On November 9, 1989, the Wall crumbled under popular pressure. It was the beginning of the end of Soviet-style communism and the cold war. Thousands of Germans climbed the Wall, now without fear, and with sledge-hammers joyfully smashed large parts of it to pieces. East Germans, held behind the Wall for decades, ran over the rocky remnants of communism, rushing with pell-mell abandon to the West. It was an unforgettable sight, and it was now only a matter of time before freedom, like lightning, would crack over the rest of Eastern Europe and, very soon, over the Soviet republics, too.

At the head of this political stampede were the Baltic republics, which put forward a bold "national front" agenda for political freedom and independence. They were restless and courageous. On August 23, 1989, the fiftieth anniversary of the Hitler-Stalin Pact, more than 2 million people from Estonia, Latvia, and Lithuania held hands in an eye-catching, 370-mile, cross-border human chain. It was defiant testimony of the Baltic's determination to break loose from Moscow. U.S. ambassador to Moscow Jack Matlock later wrote that they acted like "psychologically free people."[8]

The United States had never officially recognized Soviet control over the so-called "captive nations" of Estonia, Latvia, and Lithuania. Technically, therefore, Matlock, as the American ambassador, was not supposed to meet with representatives of the Baltic republics. But when it became clear that the three republics were now seeking independence from Moscow, and their representatives wanted to meet with him, Matlock immediately agreed and invited them to Spasso House, his Moscow diplomatic residence. He asked the obvious opening question: How did they think the Russians were responding to their demands for independence? The Lithuanian representative replied in surprisingly blunt terms. "They will do their best to block us," he began. "But we believe that if we do not yield to provocation, we can succeed." He seemed upbeat, even at the prospect of a possible Russian crackdown on their demonstrations. "They would have to kill thousands, maybe tens of thousands to stop us. And if they do that, it is the end of *perestroika*, the end of Gorbachev. We think they know this."[9] He was saying, in effect, that if Gorbachev reacted with violence, the Soviet leader would be seen as another Stalin—younger, but just as brutal—and he would lose all credibility, not only in the decaying Soviet Union but throughout the world. In other words, at that moment, the very vulnerability of the Baltic states reflected their inherent strength.

On March 11, 1990, Lithuania declared its independence from the Soviet Union. It was a daring political act, but no longer a total surprise, and it touched off, among other things, economic chaos. The rate of inflation zoomed to 100 percent. Lithuanians took to the streets—in the tens of thousands, both pro- and anti-government, most demanding change, some clinging to their Soviet roots. Tensions rose, inevitably violence followed. Gorbachev, though viscerally opposed to violence, feared that the Soviet Union was on the edge of falling apart. He warned Lithuanian leaders that they were playing with fire, adding that the Soviet army might have to intervene to restore order.

In June 1990, Soviet troops, which had been surrounding Vilnius, threatening invasion, moved into the capital. Did Gorbachev order their attack? Or was he blindsided by his generals? At the time, no one seemed to know, but tension in summertime Vilnius was as heavy as a winter blanket. Months passed. Public protests became a daily happening. Confrontations between demonstrating Lithuanians and outside troops could not be avoided. Overnight on January 12–13, 1991, shots were fired, and when the smoke cleared, bodies lay in the central square, circles of blood, victims of an irreconcilable hatred. Fourteen people were killed that day, 700 were injured. The story dominated world news. The flow of blood seemed to sanction the Lithuanian drive toward independence.[10]

For a time, the news from the Baltics even overshadowed the tumult in the Caucasus, where Azeris and Armenians fought for control of Nagorno-Karabakh, an Armenian-majority enclave in Azerbaijan. Neither side won, but their struggle underscored the continuing volatility of the nationality problem, which had dogged Soviet leaders since the 1917 revolution. As soon as the national minorities recognized that Moscow was no longer to be feared, that indeed it was losing its clout, they rushed to put distance between themselves and their Russian overlords. They tested the waters of permissible dissent and discovered, to their surprise and joy, that they could go for independence—and get it. It was the Baltic defiance, more than anything else, that caught this wave of history, and, in a relatively brief period of time, by December 1991, the whole Soviet empire collapsed—with Ukraine playing a decisive role.

Ukraine, Cautious as Ever, Finally Acts

Ukraine was not destined to play this role. It was not the race horse, bursting out of the starting gate, eager to set the pace for the other Soviet republics to declare their independence. Throughout the East European turmoil of the late 1980s and early 1990s, Ukraine moved with exceptional caution. Were it not for Moscow's decline, communism's failure in Eastern Europe, and the Baltic drive for independence, Ukraine might well have remained a Soviet republic for a long time. But Ukraine, like all of the other Soviet republics, got caught up in the revolutionary changes sweeping through the region. The Soviet Union was dying, its empire disintegrating. What would replace it? The train had left the station, and Ukraine was a passenger.

The Popular Movement of Ukraine for Perestroika, known simply as

Rukh, meaning "The Movement," grew out of informal meetings at the Writers' Union in late 1988. Not until a year later did Rukh organize a founding congress. Its membership then was 280,000, a respectable number. Rukh was not a revolutionary party, and it was not yet pushing for independence. Its platform was a benign mixture of political pablum, promoting democracy and human rights. Rukh attracted green environmentalists, political activists, and Russian-speaking democrats from the region's eastern and southern sectors. As its influence spread, communism's contracted. One sign was that nearly 500,000 miners in the Donbas went out on strike, demanding higher wages from a government and a party claiming to represent workers' rights. They also demanded that local party leaders resign. Rukh was beginning to delve into politics, but it never blossomed into a movement on the order of Poland's Solidarity.[11]

Popular rallies and demonstrations, encouraged by Rukh's modest success, sprouted all over Ukraine, elbowing the Communist Party to a corner of the village square. Party defections went from 6,200 in 1989 to 250,951 in 1990. People were looking for an alternative. In public protests, Lvov led the way, Kiev followed, as tens and perhaps hundreds of thousands of people took to demonstrating for a deeper appreciation of Ukrainian culture and history. They were still not demanding independence from Moscow, even though they could see that Gorbachev's Kremlin was shriveling into political impotence. Among the Soviet elite, many seemed to believe Ukraine was angling for advantage, hoping to strike a good deal for itself in whatever replaced the old Soviet Union.

"No. Absolutely not," declared Alexander Bessmertnykh, briefly one of Gorbachev's foreign ministers, when asked whether he thought Ukraine was heading toward independence. "Ukraine was using the opportunity to obtain more for itself as a republic, but not even the most nationalistic Ukrainians were thinking that far ahead."[12] The Bessmertnykhs of Moscow might have been right, or they might have been living in a dream world, misreading the strong currents of nationalism in the Soviet republics.

Rukh joined forces with the Green World, the Ukrainian Language Society, and other opposition groups to form a unitary Democratic Bloc. In legislative elections in March 1990, the Bloc won 100 seats in a 450-seat parliament, or Supreme Rada. In their way, the elections were impressive and represented a big step forward for Ukrainian politics. Even though most Rada members were still communists, they were clearly struggling to come up with a revised definition of party loyalty.

In July the Rada, now a player at Ukraine's political table, decided that it needed a chairman, someone who could represent legislative power and at the same time talk to political power, and it plucked Leonid Kravchuk, a relative newcomer, out of the Ukrainian Communist Party and elected him to the post. At the time, the Rada did not realize it had just selected the first president of an independent Ukraine.

Kravchuk was clever, was well-connected, and spoke fluent Ukrainian. While his special sphere within the party had been communist ideology, he also proved himself to be a flexible operator. He represented those moderate communists who were thinking about shifting their loyalties from the party to the Rada. What is more, they were also thinking about shifting their loyalties from Moscow to Kiev, from the communist center to a regional capital moving toward independence from the center. Kravchuk later recalled that he heard some Rada members wonder aloud: "Maybe it really would be better to separate [from Moscow]."[13]

Party hard-liners were not yet ready to surrender the day to Kravchuk's moderate faction. They still controlled the army, the police, and the bureaucracy—the pillars of state power—and they decided to use them to block further moves toward independence. They passed emergency legislation banning demonstrations near the Supreme Rada, they temporarily suspended broadcasts of Rada proceedings, and they stripped political critics of their legislative immunity.

Especially among students, this conservative rollback proved extremely unpopular because it threatened their hopes for a new Ukraine. In October 1990, in moves that were to be repeated during antiregime protests in early 2014, thousands put up tents in Kiev's main square and went on a hunger strike. Tens of thousands of people from Kiev's middle class joined the students. Before long, there were hunger strikes in other cities. The students were serious about change. They had a list of specific demands: holding new Rada elections, stationing Ukrainian conscripts only in Ukraine, and nationalizing all communist property. Their demands struck a sympathetic chord among many. Kravchuk had a choice. He could have cracked heads, as hard-liners urged him to do, or he could have invited student leaders to a dialogue about the future. He chose the latter course, wisely welcoming student leaders to his office, even asking them to address the Rada. When they spoke, the Rada listened. Still, differences remained, not only between the students and the Rada but, as important, between communist leaders in Moscow and those in the regional capitals, most especially in Kiev.[14]

CHAPTER 12

Yeltsin versus Gorbachev

Misfortune awaits the Ukrainians.
MIKHAIL GORBACHEV

IN MOSCOW, TWO COMMUNIST LEADERS were competing for power in 1990–91: Mikhail Gorbachev, who still remained the boss of a fraying empire, and Boris Yeltsin, who was president of the Russian Soviet Federative Socialist Republic, the largest and most prestigious of the fifteen republics in the Soviet Union. Like all of the other republics, Russia had a president, a parliament, and all of the other trappings of government, except, pre-Yeltsin, it had no power. It was an empty shell. But when the Soviet Communist Party, the once-feared center of Soviet power, began to lose its clout in the late 1980s, Yeltsin moved into the developing vacuum, claiming that, as president of the Russian republic, he, more than any other Soviet leader, had the power to lead a new Russia—a Russia that would soon be at the head of a new constellation of Slavic nations. It was a bold presumption, but Yeltsin was attuned to the times.

A small, but important, example of the changes in Kremlin politics was obvious in November 1990 when Yeltsin flew to Kiev as Russia's president. He acted as though the Soviet Union no longer existed. So did his host, Leonid Kravchuk, who had (overnight, it seemed) become an ardent fan of Ukrainian independence. Yeltsin and Kravchuk reached agreement on a wide range of economic issues—two leaders of two entities still, at least theoretically, part of the Soviet Union.

Gorbachev, caught in this rising tide of nationalist revolt, found himself on shaky grounds. The Soviet empire was falling apart, and Yeltsin was rushing to replace him. Gorbachev feared Yeltsin, while Yeltsin never concealed his contempt for Gorbachev, his onetime Politburo ally. One close observer, Leonid Kravchenko, a prominent journalist in the Kremlin's employ, later said their competition "looked childish, like little boys battling for domination, but it was based of course on the instinctive fear that Yeltsin was acquiring an authority with the people which threatened Gorbachev's own survival."[1]

In late 1988, Gorbachev had proposed a new, national treaty that would have extended broad autonomy to all the Soviet republics while preserving Moscow's ultimate control over foreign affairs, military matters, and the national economy. He thought it made sense, given the spreading turmoil, but it got nowhere. In March 1991, an increasingly desperate Gorbachev organized a national referendum on a basic question: Should the USSR itself be preserved? That he felt he needed the referendum was proof, in retrospect, that his days were numbered. Six of the fifteen Soviet republics—Armenia, Estonia, Georgia, Latvia, Lithuania, and Moldova—refused to participate in the referendum, but 76 percent of those who did vote supported preservation of the union.[2]

Surprisingly, even though the Soviet Union was teetering, on August 4, 1991, Gorbachev went on vacation in the Crimea. Like many in the Russian communist upper crust, he could not imagine August without a dip in the Black Sea. With his family, he vacationed in a new villa, built just for him. It was called the Sunrise Dacha. On August 18, the last day of his vacation, his wife went for a swim after breakfast, and he sat on the beach, complaining of lumbago while editing a speech he was to deliver on August 20 on the new union treaty he had spent many months negotiating with the increasingly rebellious Soviet republics. Gorbachev had finally won Yeltsin's consent to such a treaty.[3]

At 4:30 p.m., Gorbachev was back at the dacha, when he learned that the KGB had cut his telephone lines. He was stunned. Something had just gone terribly wrong. But what was it? A conspiracy of some sort? Yeltsin was always a problem for Gorbachev; what was he up to? At 4:45 p.m., four emissaries from Moscow, including his own chief of staff, two secretaries from the party's Central Committee, and the commander of Soviet ground troops—General Valentin Ivanovich Varennikov—barged unannounced into his office.

A coup d'état, obviously! They demanded that Gorbachev declare a "state of emergency," transfer his powers temporarily to a Presidium colleague, and remain in the Crimea for "health reasons." Gorbachev, for just a moment, thought about how Rumania's communist leader, Nicolae Ceausescu, had been brutally executed in late 1989; and how one of his own predecessors, Nikita Khrushchev, had been dismissed from office but allowed to live on in a government-provided dacha. Gorbachev decided to "negotiate" with the coup emissaries. He played to his strength, lawyer to clients.

Why a "state of emergency?" he asked. "Let's discuss and decide," he went on, not waiting for an answer. "But let us act only within the framework of the constitution and under the law. Anything else is unacceptable to me."

The coup plotters, feeling "confused and depressed," had assumed Gorbachev would fold under pressure. In fact, he seemed amazingly calm, given what had just happened. The emissaries, somewhat bewildered, departed for Moscow. Gorbachev and his family were left behind, imprisoned in their own dacha. The following day, August 19, at 6 p.m., Soviet media broke the news of Gorbachev's ouster.[4]

When informed of the coup, Yeltsin surprisingly came to Gorbachev's defense. "That's illegal!" he snapped. He had heard whispers of coup plans, but didn't believe them. Now, what could he do? Yeltsin decided that he would immediately leave his suburban dacha and drive to the Russian federation's White House, a large modern building near the American Embassy in central Moscow. From there, Yeltsin would assume command of the political opposition to the coup. It was a decision fraught with symbolism, danger but also opportunity. Only the leaders of the three Baltic republics and Moldova joined Yeltsin in opposing the coup. He impetuously called for a general strike, but it never developed. The coup organizers, led at the time by Defense Minister Dimitri Yazov and KGB chief Vladimir Kryuchkov ordered 4,000 troops, 350 tanks, 300 armored personnel carriers, and 420 trucks to hurry to the Soviet capital. The defense minister and the KGB chief felt they were in charge, and the coup would succeed.

But Yeltsin, always at his best during a crisis, posed a formidable roadblock. Even though he disliked Gorbachev, he repeatedly denounced the coup, calling it "unconstitutional" and issuing decrees saying that he, and no one else, had the authority to give military orders. "He is working constantly," his daughter, Tatiana, told her mother, "and he is in a fighting mood."[5] Yeltsin did what he felt he had to do. He loved the political stage, and the Moscow coup had provided a beautiful one. He jumped on top of a tank and, with his chin jutting forward, urged a huge crowd of cheering Muscovites to protect the White House; it provided a photo in an age of imagery that was worth a political fortune. He also performed in a similar scene from a central balcony in the White House, standing behind a bulletproof shield, yielding another photo worth a mint. Close to 100,000 people watched in admiration. "Yeltsin, we support you," the people shouted. "Russia is alive," they continued. "Put the junta on trial." Fear, that constant companion of the Soviet past, was amazingly AWOL. Former foreign minister Eduard Shevardnadze spoke to the crowd. So did the popular poet Yevgeny Yevtushenko, cellist Mstislav

Rostropovich, and human rights activist Elena Bonner. Their message was the same: The coup was proof that the communist system had to be discarded and thrown into the dustbin of history.

On August 19, Yeltsin telephoned President George H. W. Bush, who agreed that the coup was "extra-constitutional" but approached the unfolding crisis with understandable caution. Bush belonged to the "realist" school of foreign policy. He favored good relations with Moscow, if at all possible, even if that offended the new leadership in Kiev. Meeting with his aides, Bush raised many questions about the coup. Russian troops had fired on non-Russian rebels in Nagorno-Karabakh and Vilnius, but would they fire on other Russians? That was a key question. (It would be the same question in southeastern Ukraine during the turbulent spring and summer of 2014.) Another key question: Would the coup succeed, or fail? The CIA gave Bush its best judgment: The coup probably would not succeed, because there were too many loose ends. "Mr. President, this does not look like a traditional coup," said deputy chief Richard Kerr.[6]

Soviet ambassador Viktor Komplektov provided the "official" reason for the coup during a visit to the State Department. "There has emerged a situation of uncontrollability with too many centers of power," he explained. "There has also been a real threat of the country's disintegration. . . . A disintegration of the USSR would have gravest concerns not only internally, but internationally as well. Under these circumstances we have no other choice but to take resolute measures in order to stop the slide towards catastrophe."

Bush decided, Komplektov notwithstanding, that the United States would go public in supporting Gorbachev and condemning the "unconstitutional resort to force." Bush admired Gorbachev and hoped that he would survive. Bush feared chaos would envelop Eastern Europe if the coup were to succeed.[7]

Earlier in August, Bush had visited the Soviet Union. The White House later described his talks with Gorbachev about the rebellious republics as "fruitful." On a stopover in Kiev, Bush surprisingly echoed the Gorbachev line. Here was an American president in open support of a Russian president's policy toward Ukraine, something unimaginable now. Speaking to a special session of the Rada, Bush cautioned Ukrainian nationalists not to pursue the "hopeless course of isolation." He also stressed that "freedom is not the same as independence. Americans will not support those who seek independence in order to replace a far-off tyranny with a local despotism. They will not aid those who promote a suicidal nationalism based upon ethnic hatred."[8] "Suicidal nationalism?" The phrase leaped out of the president's text. "Far-off tyranny?" What did he mean? "Ethnic hatred?" Did Bush mean that Ukrainian independence would be an example of "suicidal nationalism"? Did he mean that the United States and other Western nations would not help Ukraine, were it to declare its independence? No doubt, Bush was doing his best to discourage Ukraine's move toward independence and, by implication, to support Gorbachev's new union proposal. Conservative *New York Times* columnist William Safire quickly smacked the label "Chicken Kiev" on Bush's intriguing speech.

These days, if an American president were to urge Kiev to avoid "suicidal nationalism," he would be skewered by the media and possibly defeated in his next election. And worse, if he advised Kiev to follow a Russian president's lead, he would possibly expose him or herself to being impeached. We have come a long way since 1991, the year of Ukraine's declaration of independence!

With the status of the attempted coup against Gorbachev still unclear, an obviously jumpy Yeltsin again called Bush on the evening of August 20 and reported that units of the Soviet military were about to attack his White House. "I expect a storming at any moment," he said. "We have been here twenty-four hours. We won't leave. I have appealed to a hundred-thousand people standing outside to defend the legally elected government. Basically this is a right-wing coup."[9] From intercepted telephone calls, Bush knew that coup leaders were wavering on the wisdom of such an attack, but he was uncertain which path they would ultimately follow. The fate of the coup—and Russia—hung in the balance. An attack would produce bloodshed and headlines, but it would likely ensure the coup's success, at least in the short term. A decision not to attack would surely guarantee its failure. That would be a sign of confusion and cowardice.

The attack was to start at 3 a.m. on August 21. Or at least so the coup plotters had planned! But the shooting began hours earlier. Armored troop carriers fired indiscriminately at the White House. Yeltsin's troops fired back. Everyone seemed to be shooting, but not necessarily at one another. Three people were killed, many others wounded. When Defense Minister Yazov learned of the casualties, he ordered his deputy: "Give the command to stop." The shooting stopped. Kryuchkov, dumbfounded, accused the army of cowardice, but in fact his own KGB troops were also refusing to engage their fellow Russians. He soon realized that his efforts to overthrow Gorbachev were falling far short of his goal. He decided to abandon the fight. The next morning, at 8 a.m., Yazov ordered a complete withdrawal of all troops from Moscow. The coup had failed.

On August 21, 1991, it was clear the Soviet system had survived, but it was unclear at that moment just how long it could continue to survive. Gorbachev had also survived as the leader of the Soviet Union, if only temporarily. In this context, however, survival did not ensure security.

Who Me? KGB?

At the time the coup unfolded, Vladimir Putin was a 38-year-old former KGB lieutenant colonel serving as deputy mayor of St. Petersburg. He reportedly asked Mayor Anatoly Sobchak, a Yeltsin backer, to call KGB chief Kryuchkov and ask what had happened to his letter of resignation. According to this weird tale, Putin supposedly had resigned from the KGB the year before, and he now wanted confirmation. Why he imagined that Kryuchkov, in the midst of managing a spectacularly uncertain coup, would have had the time, or inclination, to check on having received such a letter is baffling.

Putin, according to another tale, was supposed to have submitted a second letter of resignation as well. If this is true, which is questionable, he obviously would have wanted the record to show that his allegiance was to Sobchak and, by inference, to Yeltsin—and not to the discredited KGB. Putin later said that he respected Kryuchkov, but never said why. "When I saw the criminals on the screen" (presumably the coup leaders during a televised news conference), he later said, "I understood immediately that it was all over; they were done for."[10]

Soviet Union—"Null and Void"

Unlike Yeltsin, Ukraine's Kravchuk took a very cautious approach to the coup. He wanted to see what others would do. From Moscow had come orders from the Soviet Communist Party and the Ministry of Defense that Ukraine was to ignore Gorbachev and follow the dictates of the "Emergency Committee." On August 19, General Varennikov visited Kravchuk in Kiev, hoping to win his unqualified support for the coup. Kravchuk, as always, was polite and understanding, but he also remained noncommittal. Twice that day, he spoke on television, explaining the crisis but refusing to commit himself either to Gorbachev or to Yeltsin. "In such extraordinarily serious political circumstances," he said, "we mustn't make haste with judgments. . . . I call on you, dear comrades, to show calm and moderation. . . . In Ukraine, no emergency situation has been declared."[11] The opposition group Rukh, on the other hand, joined other opposition groups to denounce the coup, call for a general strike, and demand an emergency session of the Rada.

On August 20, mass protests jammed Khreshchatyk Boulevard, the beautiful thoroughfare that runs through central Kiev. Though Kravchuck was still playing it safe, shifting awkwardly from one side to the other, the Ukrainian people saw a clear path to national independence. They had lost confidence in communism. The Rada wanted an up-or-down vote on independence.

August 21 was devoted to more public protests and private politicking, the necessary preliminaries to Kravchuk's announcement the following day that the Rada would be convened in emergency session on August 24. Why? He did not say, but everyone assumed the reason was to vote on independence.

Meanwhile, on August 23, Kravchuk flew to Moscow to hear Gorbachev, just back from Crimea, looking haggard but determined, beg for Ukrainian support for his new union treaty. This time, Kravchuk, feeling unaccountably self-confident, waved him off. Gorbachev no longer represented power. Yeltsin, before a TV audience, had humiliated the man who was still head of an all-but-defunct Soviet Communist Party. Kravchenko, the journalist, recalled that Gorbachev "had become like a little puppy dog doing whatever Yeltsin told him and signing every bit of paper put under his nose."[12] It was the sort of public humiliation no proud man would ever forget. Yeltsin then announced that he had banned the Communist Party of Russia, technically still under Gorbachev's Soviet Communist Party's nominal control. Gorbachev could do nothing about it.

On August 24, Kravchuk claimed he had always opposed the coup, a claim no one believed. Then, after the communists and the democrats met in separate sessions, the Rada reconvened and, in a brief declaration, announced the independence of Ukraine. The vote was overwhelming: 346 yes, 1 no, and 3 abstentions. In its historic declaration, the Rada pronounced that Ukraine was now a "fully independent" state "in view of the mortal danger surrounding Ukraine in connection with the state coup in the USSR on August 19, 1991." Six days later the Rada outlawed the Communist Party of Ukraine, a reflection of the fact that the party no longer commanded a majority in the Rada.[13]

Still, the Rada seemed oddly defensive. It voted to hold a national referendum on December 1 to support its declaration of independence. One might argue that such a referendum was entirely unnecessary. The Rada had just voted unmistakably for independence. So why an additional vote? One reason was that the Rada vote was so incredibly important. It was saying that Ukraine, which had always been so closely entwined with Russia—indeed for centuries it was a part of Russia—was now stating that it was "fully independent" of Russia. That was, for many Ukrainians, an awesome, almost unbelievable thought.

On the same day, December 1, Ukrainians would also be asked to vote for a president of their newly independent country. Kravchuk was the runaway favorite.

During the run-up to the December vote, in the fall of 1991, Kravchuk showed the flag in well-publicized visits to the United States, Canada, and France; in each visit he dangled the prospect of profitable commerce and exciting new market opportunities. Perhaps he really believed the seductive myth then floating over newly independent Ukraine—that with communism gone, with Moscow's grip on its rich natural resources now lifted, Ukraine could prosper, consumer goods could pop up like buds in spring, and people could finally enjoy a much higher standard of living. Ukrainians wrapped themselves in a new optimism, many believing that they had finally discarded their Russian greatcoat.

On Sunday, December 1, Ukrainians went to the polls. Kravchuk, in a race for president, was among the first to cast a ballot in a nation known for early voting. "This is a great day," exulted election worker Olga Ovsiyenko, "it is the flowering of our soul."[14] Throughout the country, the turnout exceeded expectations. Galicia, in the west, where Ukrainian nationalism burned most brightly, registered a 97 percent turnout. Even in the east and south, where pro-Russian sentiment was strong, the turnout was remarkable. In Luhansk, for example, support for independence reached 83 percent. In neighboring Donetsk, it was 77 percent, and in Odessa and in the Crimea, 85 percent. A week earlier, Kravchuk had brushed aside Rada member Stepan Khmara's prediction that there would be a 90 percent-plus vote for independence, saying the gulag survivor had lost his mind. But, in fact, Khmara's faith in Ukraine's yearning for national independence was fully justified. The nationwide turnout averaged 84.2 percent, with 90.32 percent voting for independence. On the vote for president, Kravchuk received 61 percent, and his opponent, Viacheslav Chornovil, a gulag survivor, also a passionate nationalist, got 23 percent. To no one's surprise, Kravchuk had kept his job.[15]

"A full-fledged nation of the Ukraine," wrote *New York Times* reporter Francis X. Clines, "a fragile dream across centuries of alien oppression and warfare abruptly came within reach with the collapse of central authority."[16]

Gorbachev, when informed, could not believe the news. He had expected, in fact predicted, a suspect vote because of local violence and ethnic strife. He had reluctantly prepared a speech offering congratulations to the people of Ukraine. Then he changed his mind and had the speech redrafted to express his anger and disappointment. "All are independent," the new draft read, "but not all turn independence into a weapon against the union. . . . Misfortune awaits the Ukrainians—both those who live there and those scattered around the country." Gorbachev still entertained flickering hopes that his formula for a reconstituted union, which would include Ukraine, could somehow be salvaged. But that was not to be. The Ukrainian vote effectively smothered not only his new union but the Soviet Union as well.

And yet, among politicians, hope still prevailed that one day their horse would win. Gorbachev telephoned Yeltsin and proposed a five-way meeting, involving him as head of the Soviet Union plus Yeltsin and the leaders of Ukraine, Belarus, and Kazakhstan. The Russian president shook his head. "Nothing will come of it," he said. "Ukraine is independent." Yeltsin now had to adjust his plans. He offered a proposal of his own, similar to Gorbachev's but different enough to guarantee its rejection. He proposed a four-nation summit, including Russia, Ukraine, Belarus and Kazakhstan—and Gorbachev, but as a leader who lacked a specific portfolio. "And what would be my place in it?" asked Gorbachev with seething anger. "If that's the deal, then I'm leaving. I'm not going to bobble like a piece of shit in an ice hole."[17] Gorbachev refused to play a supporting role. Behind his refusal, though, was the continuing, fundamental dispute about the shape of the new Russia.

In a telephone talk with Bush, Yeltsin explained his thinking. At the moment, Gorbachev's draft treaty for a new union, Yeltsin explained, contained seven republics—five Islamic and two Slavic. There were fifteen in the old Soviet Union. Without Ukraine, Yeltsin believed, Russia would be in serious trouble, overwhelmed on each vote by an Islamic majority, consisting of Azerbaijan, Kazakhstan, Uzbekistan, Tajikistan, and Kyrgyzstan. "We can't have a situation," he continued, "where Russia and Byelorussia would have two votes as Slavic states against five for the Islamic nations." Ukraine was the key. With it, the Slavic soul of the new Russia would glow like a bright star over the newly reconstituted nation. Yeltsin thought Ukraine would be where it always was and should be—with Russia. The Slavs would prevail in all decisionmaking. Without Ukraine, Yeltsin feared, the new Russia would no longer remain Slavic in language, tone, and character. "Our relations with Ukraine," he said, stressing the obvious, "are more significant than those with the Central Asian republics."[18]

On December 2, Yeltsin extended formal Russian recognition to Ukraine. He was among the first to do so; only Poland and Canada beat him to it. That must have been difficult for a Russian nationalist to accept, to imagine, much less to say: an independent Ukraine. It had always been Russia's "little brother." Now, suddenly, it was an equal, another former Soviet republic proclaiming its independence. Yeltsin then invited Kravchuk to Minsk, the Belarus capital, where the Russian president was scheduled to meet with Stanislau Shushkevich, speaker of the Belarusian parliament, on December 7. Yeltsin wanted to negotiate the terms of a new state-to-state relationship with Kravchuk, but in a place where Gorbachev could not possibly cast a shadow over their deliberations. Such a place was the Viskuli hunting lodge in the forests of western Belarus. Khrushchev had built it and gone hunting there, and so had Brezhnev. "Why Viskuli?" asked a surprised Kravchuk. Because, his host responded, it's the perfect place to get away from government ministers, journalists, and TV cameras.

All of the negotiators had ideas about what a new union should look like. Yeltsin had two ideas, both inspired by an article written by Nobel Prize–winning author Alexander Solzhenitsyn and published the year before in *Komsomolskaya Pravda*, Russia's largest circulation newspaper. It began, "The clock of communism has stopped striking. But its concrete building has not yet come crashing down. For that reason, instead of freeing ourselves, we must try to save ourselves from being crushed by its rubble." Solzhenitsyn was an old-fashioned Russian nationalist. His vision of a new union was narrowly Slavic—Russia, Belarus, and Ukraine, plus "southern Siberia," or the northern strip of Kazakhstan, colonized by the Russians in the nineteenth century.[19]

Yeltsin updated Solzhenitsyn's treatise. One of his proposals was for a new union, or confederation, of all former Soviet republics, save the Baltics; another of his proposals was more selective: Russia, Belarus, and Ukraine, plus all of Kazakhstan. When, earlier in the year, he had laid these two ideas before Gorbachev, Yeltsin got a quick rejection. When he proposed a skeletal union of only the three Slavic republics—Russia, Belarus and Ukraine—he got the same response. The relationship between Gorbachev and Yeltsin had become so poisonous that neither could work with the other, even as both understood, in rational moments, that the fate of Russia lay in their hands.

By the time Yeltsin met with Kravchuk and Shushkevich in snowy Viskuli in December, he had come to one inescapable conclusion: He needed Kravchuk desperately. Ukraine was the key to Yeltsin's plans for the hoped-for confederation. As Harvard's Serhii Plokhy told Deborah Kalb's *Book* blog: "Keeping Ukraine in the Russian sphere of influence [was] crucial for whatever plans there [were] for Russia as a major power."[20] Plokhy's research on the death of the Soviet Union is especially impressive, providing insight into the politics and personalities of this historic moment.[21]

Dinner found Yeltsin seated opposite Kravchuk. They dominated the conversation. Everyone else was merely there as a witness to history. Dinner, soaked in vodka and wine, took less than an hour. By toast time, Yeltsin asked if Kravchuk would sign Gorbachev's draft of a new union constitution, knowing in advance that Kravchuk would likely say no. And Kravchuk did say no, adding that the December 1 Ukrainian referendum was remarkable, because it appealed to all Ukrainians, including 14 million Russians, Jews, and Tartars.

Yeltsin was impressed. "Did the Donbas also vote for it?" he asked.

"There is no region in which the votes were fewer than half," Kravchuk replied, enjoying the power and confidence he seemed to derive from the referendum vote.

According to Petr Kravchenka, the Belarus foreign minister, who was taking notes, "Kravchuk was unyielding." Kravchenka added: "Smiling and calm, he parried Yeltsin's arguments and proposals. Kravchuk did not want to sign anything. His argumentation was as simple as could be. He said that Ukraine had already determined its path in the referendum, and that path was independence. The Soviet Union no longer existed, and parliament would not allow him to create new unions of any kind. And Ukraine needed no such unions; the Ukrainians did not want to exchange one yoke for another."[22]

Kravchuk, with his rigid insistence that the Soviet Union no longer existed, brought the conversation to a screeching halt. He explained "a hundred times that for Ukraine there was no [question] of a union treaty—it simply did not exist and no integration was possible," Gennadi Burbulis, a top Yeltsin aide, later recalled. "It was out of the question: any union, even a reformed one, with or without a center."[23] By "center," he meant Moscow. Kravchuk then unnecessarily needled Yeltsin. "Who will you be when you return to Russia?" asked the Ukrainian leader. "I'll return to Ukraine as the president elected by the people, and what will your role be—that of Gorbachev's subordinate?" Yeltsin, famous for his notoriously short fuse, could have exploded in anger and stormed out of the negotiation. Instead, he tried calmly to mollify Kravchuk, saying in effect that if he were Ukraine's president, he wouldn't sign Gorbachev's draft either. He then suggested that the three Slavic republics, those represented at the Viskuli summit, get together and come up with a completely new draft. Kravchuk's prime minister, Vitold Fokin, expected his boss summarily to reject Yeltsin's proposal. Reaching into his bag of political goodies, he surprised everyone by pulling out, of all things, Rudyard Kipling's "call of blood," "the unity of fraternal peoples," and the argument that "we all have the same roots." Fokin urged Kravchuk to return to his Slavic "roots." In this way, Kipling helped Fokin try to persuade Kravchuk that the "call of blood" and the "same roots" were reasons enough for the three Slavic leaders to work together. Kravchuk accepted Yeltsin's proposal.

Yeltsin directed his top aides, working with aides to Kravchuk and Shushkevich, to labor all night, if necessary, and create a new draft. Yeltsin then thundered that Gorbachev—and everything he represented, including his draft reform of the Soviet empire—had lost all credibility at home and abroad. "Gorbachev has to be removed. Enough!" he screamed. "No more playing the tsar!" It was time for a few more drinks. Later reports on this Slavic summit said everyone then got drunk and sweated in a sauna.

On the morning of December 8, 1991—on what was to be the last day in the life of the Soviet Union—the "young Turks" finished drafting a new treaty, called "Agreement on the Creation of a Commonwealth of Democratic States." They used the word "commonwealth" instead of "union" because Kravchuk had strenuously objected to "union," which he demanded be "stricken from the lexicon, from consciousness, from experience." It reminded him of the "Union of Soviet Socialist Republics." Before taking a needed nap, the "young Turks" listened to Moscow Radio at 6 a.m. It began, as it did every morning, with a choir singing "'Great Rus' has forever bound together the indissoluble union of free republics." The choir soon would need to look for new lyrics.

Before breakfast, the Ukrainians edited the title of the draft treaty. They insisted that the word "democratic" be changed to "independent." Everyone accepted the change, agreeing that it would be a long time before the former Soviet republics would be democratic.

After breakfast, Kravchuk injected drama into the summit proceedings. He cavalierly discarded the draft treaty, refusing even to read it, but he made clear he was not discarding the idea of a new treaty. He "took a blank sheet of paper, a pen," he later recalled. "That was how we began. We wrote, and edited ourselves, without assistants. According to the old protocol, there had never been anything like it—heads of state writing government documents themselves." Kravchuk had a few legacy drafts of union treaties, which he had studied until 3 a.m. Yeltsin's aide Burbulis had a few drafts of his own, too. After several hours of intensive writing, researching, and negotiating, Yeltsin, Kravchuk, and Shushkevich agreed on a fourteen-article treaty, called "The Agreement on the Establishment of a Commonwealth of Independent States." They toasted one another with champagne, at which point Burbulis pricked this bubble of euphoria with the dismaying announcement that the draft treaty lacked one essential article, without which all of the others, he maintained, lacked legal authority. And what article would that be? everyone was eager to know. "We should begin by denouncing the union treaty of

1922," he responded. "Only then will our accords be absolutely correct from the legal viewpoint."

The 1922 treaty established the USSR, which then consisted of the three Slavic republics, plus another called the Transcaucasian Federation, which included the future Soviet republics of Georgia, Armenia, and Azerbaijan. Unless the 1922 treaty was formally dissolved, the "Soviet Union," lawyer Burbulis insisted, would continue to exist. If it existed, Gorbachev would remain its leader. This Yeltsin could not tolerate. Gorbachev had to go, meaning the union, as formally constituted, had to be dissolved, so Yeltsin could be president of the newly created commonwealth. It wasn't that Yeltsin had a clear, step-by-step plan of action. Even so liberal a Russian writer as Tatyana Tolstaya observed at the time: "Having rushed to 'seize' Russia, he didn't know what to do with it."24

Still, at key moments, Yeltsin moved history along. His agreement with Kravchuk and Shushkevich opened with the historic announcement that the Soviet Union no longer existed. "We, the Republic of Belarus, the Russian Federation (RSFSR), and Ukraine, as founding states of the USSR that signed the union treaty of 1922 . . . hereby establish that the USSR as a subject of international law and a geopolitical reality ceases its existence." All Soviet laws would henceforth be declared null and void in the nations of the new commonwealth, but all international obligations of the Soviet Union would be honored. The territorial integrity and the existing borders of each nation in the commonwealth would be officially recognized.25

The agreement was signed at 2 p.m. on December 8 in the Viskuli hunting lodge. Each article was toasted with champagne, and reporters invited to witness the ceremony couldn't help but notice that Yeltsin was getting quite tipsy. He wanted to hold a news conference, but Shushkevich vetoed the idea. "Boris Nikolaevich," his spokesman said, "there is no need to say anything. Everything is clear." Yeltsin yielded. "If it's all clear to you . . . ," he mumbled, and left the room. Somehow, after a brief time, a composed Yeltsin managed to call President Bush and tell him about the summit and its results. He had one reason in mind, in particular. As Kravchuk later explained, "It was done so that the world would know where we were and what documents we were approving." He added: "For any eventuality, as they say." Yeltsin informed Bush that the Viskuli summit decided that the Soviet Union no longer existed, Gorbachev was no longer president, and nothing could change that fact. "This is very serious," Yeltsin said. "These four states (the original three, plus Kazakhstan) form 90 percent of the national product of the Soviet Union." Yeltsin stressed that the new commonwealth would honor existing international obligations of the Soviet Union and would maintain joint control over all Soviet nuclear stockpiles.

The call to Bush having been concluded, Yeltsin thought Gorbachev should now be told that his world had just ended—that his country no longer existed and he was out of a job. Neither Yeltsin nor Kravchuk wanted to be the messenger, so the task was left to Shushkevich, technically host of the summit. He telephoned Gorbachev and in simple words broke the news.

Gorbachev exploded. "Do you realize what you've done?" he shouted. "Do you understand that the world community will condemn you? Angrily!" Gorbachev worried especially about the American reaction. "Once Bush finds out about this, what then?" Gorbachev asked.

Shushkevich replied, "Boris Nikolaevich [Yeltsin] has already told him; he reacted normally." Gorbachev then "made a scene. . . . And we said goodbye."[26]

Gorbachev called Yeltsin. "What you have done behind my back with the consent of the U.S. President is a crying shame, a disgrace!" He demanded that Yeltsin, Kravchuk, and Shushkevich fly to Moscow immediately. He wanted to talk to them. Yeltsin, who lived and worked in Moscow, had little choice but to accept the idea of a meeting, but he worried that Gorbachev might try to shoot down his plane. Kravchuk had the same worry. In fact, Gorbachev attempted to reach key military commanders that evening. However, since the attempted coup and Defense Minister Yazov's resignation, the Soviet military refused to obey Gorbachev. He had become a shadow president without a country. He could not find a single regimental commander who remained loyal to him.[27]

When Kravchuk returned to Kiev, he told his wife, Antonina, what had happened at Viskuli. She asked, "So we are no longer in the union? What, is it all over?" Kravchuk replied, "So it would seem."[28]

CHAPTER 13

"Ukraine Has Arrived!"

[Ukraine is] a pastiche . . . of peoples and cultures and narratives
that, like the phoenix, is still waiting to be born.
YURII ANDRUKHOVYCH, UKRAINIAN WRITER

UKRAINE HAS BEEN INDEPENDENT since 1991, having survived corruption, failed leadership, and relentless pressure from Moscow. Ukraine's independence was not the result of a popular revolution, Ukrainians with bloodied headbands rushing to the barricades of freedom. Rather, it was the result of the disintegration of the Soviet Union.

There was, too, the happy coincidence of a Mikhail Gorbachev, without whom the disintegration might well have been delayed for another decade or two. Uncharacteristic of a Soviet leader, he abhorred violence and saw tomorrows of potential and promise in a truly reformed Russia. The courage of the Baltic peoples, who lit a bonfire of hope and rebellion in the Soviet republics, encouraged the protesters in Kiev's Maidan Square to believe that Ukraine's independence was a realistic goal. And finally, in Ukraine—as communism retreated to the sidelines of power and influence—a sufficient number of democratic nationalists rose in the Rada to say the time had come to shout the nation's independence from the rooftops of Europe. "Ukraine has arrived!" But because the new democrats had been communists, or in many cases were still officially members of the Ukrainian Communist Party, when independence was finally proclaimed, Ukrainians found that the old elites remained in charge of their politics and their economy. Those who had tried to build communism, and failed, were now trying to build a free market democracy, and they hadn't a clue about how to do it.

Like Douglas MacArthur's "old soldiers," communism did not "die"—here one moment, gone the next—it just "faded away." New problems, demanding urgent action, crowded the daily agenda of the new president, Leonid

Kravchuk, slowing progress on his efforts to dismantle the communist past. One was this matter of national identity, which seemed for a time to loom above the others: What was Ukraine?

That question had rumbled through Ukrainian history for centuries, seeking an answer but never quite finding one. Borders changed with unsettling regularity. After World War II, Ukraine was fattened with land that had been part of Poland, Czechoslovakia, Romania, and Russia. Which was the legitimate Ukraine—the one before or after? Or was the only authentic Ukraine the one that went back to the Cossacks of the seventeenth and eighteenth centuries? The upshot was that Ukrainians never enjoyed a true sense of nationhood. The land they occupied—from Lvov in the west, to Kiev in the center, to Odessa in the south, to Donetsk in the east, the largest land mass in non-Russian Europe, 233,062 square miles of newly proclaimed sovereignty—featured many national and cultural traditions, all with a Slavic flavor. Most important among them were Russian and Ukrainian.

If there was a bond common to all Ukrainians, it was, without doubt, their language. Most spoke Ukrainian, and many spoke Russian, and almost all spoke a mix of the two languages. "Language is the foundation of any national identity," said Pavlo Movchan, a Rada member. "It's impossible to imagine the French without the French language, or the English without the English language. . . . It is just as impossible to imagine Ukraine without the Ukrainian language. Ukraine must speak in Ukrainian."[1] The first decision for Kravchuk's postcommunist regime: Ukrainian was proclaimed the official national language, but—added carefully—Russian would be "guaranteed" and "protected," too.

History, like language, also contained answers to the question of national identity. From some shadowy moment in the ninth century, Slavs have lived in those parts of Europe that we now call Ukraine and Russia. Their fates have been closely intertwined ever since. In fact, from the early eighteenth century to the 1917 Russian Revolution, Ukraine was an integral part of Russia, recognized and understood as such by all parties. Not surprisingly, then, after the 1991 proclamation of Ukrainian independence, a form of hybrid nationalism emerged, which blended a new Ukrainian nationalism with an existing, and widely appreciated, Russian culture. Ukraine developed a split personality, looking first one way and then the other, before making any major decision.

Yurii Andrukhovych, the Ukrainian author of the 1993 novel *Moskoviada* ("The Last Days of Moscow"), wrote about Ukrainians being drawn irresistibly to Moscow, even while being repelled by many things they found there. Many Ukrainians, including writers and laborers, lived in the Russian capital, married Russians, and worked in Russia—yet always considered themselves Ukrainian. Likewise, many Russians lived, married, and worked in Ukraine, while never losing their emotional attachment to their "homeland."

In Chekhov's play *Three Sisters* every major character dreamed of a journey to the Russian capital. "To Moscow," they cried, "to Moscow," believing Moscow was the heart of Russian culture. It was the destination they prayed one day to reach, the rural Russian yearning for a day in the urban capital. In a similar fashion, in psychological terms, many Ukrainians, the "little Russians," regarded themselves as the eternal provincials when compared with the sophisticated "Russian" aristocrats in Moscow. Ukraine, after all, meant "borderland," the Ukrainian looking from the border of Russia, through a hazy window, into Russia's heart and soul.

In another of Andrukhovych's novels, called *Perversion*, the hero described Ukraine as "a pastiche . . . of peoples and cultures and narratives, that, like the phoenix, is still waiting to be born." He meant that, in his view, there was nothing distinctively Ukrainian anywhere. He was writing in 1997, six years after independence.[2] Or critic Roman Kis, who thought of his fellow Ukrainians as living in "two worlds." "Ukraine on the border of two worlds," he wrote, "is a profoundly dangerous [idea], insofar as he who finds himself only on the border of two worlds has no powerful world of his own." Kis wanted Ukrainians to develop "our own integral Ukrainian cultural-civilizational complex." (Few studies better explain the links between Ukrainian and Russian culture and history than Andrew Wilson's *The Ukrainians: Unexpected Nation.*)

The modern Ukrainian, argue a number of writers and scholars, needs to develop a native culture strong enough to compete with a lingering nostalgia for Russian culture. Without it, Ukrainians may be consigned to living in "two worlds."

It may yet prove to be the height of historic irony that Putin's relentless pressure on Ukraine, his drive to peel off parts of the country to satisfy his dream of a "greater Russia," may help crystallize a new Ukrainian nationalism. It would not be the first time that war has sharpened a nation's sense of pride or grievance. But, even so, one relevant fact cannot be ignored: 11 million Russians still live in Ukraine, 57 percent of whom were born there. They want their piece of the pie, too. They want Kiev authorities "to recognize Russians alongside Ukrainians as an indigenous people in Ukraine."[3]

Defining national identity can be a tricky business, particularly in the current fevered context. "The idea of independent Ukraine as a state for ethnic Ukrainians, where their language and culture should finally become dominant," wrote historian Serhy Yekelchyk, "is common in the country's media and political discourse, but it usually reflects a protest against the persistent influence of 'imperial' Russian culture rather than exclusive ethnic nationalism."[4] The balance between the two is a daily headache for Ukraine's political leadership. There is no way to avoid history: Russia and Ukraine grew up together. Ukraine was part of Russia for centuries. A clean, definitive rupture between the two may be unrealistic—and may remain so, even with the current de facto war between them.

Kravchuk's new Ukraine was able easily to adopt the state symbols of independence: the blue-and-yellow flag, for example, the trident as the state coat of arms, and a national anthem, which begins on an oddly defensive note, "Ukraine Has Not Perished Yet." Still, Kravchuk, looking over his shoulder, already could see Yeltsin's Russia pushing for a form of regional dominion over neighboring states that were once part of the Soviet Union. Fresh from his victory over Gorbachev, Boris Yeltsin was busy implementing plans for a new Commonwealth of Independent States (CIS). He obviously assumed that because he ran the most powerful of the states, he would be able to control the others within the Commonwealth, none more important than Ukraine.

Kravchuk had other plans for Ukraine. He wanted, more than anything, to underscore his country's independence—its separateness from Russia. Though a founding member of Yeltsin's Commonwealth, he made it clear that he opposed a number of Russian proposals. Yeltsin thought everyone should be a "citizen" of the Commonwealth; Kravchuk disagreed. Yeltsin believed the Commonwealth should set up a joint security pact; Kravchuk disagreed. Yeltsin proposed an interparliamentary assembly; Kravchuk disagreed. In every case, Kravchuk suspected Yeltsin was seeking indirectly to assert Russian control over the Commonwealth, including Ukraine, and his instincts proved to be correct. Part of the reason, from Kiev's perspective, was that many Russian diplomats and politicians had trouble conceiving of Ukraine as a truly independent nation. They thought they could offer a proposal, and Ukraine would automatically accept it, as it had always done during the Soviet era. After a while, the Russians would be ready, however reluctantly, to accept the idea of an independent Ukraine, so long as Ukraine did not raise obstacles to Russian policies and needs.

For a time, no problem produced greater tension between the two countries than control over Crimea and the Black Sea fleet. Nikita Khrushchev had transferred control of Crimea to Ukraine in 1954. His action proved to be a bone in the throat of every Russian politician in 1992. Their argument was that in 1954 control of Crimea was a mere formality because every province or city was really a part of the Soviet Union, no matter which one of the Soviet republics it might be in. But in 1992 control of Crimea by an "independent" Ukraine would run the risk of Russia losing control of the Black Sea fleet, a national treasure, based in the port city of Sevastopol, which Moscow simply assumed had been and always would be Russian.

During the Crimean War of the 1850s and again during World War II, the Russians had heroically defended Sevastopol and Crimea. The battles there had become part of Russian military and political mythology. When Kravchuk made noises in 1992 about maintaining Ukrainian control over Crimea, Sevastopol, and the Black Sea fleet, Moscow erupted angrily. An intense dispute arose, revealing deep antagonisms on both sides. Crimea was a kind of "third rail" in Russian-Ukrainian politics. As it was to do again in 2014, Moscow encouraged the Russian majority in the Crimean parliament to pass a declaration of independence, which it did, but oddly soon after rescinded when the Russian Duma passed a resolution declaring the 1954 transfer of Crimea to Ukraine to be "unconstitutional." What now? Would Russian sailors in Sevastopol, there to man and maintain the Black Sea fleet, now move to reestablish Russian control over Crimea? Ukraine could not stop them; it had no military force capable of resisting the Russians. In fact, the possibility of Russian action was considered, but dropped. Yeltsin decided the timing was not right. He was then trying desperately to build a new country and rebuild Russian authority in its corner of the world. His solution was diplomacy.

Yeltsin and Kravchuk held two emergency meetings in the summer of 1992. They were trying to defuse tension and delay decisions. They compromised and agreed to establish joint Russian-Ukrainian control of the Black Sea fleet, but limited this agreement to three years. Ownership would be determined later in the decade.

Just as they postponed the solution of one problem, another unavoidably popped up in Kiev, where Kravchuk was trying to create a Ukrainian Ministry of Defense, which in Soviet times Ukraine did not need. Defense had always been Moscow's responsibility. The immediate problem for the new ministry was jurisdiction over more than 700,000 Russian (formerly Soviet) troops stationed in Ukraine. There was also the question of jurisdiction over more than 6,500 tanks, 1,500 combat aircraft, and 5,000 nuclear weapons, including both long-range and tactical missiles and warheads. Ukraine had the world's third-largest nuclear stockpile. The new minister of defense, 47-year-old Major General Kostiantyn Morozov, was, until Ukrainian independence was proclaimed, the Soviet chief of air force operations in Ukraine. He had switched sides in the chaos, now pledging his loyalty to an independent Ukraine. His new job was obviously stimulating, but his responsibilities were awesome. What to do with the troops and the nuclear weapons?

Morozov, at first, supported the Soviet Union's pre-independence policy of Moscow retaining control of the nuclear weapons based in Ukraine. That is, until he had a meeting with Henry Kissinger, who was visiting Ukraine. One question from the former secretary of state seemed to change Morozov's mind and Ukrainian strategy. "And what then is independence?" was the question. Kissinger was asking, in effect, how could Ukraine assert that it was an independent nation if it allowed another nation, in this case Russia, to control nuclear weapons on its own territory? Morozov, impressed by Kissinger's logic, flipped Ukrainian policy on its head. Instead of accepting the policy of Russia retaining control of all of the former Soviet Union's strategic weapons based in Ukraine, henceforth if Russia wanted to retain control of these weapons, it would have to move them into Russia. Ukraine would, under this new arrangement, assume control of all weapons systems on Ukrainian territory.[5]

But there were to be many "buts" in fast-moving, newly independent Ukraine. Not so fast! interjected Kravchuk. If Ukraine was to change its policy, then he wanted upfront compensation—specifically, an American guarantee of Ukraine's territorial integrity plus a substantial aid package. Kravchuk understood that Ukraine, on its own, could not afford to maintain those Soviet-era weapon systems that were left in Ukraine. A natural dealmaker, he sniffed the possibility of a good deal. Negotiations soon followed, and an agreement was ultimately reached in December 1994—a few months after Kravchuk had lost his bid for reelection to Leonid Kuchma.[6]

At a meeting in Budapest, including Ukraine, Russia, and the United States, Ukraine formally agreed to give up its nuclear arsenal in exchange for the delivery of inexpensive Russian fuel for Ukraine's nuclear power plants and for an American guarantee that the "threat" or "use of force" against the "political independence" and "territorial integrity" of Ukraine would be countered by unspecified U.S. action.[7] When, twenty years later, Russia seized Crimea, Ukraine objected strenuously, arguing that Russia had clearly violated the so-called Budapest Memorandum. Russia ignored Ukraine's objection, saying it was only responding to the appeals of the Russian majority in Crimea, and the United States strongly condemned Russia and imposed economic sanctions against the government and some of Putin's associates but ruled out the use of force.

At the time of the nuclear weapons agreement, in the mid-1990s, the

United States usually sided with Russia whenever these East European squabbles arose. The region remained wildly unstable, and Washington believed that only Russia, the strongest of the post-Soviet states, could ensure political stability in the area. That was one reason why Washington joined Russia in encouraging Ukraine to accept the terms of the Budapest Memorandum.

Washington often guessed wrong on its Russia policy, pursuing hazy goals in an uncertain time. It tended to anchor its East European policy on Russia, a country in totally unpredictable transition, and this proved to be a mistake. Not just Ukraine but all of the former Soviet republics were fumbling with volatile political systems, swinging wildly from communism to something between socialism and capitalism. "A mean and shabby thing it is," wrote reporter Jon Sawyer, after a swing through Ukraine, "with corrupt Communist holdovers in office, worthless currency and mounting tension with Russia." He was then Washington bureau chief of the *St. Louis Post Dispatch* before becoming director of the Pulitzer Center.[8]

The standard of living in Ukraine plummeted. Sawyer said that it "looked like a country sliding toward national collapse." Its economy, based on agriculture and heavy industry, had depended to a large measure on Russia buying its products. For example, Russia had purchased 80 percent of Ukrainian arms production. That was the traditional model. There was no new model, yet. Chaos in the marketplace clearly frightened the average shopper. Food was scarce, and prices soared. Inflation reached an annual rate of 2,500 percent in 1992. The government pulled out of the ruble market in November 1992. It created a new currency, called the *karbovanets*. It tried to impose a belt-tightening program of economic reform. Unfortunately, nothing worked.

In June the following year, the Donbas coal miners, unable to make ends meet, seriously disillusioned with the postcommunist improvisations, went on strike, throwing the whole economy into an unmanageable tumble. Kiev printed as much money as it could to meet worker demands. The result was hyperinflation, jumping to incredible heights—10,115 percent for the calendar year 1993. Coins lost their value as well.[9]

In this turmoil, it was natural that the far-right wing of Ukrainian politics would rear its head, and it did, waving a Cossack banner of ultranationalism, reminding many of its collaboration with the Nazis during World War II. The Banderite wing of the Organization of Ukrainian Nationalists, calling itself the Congress of Ukrainian Nationalists, demanded a place at the table, but got only a small one. Many young radicals, unemployed, frustrated, feeling they had nowhere else to turn, fled to the western part of Ukraine, where they joined the neo-fascist Ukrainian National Self-Defense Force, similar to the one that had fought alongside the Nazis. They nostalgically looked back into Ukrainian history for *Hetman* inspiration, eager for a Christian crusade against the foreigner and the infidel.

Unable to manage his domestic economy, Russian president Yeltsin sought solace in foreign policy, putting the heat primarily on Russia's "near abroad," those former Soviet republics or satellites that Yeltsin felt should continue to follow Moscow's lead. In their weakened state, they often could do little but submit to Russian pressure. In a Harvard report, released in early 1994, scholars Fiona Hill and Pamela Jewett wrote that "the sovereignty of each of the former republics of the Soviet Union has been compromised, forcing them into a dependent relationship with Moscow."[10]

For Yeltsin, Ukraine was always the key to Russian success, the country most likely to bolster Russia's future as a great power. Zbigniew Brzezinski, who served as President Jimmy Carter's national security adviser, wrote: "It cannot be stressed strongly enough that without Ukraine, Russia ceases to be an empire, but with Ukraine suborned and then subordinated, Russia automatically becomes an empire."[11] If Yeltsin's relations with Kravchuk were often irritating, so too were those with Leonid Kuchma, who defeated Kravchuk in July 1994 elections. Kuchma was a bright, ambitious engineer, a communist bureaucrat who favored reform but succumbed ultimately to the deep corruption in full Ukrainian bloom. He ran on a platform of improving Ukraine's relations with Russia and protecting the Russian language, a platform that helped him get votes in the eastern and southern parts of the country.

Both Yeltsin and Kuchma made a determined effort to solve the many problems plaguing their countries, but the problems persisted, like thorns on a rose bush. After two years of on-again, off-again negotiations, they finally agreed in 1997 to sign a Friendship Treaty. At the Tomb of the Unknown Soldier in Kiev, "this sacred place," intoned Yeltsin, they pledged to cooperate in political and economic matters and to postpone their running dispute about which side really owned Crimea and the Black Sea fleet. For the time being, anyway, they decided to divide up the fleet: 18 percent going to Ukraine and the rest to Russia with the promise that the Russian fleet could continue to use Sevastopol's port facilities. Yeltsin, wanting to smooth the ruffled edges of Ukrainian insecurities, told Kuchma that Ukraine was "a priority of priorities for us," and "we respect and honor the territorial integrity of Ukraine."[12] Kuchma could be excused if he had musically mumbled the line from *My Fair Lady*: "Words, words, words, I'm just sick of words."

Why was Yeltsin so accommodating? First, because he was concerned about NATO expansion into eastern Europe, and, second, because Ukraine had just joined NATO's Partnership for Peace program and signed an unusual Charter on a Distinctive Partnership with NATO. And, most important, there were rumors, all too energetically denied by Kiev, that Ukraine might actually be interested in joining NATO. Yeltsin wanted to discourage any such thought. "Ukraine is not going to join NATO now," promised Volodimyr Horbulin, Ukraine's top military official, hoping the Russian president was listening.[13] Yeltsin definitely heard the word "now," but he must have been left wondering: "If not now, when?"

Building Ukrainian Independence

For the rest of the 1990s, Kuchma faced two urgent priorities. The first was to stem a desperate economic crisis, to give people hope that tomorrow would be better than today. The second was to create the image, and it was hoped, in time, the reality, of an independent Ukraine, disconnected from Russia and accepted by the world.

Year after year, Kuchma tried just about every formula for economic growth, but there were few signs of success. Ukraine was so tightly tied to Russia, so dependent upon Russia as a market and as a source of oil and gas, that even when it attempted to break loose from Russia, to cozy up to the European market, for example, it failed. When Russia itself ran into severe economic problems in August 1998, forced to devalue its currency and default on its foreign debt, Russia's trading partners, starting with Ukraine, felt the impact almost immediately. If Russia could not buy, Ukraine could not sell. If Ukraine could not sell, it could not eat. It was the equivalent of the old Asian saying that when China sneezes, the rest of Asia catches its cold. Fortunately, for Kuchma and Ukraine, the Russian crisis eased within a year, largely because global oil prices skyrocketed and Russia, one of the world's biggest oil producers, suddenly found itself rich with extra rubles. When Russia's economy improved, so too did Ukraine's.

Another deeply ingrained problem was Ukraine's crony capitalism, which crimped most efforts at reform. Shortly after taking office in 1994, Kuchma launched a series of economic reforms, including privatization of heavy industry and a new, stable currency, called the *hryvnia*, but he ran into a stonewall of opposition from a gaggle of oligarchs, or businessmen, who had become billionaires through shady dealings with the government. They did not welcome change. One, Pavlo Lazarenko, even rose to be prime minister under Kuchma, until a number of his competitors charged him with extortion, the charge stuck, and he was forced to flee to the United States, where he was imprisoned on money-laundering and other charges.[14] Other oligarchs became notorious regional autocrats, striking nefarious deals with Kiev-based politicians, even presidents, who did their bidding without excessive complaint.

Corruption became a way of life in Ukraine, sinking deep roots into the economy, blocking legitimate reform, and paralyzing political change. It was, in fact, so pervasive that Ukraine could not find a way out of its impasse between intolerable communism and unachievable capitalism.

When Kuchma sought assistance from outside sources, he met with only modest success. The United States responded sympathetically, sending an estimated $2 billion in economic aid to Ukraine from 1992 to 2000. Washington hoped that a vibrant Ukraine would be a bulwark against any possible Russian expansion. It was a serious effort. But given the Alpine dimensions of Ukraine's economic crisis, Washington's aid, while welcome, was unable to do the job. The International Monetary Fund also contributed substantial sums to Ukraine, but it attached so many unrealistic conditions on inflation control and interest rates as to make compliance virtually impossible.

Enter Yushchenko and Tymoshenko

Ukraine desperately needed reform, but it was stuck in a quicksand of corruption. As it approached the 1998 elections, street corner unhappiness with Kuchma and his cronies deepened. The communists were making a comeback. Kuchma swung to the right, rallying conservative and centrist politicians, and won 56 percent of the vote. His victory only brought him back to Ukraine's old problems, which had worsened to the point where its foreign debt reached $12.4 billion, a historic high, and the IMF, the World Bank, and Russia demanded fiscal discipline. Washington suggested belt-tightening. A Ukrainian default loomed as a distinct possibility.[15]

In December 1999, Kuchma appointed Viktor Yushchenko as prime minister. It was a roll of the dice. Yushchenko, a successful banker known for his pro-Western, liberal policies, was head of the National Bank, familiar with Ukraine's problems, and married to an American from Chicago; he was the perfect person to negotiate with Western donors. Kuchma probably figured that Yushchenko, after a year or so, like a number of his predecessors, would tire of the thankless chores, amass his own fortune, and leave.

But, miracle of miracles, Yushchenko turned out to be a serious, honest reformer, and he made things happen. He rescheduled debt payments, cracked down on the illegal resale of Russian oil and gas, and ended the highly questionable practice of tax exemptions for favored oligarchs. Working with Yulia Tymoshenko, a rising firebrand who had made her fortune manipulating gas exports for Lazarenko's financial empire, Yushchenko lowered income taxes for Ukraine's small but growing middle class. The effect was twofold: more money spent on consumer goods, which stimulated investment in small businesses; and more of these small businesses emerging from the "shadow economy" and then contributing personal and business taxes to the national economy. Lo and behold, his reform program raised billions, and Ukraine's GDP shot up to the highest it had been throughout the 1990s. Yushchenko and Tymoshenko became instant political darlings. They had squeezed the oligarchs, thus restoring a degree of social justice, and directed increased funding for worker pensions. Kuchma's favorite oligarchs, watching anxiously from the sidelines, urged him to get rid of his twin reformers. Enough! they insisted. Kuchma shared their opinion. In fact, he was ready to sack Yushchenko and Tymoshenko, both already being touted as promising democratic prospects for the next presidential election. But, inexplicably, Kuchma delayed, and suddenly he found himself besieged by other more pressing problems.

One of them was Kosovo, a beleaguered province of Serbia. Since 1991 a guerrilla force known as the Kosovo Liberation Army, armed by neighboring Albania, had been undermining Serbian authority in Kosovo, attacking military bases and trading posts. Serbia had thought of itself as leader of a new Balkan conglomerate, a new master of all the pieces of old Yugoslavia, including Kosovo. At first Serbia swatted away the guerrilla attacks, but as they persisted with irritating and embarrassing frequency, Serbia struck back with merciless cruelty, killing so many Kosovars that this mini-war in Kosovo began to attract international attention. The United States and NATO leveled sharp criticism at Serbia, while Russia and the rest of the Slavic world, including Ukraine, rushed to support their brethren in Serbia. As had been the case during the recently concluded cold war, East and West split over Kosovo. In early 1999, while Albania increased its military aid to the guerrillas, the United States, under a NATO umbrella, began bombing Serbian positions in Kosovo.

For Kuchma, Kosovo represented an unwelcome intrusion into his efforts to solicit bigger and better aid packages from the West. He, like Yeltsin, felt the need to criticize U.S. and NATO policy toward Serbia, even while knowing that his criticism of the West would surely sour its desire to help Ukraine. Kosovo touched an emotional nerve among Ukrainians, who sympathized with fellow Slavs under American air attack. Up until Kosovo, Ukrainians had expressed warm sentiments toward the United States, even toward NATO. But then in 1999, with surprising speed, their attitude changed dramatically.

According to the International Institute of Sociology in Kiev, a well-regarded research center, 61 percent of Ukrainians voiced a "lack of confidence" and "trust" in the United States and NATO. Only 15 percent voiced confidence in them. In 2000 the institute asked a slightly different question: Which country do you trust more—Russia or the United States? Seventy-five percent of Ukrainians polled said Russia; 14 percent said America. Sixty-nine percent supported the new Russian president, Vladimir Putin, knowing little or nothing about him then. Sixty-one percent, reflecting a sudden anxiety about Western policies, even voiced support for a "union" between Russia and Ukraine.[16]

Kosovo proved yet again that Ukraine, though traditionally split along pro-Western and pro-Russian fault lines, would likely swing toward support of Russia when facing a Western military challenge. This flips when Russia represents the challenge to Ukraine. Then Ukraine turns toward the West. It has nowhere else to go.

Early Days of the First Orange Revolution

Twice, between 2004 and 2014, Ukrainians went into the streets demanding a more honest and productive government. Hundreds of thousands voiced their disgust and impatience with the selfish and ineffective politicians running their government. In both cases, their voices were heard: They got a change of government, but not necessarily the one they wanted. Corruption was still rampant, fortunes routinely made under the table, its neighbor, Russia, continually an oppressive irritant; but Ukrainians were beginning to see something new, possibly promising. They were beginning to see themselves as a nation—one with a largely uncharted agenda, disappointing leadership, and an uncertain future, but a nation nonetheless. The nagging, often embarrassing, question of national identity seemed finally on the road to being settled.

Their borders, though crudely violated by Russia in 2014, seemed real—indeed, recognized by much of the world. Their flag of yellow and blue hung alongside the red, white, and blue in international chanceries, and diplomats knew, without thinking twice, which country each represented. Their diplomats, suddenly showing up at conferences and summits, came to be respected. Their president addressed the U.S. Congress and received a standing ovation.

Ukraine had arrived. It could not escape its geography, nor ignore its history, but it was finally being recognized as a nation, deserving international respect.

Kuchma, like Kravchuk and the communist chieftains preceding both, governed with bribes, arm-twisting, and ballot-stuffing. Democrats they were not, but they used the deceptive framework of democracy, filling it with substance only one little bit at a time. In an April 2000 referendum, Kuchma's proposals won 82 percent to 90 percent of the vote. Turnout was 81 percent. These were numbers any unprincipled autocrat would embrace with pleasure, but they were misleading. As his numbers rose, pumped up artificially by political gimmickry, his popularity dropped. When a scandal developed in the fall of 2000 over the strange disappearance of a popular Georgian journalist, Georgiy Gongadze, Kuchma lost more than his popularity. He also lost his credibility. Gongadze's headless body was discovered near Kiev, and everyone wanted to know who killed him. One of Kuchma's security advisers, Major Mykola Melnychenko, planted a bug in Kuchma's office (for reasons never known for certain), and the so-called Melnychenko tapes later proved that Kuchma three times had asked the major and his interior minister to "take care" of Gongadze, probably because he feared the journalist's reports were getting close to implicating him in fraud and embezzlement.[17]

Popular demonstrations sprung up in Kiev and other cities. "Ukraine without Kuchma" was the slogan of choice. Kuchma's supporters figured they needed a new president, and they pressed for changes. Tymoshenko was dismissed in February 2001, but she wasted little time joining the street protests, and before long, she emerged as a genuine threat to the Kiev establishment. She seemed destined for big things. A few months later, Yushchenko was ousted from Kuchma's government. He too wasted little time jumping into the political ring. He organized a center-right party, called "Our Ukraine," and he promoted a program of clean government and economic reform, attracting the financial support of a few oligarchs, including Petro Poroshenko, who made his billions selling chocolate.

Kuchma created his own party, called "For a United Ukraine," but it did him little good. His role in the Gongadze scandal had robbed him of any popular appeal. It also offended the new American administration of President George W. Bush, and it left him vulnerable to pressure from the new Russian administration of President Vladimir Putin. Bush strongly disapproved of Kuchma's illegal $100 million arms sale to Iraq, and he was furious when he learned that Kuchma was also selling high-tech radar systems to Iraq. Hoping to win back Western support, Kuchma went to a NATO meeting in Prague in 2002, though he had not been invited, selling the story, like an itinerant salesman, that Ukraine would love to join NATO and send troops to Iraq, if needed. Putin, for his part, wanted Ukraine, invited or uninvited, to return to the Russian sphere of influence—if not, to be prepared to pay higher prices for gas and oil. Kuchma reluctantly bowed to the pressure, forcing the Rada to vote in favor of Ukraine joining Russia, Belarus, and Kazakhstan in a new "Common Economic Space."[18]

Kuchma's time in office, measured in political clout, was decidedly limited, though he still had two more years of political privilege. The next election was set for 2004. His crony oligarchs began searching the political underbrush for an obliging successor. They went to the coal-rich east and came up with Viktor Yanukovych, a remarkably unimpressive former governor of Donetsk who had retained his tight ties to powerful clans in the city of Dnipropetrovsk as well as his emotional ties to Russia. They propelled him to national prominence and persuaded Kuchma to appoint him as prime minister.

He was, in many ways, an odd choice. He was born and raised in the Donbas, in the eastern half of Ukraine. He spoke Russian fluently, Ukrainian with a distinct accent. He had a criminal record, having twice been convicted of theft in 1967 and assault and battery in 1978. He had limited education, and had been forced, when facing an election, to buy an engineering degree and a professorial title. He wrote with difficulty; his spelling was awful. When he registered as a candidate for the presidency, scholar Yekelchyk reported, "He misspelled his title of professor as 'proffesor'. . . . When he appeared on television, he stumbled in search of words, especially in Ukrainian."[19]

Yanukovych was prime minister for the remaining two years of Kuchma's second term in office, giving him a launching pad for a presidential run. He faced tough competition in Yushchenko, who spoke excellent Ukrainian, had a sparkling personality, and ran as a devout Orthodox Christian. Yushchenko hired a campaign team that produced appealing television commercials, reached into the Internet for youthful support, and plastered handsome posters all over the country. Also, obviously inspired by the 2003 Rose Revolution in nearby Georgia, his team came up with the color and the slogan for what they called the 2004 Orange Revolution. Everything was in orange—their banners, scarves, hats, and handouts. Yushchenko's campaign functioned like a Swiss watch, and he consistently led Yanukovych in the polls. He seemed the likely winner.

Desperate, Yanukovych asked Putin for advice. The Russian president's PR people offered a few suggestions. First, favor close relations with Russia, not with the West. Second, make Russian the second official language of the country. And third, run as a proud Ukrainian nationalist, not as an American puppet. One poster quickly showed up on billboards: the faces of Yushchenko and Bush with the word "Bushchenko" splashed across them. Toward the end of the campaign, Yanukovych proposed dual citizenship—Ukrainians could also be Russian, and Russians could be Ukrainian—and the doubling of state pensions. In the eastern and southern parts of Ukraine, Yanukovych did well, but not in Kiev and not in the western parts of the country. Putin's personal popularity in Ukraine stood at 66 percent, not bad for a Russian. He was a frequent visitor and an unapologetic supporter of Yanukovych, having contributed an estimated $300 million to his campaign to buy votes, pay bribes, and pay for staff. He favored Yanukovych because he was certain that, as president, Yanukovych would ally Ukraine with Russia. That had always been Putin's plan.

On September 5, 2004, Yushchenko did something he was later to regret. He drove to a Kievan suburb for a secret dinner meeting with the chief of Kuchma's secret service. They ate and drank, all seemed to be going well, but on the drive back to Kiev, Yushchenko got terribly sick. His stomach pain was intense. Food poisoning was the likely reason, but no one had proof. An oligarch airlifted Yushchenko to a private clinic in Austria, where he stayed for three weeks. He slowly got better, but he had paid a terrible price. His face was left forever scarred by unexplained lesions, but he refused to pull out of the campaign. Later tests by German and Austrian doctors confirmed he had been poisoned by the chemical dioxin.

It was a big story all over the world. Did Kuchma order the poisoning? Did Putin? No one would say.

There were actually twenty-four candidates for the presidency, but only two mattered: Yanukovych and Yushchenko. The first round ended in predictable controversy. The vote was 39.9 percent for Yushchenko, 39.3 percent for Yanukovych. The experts judged, "too close to call." Besides, Yanukovych's people had somehow gotten into the Central Electoral Commission's database and "corrected" the results, which invalidated the first round.

For the second round, on November 21, both candidates campaigned relentlessly, spending lots of money. Yanukovych appealed for, and obtained, more Russian and pro-Russian support. His goal was to buy favorable exit poll data. It was just a matter of money. Yushchenko attracted pro-Western support. He bought many television ads with the additional funding. The two candidates seemed to represent an electoral cold war.

On election night, with 65 percent the vote counted, the exit polls showed Yanukovych with 53 percent of the vote and Yushchenko with only 44 percent. The official vote, later in the night, was closer, but the result was the same: Yanukovych 49.5 percent, Yushchenko 46.9 percent. Yanukovych had won.

But had he? Yushchenko had phone records (illegally obtained), proving that once again Yanukovych's people had manipulated the Central Electoral Commission's database and had engaged in massive fraud, exactly what Yushchenko had feared. Huge protests by his supporters began almost immediately. A stage was constructed in Independence Square, popularly known as the Maidan. Large plasma television screens were installed. Fifteen hundred tents were set up on Kiev's central boulevard, the beautiful Khreshchatyk. Busload after busload of protesters rode into the capital. They stayed in the tents or with friends. They had anticipated electoral finagling, and they were ready to move.

The next morning, more than 200,000 Ukrainians gathered in the Maidan, protesting the election results. Putin, who liked the results, and helped produce them, was first to congratulate Yanukovych; few other world leaders even bothered. The election was a joke.

On November 26, the presidents of Poland and Lithuania, Aleksander Kwasniewski and Valdas Adamkus, joined the foreign policy chief of the European Union, Javier Solana, and the speaker of the Russian Duma, Boris Gryzlov, in Kiev, where they arranged a few negotiating sessions with Kuchma, Yanukovych, and Yushchenko. No one expected a breakthrough, and none was achieved. Kuchma, wanting to leave something on the table, pathetically proposed an election rerun. Everyone else decided to wait for the Supreme Court to render a decision. They were all concerned about a possible outbreak of violence. Yanukovych had coal miners from the Donbas bused into Kiev, ready for a fight with the Orange protesters. He (and Putin) had reportedly proposed that military force be readied for use against the protesters.

On November 27, the Rada passed a resolution protesting the election results. Yanukovych's supporters objected, warning they would propose the "separation" of eastern Ukraine from the country. Eastern governors proposed the "federalization" of the whole country. The effect would have been the same as separation. The Western press checked the political horizon and sensed the prospect of civil war.

On December 3, the Supreme Court ruled that the election had been a fraud, called the results invalid, and proposed a runoff on December 26. Usually, the Ukrainian courts never did anything to offend the financial oligarchs. This time, Yanukovych's oligarchs had been stumped, clearly—their candidate's "victory" had been upended. Still, surprisingly, they chose to accept the ruling for a runoff and not challenge it.

From all over the world came foreign observers—12,000 of them; and all over Ukraine monitoring teams were set up—300,000 monitors in all. It was to be the most observed election in history. Finally, when election day came, observers and monitors were in place, and the people voted without major trauma. The results this time were clear. The election returns paralleled the exit polls—51.99 percent for Yushchenko, who carried the Ukrainian-speaking west, and 44.19 percent for Yanukovych, who carried the Russian-speaking east and south. With the exception of Putin, who feared "people power" and distrusted the Orange Revolution, everyone took a deep breath, President Bush among them. He was among the first to call Yushchenko with congratulations for "democracy's victory."

On January 23, 2005, Yushchenko was sworn in as Ukraine's third president, the winner of the Orange Revolution. Now he had to prove that he could run Ukraine, one country divided along linguistic, cultural, and political lines, often acting, however, like two countries wrapped in a single blue and yellow flag.[20]

Yushchenko's Collision with Putin

Yushchenko wanted, in his first year as president, to open a new chapter in Ukrainian foreign policy—not to balance Ukrainian interests between East and West, tilting slightly to the East to satisfy Russian anxieties, as was usually the case, but to swing dramatically, unmistakably to the West. He wanted to align Ukraine with Western interests, values, and policies and naively thought he could effect this radical swing in policy without offending Putin. How wrong he was!

It had always been the case that a new Ukrainian leader, communist or postcommunist, would make his first foreign journey to Moscow, a way of showing respect to the "tsar." The tradition was enshrined in the uneven relationship between Ukraine and Russia—Ukraine the "little Russian," Russia the big bear. For a very brief time, Yushchenko considered breaking this tradition and flying first to the West, his way of telling the tsar that there was a new leader in Kiev, a Ukrainian president brave enough to have a new policy with new priorities. But several of his advisers, a few of them oligarchs with long-standing business ties to Moscow, persuaded Yushchenko that it made no sense needlessly to offend Putin. Everyone knew that he had no respect, and certainly no admiration, for the youthful democrats who had put the Orange Revolution on the European map. Putin feared Kiev's message of successful revolution. "Putin sincerely believed that the 'Orange Revolutions' in

Ukraine were instigated by the U.S. State Department," said Russian political analyst Andrei Piontkovsky."[21] If it could happen in Ukraine, Putin must have thought, it could happen in Russia; it had to be stopped. Probably because, in the final analysis, it indeed made no sense needlessly to offend Putin, Yushchenko decided to fly first to Moscow, explain Ukraine's new policies to Putin, try to calm his obviously ruffled feathers, and only then show the flag in Brussels, London, and Washington.

When Yushchenko met with Putin, he realized that his decision to fly first to Moscow made no real difference. Putin still saw Yushchenko's pro-Western policies as a threat to Russian interests. He imagined the Orange Revolution to be part of a nefarious Western conspiracy, hatched by the CIA, and Yushchenko's new regime to be home for far-right, ultra-nationalist, anti-Russian, fascist politicians. But, Putin argued, if Ukraine saw the light and joined his Eurasian community of Slavic nations, plus Kazakhstan, that would be a move benefiting everyone—economically, politically, and militarily. Yushchenko, polite but unintimidated, carefully explained that, in his view, good relations with the West would benefit Russia as well as Ukraine. It was not a zero-sum game, he stressed. Everyone could win. Putin dismissed his argument. If Yushchenko insisted on pursuing what Putin regarded as a misguided policy, Ukraine would suffer. Russia, fulfilling its Slavic destiny, would prosper. Their summit ended on a sour note of distrust and deadlock. Yushchenko had extended a hand of friendship to Putin; the gesture had not been welcomed. It had, in fact, been waved off. Yushchenko, having paid his respects to the tsar and having satisfied his oligarchs, then flew off in a westerly direction, perhaps thinking Putin and Putinism be damned!

Yushchenko appointed a decidedly pro-Western foreign minister, Borys Tarasiuk, chair of the Institute for Euro-Atlantic Cooperation, who favored Ukraine's admission to NATO and the European Union. He created a ministerial post for "European integration." He traveled to Brussels in February 2005 to address the European Parliament. "After the fall of the Berlin Wall," Yushchenko said, linking one historic event to another, "we now also have the Orange Revolution." He made it clear that "we have chosen Europe," but "we also want to deepen relations with Russia," as if, realistically, given Putin's conspiratorial vision of Western policy, Ukraine could embrace both Europe and Russia at the same time. "Moving closer to Europe," Yushchenko explained, "does not prevent closer cooperation with Russia. Ukraine's membership in the EU and NATO is not against Russian interests—on the contrary, a stable Ukraine could help bring Russia closer to Europe."[22]

In March, Yushchenko played host to a visiting congressional delegation, including Senate Majority Leader Harry Reid, who burst with excitement about the Ukrainian's victory. Yushchenko, he said, is "an international hero."[23] Republican leaders could barely contain their enthusiasm for Yushchenko, publishing a glittering PR packet, called "Promoting a Robust U.S.-Ukraine Agenda."[24] Shortly thereafter, in April, when Yushchenko arrived in Washington, he was greeted with the pomp and circumstance reserved for popular kings or democratic pin-ups, such as Lech Walesa, Nelson Mandela, or Pope John Paul II—he was invited to address a joint meeting of Congress, where he spoke boldly about helping Bush and the United States promote democracy and freedom in neighboring Belarus and Castro's Cuba. "Yushchenko! Yushchenko!" members of Congress roared, ten times rising to their feet in rapturous applause for this newly elected symbol of democracy on the rise in eastern Europe. Yushchenko decorously responded with a call for a "genuinely strategic partnership" with the United States, quietly hoping that Ukraine would not become a football in an East-West competition.[25]

In that same year, Lebanon experienced the "Cedar Revolution" and Kyrgyzstan toyed with its "Tulip Revolution." If Yushchenko chose a message designed specifically to irritate Putin, he had hit pay dirt. His "orange" overtures to the West irritated Putin and his entourage. Moscow seethed with anger, deepening its suspicions about Ukraine's ultimate game. Putin must have believed that Yushchenko was deliberately using his Orange Revolution to encourage uprisings in other countries, a few of them neighbors of Russia.

And was it possible, Putin likely wondered, that Yushchenko was actually trying to stimulate an Orange rebellion in Russia? This kind of question flowed logically from Yushchenko's support for GUAM—a loose grouping of four former Soviet republics, Georgia, Ukraine, Azerbaijan, and Moldova, all professing a desire to break free of Russian control. Also, Yushchenko joined Georgia's President Mikhail Saakashvili in August 2005 to create the Community of Democratic Choice, another loosely organized group eager to promote democracy in countries bordering Russia.[26] Putin profoundly disliked Saakashvili—and anyone or group with whom he was associated. Through his own "Rose Revolution" starting in November 2003, the Georgian had stormed to power—"people power," he called it—and it had sent a chill down Putin's spine. Rising tension already existed between Russia and Georgia over control of two so-called breakaway provinces in Georgia—South Ossetia and Abkhazia. In 2008 a suspicious Putin would send the Russian army into both provinces, declaring them to be independent. Actually, they ended up becoming Russian satellites, frozen in place and position by Russian arms. Putin also sent the Russian army into Georgia, only to pull back. The United States objected, but essentially did nothing. A pattern of Putinesque aggression was being established: Whenever Putin felt the need, for whatever reason, to extend Russian power and control, as he would do in Ukraine in 2014, he would send his army into the region, freeze his military conquest, and then claim that Russia had nothing to do with its latest conquest.

By his words and actions, deliberately or not, Yushchenko had seeded Putin's already dim vision of Ukraine with images of Western conspiracies and CIA plots designed to undermine Russia.

If Yushchenko had focused his attention on swinging Ukraine to the West, no matter what Putin preferred, he might actually have achieved some success. In less than year, however, he learned that in addition to foreign affairs, he had to master political and economic problems much closer to home—all of them steeped in a mix of Ukrainian corruption and illegalities so pervasive that accomplishing anything was almost impossible. He found, much to his disappointment, that while he could attract enough votes to win the presidency, he could not attract enough support for his economic and political reforms. As a president, Yushchenko was a flop.

Yulia Tymoshenko, known popularly as Yulia, a dynamic politician, tried to revamp the entire political system. She wanted to create a new political elite, and to an extent she succeeded. In a few short months, with Yushchenko's backing, she fired roughly 18,000 middle- and low-level bureaucrats and replaced them with budding politicians loyal to her. After a while, the new bureaucrats came to be as corrupt as the ones she had replaced.

Dealing with the oligarchs proved to be much tougher. Tymoshenko started a program called "reprivatization," which essentially meant nationalizing a number of the big enterprises that President Kuchma had privatized and then selling them again to other oligarchs willing to pay a higher price. This program unsettled both Ukrainian businessmen and foreign investors, forcing Tymoshenko to sharply reduce the number of enterprises to be reprivatized. When it impacted Kuchma's favorite oligarchs, the former president brashly intruded into the process and effectively shut it down.

Overall, the economy was beginning to slow down anyway. Inflation was rising, new investments were slipping, and the cost of imported oil and gas, controlled by Putin's cronies, was increasing. Apparently, the more Yushchenko's government annoyed Putin, the higher the prices climbed. Ukraine's middle class, Yushchenko's pride and joy, the basis of his popularity, suffered for an unromantic reason related to the dollar exchange rate. Many in the middle class, playing it safe, kept their *hryvnias* in U.S. dollars, but when the government raised the exchange rate, people got less in return; and their disappointment in Yushchenko and Tymoshenko deepened.

Moreover, in the back rooms of Kiev's power structure, Tymoshenko was absorbed in a bitter struggle with Petro Poroshenko, one of Yushchenko's favored oligarchs. The issue was power: Who had how much? Poroshenko wanted Tymoshenko's job as prime minister but instead got the job of secretary of the Council of National Security and Defense, an important position but certainly not as important as prime minister. Poroshenko then used his clout with Yushchenko to enhance his power throughout the government, challenging Tymoshenko's position as prime minister.

Their struggle soon broke into the open and dominated the political environment in Kiev. Yushchenko did little to stop them. His power and position began to wither. Ukrainians judged their president to be a nice man, but a weak leader. When his son, a university sophomore, began driving around Kiev in a car valued at $150,000, using a cell phone costing $50,000, he became titillating copy for every journalist struggling to make it to the front page. Yushchenko, instead of moving to change his son's lifestyle, responded to the avalanche of gossip by calling one reporter an "ugly mug" and another a "hired killer." Suddenly the politician who had been a champion of freedom of the press, during his run for office, became a scowling Nixon-like enemy of the press while in office. Corruption, it appeared, had crept into the president's inner circle.[27]

Yushchenko could not fire his son; so he fired his prime minister and his secretary for security and defense policy, opening yet another ugly chapter in Ukrainian politics. Not even the game of musical chairs could accurately describe the silly up-and-down, in-and-out mystery of who held what job. It became a sick joke ("Wanna know who's prime minister? Tomorrow, we'll know."), and the president's once-bright halo dimmed, until he was no longer seen as a hero, only as another politician. Foolishly, he plunged into the Tymoshenko-Poroshenko bloodbath, accusing both of corruption. Tymoshenko, always ready with hot rhetoric, attacked the president, charging that his policies had caused the economic slowdown and, worse, that he had betrayed the ideals of the Orange Revolution. Poroshenko kept his cool, dropping pellets of poison into the dialogue whenever it suited his purposes but otherwise standing on the sidelines, biding his time while trying to appear statesmanlike.

As Yushchenko opened the second year of his presidency, he found himself in serious trouble. He had his chance to fight corruption and launch a major program of economic and political reform; after the Orange Revolution, he had even had his chance to rise above politics and become a Ukrainian Mandela. But, in almost every respect, he fell short. Moreover, hovering like a dark shadow over him, and Ukraine, was Putin's Russia. Yushchenko would have wanted Ukraine to turn away from its increasingly frustrating relationship with Russia, and throw its chips in with the West, but he lacked either the vision or the guts to steer his ship-of-state in a pro-Western direction. Instead of elevating the Russian-Ukrainian dialogue, he found himself submerged in a street-corner argument about the price of natural gas. Since Putin controlled the price, he could control the agenda and, he felt, the outcome. Putin wanted Ukraine to become a member of his Eurasian coalition; he placed a top priority on Ukraine remaining in a Slavic world run by Russia. Since Putin held the levers of economic and military power over Ukraine, he saw no reason why he should lose the argument. In fact, he was determined to win it, and he pushed his advantage whenever he could.

If Yushchenko had been an effective autocrat, he might have run an effective government. But he was not an autocrat, and he certainly was not effective. Between 2005, when he took power, and 2010, when he lost it after a humiliating electoral defeat, he consistently failed the basic tests of political leadership, and Ukraine lost an opportunity to turn a corner and seriously address its problems. Instead, it continued to flounder in corruption, economic retreat, and political gamesmanship.

Take, for example, the fact that Yushchenko's first cabinet was in office for less than a year. After Tymochenko came Yurii Yekhanurov, a caretaker bureaucrat of little distinction, willing to bend to the wishes of the nearest oligarch. He was also in office for less than a year. Parliamentary elections followed in early 2006, with results embarrassing to Yushchenko. Yanukovych's party led the parade, Tymoshenko's was second, and Yushchenko's fell into third place. When, not surprisingly, the parliament could not agree on a governing coalition, Yushchenko was forced to invite his arch enemy, Yanukovych—Putin's favorite Ukrainian politician—to form a new government. For the next year, they fought over every issue, and nothing was accomplished. In 2007, in desperation, Yushchenko called for yet another parliamentary election. This time, though Yanukovych's party again came in first, Yushchenko was able to ease him out of power by forming a coalition government with Tymoshenko, whom he distrusted and despised, after promising her the job of prime minister. She accepted. For the next year, until September 2008, the Tymoshenko-led government sought to balance Ukraine's troubled relations with Russia with its desire for closer ties with the European Union. Every time Ukraine so much as smiled toward the West, Putin frowned, and the Russian-Ukrainian relationship went into another of its periodic nosedives. Putin was at the time distracted by his war with Georgia. He was not in an accommodating mood.

Yushchenko dismissed the Tymoshenko cabinet and again called for new elections. But they had to be cancelled. The government was bankrupt. One result was that no one was in position to manage the process. What could Yushchenko do with this mess he had helped create? He hated Yanukovych and his oligarchs from the eastern and southern sectors of Ukraine, and he thoroughly distrusted Tymoshenko; but he had to have a prime minister and a new government. With no options, Yushchenko turned to the politician he distrusted rather than to the one he hated—there was no one else, he was president, and Ukraine needed governing guidance. Tymoshenko agreed to join Yushchenko and a few others and form a new government. It too lasted only a brief time, until January 17, 2010, when Ukrainians went to the polls to elect a new president.

Yushchenko got the bad, but hardly surprising, news in the early evening. He had received only 5 percent of the vote. He was finished. From the glory days of the Orange Revolution in 2004 to the dark winter of 2010, Yushchenko had shrunk into political ignominy, a politician of promise who had failed to deliver on a single reform. Many Ukrainians believed that if Yushchenko could not deliver, no one could. Their disillusionment with government deepened into a hard cynicism. Yanukovych got 35 percent of the vote, and Tymoshenko 25 percent. Because neither got a majority, a runoff election was held on February 7, 2010, and the results ran along regional lines. Yanukovych polled strongly in the east, winning 48.95 percent of the vote, and Tymoshenko polled strongly in the west, winning 45.47 percent of the vote.[28] Again, as so often in the past, Ukraine was split between east and west, neither candidate able to win in both parts of the country. Yanukovych took the presidency, a victory for the east, a defeat for the west, a relief for Putin.

Totally dissatisfied was Tymoshenko, who declared the runoff to be fraudulent, even though many observers judged the election to be fair. She refused to recognize the results, and she and many of her supporters boycotted Yanukovych's inauguration on February 25. What followed was inevitable: Tymoshenko was booted out of her job as prime minister, and a Yanukovych ally, Mykola Azarov, replaced her. And Yanukovych put a smile on Putin's face by quickly recalibrating Ukraine's policy toward Russia.

In April 2010, after a bitter parliamentary debate, Ukraine extended Russia's lease on the naval base at Sevastopol, set to expire in 2017, until 2042. Putin responded in a totally predictable way: He reduced the price of Russian natural gas to Ukraine. Two months later, in June, Yanukovych announced that Ukraine would abandon its goal of joining NATO, but not its goal of one day joining the European Union. That was left vague. Clearly, Yanukovych wanted to mollify Putin's chronic anxieties about Ukraine swinging too far to the West while at the same time leaving himself a little room for future maneuvering. He knew that he still faced a vocal minority in parliament and in the public that favored closer links with the West. He also knew that Putin was looking over his shoulder.

One way of handling Tymoshenko, still a popular politician, was to jail her, which is what Yanukovych did in 2011. His cover story was that she had "abused" her power while negotiating a natural gas deal with Russia in 2009. She was sentenced to seven years in prison. A few months later, her former interior minister, Yurii Lutsenko, was also arrested, convicted of abuse of power, and sentenced to four years in prison. (Why not also seven years was never explained.) These arrests were widely considered illegitimate, and many protested Tymoshenko's imprisonment. When Ukraine cohosted the European soccer championships in the summer of 2012, a number of member nations of the European Union boycotted the tournament, demanding that Tymoshenko be released immediately. She was not released, not then, but Lutsenko was released in April 2013, a gesture toward the European Union.

Yanukovych had been in serious negotiations with the EU, so serious, in fact, that everyone, everywhere, was expecting Yanukovych to sign a formal agreement with the body in November 2013, which could have locked Ukraine into a pro-Western policy certain to anger and disappoint Putin, already under pressure from a slowing economy and more questions over his Ukraine policy from some advisers.

But, at the last minute, feeling the heat from Putin and local oligarchs, Yanukovych changed his mind. He refused to sign the EU agreement, ending one troubled chapter in Ukraine's modern history and opening another. Once again, hundreds of thousands of disenchanted Ukrainians rushed to the streets. Days later, an elected president fled in terror, and Putin sent "little green men" into Crimea and eastern Ukraine, starting a bloody battle with historic implications for Ukraine's future—and Russia's.

According to Vladimir Frolov, president of a Russian PR and government relations company: "What looks like audacity and forcefulness is more often merely the byproducts of improvisation, knee-jerk reactions unrestrained by due government process."

CHAPTER 14

A Very Uncertain Future

What was called Novorossiya, back in the tsarist days, Kharkov, Lugansk, Donetz, Kherson, Nikolayev, and Odessa, was not part of Ukraine back then. The territories were given to Ukraine in the 1920s by the Soviet government.
VLADIMIR PUTIN

IT COULD BE CALLED THE second Orange Revolution. The first one, nine years earlier, ended with a new president emerging from a contested election and promising the Ukrainian equivalent of "peace and prosperity," which, if he had delivered, would have made the second revolution totally unnecessary. But he did not deliver, his successor was not delivering, and many Ukrainians, as disappointed as they were disillusioned, again took to the streets. It was November 2013, as fall slipped into a bitterly cold winter.

This time the Ukrainians were demanding more than a fair election. They were also demanding a signed-and-sealed agreement that Ukraine would be able to join the West, not in terms of an irrevocable revolt against Moscow but rather as an independent nation making an important decision about its own future.

In the process, as tens and then hundreds of thousands of Ukrainians returned to Independence Square, or the Maidan, as it was popularly called, they got more than they had ever imagined. They got a new president—that was relatively easy, but in addition they also got a cruel civil war pitting Ukrainians from Kiev against Ukrainians from Donetsk; a Russian leader who seemed, in both style and action, to blend Stalin with the worst of tsars; and a world that went topsy-turvy, hurtling to the very edge of a new cold war. The second Orange Revolution, or the Maidan Revolution, as some have called it, opened a new chapter in Russian-Ukrainian relations against the backdrop of a turbulent and dangerous twenty-first-century world.

The Maidan in Revolt, Again

It started innocuously enough when roughly a thousand Ukrainian activists, drawn together by social media, gathered in the Maidan on November 21, 2013, to demand that President Viktor Yanukovych do what he had been promising for the past year—sign an association agreement with the European Union. For several years, pro-Western Ukrainians had been pressing their government to stop diddling and sign the agreement—to affirm, once and for all, that Ukraine was institutionally a part of the Western world. But for President Yanukovych diddling was not dawdling—sometimes it reflected serious strategic risks and concerns. It was his way of containing Putin's wrathful impatience while at the same time cozying up to the EU. If Yanukovych, or Putin, ever thought that the demonstration of November 21 would prove to be a one-night boom-and-bust, they were wrong. An activist reporter, Mustafa Nayyem, had bigger plans in mind. "As soon as there are more than 1,000 of us," he emailed his friends, "we will start organizing."[1]

A colleague, Yuri Andreev, a journalist for Korrespondent.net, then tweeted his pro-Western friends that another demonstration would be held in the Maidan at 10:30 p.m. the following evening.[2] More than 2,000 protesters showed up for speeches and drinks, enough to "start organizing." The atmosphere was warm, serious but in no way violent. The word spread. On November 24, the Maidan crowd ballooned—anywhere from 50,000, according to the police, to 200,000, according to protest leaders. They marched and carried banners, screaming their message, "Ukraine is Europe," and some even stormed City Hall, hoping to occupy it. The police, who had been alerted, fired tear gas at them, and the protesters fired tear gas back at the police. Fistfights ensued. Batons came smashing down on unprotected heads. TV cameras from all over the world recorded the scene, sending pictures of the bloody encounter to viewers everywhere.[3] Ukraine was again becoming a big story. Would Yanukovych embrace the West or again bow to the East? In the meantime, would he be able to mollify the protesters, or, as Putin had encouraged him to do many times, crush them?

For a time, Yanukovych tried striking a middle ground. As a gesture to the protesters, his prime minister, Mykola Azarov, promised that the EU negotiations would continue and "not stop for a single day" until agreement was reached. He set up heated tents for students. He fed them. But, at the same time, Yanukovych warned the protesters that by blocking the main thoroughfares, they were undermining Christmas preparations and they would have to move. And if they didn't, the obvious question was, then what?

Yanukovych waited a few days before acting. Then, on November 30, at the unlikely hour of 4 a.m., he ordered his special forces and police to storm the Maidan and disperse the sleeping or sleepy protesters. Not surprisingly, once fully awake, they refused to leave. What followed was more tear gas, more batons to the head, more stun grenades; whatever the police did or used, nothing seemed to work. Protesters held new banners aloft, some carrying the urgent message of "Revolution!" Another made clear, "Won't Disperse!"[4]

Word of the police attack quickly spread. By December 1, the demonstrators, far from being discouraged, again tried to occupy City Hall, this time wearing construction hats and bicycle helmets and carrying sticks, bats, and hammers, looking as if they were expecting a fight. Swelled by thousands of students, the crowd grew and tempers flared. The BBC reported that the Maidan, by now filled with hundreds of thousands of protesters, was beginning to look like a "military camp,"[5] But the mood, said the *New York Times*, was "oddly festive."[6] First on the fringes but then closer to the center were right-wing groups holding red-and-black flags and mouthing ultra-nationalist slogans that would have made the Nazi-era Gestapo look like a happy band of bigots and bandits.

The Western reaction was one of contained outrage. The EU's number one diplomat, British-born Catherine Ashton, made clear that her sympathies lay with the protesters. "The authorities did not need to act under the cover of night," she said. Secretary of State Kerry expressed "disgust," adding: "As church bells ring tonight amidst the smoke in the streets of Kiev, the United States stands with the people of Ukraine. They deserve better."[7]

The larger question of "whither Ukraine?" was already being etched into the barricades of the Maidan. No one knew for certain. The demonstrators wanted Ukraine to be closely associated with the West. In the eastern Donbas region, the mood was gloomy, but attitudes tipped unmistakably in a pro-Russian direction. Again, Ukraine was split in two. Looking in on the unfolding crisis was the rest of the world, and here attitudes had already hardened. The West enthusiastically threw its support to Ukraine, framing the issue as one of democracy vs. authoritarianism, of good guys vs. bad guys, of national independence vs. Russian oppression, and describing Russia, as personified by Putin, already being compared to Hitler, as a bully nation driven by aggressive, irredentist, and dangerous impulses.

Russia saw the evolving Ukrainian situation in an entirely different light. In its view, Ukraine was a kind of wayward, misguided cousin, the victim of Western shenanigans out to subvert its independence, absorb it into NATO, and undo its historic ties to Russia.

This West vs. East comparison was hardly a serious description of the problem, but it was one often heard in diplomatic chanceries and read in morning newspapers. In both Washington and Moscow, it was apparently easy, perhaps even too easy, to resurrect the language and mood of the cold war and then adjust foreign policies to conform to the budding confrontation. Reporters who had covered the cold war in both Washington and Moscow were amazed by the speed of the sudden decline in East-West relations.

A Putin Feint

The Maidan protests continued. On occasion, angry demonstrators threw firebombs at the police, and the police responded with gunfire. Pictures of the dead and wounded further inflamed passions. On December 6, as though to break the cycle, Putin summoned Yanukovych to Sochi for a meeting to discuss their "strategic partnership."[8] The wording sounded important, but meant little. The concluding communiqué was similarly opaque, but reporters picked up rumors that Yanukovych had been invited to the Kremlin on December 17 for a "signing ceremony." Signing what? Meaning what? The questions were asked; no answers were given. When these rumors hit the Maidan, the protesters were instantly convinced that Yanukovych had been sucked into an evil Putinesque plot to strip Ukraine of its dignity and independence, and he was too stupid to appreciate what was happening.

In less than two weeks, indeed on December 17, as rumored, Yanukovych was in the Kremlin, seated beside Putin. A wonderful photograph caught a playful moment in an otherwise complex negotiation—Yanukovych, a large man, was looking down at the smaller Putin, and winking. Putin was smiling like a Cheshire cat, but he did not wink back. He had just agreed to buy $15 billion in Ukrainian government bonds, a kind of loan to Kiev's troubled economy, while also pledging to cut by more than 30 percent what Ukraine was paying for Russian natural gas.[9] The immediate, and completely understandable, speculation was that Putin had just purchased not bonds but Ukraine's allegiance to Moscow, the subtext being that Yanukovych had abandoned his long-standing hope of one day seeing his country join the EU.

That was precisely what the Maidan protesters had feared would happen. In response, they demanded Yanukovych's resignation. When issued, it was more a cry from the heart than a realistic demand. "Down with the gang," they chanted, the "gang" being all the "crooks" surrounding their president, whom they considered Crook No. 1.

At a news conference following their meeting, Putin, with a straight face, told reporters that he had acted to help solve "the problems of Ukraine's economy." He cared about the "welfare of the people," he added. They had not discussed the idea of Ukraine joining Moscow's Eurasian customs union, he assured Ukrainian journalists. Yanukovych beamed, the student who had just earned an "A." Looking at Putin, he crowed, "This work wouldn't have been accomplished with such optimal speed but for [Putin's] political will." They kissed in Slavic fashion and parted.[10] Did Putin buy Ukraine's allegiance? He certainly hoped so. This was a brewing crisis he did not want, but one he still thought he could manage. In due course, he was to learn he was wrong. Ukraine proved to be fertile ground for further misjudgments by the Russian president.

In Kiev, opposition politician Oleg Tyagnibok was not buying any of the rhetorical fluff. "The deals Yanukovych struck in Moscow," he said, "are the price Moscow paid him for rejecting European integration." Vitali Klitschko, the boxer, said that "the biggest fight of my life is going on now, and my opponent is Yanukovych." From eastern Ukraine came a different perspective, the Russian perspective. Lawmaker Alexander Volkov praised the Moscow deal, saying "our economy can get a second breath and start climbing out of its stupor."[11]

The Olympics as a Prelude to Action

The Russian apex of 2014, in Putin's mind, was to be a glorious extravaganza—the Winter Olympics at the Black Sea resort of Sochi. The Games, which the Russians had bid for and won seven years earlier, were part of a broad strategy soon to unfold. The Olympics were to project the image of a "new Russia," sleek, swift, and optimistic—Putin's Russia, back from the muck and misery of the post-Soviet chaos, ready once again to take its place in the pantheon of great powers. If the rest of the world still thought of Russia as a dark and musty backwater of a country, they would soon learn they were mistaken. Putin's hope was that the Olympics would obliterate old negative images and create new positive ones.

The Winter Olympics were Putin's version of "shock and awe." He was warned they would be expensive—they ended up costing an estimated $51 billion. No other Olympic Games, whether winter or summer, had ever cost more. But, like Peter the Great building his capital of St. Petersburg, Putin was indifferent to cost. He was warned that terrorism was "a clear and present danger"—Sochi was very close to the Islamic tumult in the northern Caucasus—but he was certain the problem could be managed. Putin saw the benefits in global imagery and glory, in a return of national pride, in business opportunities, in boasting rights. If Russia was soon to feel the need to indulge in an adventure or two, perhaps the world would be more understanding.

Putin threw himself into the project. He flew to Guatemala City on July 4, 2007, hoping to persuade Olympic bigwigs that Sochi was their best bet for 2014. He delivered his speech in English, which took a good bit of time and preparation. His pitch was that he represented a "new Russia," a phrase he was to use again and again. It sounded perfect—forward-looking, cooperative, possibly even democratic, just what the world needed. As deputy mayor of St. Petersburg in the uncertain 1990s, he had impressed Western businessmen as the only Russian who could get things done; and so, similarly, he impressed the Olympic officials in 2007. Sochi was their choice. Putin's salesmanship had won the prize.

No one was more elated than the oddly messianic president of the "new Russia." No matter the cost, he seemed to be saying, the Olympics were a national priority. The job had to be done, and done on time. Like Stalin building the Russian atomic bomb after World War II, Putin utilized every resource of his vast country—talent, muscle power, and resources. As a consequence of his dogged determination, the Olympics opened in a prime-time blaze of televised glory on February 7, 2014, the start of a fifteen-day run. The pressure was on every Russian athlete to win—it was more than picking up another trophy; it was a matter of national pride, proof the "new Russia" had arrived and henceforth would be a contender on the world stage.

In Putin's planning, the "new Russia" theme was central to his resurrection of the nostalgic concept of *Novorossiya*, which, as earlier noted, harkened back to the mid-eighteenth century and defined Russian hegemony over an arc of land running from western Ukraine down to the Black Sea, including Crimea, and then rising northeast into the Donbas. Putin believed that this was all Russian land, rightfully, legally, historically. In Putin's strategic calculations, the fact that most of *Novorossiya* was now in a nation called Ukraine was a nuisance, but not an insurmountable one, in part because he never viewed Ukraine as a truly independent country.

"I would like to remind you," Putin said in a nationally televised call-in broadcast, "that what was called *Novorossiya* (New Russia), back in the tsarist days, Kharkov, Lugansk, Donetsk, Kherson, Nikolayev, and Odessa were not part of Ukraine back then. The territories were given to Ukraine in the 1920s by the Soviet government." When Lenin and Stalin created the Soviet Union in 1922, Ukraine was made a Soviet republic, and these cities were made part of it. "Why?" Putin asked rhetorically. "Who knows?" he responded with casual indifference, as though he were saying that Lenin's decisions in 1922 had no relevance now.[12] Now it was Putin's time.

What did have relevance, in Putin's mind, was the supporting historical work of the Russian Academy of Sciences, which, under his personal direction, was producing a 1,000-page "History of the New Russia (Novorossiya)."[13] Because historians in Putin's Russia no longer adhered to the standards of objective scholarship, instead producing works consistent with the party line—as during the Soviet era—the new study would likely produce a narrative "proving" that *Novorossiya* was linked historically to the "new Russia" and therefore belonged to the "new Russia." U.S. think tank experts had recently left meetings in Moscow disappointed by the politically motivated shallowness of current Russian scholarship, remembering wistfully that, once upon a time, in tsarist times, Russian scholars were regarded as among the best in the world and their work was read with respect. No longer. Now their work was seen as little more than a Russian version of an op-ed polemic.

In the Olympic Shadow

The date February 23, 2014, was a special day in Putin's calendar. At the time the reason was known only to a handful of Russian generals. But up until February 23, so far as everyone else was concerned, it was a time for the skiing, skating, and slaloming wonders of the Winter Olympics. As hundreds of millions around the world watched the games in Sochi, Putin was watching the demonstrations in Kiev, which he thought represented a threat to Russia; in his view, they were getting out of hand. Just as his attendance at the Beijing Olympics in 2008 had served as a handy distraction from a Russian mini-war against Georgia—resulting in the subsequent occupation of two formerly Georgian provinces, Abkhazia and Ossetia—now the Sochi Olympics would serve a similar purpose. While the games were under way, Putin reportedly raised the alert status for Russian military action against Ukraine, starting in Crimea but moving swiftly into the Donbas. His Special Forces already had been put on alert when the second Orange Revolution started several months earlier. The sight of hundreds of thousands of protesters demonstrating in the Maidan against the pro-Russian government of President Yanukovych profoundly disturbed Putin. The demonstrations had turned violent and anti-Russian. Putin saw the possibility of a wobbly Ukraine deteriorating into a contagious crisis capable of infecting his own people. That had been his fear in 2004 during the first Orange Revolution, and that again was his fear in the fall of 2013 and early months of 2014. Action of some sort, he believed, would have to be taken.

By 7 a.m., on February 23, having conferred with "the leaders of our special services and the Defense Ministry" all night, Putin made two decisions: one was to save Yanukovych's life, and the other was "to bring Crimea back into Russia." Yanukovych had already made his way to Donetsk. "We got ready to get him right out of Donetsk by land, by sea, or by air," Putin disclosed a year later. "Heavy machine guns were mounted there so that there wouldn't be much discussion about it." Nor would there be much discussion about his conquest of Crimea, when it happened.[14]

Putin, like most autocrats, only adores a crowd when it is his crowd, like the Olympic crowd in Sochi. Otherwise, he fears crowds, and he distrusts the "masses." They may embark—who knows? he asks—on wild adventures, producing unpredictable coups d'état and uncontrollable violence. His return to the presidency in 2012 had been preceded by massive anti-Putin demonstrations, starting in Moscow and spreading to St. Petersburg and other Russian cities, and they terrified him. They represented, to him, an existential threat to his power, and as an ex-KGB apparatchik, he was not above using force to crush a popular uprising, even a popular demonstration. Yury Andropov, once head of the KGB, held a lesser KGB job in Budapest in 1956, and he also supported the use of the Red Army to smash a popular uprising there.

"The battle for Russia continues," Putin told a sympathetic crowd. "The victory will be ours." Those who opposed him, he argued, were really seeking to destroy Russia. He returned to the presidency, wrote Maxim Trudolyubov, an editor of *Vedemosti*, "a changed man, full of messianic fervor and eager to pick a fight."[15]

One of Putin's first acts, on returning to the Kremlin in 2012, had been to make such demonstrations difficult to organize and soon impossible to organize without his personal prior approval.

"Moscow Is Silent"

Putin's biographers have written about anticommunist mobs storming KGB headquarters in Dresden in the moribund German Democratic Republic, where Putin worked in the late 1980s, even as the Soviet Union was falling apart. "These people were very aggressive," Putin recalled. "It was a serious threat." He felt "outraged." Putin spent his time, according to reporter Masha Gessen, "shoving papers into a wood-burning stove until the stove split from the excessive heat. He had destroyed everything he and his colleagues had worked to collect: all the contacts, personnel files, surveillance reports, and probably endless paper clippings."

Putin was desperate. He called for help, but none came. Not from the KGB troops, still in East Germany. Not from the Red Army. "I remember," he said, "that 'Moscow is silent,'" a phrase that apparently left him disoriented and more than a bit frightened. "I realized that the Soviet Union was ill. It was a fatal illness called paralysis. A paralysis of power."[16] Gorbachev's Moscow might have been "silent," as this former KGB operative remembered; but if he had his way, Putin's Russia would never be "silent," never be paralyzed by demonstrating mobs challenging the authority of the state. Putin's narrative has always been that his Russia would be proud, powerful, and unafraid—the master of its own destiny. If a threat loomed on the near horizon, as Putin viewed the increasingly violent, anti-Russian Maidan demonstrations, then Russia had an inherent right to rise, preemptively, if necessary, against the Ukrainian threat and destroy it. No excuses were necessary. National self-interest demanded action. The sole remaining questions were: What kind of action? Where? And who would decide?

First Crimea, A Historic Prize

Crimea has always evoked powerful emotions among Russians tuned into their history. As we have seen, it was the place where such writers as Pushkin drew inspiration for their poetry, where thousands of Russians died gallantly in the nineteenth and twentieth centuries, defending the "homeland" while fighting Turks and Germans, and where Stalin negotiated the shape of post–World War II Europe with Roosevelt and Churchill. It was, in brief, a treasured piece of real estate. Though Khrushchev had given it to Ukraine in 1954—a foolish, reckless gesture, according to Putin—it remained, in Kremlin calculations, still part of Russia, still the indispensable base for Russia's Black Sea fleet, still home for the Russian majority who lived there. Putin circled Crimea on an imaginary map. Here Russia would act. Here Russia would begin to recapture her former glory as a great nation.

His reasoning smelled partly of an ad hoc response to the building crisis in Kiev but mostly of old-fashioned European power politics, the sort Peter and Catherine had played in the eighteenth century. If Yanukovych, his man, was going to be kicked out of power by rioting anti-Russian, pro-Western protesters, then Russia would be facing a new regime, almost sure to be right wing, possibly even fascist, that would quickly align itself with NATO and the European Union and become a Western dagger pointing at Russia's heart. The new regime, encouraged by NATO, might even seek to expropriate the Russian naval base at Sevastopol and bottle up the Black Sea fleet on the assumption that the base and the fleet were in Ukraine's domain, and not Russia's. Or, at least, it might attempt to.

In Putin's view, all of this constituted a genuine threat, and Crimea had to be "protected." That was the word he used. The Russians living there also had to be "protected." For reasons both domestic and diplomatic, he persuaded himself that Crimea had to be brought back into the fold.

—Domestic reasons: Retaking Crimea would certainly rekindle national pride; it would sidetrack the obvious need for economic reform; it would solidify his political base; and it would send a strong signal to Kiev's new leaders not to mess with Russia.

—Diplomatic reasons: It would guarantee continued Russian control of its strategically vital naval base and fleet, and it would ensure Russian access to a warm water port, a strategic goal that had influenced Russian policy for decades, even centuries.

At the time Putin ignored the likelihood that a Russian seizure of Crimea would ignite strong nationalist feelings in the rest of Ukraine. It would also generate an anti-Russian diplomatic campaign, reminiscent of the days of the cold war, but this too, Putin thought, could be weathered. He could portray the West, especially the United States, as hostile, seeking once again, as in cold war days, to suffocate Russia with sanctions, boycotts, and military threats. Why else then would the United States have led the way in expanding NATO to Russia's borders? Why would Western leaders ponder incorporating Georgia and Ukraine into their strategic clutches? But even if, as a consequence of Russia retaking Crimea, Putin's relations with the West suffered, even if life for Russia's rising middle class turned sour, he was convinced Russia could survive the West's best punch, and in time prosper once again. Russians had what he called "a unique and very powerful genetic code," which prepared them for self-sacrifice.[17] Putin came therefore to believe that Crimea could— and should—be reabsorbed into Russia. It would show the Ukrainians that, though they might think of themselves as independent, they still live in Russia's shadow and must accommodate themselves to the realities of geography, power, and politics. Their future as a successful nation, he was convinced, could only be ensured when Russia was satisfied that its national interests were not being threatened by the policies or actions of a nation that for most of its existence was part and parcel of the Russian empire, whether in tsarist or communist times.

In late January 2014, when the Olympics were still a week or so away, Putin

was invited to an EU summit meeting in Brussels. It was there that he demonstrated for the first time his on-again, off-again strategy for negotiating an
acceptable outcome to the Ukraine crisis. It was going to be a rough East-West
ride, but unless the West took Russian interests into account, no deal was
possible. Just a month earlier, Putin had promised Yanukovych a $15 billion
loan. Now, he told his fellow summiteers, there was a problem—one not of
his making, he assured them. Apparently, there had been a cabinet meeting in
the Kremlin a few days earlier. Putin said that he had told his colleagues that
he intended to live up to his $15 billion promise to Yanukovych. "I ask the
government to carry out these agreements in full," said Putin, whose orders
were not usually questioned. But, in this tale, Prime Minister Dmitri Medvedev rose to challenge Putin and suggest that the promise to Yanukovych could
be fulfilled "only when we know what economic policies the new government
will implement, who will be working there, and what rules they will follow."
How did Putin react to his puppet prime minister's challenge? According to
this rendition, he agreed with him. "That's reasonable," he is supposed to have
said. And that was that.[18]

The official Russian news agency, Itar-Tass, immediately put out the story
that the Medvedev tale meant that the promised aid would not be delivered.
In addition, the deputy director of Gazprom, the state-owned monopoly, disclosed that Ukraine had failed to make payments on a $2.7 billion debt, and,
therefore, no further natural gas deliveries would be made. Finally, Russian
customs agents decided, under orders from the Kremlin, no doubt, to increase
border checks on Ukrainian trucks entering Russia with Ukrainian produce, an essential segment of the overall Ukrainian economy. This of course
delayed deliveries by a week or two, spurring unhappiness among consumers
and hurting the economy.[19]

Putin, in this way, had clearly wanted to pressure Yanukovych to steer clear
of the EU, while trying to persuade EU leaders that he really wanted to help
the Ukrainian people. But his cabinet raised "reasonable" questions, which,
he said, he had to answer. The EU did not buy Putin's story nor his explanation. The EU's usually obliging hosts showed their irritation by cancelling
a dinner in honor of the Russian leader, a mild gesture that stretched the
EU's definition of toughness to its outer limits. "Business as usual" was no
longer possible, a spokesman explained—certainly not when a former Ukrainian president, Leonid Kravchuk, scanned the horizon at the same time and
lamented to reporters that his country stood "on the brink of civil war." In the
streets outside of EU headquarters, bare-chested female demonstrators from
Ukraine, mimicking Putin who enjoyed bare-chested posturing, eschewed

diplomatic niceties. They denounced the Russian president, carrying placards reading "Putin—Killer of Democracy" and "Viva Putin—Viva Killer."[20]

Kravchuk's crystal ball enjoyed exceptional clarity. Within a month, almost to the day, the Ukrainian civil war began. Though both sides had made gestures toward accommodation, Yanukovych and the Maidan protesters could not reach an agreement on anything. This story of failure, tracked day by day, conveyed the urgency of a front-page news story.

—On January 28, Prime Minister Azarov resigned, apparently Yanukovych's way of saying to the protesters: "Let's be friends." But the protesters wanted nothing to do with Yanukovych. They wanted *him* to resign. Putin reportedly urged Yanukovych to crack down on the protesters, but he held back. He was never certain he had the support of his security forces.

—On January 29, the Rada, filled with many Yanukovych supporters, annulled an antiprotest law, promising to drop charges against all who had been arrested, on the condition that the protesters abandon the government buildings they had been occupying for weeks. They rejected the condition.

—On February 14, when the Olympics were still in progress and few people paid much attention to events in Kiev, Yanukovych and the Maidan protesters made parallel conciliatory gestures. The president released all 234 protesters who had been arrested in December, and the demonstrators, in an apparent quid pro quo, abandoned Kiev's City Hall, which they had held since December 1.

—On February 16, secret reconciliation talks were reportedly under way, and tensions seemed to ease in and around the Maidan.

—On February 18, clashes erupted once again. It was clear extremists on both sides feared a possible reconciliation and wanted to exploit current tensions. They had weapons. The demonstrators acted first, according to local reports, attacking police lines and lighting a bonfire outside the Rada. The police responded forcefully. By nightfall, twenty-four people had been killed, including seven police officers, and hundreds of people had been wounded. Each side accused the other of triggering the violence.

—On February 20, eighty-eight people were killed in the worst day of Kiev violence in more than seventy years. A visiting Baltic politician said she was told the demonstrators opened fire, apparently to instigate a confrontation, but video that evening showed uniformed snipers shooting down at protesters, protected by little more than makeshift shields. Both sides now seemed to have crossed the Rubicon, from grudging concessions to outright violence.

—On February 21, in a dramatic last-ditch effort to contain the spreading violence, Russian, German, French, and Polish ministers flew into Kiev and urged Yanukovych and three of his principal political opponents to meet and agree to end the violence. Enough! the world seemed to be saying. Poland's foreign minister Radoslaw Sikorski warned both sides that they had little choice but to meet, to compromise, and to negotiate a deal. "If you don't support this," he said, "you will have martial law, the army. You'll all be dead."[21]

Yanukovych and his opponents met and argued for many hours and then, to the relief of the visiting ministers, reached what the EU described as a "temporary agreement." The Russian minister, however, refused to sign it, an indication of Moscow's continuing displeasure. Putin saw the agreement as Western arm-twisting and, in the final analysis, detrimental to Russian interests. Yet, for months thereafter, he cited the "temporary agreement" as the basis of a deal that Kiev subsequently sabotaged. The other foreign ministers did sign it. The highlights: a plan for early elections in December 2014, and, in the meantime, a new unity government. The balance of power would shift back to the Rada, where it had been up until Yanukovych's election in 2010. The Ukrainian president, on the defensive, yielded on a number of major demands, apparently in a pathetic effort to hold on to power for a few more months and see what might transpire. Everyone in the negotiation understood that the "temporary agreement" was a fig leaf to cover a staged presidential abdication.

Yanukovych called Putin and said that "the situation had stabilized," and he would soon be leaving for a conference in Kharkov, in northeastern Ukraine. "A conference in Kharkov?" Putin asked. Months later, as he told the Valdai Discussion Club meeting in Sochi, "I did not think everything would be fine," and, in any case, "I do not think you [Yanukovych] should withdraw the law enforcement forces from Kiev. . . . He said he understood," but withdrew the forces anyway—much to Putin's annoyance. [22]

Though opposition leaders signed the agreement, many of their Maidan backers turned their backs on it. "Too little and too late," they seemed to be saying. What they demanded, unconditionally, was Yanukovych's resignation and then his trial before the International Criminal Court.[23] The Rada, reflecting the mood of the moment, discussed a plan to strip Yanukovych of all power and bring him to trial.

—On February 22, the earth shook, and Kiev was left in a power vacuum. By dawn, Yanukovych had vanished, and the peace agreement, so painfully negotiated the day before, got caught up in the Maidan firestorm, and it too simply vanished.

In the dead of night, just a few hours earlier, Yanukovych and his family had fled from the luxurious presidential palace in a fleet of helicopters and limousines, ending up somehow in Donetsk. Putin's later rendition of what then happened was a typical mix of fact and fancy. Putin said Yanukovych called and asked for a meeting. Putin agreed. Where? Rostov, not too far from Kiev. What about the Kharkov conference? Impossible—things suddenly too dangerous. "They were beginning to use force against him already," Putin related, "holding him at gunpoint." But whoever held him "at gunpoint" allowed him to escape, which made no sense. Putin admitted, "We helped him move to Crimea, where he stayed for a few days. . . . The situation in Kiev was developing very rapidly and violently. . . . People were killed, they were burned alive there. They came into the office of the Party of Regions [Yanukovych's party], seized the technical workers, and killed them, burned them alive in the basement. There was no way he [Yanukovych] could return to Kiev. . . . He asked us to help him get to Russia, which we did. That was all."[24]

With Yanukovych gone, the demonstrators took command of government buildings, and the Rada, claiming it was now the only game in town, voted formally to oust Yanukovych from power—by vote of the Rada, he was no longer president—and to hold new elections on May 25, 2014. Whether the Rada's actions constituted a coup d'état (Putin said yes, the West said no) became a core issue in future arguments over ways of defusing the Ukraine crisis.

Shortly thereafter, the indestructible Yulia Tymoshenko, imprisoned by Yanukovych three years before, was sprung. She drove immediately to the Maidan, where she delivered an impassioned plea for "national independence." For a moment, she represented post-Yanukovych Ukraine.

In the early evening, Yanukovych appeared on television to denounce the Rada's decisions. He had residual clout in the Donbas. He could command TV time, and get it. "I am a *legitimately* elected president," he pronounced clearly and accurately, putting special emphasis on the word "legitimately." His election in 2010, though contested by his political opponents, was legal. It was the last presidential election. "What is happening today, mostly, it is vandalism, banditism, and a coup d'état."[25]

—On February 23, one day after the Winter Olympics ended, Putin unveiled his surprise, but in a way so oblique and startling that not everyone could quickly recognize its importance. Crimea was about to change ownership. Eastern Ukraine was about to descend into civil war.

The Rada, in Kiev, seemed not to appreciate what was happening in Crimea. Everyone was deliriously absorbed with domestic politics. The Rada handed presidential powers to its speaker, Oleksandr Turchynov. It also voted to resurrect a ten-year-old constitution, granting greater powers to the Rada. An arrest warrant was issued for Yanukovych, mostly to satisfy the Maidan protesters. Arseniy Yatsenyuk, a young English-speaking, anti-Russian, fiercely nationalistic politician, was appointed prime minister. He was soon to become an international superstar, representing the new Ukraine at diplomatic gatherings covered by the global media.[26] If this tick-tock of one event after another suggested the Rada was functioning with Swiss efficiency, freed finally from Yanukovych's stifling grip, that would be a mistaken impression. In fact, not just the Rada but all of Ukraine had been thrown into a cocked hat: Politicians reaching for more power, oligarchs for new business opportunities, and ordinary people for simple answers, of which there were very few. No one knew what would happen from one day to the next. Ukraine was gripped by a whirlwind of unpredictable change.

From Moscow came word that Putin, like Yanukovych, believed that Kiev's political circus had just pulled a coup d'état out of its center ring, but it was not a coup to his liking. It was a right-wing coup, one lacking all legitimacy, disrespectful of Russian interests, and open to Western seduction. Because some of the participants belonged to extremist political parties and militia, taking their inspiration from anti-Russian movements in World War II, Putin branded them as fascist. Medvedev, of course, agreed with his boss's description, adding they constituted an "armed mutiny . . . Kalashnikov-toting people in black masks."

In Kiev, Putin saw Western conspiracies everywhere. He now expected NATO to make a play for Ukraine, and the International Monetary Fund (IMF) to become Ukraine's sole banker. If one is to believe Putin, he disclosed a year later that he actually thought the West might launch a military attack on Russia and, for this reason, considered putting his nuclear arsenal on alert.[27] Putin had clearly suffered a setback in Kiev: He had underestimated the resilience and strength of the anti-Yanukovych demonstrators, and he had obviously overestimated Yanukovych's political skills.

Unlike Gorbachev and Yeltsin, though, Putin refused to play the part of a loser. But what specifically would he do? He decided to raise the voltage on Ukraine. He would risk a new confrontation with the West. He wanted the coup-plotters and -planners (he was certain the United States had a big hand in this coup) to understand that Putin's Russia would have to be respected, honored, and brought into any negotiation designed to reach a settlement. He had many cards he could play in Ukraine: political, economic, and military. And if he had to lie, cheat, and steal in this game, then he would do that too. He was convinced he would end up on top. He was a risk-taker supreme, an opportunist, a gambler. Just look at history, he would say. Look at geography. He would start first in Crimea, and go on from there.

Obama's Vision of Putin

The two presidents—Obama and Putin—spoke a few times during the twilight days of Yanukovych's time in office. On one occasion, Obama picked up the phone and proposed "broker[ing] an agreement that would quell the violence" and, in his words, "allow Yanukovych to play out his term but would devolve power to the Rada."[28] The proposal was similar in frame and intent to the one that evolved into the February 21 "temporary agreement." It was based on an assumption that Yanukovych was no longer acceptable to a majority of Ukrainians, but he could not be run out of town like a criminal escaping justice. He was the elected president. He had to be given a degree of respect.

Gradually reduce the violence, Obama argued. Shift power slowly but definitely to the Rada, and then, further down the line, hold presidential elections. But Putin shot down Obama's proposition, basically because, no matter how it was sugarcoated, the end result was that it took power from his man in Kiev and gave it to his political opponents. Even if Obama had been able to persuade Putin to accept his proposal, protesters at the Maidan were too impatient to wait for negotiations to produce a political miracle. They wanted action. They wanted Yanukovych out, stripped of power and brought, manacled, if necessary, before a court.

Obama wanted to understand Putin, even when it came to the Ukraine problem, but he failed time and again to grasp Putin's obsession with the idea that the United States was trying to "punish Russia, to isolate Russia," a perceived course of action Russia could not accept.[29] Obama told *New York Times* columnist Friedman that Putin had "genuine concern" about a number of American decisions, including "NATO expansion, missile defense, our unilateral pullout of ABM treaty, our decision to go into Iraq, . . . and Libya," regarding them as "examples of the U.S. throwing its weight around in ways that are contrary to Russian interests." Although Obama disagreed with him, he recognized that Putin could "make a rational argument."[30]

But, having paid his respects to diplomatic protocol, Obama then went on both to criticize and judge Putin's policy. The huge pro-democracy demonstrations in Moscow prior to Putin's return to the presidency in 2012 unnerved Putin, in Obama's view, to the point where he believed "he was losing control." Putin quickly infused his administration with an "anti-American and anti-Western, . . . proto-Russian nationalist, almost czarist" attitude, which improved his political position at home but complicated his foreign policy, especially his dealings with the United States. It also put Moscow on edge, Putin insiders looking anxiously over their shoulders, concocting Western conspiracies, imagining NATO threats. And then came the unrest in Kiev, marked by an anti-Russian and anti-Putin energy that deepened Putin's sense of insecurity.

"I actually think the situation in Ukraine caught him by surprise," Obama said, reflecting the judgment of many Washington experts, who seemed consistently to undervalue the importance Putin placed on Ukraine remaining a vital part of Russia's post-communist world. "This wasn't some grand strategy."[31] Here was yet another time when Obama misjudged Putin—it was, indeed, part of a "grand strategy," but one that slipped past Obama's radar.

"The notion that Putin is an opportunist, at best an improviser, but not a strategist, is a dangerous misread," wrote Fiona Hill and Clifford G. Gaddy, two superb analysts of the Putin era. "Putin thinks, plans, and acts strategically."[32] Putin might not have imagined that the Kiev situation would have collapsed as swiftly as it did, but he knew that the situation was volatile, anti-Russian, and that action of some sort would have to be taken—and he prepared to take action, and ultimately did. Putin, one analyst said, was influenced by a "smaller and smaller circle . . . of fierce Russian nationalists." A burst of jingoism set Russia on a course to take Crimea and destabilize Ukraine. That would "set us on a course," said Obama, "not to a new cold war but trying to find our way back to a cooperative, functioning relationship with Russia during the remainder of my term will be much more difficult."[33] But if the United States truly believed that one nation crossing the borders of another was indeed a gross violation of international law, as it repeatedly stated, then obviously a Russian move into Ukraine would be more than a "new cold war"; it might also be the first step toward a new hot one. Yet, Obama chose to sidestep the dangers Putin posed, instead choosing a more diplomatic approach.

The rest of 2014 saw what many in the West regarded as a Russian "invasion" of Ukraine, not in the way the Germans had invaded Poland on September 1, 1939, but rather in the way Russia seized Crimea in February–March of that year, as though operating on cat's paws while no one watched. Putin, of course, denied that he had invaded any country, even after journalists interviewed Russian troops in the Donbas, even after NATO produced proof of Russian support, even after Russian casualties were returned to their grieving families. He was expecting another Crimea-like success—"little green men" instigating an uprising of Donbas nationalists who would welcome a new, close association with Moscow.

But after a few months it was clear that once again Putin had miscalculated. In Crimea, a majority of the people rose in support of a quick association with Russia. They were, after all, ethnic Russians. In eastern Ukraine, that was not the case. There were many Ukrainians who spoke Russian, felt an emotional kinship with Russia, and could not imagine themselves to be in conflict with Russia, but still considered themselves Ukrainians. This chronic confusion about "national identity" affected Russian and Ukrainian leaders alike, propelling them to change their policies and tactics time and again.

As 2014 came to a close, the situation in Ukraine remained unsettled, fluid, and dangerous.

CHAPTER 15

The War in Ukraine

The American people are not going to war with Russia over Ukraine, full stop.
SENIOR U.S. OFFICIAL

IN THE WEST, the post-Yanukovych government in Kiev seemed like heaven on Earth, a place for the birth of democracy; in Moscow, it seemed like hell, an anti-Russian cabal in its own backyard. "Unacceptable" was Putin's response. He had a plan, and he had every intention of putting it into effect.

On February 26, 2014, three days after the Winter Olympics dropped its final curtain, hundreds and then thousands of pro-Russian demonstrators began appearing on the streets of Simferopol, the capital of Crimea, demanding that Crimea become part of Russia. They seemed to come out of nowhere. Within hours, pro-Kiev demonstrators took to the streets, arguing that Crimea remain part of Ukraine. They were ethnic Ukrainians, joined quickly at the hip by Muslim Tartars, who were deeply suspicious of anything Russian. Soon emotional clashes erupted between pro-Russian and pro-Kiev mobs—fistfights followed by angry scuffles, each side denouncing the other's agenda and intent. At the time the clashes attracted little attention in the world's newsrooms, worth no more than a four-sentence account on one agency wire.

On February 27, the next day, matters began to escalate. Again, thousands of demonstrators, pro- and anti-Russian, fought in front of the regional parliament. An old woman was trampled to death; three people were injured. Nearby, armed gunmen seized two government buildings and planted a Russian flag on top of one of them.

In Kiev, on February 28, acting president Oleksandr Turchynov ordered the Ukrainian army, a force more in name than power, to stand by for action against "potential aggression." This was a sad joke, for everyone knew that the Ukrainian army was in shambles, unable to engage in a serious fight. In

Simferopol, the pro-Russian governor, Sergiy Aksyonov, newly appointed to the job, asked Putin for "help" to ensure public security. This was part of an obviously rehearsed scenario. He also closed the air space over Simferopol, as reports circulated that Russian transport planes were flying into the capital.

In Washington, a suddenly wary Obama called Putin to warn him that "there will be costs" should Russia persist in intervening in Crimea. One of the likely "costs" was the United States applying economic sanctions against Russia. No one ever seriously considered the United States using its military power to stop Russia. "The American people are not going to war with Russia over Ukraine, full stop," said one senior administration official.[1]

By daybreak, on March 1, the world seemed to have turned a corner. Putin had brazenly flown "little green men" into Crimea. Within hours, it seemed, without firing a shot, they occupied the entire peninsula, seizing control of government buildings, airports, and communication centers.[2]

In Moscow, Putin went through the motions of asking his tame Federation Council for permission to use Russian troops "in connection with the extraordinary situation in Ukraine and the threat to the lives of Russian citizens." The troops would remain in Ukraine "until the normalization of the political situation." It was immediately noted in Western chanceries that Putin was speaking of "Ukraine," not just Crimea. Within hours, the Duma gave its permission.[3]

Obama, alarmed by the news, again picked up the phone and spoke with Putin for more than an hour. According to a White House briefing, the president expressed his "deep concern" about "Russia's clear violation of Ukrainian sovereignty and territorial integrity." He warned the United States would pull out of a planned June G-8 summit meeting in Sochi, adding that Russia's "continued violation of international law will lead to greater political and economic isolation."[4] Putin denied that Russian troops had invaded Crimea while stressing his "concern" about "real threats" to Russian citizens in Ukraine. "Frankly, this is our historical territory and Russian people live there," Putin later explained. "They were in danger, and we cannot abandon them."[5]

Later on March 1, a statement issued by Putin's office said that "in the case of any further spread of violence to Eastern Ukraine and Crimea, Russia retains the right to protect its interests and the Russian-speaking population of those areas."[6] Critics instantly recalled Hitler's explanation for the German annexation of the Sudetenland in 1938. For the record, critics also noted that there were no reported "threats" to the "Russian-speaking population" of Ukraine. None. Putin had created a pretext.

An international chorus of "concern" ensued. Britain's Prime Minister David Cameron contributed his "deep concern," saying "everyone must think carefully about his actions."[7] The UN Security Council met in emergency session, and the spokesperson for Secretary General Ban Ki-moon appealed for "an immediate restoration of calm and direct dialogue."[8]

Over the tumultuous weekend of March 1–2, Putin ignored such appeals for "calm" and "dialogue." He saw a "threat" to Russian interests in the new pro-Western regime in Kiev. He felt the need to crush it, even if the cost was Western economic sanctions. Having seized Crimea, he moved into the Donbas region of Ukraine, where pro-Russian sentiment was traditionally strong. Again, overnight, it seemed, pro-Russian rallies popped up in Donetsk, Kharkov, Luhansk, Mariupol, and even the southern port city of Odessa, instigated by Moscow and organized by Russian special forces in the region. More than 7,000 demonstrators tried to occupy City Hall in Donetsk, but they failed, repulsed by Ukrainian police. However, they succeeded in hoisting a Russian flag in the center of the city. They sang Russian folk songs, while denouncing the Kiev regime as "right wing" and "fascist." In Kharkov, Ukraine's second-largest city, as many as 100 people were injured during rival demonstrations by thousands of pro- and anti-Russian throngs. For a time, supporters of the post-Yanukovych government in Kiev were flushed out of City Hall, and a Russian flag was run up the flagpole atop the building. For centuries, this region of Ukraine has been the heart and home of many ethnic Russians. Therefore, Putin imagined he could quickly win their sympathy and support, and take control of the Donbas, just as he had Crimea. But the Donbas proved to be a much more daunting and complex challenge. Ethnic Ukrainians, Tartars, and others objected to Russian intervention. They rallied against the Russian rebels, forcing Putin to adjust his tactics. He learned to play musical chairs. Sometimes the Russians took charge of rebel operations; at other times, they needed to be more discreet.

Putin soon came to realize that it made much more sense for Russia to control Ukraine than occupy it. Not only would occupation be costly, it would also be bloody. What Putin wanted was a friendly, obliging government in Kiev. But, much to his regret, the moment he seized Crimea, he lost Ukraine, certainly the western half of the country. For many Ukrainians, the loss of Crimea stoked their nationalist, pro-Western sentiment, aligning them strategically with the European Union and even NATO. As Putin viewed this shift in Ukrainian sentiment, he had now to control the southeast quarter of Ukraine, meaning first to seize it, and then freeze it, much as he had frozen Abkhazia and South Ossetia in his mini-war with Georgia. Then, all other things being equal, he could arrange an acceptable modus vivendi between this corner of Ukraine and Kiev. In the process, Russia would have to be assured that Ukraine would not adopt anti-Russian policies and programs.

The Annexation of Crimea

Occupying Crimea was only half the job; the remaining half was to formally annex the peninsula. Putin wanted it all to appear to be a legitimate exercise, a natural extension of popular will. At a March 4 news conference, the question arose about the "legitimacy" of Russia's actions in Crimea. This bugged Putin. "We are often told our actions are illegitimate, but when I ask, 'Do you think everything you do is legitimate?' they say yes." It was time for Putin to point to his favorite bête noire. "Then," he continued, "I have to recall the actions of the United States in Afghanistan, Iraq, and Libya, where they either acted without any UN sanction or completely distorted the content of such resolutions, as was the case with Libya."[9] He was also asked about the presence of Russian troops in Crimea, a question that was to plague him throughout the enfolding crisis. (The Pentagon had just disclosed that as many as 20,000 Russian troops had entered Crimea.)[10]

"The people who were blocking the Ukrainian army units in Crimea were wearing uniforms that strongly resembled the Russian Army uniform," a Western journalist noted. "Were those Russian soldiers, Russian military?" he asked.

"Why don't you take a look at the post-Soviet states," Putin replied. "There are many uniforms there that are similar. You can go to a store and buy any kind of uniform."

"But were they Russian soldiers, or not?" the journalist persisted.

"Those were local self-defense units," Putin said.[11] That was a lie. The next day, the U.S. State Department listed it as number one of ten "false claims" Putin made about Ukraine.[12]

Likewise, the Russian minister of defense, Sergei Shoigu, when asked a similar question, responded with a two-word, back-of-the-hand dismissal: "Complete nonsense," he hissed. But, journalists pressed on, what about the Russian equipment? What about the armored vehicles with Russian military license plates? The minister replied that he had "no idea."[13] (Six weeks later, Putin would correct the record, admitting that there had been Russian troops in Crimea from the beginning.[14] Time and again, when trapped in a blatant lie, he would tell the truth, but only if it suited his purposes.)

To satisfy Putin's desire for a fig leaf of legitimacy, the newly installed pro-Russian leaders announced that there would be a referendum in Crimea. A simple set of questions would be put to the voters, a majority of whom were ethnic Russians: Do you want to remain part of Ukraine, or do you want to become part of Russia? On March 16, the day of the referendum, huge crowds formed in Simferopol's Lenin Square. They celebrated, many shouting "Russia! Russia!" while others carried the tricolored Russian flag. It was the same scene in Sevastopol, the naval base for Russia's Black Sea fleet. When exit poll numbers were aired later that evening, showing well over 90 percent had voted for union with Russia, everyone cheered, pumping their fists in the air.[15] (Skeptical scholars in Washington later came upon contradictory evidence, suggesting the percentage was much smaller.)

"We're Russian," one businessman told a reporter, "and we want to live in Russia." A film director echoed a similar theme, but added religion to his comment. "I'm Orthodox, and Orthodoxy began in Crimea," he said, referring to the conversion and baptism of the Kievan prince Vladimir the Great in 988. "Orthodox people must be reunited." He meant the Slavic, Orthodox union of Russia, Belarus, and Ukraine. "This is all Russia—greater Russia, minor Russia, and white Russia."[16] These strong sentiments upholding Slavic unity help explain why so many Russians have difficulty in viewing Ukraine as a separate, independent nation.

On Russia's border with eastern Ukraine, thousands of Russian troops began bivouacking, raising questions about a possible Russian drive into Ukraine, while across the border many thousands of pro-Russian demonstrators in Kharkov scuffled with police and shouted "Putin! Putin! Putin!" and "Crimea, we are with you." The demonstrators tried smashing into the governor's office, but they were repulsed, at least on this Sunday, and they then marched to the Russian consulate, according to a *New York Times* reporter, "carrying Russian flags and freshly made red banners that read 'Russian Spring.' "[17] Obama, in a call to Putin, stressed that the United States would not recognize the Crimean referendum and warned that Russia would now face "additional costs."[18] The "costs" were in a set of mild economic sanctions against Russia announced later that day by the White House. They included travel bans and asset freezes on several Russian officials, but not Putin.[19] Secretary Kerry, in a parallel call to Russian foreign minister Lavrov, pointed to "continuing provocations" in the Donbas and accused the Russians of fomenting unrest there.[20]

Both sides had already begun to talk past each other, volume going up, mutual understanding going down. They were to continue to follow that pattern, with only minor exceptions, for the rest of 2014 and well into 2015.

On March 18, 2014, Russia officially annexed Crimea, and Putin delivered Russia's explanation in the form of a history lesson, as much a Rorschach test on Putin's psyche as it was a justification for Russian irredentism. In the West Putin was demonized, but in Russia his poll numbers jumped to new highs. He had accurately read the mind of the Russian people. They needed a psychological boost, and Putin provided one.

"Today, there is a kind of renaissance. People are feeling that their country is strong again, but it is not about aggression," said Olga Kryshtanovskaya, a sociologist exploring Russia's political elite. "After the Soviet Union collapsed, we were losing territories—losing and losing and losing. Now, Crimea is a symbol that we have stopped losing, we are gaining."[21] Yet, at the time, it was not entirely obvious that Crimea was a win-win for Russia. Many in the West worried that a full-blown civil war could yet erupt in Ukraine, dragging Russia and the United States into a proxy conflict of no benefit to either country. Others, with a bent toward history, anguished over the prospect of Russians killing Ukrainians and Ukrainians killing Russians, knowing all the while that both peoples shared a common Slavic tradition, an Orthodox Christian faith, and an allegiance to a core history harkening back to tenth-century Kievan Rus'.

Though Ukrainians and Russians share a common faith, they have, since 1992, seen a split develop between their church hierarchies. Ukraine's Orthodox patriarch, Metropolitan Filaret, announced the creation of a new Ukrainian Orthodox Church, known as the Kiev Patriarchate. It was to stand on its own, independent of the Russian Orthodox Church—a religious divide reflecting the political divide that persists to this day.[22]

The prevalent fear in Ukraine was that Russia would never acknowledge its status as a free, independent, and sovereign nation. The prevalent fear in Russia was that the new regime in Kiev would be chronically pro-Western and anti-Russian, unable to see the inherent benefits of friendly relations with Russia. In fact, according to reliable polls, 68 percent of Ukrainians favored being both independent of and friendly toward Russia.

From Crimea to the Donbas

Over the next few weeks, the crisis in, and about, Ukraine deepened. Putin, having pocketed Crimea, ordered more Russian troops to the Ukrainian border (the number now approached 30,000) and dispatched small numbers of special forces, plus military equipment, across the border to such pivotal cities as Donetsk, Luhansk, and Kharkov. There they would, over the next few weeks, help organize a Donbas rebellion against the Kiev regime. Once again, Obama urged Putin to "move back [Russian] troops" from the Ukrainian border as a way of lowering tension.[23] He was baying at the moon. Obama was still of the view that he could offer Putin an "off-ramp," a way of de-escalating the crisis, and he would accept it. It was a naive view. The president and other Western leaders were angry at Putin and baffled by his aggressive actions. They were absorbed by one question: Was Putin planning to occupy all of Ukraine, or just the Donbas? Their uncertain answer: He coveted only the Donbas, but . . . would he then move against all of *Novorossiya*?

Everyone seemed to agree that Putin's strategy was to instigate a pro-Russian rebellion in the Donbas. There would be violence—that was assumed. Kiev would fight—if for no other reason than to retain its clout in this vitally important region. Putin was banking on local support, believing that ethnic Russians in the Donbas would be cheered by the Crimea takeover, thrilled by this show of Russian power and daring, and, in the belief that they had boarded a train of destiny, try to duplicate the Crimean fait accompli in southeastern Ukraine. They would first organize mass demonstrations. Then they would seize City Hall. And, finally, they would hold a referendum, a popular display of democratic legitimacy. That appeared to be Putin's plan, and, for the most part, it worked. From time to time, Putin needed to improvise, to coo one day and shout the next, to be belligerent and then accommodating. But, in the larger scheme of things, he stuck to his guns.

In Donetsk, on April 6, more than 2,000 pro-Russian demonstrators stormed City Hall and demanded a Crimean-style referendum. The sooner the better, they shouted. This time, they succeeded in occupying the first and second floors. They declared themselves to be a "People's Republic," proudly pro-Russian. They wanted nothing to do with Kiev, which they described as "foreign" and "fascist."

On the same day, in Kharkov and Lugansk, in an obviously well-coordinated operation, thousands of pro-Russian demonstrators went through the same motions. They too stormed City Hall, occupied the first and second floors, demanded the setting up of a "People's Assembly," and announced two referendums—one on May 11 for the "autonomy" of their region and the other on May 18 either for a declaration of independence or a joining up with Russia. In neither proposed referendum was there the option of remaining in Ukraine.

Over the next few days, separatist demonstrators echoed the same demands in other east Ukrainian cities, such as Mariupol, Horlivka, and Sloviansk, whose mayor, Nelya Shtepa, expressed the feelings of many Donbas natives. "I cannot object to them (rebels)," she said, "since [they] consider Russia [their] elder brother, and we cannot fight with Russia." Shtepa was later abducted temporarily by the rebels; then after her release the Kiev government accused her of supporting the rebels.[24] That in time was to change. Everyone understood that the separatists represented Russian policy and interests. Indeed, among the separatists were Russian "advisers." Everyone spoke Russian, which eased communication between the advisers and the advised.

On April 7, Ukrainian army and police regained control of the city halls in all the rebellious cities. There were casualties, but not too many. In Kiev, government officials, hearing of these mini-victories, entertained the notion that the rebels could easily be defeated. Without Russian backing for the rebels, yes—they could be defeated; but with Russian support, no—they could not be, and for one simple reason: Russia was the stronger party. During the summer, Kievan officials were to learn that Ukraine was no military match for Russia.

Proxy War

From April to September 2014, the Ukrainian civil war lurched forward, then stumbled backward, but followed an essentially predictable path—with each step, unfortunately, drawing the Russians and the West into deeper commitments to incompatible goals: for the Russians, a totally submissive Ukraine; for the West, a free and independent one. Neither side's goal could be realized without a bigger war—which neither side wanted.

At the start of what was to become a civil war in Ukraine, the rebels, working with Russian advisers, seemed to carry the day, occupying government buildings in one village, town, or city after another. April 12 was a particularly successful day, their pro-Russian message spreading through the Donbas. Kievan leaders were alarmed, realizing, perhaps for the first time, that the rebels were laying down a serious challenge to their rule over Ukraine's eastern half. Because they knew the Russians were supporting the rebels, they wondered how far Putin would go.

On April 15, fearing there was no option, Ukraine's acting president, Turchynov, announced the start of "an antiterrorist operation" against pro-Russian separatists.[25] The announcement sounded impressive, but it fooled no one. The Ukrainian army was simply not up to the task. Just as the rebels had been calling the Kiev leaders "fascists," Kiev was now referring to the rebels as "terrorists." Invective and bullets then began to be the only means of communication between the two sides.

Within a few days, however, the "anti-terror operation" stalled, when rebel separatists seized six armored vehicles in the town of Kramatorsk, taking the steam out of Kiev's "offensive."

Diplomats, meeting urgently in Geneva on April 17, mumbled about the need for "de-escalation" of the crisis, fearing a wider war. But the fighting seemed only to escalate when three Ukrainian police were killed in Mariupol and three rebels were killed near Sloviansk. Each side blamed the other for the increasing violence.

On May 1, Kiev upped the ante, when it reinstated conscription and warned that Ukraine was now on "full combat alert." That meant Ukraine was preparing for all-out war, adding organized, ultra-conservative, anti-Russian militias to the weak regular army. Whether this also meant that Kiev had struck a political deal with extremist, right-wing parties was not known.

On May 2, the civil war spread to Odessa, the jewel on the Black Sea. Pro-Russian and pro-Kiev demonstrators clashed. They carried flags and banners, shouted at one another and engaged in limited shoot-outs. Many were hurt, dozens arrested. In the ensuing mayhem, forty-two people were killed, many burned to death when the building in which they had sought safety was torched. Over the next few days, Odessa lived in violence and fear. Pro-Russian rebels went on a rampage, claiming they were defending the "Russian homeland." They beat Ukrainian officials and attacked police headquarters.[26] There was a growing fear, not just in Kiev but also in Moscow, that the fighting was now getting out of hand.

At this moment in the crisis, for the first time, Putin did what he was to do several times over the next few months: he adjusted his policy, while not abandoning his ultimate goal. He met in the Kremlin on May 7 with the Swiss president, Didier Burkhalter, who happened also to be the head of the Organization for Security and Cooperation in Europe (OSCE), and told him that Russia opposed the May 11 referendum, putting him in direct opposition to the rebels. He also said he favored "direct dialogue" between Kiev and the separatist rebels—which had always been his position, but not that of the rebels—and considered the upcoming May 25 presidential elections in Ukraine to be a step "in the right direction" (he had earlier opposed the elections). Putin also promised that Russian troops maneuvering near the Ukrainian border, a cause of considerable concern in the West, would be "withdrawn." "They are now not near the border," he assured the Swiss president.[27] For those in need of a sound-bite, Putin then summarized his position: "cease-fire, de-escalation of tensions, dialogue, and elections."

Putin struck all the right chords—welcome music to the ears of anxious Western diplomats who yearned for peace and harmony. If his intent was to head off another round of Western sanctions, which were then being threatened, he succeeded, at least for the time being. Prime Minister Arseniy Yatsenyuk, who had a way with words, dismissed Putin's new and nuanced position as "hot air."[28] Kiev's Foreign Ministry added that while Ukraine favored "a full-scale national dialogue," it would be "impossible and unthinkable with terrorists," meaning that Kiev would not talk to the rebels, not then anyway.[29]

In any case, there were two immediate questions: would the rebels obey Putin and postpone their May 11 referendum, and would Russian troops actually be withdrawn from the Ukrainian border? A rebel spokesman in Donetsk, patronizingly describing Putin as a "balanced politician," said he would have his answer in twenty-four hours. It was to be a "no"; the rebel referendum would be held as scheduled, suggesting an uneven, unpredictable relationship between the rebels and Putin. He did not have them under his complete control. Indeed, a number of rebels read Putin's objection to their May 11 referendum as a form of "betrayal." "So Russia has abandoned us as well," moaned one rebel spokesman. "Well, we will just have to fight the fascists on our own." Another rebel, describing Putin as a "coward," said: "Instead of helping the Russian people here, he is betraying us. He will pay for this with a revolution in Red Square."[30]

And his troop withdrawal promise? The United States and NATO said there was no evidence of a withdrawal. This was to happen again and again—a Putin promise of withdrawal, followed by either no action or such limited action as to be inconsequential.

A Brief Respite for Elections

May 25 was Election Day in most of Ukraine, except in the rebel-held southeast, and, not surprisingly, the man with the money won the presidency. Petro Poroshenko, known as the "Chocolate King"—a billionaire who owned a chocolate empire, a TV station, and many manufacturing plants—won 56 percent of the vote and became Ukraine's president at a testing time of war, economic chaos, and regional alienation. He also had extensive business interests in Russia, which reflected the closeness of Ukraine's economic relations with Russia but which also raised hope that he, better than other Ukrainian politicians, could somehow work with Putin and end the war. Actually, Poroshenko, who spoke both Russian and English, did establish a working relationship with Putin, and they did manage to arrange a fragile cease-fire in early September. But they did not trust each other (naturally, they represented the two sides of a bloody civil war), and they could not summon up the magic formula for ending the war. Two days before Poroshenko's election, Putin said he would "respect" the results, which was not as strong as "recognizing" the results, but, in the world of diplomacy, it was better than nothing.

Poroshenko, in his first TV address, promised to devote himself to bringing "peace to a united and free Ukraine," a phrase loaded with not quite hidden conditions: "united," meaning he would not allow the Donbas to break away from Ukraine; and "free," meaning a Ukraine free of Russian control. He had been in Ukrainian politics for a long time, and he knew the words and phrases that were red meat for Ukrainian nationalists. Like any pro, he tried to sound both firm and flexible. He pledged to visit the Donbas, while stressing that the "sovereignty and territorial integrity" of Ukraine would never be sacrificed. He announced new parliamentary elections on October 25, and he implied that he would negotiate with the rebels. He did not call them "terrorists."[31] Interestingly, in the next few days, the Ukrainian army, bolstered by unofficial alliances with right-wing militias, went on the offensive. Using combat jets, helicopters, and airborne troops, the army attacked a number of rebel positions, including a contested area near Donetsk airport. More than forty separatists were reportedly killed.[32] The rebels fought back. They shot down a Ukrainian helicopter near Sloviansk, killing fourteen troops, including a general, and they battled their way into two Ukrainian military bases near Luhansk, and occupied them.[33] Even before this round of fighting, NATO, encouraged by the Ukrainian offensive but wary of Russia's ultimate objectives, pledged to increase its force levels in Poland and the Baltics, partly to ease the concerns of allies close to Russia, partly to be ready if Russia moved to the west.[34]

An Estonian Nightmare

One nightmare in Washington at the time was that Putin would instigate pro-Russian demonstrations in Estonia, a NATO country where 26 percent of the population are ethnic Russians. Under this scenario, the demonstrators would allege anti-Russian persecution and request Russia's help. Putin would move a battalion of troops close to the Estonian border. He would not cross it, though he would repeat his March 18 promise to help Russians "wherever they lived." But he would do in Estonia what he had been doing in eastern Ukraine—sneak Russian "advisers" and equipment into the country. Estonia, alarmed over these developments, would seek NATO's immediate support, citing the Article 5 pledge that an attack on one NATO country would be regarded as an attack on all NATO countries. NATO would meet, denounce

Russia in blistering terms, perhaps even bolster Estonia's air force with the delivery of a half dozen American jet fighters, send a few warships to the Baltic waters, but in the end it would not send troops. The demonstrations would continue. Requests for Russian assistance would also continue, and Russian help in modest but unmistakable ways would be detected.

So what would NATO do? What would the United States do? If they did little to nothing, what would be the value of NATO? NATO, in fact, would be seen as toothless and irrelevant, and the United States would be seen as a "pitiful, helpless giant," to quote Richard Nixon when he announced the U.S. invasion of Cambodia in 1970.[35] The United States would be humiliated as Putin played cat-and-mouse games with President Obama.

In Washington, this would be regarded as a realistic war game, and the White House would not appreciate the outcome, but could do little about it. After the wars in Iraq and Afghanistan, and now suddenly countering the Islamic State in Iraq and Syria, Americans had no appetite for another war.

A Day of Nostalgia and Diplomacy

On June 6, 2014, the former World War II allies celebrated the seventieth anniversary of the D-Day landings in Normandy, France, but it was Ukraine that was on their minds and agendas. French president Francois Hollande made a special point of inviting Putin to the celebrations, even though he was a toxic guest as leader of a country that had recently seized Crimea and sent special forces into the southeast corner of Ukraine. Hollande noted that Russia had lost more than 20 million people during World War II, and that was reason enough for his presence. Hollande joined Germany's Angela Merkel in arranging for Putin to meet Poroshenko, who had also been invited. They did meet. They shook hands. They even discussed a possible cease-fire.[36]

Putin's spokesman, Dmitry Peskov, used positive language in briefing reporters, saying both leaders had agreed to call for "a speedy end to the bloodshed in southeastern Ukraine and to the military actions of both sides—the Ukrainian armed forces and the supporters of the federalization of Ukraine," meaning the rebels who wanted to set up independent "People's Republics" in Ukraine.[37] Once again, Putin used all of the right, reassuring words, but on the ground there was no evidence of restraint; in fact, none on either side of the fight. It was almost as though both Putin and Poroshenko felt the need at Normandy to articulate a policy of cease-fire and accommodation while knowing that the battle would still continue.

Obama had a fifteen-minute exchange with Putin. He pleaded with him to recognize the new Ukrainian leader as "legitimate" and to stop supporting the separatists in eastern Ukraine—no more sending of arms and materiel across the border! Obama did not include Russian advisers to his list, though he knew they were there. The president beseeched Putin to cooperate with Poroshenko to reduce tensions in Ukraine, else Russia would find itself facing another round of Western sanctions.[38]

Were Putin of a mind to heed Obama's calls for restraint, if he really wanted to stop the rebels, he could have done so by simply stopping the flow of Russian arms. But he did not want to stop the rebels, or perhaps could not stop the rebels even if he had wanted to. So the war not only continued but intensified, as spring slipped into summer. The Russians sent tanks into eastern Ukraine. They also sent Chechen mercenaries, trained guerrillas ordered to Donetsk by Chechen president Ramzan Kadyrov, a Putin ally. If there were Chechen casualties, the thinking went, the Russian people would not raise objections to their country's involvement in the war. They would, if there were Russian casualties.

The Ukrainians, after heavy fighting, took back Mariupol. The rebels shot down a Ukrainian military transport plane as it was about to land in Luhansk, killing all forty-nine on board. Poroshenko called it a "criminal act of terrorism" and demanded that fighting stop in a week. A rebel, identifying himself only as Pyotr, told Reuters, "This is how we work. The fascists can bring as many reinforcements as they want, but we will do this every time." In Kiev, several hundred extremist demonstrators, some wearing balaclavas, attacked the Russian Embassy, hurling eggs and petrol bombs, smashing windows, tearing down the flag, and overturning cars with diplomatic plates. One demonstrator carried a placard reading "Russia is a killer." Russia objected angrily, labeling the attack a "grave violation of Ukraine's international obligations." Police in Kiev could have intervened, but chose to stand back.[39]

On June 20, hoping to break the escalating cycle of violence, Poroshenko announced a week-long cease-fire.[40] Three days later, the rebels accepted the idea, and the cease-fire actually held for a few more days before it began to fray at the edges. But for a brief time it held, and perhaps to extend this flicker of optimism, Putin had his parliament, the Duma, invalidate one of its early wartime resolutions authorizing Putin to use military force in Ukraine.[41] He seemed to be operating on dual tracks: sustaining the rebel insurgency with arms and advisers while, at the same time, signaling the West that he would like to end the fighting. The EU applauded his move, but still warned of additional sanctions if Russia did not do more to stop the insurgency.

Of course, Poroshenko had his own strategy, focused almost entirely on linking Ukraine's future to the West, but he did make continuous, if unsuccessful, efforts to mollify Putin's obvious anxieties about his westward tilt. According to some observers, Poroshenko cared less about mollifying Putin's anxieties than about advancing his own agenda, even if that meant engaging in deception and lying, which was par for this course.

On June 27, for example, a day he described as the most important in Ukraine's history since independence in 1991, he signed an "association agreement" with the EU, the same agreement that Yanukovych had, at the last minute, refused to sign nine months earlier, triggering the Maidan revolt.[42] For the record, Poroshenko stressed his peaceful intent, saying he would extend the cease-fire. He would not rush into its implementation and thereby further alarm Russia. He would wait for a better time. But while he spoke in accommodating terms about the EU agreement, and even Putin, he displayed a cunning toughness about prosecuting the war in eastern Ukraine. Three days later, without warning, he suddenly switched tactics, canceled his ceasefire overture, and ordered the Ukrainian military to swing into an even higher gear and, if possible, smash the rebel insurgency.[43]

Though under-equipped and under-funded, relying heavily on right-wing militias to augment its offensive clout, the Ukrainian army retook Sloviansk and smaller surrounding towns on July 5 and then began advancing on Donetsk, rocketing its suburbs and killing rebels.[44] Caught by surprise, rebel separatists retreated, blowing up bridges as they abandoned fixed positions. They built barricades in Donetsk and Luhansk, as though preparing for a final stand, but they were far from giving up the fight. On July 11, one rebel battalion killed more than twenty Ukrainian soldiers near Luhansk, and on July 14, armed with sophisticated anti-aircraft missiles, they shot down a second Ukrainian transport plane flying at 21,000 feet.[45] This was not a routine kill, not "just another day at the office" during a war. The rebels could not have shot down a plane at that altitude unless they had a special kind of Russian missile. Obviously the Russians had given it to them.

Just as Poroshenko had changed tactics, so too did Putin. He recognized quickly that the battlefield balance was shifting—that the Ukrainian army was now on the attack, and the rebels were thrown into hasty retreat. Because he would never accept the idea of defeat, because he was determined to win, he ordered a major boost in Russian military supplies to the rebels—and not just supplies, but advisers and special forces too. If Poroshenko wanted a fight, Putin would give him one.

The *Moscow Times* wrote: "On Wednesday [July 16], they [rebels] claimed to have hit two Su-25 attack jets near Horlovka in the Donetsk region. On Tuesday they claimed to have downed another Su-25 near Snezhnoye in the same area. . . . Earlier, insurgents claimed to have downed several other military and transport aircrafts, including at least seven Su-25 attack jets, three Su-24 attackers, one Su-027 fighter jet, an Il-76 military transport aircraft, and at least 17 Mi-8 and Mi-24 military helicopters."[46]

CHAPTER 16

The Tragedy of a Malaysian Airliner

A retreat—or, worse yet, a defeat—in Ukraine [was] not an option.

LEON ARON, RUSSIAN SPECIALIST

NOT EVERYTHING IN WAR, or life, goes according to plan. Tragedies often intrude. On July 17, over the rebel-held town of Grabovo in eastern Ukraine, Malaysian Airlines Flight 17, en route from Amsterdam to Kuala Lumpur and flying at an altitude of 33,000 feet, with 298 people aboard, including three infants, was shot out of the sky by a Russian SA-17 antiaircraft missile (a BUK ground-to-air launcher), falling to earth in hundreds of pieces. Bodies and wreckage were scattered for miles over empty fields. No one survived.[1]

World reaction was one of horror and outrage. The United Nations went into emergency session. The White House called for a "full, credible, and unimpeded international investigation."[2] Who was responsible? The rebel separatists, using sophisticated Russian equipment, or Russians, fighting in the Ukraine war? It was a fundamental question, demanding an answer, and it hardened anti-Russian sentiment throughout the Western world, making additional sanctions almost inevitable.

The Ukrainian Security Service released audio tapes of two intercepted telephone conversations, one of them involving a Russian officer, named Igor Girkin but using the cover-name of Igor Strelkov, later identified as the military commander of rebel forces in eastern Ukraine. He was heard informing a Russian intelligence officer that the rebels had just shot down another Ukrainian transport plane, similar to the one they had shot down earlier in the week. In the second conversation, two unidentified rebel fighters, one of them speaking from the crash site, were overheard saying that the rebels had shot down a plane, which turned out to be the Malaysian airliner.[3] One Pentagon theory was that the rebels, using Russian anti-aircraft missiles, were targeting a Ukrainian military aircraft flying not too far from the Malaysian aircraft. Their missiles, according to this theory, missed their intended target and then mistakenly "locked" onto the civilian airliner and, moments later, blew it up.

No one was really certain what happened, but almost 300 people, most of them Dutch citizens, died as a result of this tragic mistake. No one believed that the passenger plane was deliberately targeted by either the Russians or the rebels. But the tragedy was proof once again that by sending sophisticated armaments to the rebels, the Russians were playing with fire—and this time they got burned.

Obama called Putin, again urging the Russian leader to stop the war. Putin agreed that "this is a completely unacceptable thing," but he expressed no remorse and blamed Ukraine for the downing of the plane. "This tragedy would not have happened," he later told a TV audience, "if there had been peace on that land, or in any case if military operations in southeastern Ukraine had not been renewed." He was referring here to Ukrainian president Petro Poroshenko's decision to go on the offensive. "Without doubt the government of the territory on which it happened (Ukraine) bears responsibility for this frightening tragedy. We will do everything that we can so that an objective picture of what happened can be achieved."[4] Putin never veered from his early belief that the government that replaced Yanukovych in late February was "illegitimate." Before his bar of justice, it was guilty of everything. Before the bar of European public opinion, though, especially after the shooting down of the Malaysian airliner, Putin was guilty, and many felt he should be punished. It followed then that, on July 29–30, the United States and the EU announced another round of sanctions against Russia, more severe than the earlier ones. These were directed at Russia's oil sector, the key segment of the Russian economy, cutting off supplies of dual technologies and advanced drilling components and limiting state-owned bank access to EU debt markets.[5]

A Summertime of Escalation

August was the bloodiest month of the war in 2014. The Ukrainians had gone on the offensive; and, for a time, as they closed in on Donetsk, the separatist capital, it seemed as if they might win. From the suburbs, now under their control, they rocketed the center of the city, where streets were empty and restaurants closed. Luhansk, the other major city under rebel control, offered similar scenes. The rebels were clearly in trouble, and, as a result, Putin faced one of the most difficult decisions of his presidency. Should he send the Russian army across the border, crush the Ukrainians, and win the war? That was one realistic option, though it would leave Russia in absolute control of Ukraine, an outcome that Putin sought at this time to avoid. Or should he pursue essentially the same policy, only now, for a limited time, take full control of the rebel cause: send a relatively small fighting force into Ukraine, 3,000 to 4,000 well-trained troops, with proper leadership and with enough sophisticated weaponry, to turn the Ukrainian offensive into a Russian victory; and with the rebels back in the driver's seat, arrange for a cease-fire. That too was a realistic option, and it was the one he chose to pursue. "A retreat—or, worse yet, a defeat—in Ukraine [was] not an option," concluded Russian expert Leon Aron.[6] The upshot, though, was a major escalation of the war.

One problem for the Russians, hardly the most important, was secrecy—how to maintain it, while large troop convoys, heavy weapons, and supplies moved across the Russian-Ukrainian border. On one occasion, 260 trucks "thundered across Russia," according to a *New York Times* report, "bearing thousands of tons of humanitarian aid for the people of the besieged Ukrainian city of Luhansk." It was hard to hide "the latest, almost farcical encounter between Moscow and Kiev."[7]

One reason why the Russians kept losing credibility was that a number of their military commanders, based in Donetsk and Luhansk, gave interviews to Western reporters. One was Aleksandr Khodakovsky, the Ukrainian-born commander of the Vostok Battalion, the largest separatist militia in Donetsk. He admitted that Russians were in his militia, but the "overwhelming majority," he insisted, were local Ukrainians. In fact, there was evidence pointing to a significant Russian presence. In a major battle near the rebel capital between his forces and the Ukrainians, forty of his fighters were killed. Thirty-three of them were Russian citizens, their bodies placed in refrigerated trucks to be returned to Russia. Khodakovsky put the Ukraine war in a broader context. "Everyone understands that this is a war between Russia and America," he said, "and we must be for one side or the other." He obviously chose the Russian side.[8] Another commander was Vladimir Antyufeyev, recently transferred from Transnistria, the breakaway, pro-Russian province of Moldova, to the Donetsk People's Republic, where he was immediately named deputy prime minister. He did not have to run for office. Antyufeyev told a *New York Times* reporter that he was a "professional," responsible for maintaining "social order . . . and state security." He explained his mission. "The people have a right to live on their land," he said, "to speak the language they want. Only a state can defend that right." Only Russia, or the Donetsk People's Republic, could provide those guarantees.

A colleague from Transnistria, Valery Litskai, added a relevant detail: "He coordinated his work 90 percent with Moscow, and he never disguised it."[9] Igor Strelkov was still another commander, but he was not enjoying the fame he accidentally earned from his role in the Malaysian tragedy. He too was a professional soldier, a former colonel of Russian Special Forces in the 2001 Chechen War. His troops in eastern Ukraine were Russian or Caucasian "volunteers"—primarily, he stressed, because he could not depend on local recruits. For a long time, in the Donbas, Strelkov was considered a hero, a brilliant strategist, an ideologist. He was the boss. When people needed information or a decision, they turned to Strelkov. One of his key advisers, Igor Druzd, told the *Daily Beast's* Anna Nemstova that Russians had to come to the Donbas in order to "prevent a revolution like the Maidan in Kiev from spreading to Moscow."[10] It was almost as if Strelkov considered the war in Ukraine to be a defensive operation designed to protect Russia.

Not surprisingly, soon after fresh Russian troops and supplies entered the fight, the tide turned decisively in the rebels' favor. Heavy fighting erupted in and around Donetsk and Luhansk in mid-August, and, for the first time in months, rebel forces, now supported by Russian armored personnel carriers, broke out of their defensive perimeter, expanding their base of operations and moving south of Donetsk to Amvrosiyivka, a small but key transit point, should the Russians decide to widen the battlefield and make a push for the port of Mariupol. In fact, this is what they did later in the month. Heavy casualties ensued on both sides, but the rebels were feeling less pain—they were on a roll and the Ukrainians were retreating. Over the next few weeks, according to Fyodor Lukyanov, editor of *Russia in Global Affairs*, the Russians destroyed 65 percent of the heavy armament that the Ukrainians had committed to the conflict.

Putin's point seemed to be the obvious one. He was signaling Ukraine and the West that they could not achieve a military victory in Ukraine—only Russia could achieve such a victory; and it was time to make a deal, one that of course would accommodate Russia's interests. This was an accommodation the West was not ready to make. The reason was simple: Russia was the aggressor, and aggressors were not to be rewarded.

Putin, in August, could have been enjoying life. His popularity remained very high, measuring in the 80s, and there were no mini-Maidan protests on the immediate horizon. But he was not blind to a number of serious problems, each raising questions about the wisdom of his Ukraine policy. One was the economy. Although in public Putin continued to sound optimistic ("The fundamental factors supporting stability are very strong, very reliable," he assured Russian financiers), he was hearing troublesome reports from his economic advisers. The ruble, always "wobbly," to quote the *New York Times*, dropped in September to its lowest level against the dollar in nearly twenty-five years. Its value had fallen 23 percent in the preceding three months. So far, the Russian stock market was down by 3 percent in 2014, while global markets had risen by 9 percent. Oil prices were down dramatically, and this drop gravely impacted Russia's budget, 50 percent of which was dependent on oil profits. Russia was, in short, mired in stagflation, with an inflation rate of 8 percent and a growth rate hovering near 0.[11] Most striking, perhaps, German Gref, head of Russia's largest bank, Sberbank, said Russia seemed again to be turning to state-run economic development, and this was bad. The Soviet Union, he said, collapsed because of the "mind-boggling incompetence of the Soviet leadership. They did not respect the laws of economic development." He decried the fact that half of Russia's economy was in "monopolized industries." "You cannot motivate people through the gulag, like in the Soviet Union."[12] Gref seemed, not so indirectly, to be criticizing Putin's stewardship of the Russian economy. Igor Bunin, head of Moscow's Center for Political Technology, offered his own grim judgment. "The economic and business elite is just in horror," he said. "Any sign of rebellion, and they'll be brought to their knees."[13]

The collective judgment of Russia's financiers and economists seemed to be that Putin's policy in Ukraine, which produced punishing sanctions, a collapsing ruble, and sharp reductions in foreign investments, had badly hurt the Russian economy and should be changed. *The Economist* headline on November 22, 2014, said Russia's "wounded economy" was "closer to crisis than the West or Vladimir Putin realize."[14]

So what was Putin's response to these seemingly dire judgments? He brushed aside all negative judgments, as though none of them was worth listening to, and, with characteristic bravado, on August 6 ordered his own sanctions on all agricultural imports from countries that had imposed sanctions on Russia. Henceforth, none would now be permitted into Russia. This decision, which could paralyze billions of dollars in trade, had the earmarks of a Putin in a rage. He too could play the game of sanctions, he was, in effect, saying to the West. In 2013 Russia imported $43 billion in foreign foodstuffs. Now Russians would have to get along without them. According to the Kremlin's website, Putin, by targeting Western food products, was ensuring the "safety of Russia."[15] Prime Minister Medvedev explained that the sanctions would stimulate the Russian economy to produce substitutes for the imported foodstuffs. Economists said that even if Russia learned to produce the substitutes, it would take many years before it could make up for the lost imports.

In mid-October, Putin met with his minister of economic development, Alexei Ulyukayev, who itemized the bad news. A recession was imminent, the minister predicted. Inflation was getting out of hand, and the ruble and oil were in free fall. Western sanctions somehow had to be lifted. They were worsening, not causing, many of Russia's economic problems. How, Putin asked, can we get them lifted? Ulyukayev replied, we were hoping you knew how. What Putin suspected was that if he altered his Ukraine policy, the West would likely ease and maybe even lift its sanctions against Russia. But for Putin, a change in his Ukraine policy remained out of the question. He asked Ulyukayev for options. One was "economic liberalization," and Putin accepted it. In essence, it was a way of easing the financial burden of corruption on all enterprises, amounting to tens of billions of dollars in bribes and kickbacks. "Wastefulness, an inability to manage state funds and even outright bribery, theft, won't go unnoticed," Putin said in mid-November. Yet, Russian economists had come to the rather gloomy conclusion that the Russian economy, as it was currently constituted, could not survive without corruption.[16]

Russian mothers were another problem. If their sons were indeed engaged in a foreign war, they felt they had a right to know. Were their sons fighting in Ukraine? Were they wounded? Were any of them killed? No official information was made available, and mothers were becoming irritable. Ever since the Russian involvement in the Afghan war in the 1980s, Russian mothers have been asking questions, and demanding answers. In the old days, when the communist system held ordinary Russians in an iron grip, few mothers (or fathers, for that matter) would have had the gumption to ask serious national security questions of government officials, let alone expect to elicit honest answers. But when Russian troops began returning from Afghanistan in the late 1980s, many wounded or hooked on dope, mothers were desperate for information about their sons. Who survived? How many wounded? Needing help?

Since then, Russia has fought two wars in Chechnya, one in Georgia, and now Russia was again fighting a war, this one in neighboring Ukraine. Mothers wanted to know what was going on, and, through the controlled media, Putin's government provided only limited, self-serving, highly nationalistic coverage of unfolding events. Mothers talked to reporters, even foreign reporters. They wrote letters. They were no longer willing to be silent spectators; they objected to news blackouts. A BBC television crew visited a family that had lost a son in Ukraine. The crew was attacked by masked hooligans, their equipment destroyed, the family threatened.[17] Poorly informed mothers constituted a restless, dissatisfied, unafraid constituency, for whom Putin was not an unapproachable god.

A Cease-fire, at Last

By the end of August, Putin and Poroshenko, each for reasons of his own, thought it was time for a cease-fire. The war was, to quote one anxious German official, "slipping out of control." The Russian and Ukrainian leaders were exchanging angry accusations in the media, while trying privately to arrange a meeting. They had not met since early June when they attended the Normandy commemoration, though they had spoken on the phone a few times since. Minsk, it was decided, would be a convenient place for a negotiation. It was where the two sides had met in 1991, when the issue was the crafting of post-Soviet independence, not war.

During the Minsk negotiations, the two sides found time to play to the galleries—propaganda always a valued commodity in twenty-first-century warfare. Rebels invited Western cameramen to take pictures of captured Ukrainian soldiers paraded through the streets of Donetsk, visual proof they were winning the war, and Ukrainian authorities gleefully released embarrassing videos of captured Russian paratroopers, who, according to Putin, were not in Ukraine. Reporters knew better and asked, how many Russians were actually fighting in Ukraine? Rebel leader Aleksandr Zakharchenko answered that there were as many as 4,000 Russian "civilians" and "soldiers on leave."[18] Other sources reported that as many as 10,000 Russian troops had been in Ukraine since the start of the war, rotated in and out, a figure that could not be confirmed.[19] The first of what was to become a series of exchanges was organized in August: ten Russian paratroopers captured in Ukraine for sixty-three Ukrainian soldiers captured near Donetsk.

Finally, Poroshenko and Putin met on August 26. They could not reach agreement on a cease-fire, but they promised to meet again. They left their respective experts behind to keep the negotiations going.[20] While the leaders talked, their troops fought, and the war widened. The rebels gained easy access to much of eastern Ukraine and began advancing to the west and south. The Ukrainian high command, for its part, announced regretfully that nearly 700 of its soldiers had just been taken captive, and the airport at Luhansk had to be abandoned.[21]

All-out war seemed just around the corner. NATO pledged to create a "rapid response force" of several thousand troops for the protection of East European members threatened by Russia.[22] As a counter-point, Russia said it had to alter its military strategy because of NATO's "infrastructure getting closer to [Russia's] borders." It provided no details.[23]

The United States tried, with warm words and quick top-level visits, to reassure the anxious Estonians, Latvians, and Lithuanians that, in their uneasy relations with Russia, the Baltic states would not be left alone. All three had been admitted to NATO in 2004. On September 3, Obama flew into the cozy, picturesque capital of Tallinn, Estonia. People there were deeply unsettled by Putin's repeated claim that Russia had a "right" to protect the interests of Russian speakers everywhere. As noted earlier, 23 percent of Estonians were ethnic Russians. (Twenty-eight percent of Latvia's population were ethnic Russians, and five percent of Lithuania's.) The fear was that if these ethnic Russians were to engage in mass protests alleging that they were being mistreated, might Russia then intervene?

The White House said that Obama wanted everyone to understand that it was "not OK for large countries to flagrantly violate the territorial integrity of their smaller neighbors."[24] Nice, decent, appropriate words, but what would the United States in fact do if Russia violated the borders of a small Baltic neighbor? Lithuania's president, the outspoken Dalia Grybauskaite, told the BBC that if NATO responded meekly to a clear Russian challenge in the Baltics, "sooner or later, we will be facing the aggressor near our border, literally."[25] Could Lithuania hold off a Russian attack? Could Latvia, or Estonia? Obviously, no; but would NATO? What in fact would NATO do? Western leaders have repeatedly pledged that NATO would act to stop Russian aggression. Yet, questions remained, and doubts as well.

Obama's next stop was Wales, the site of a NATO summit, devoted in large part to Ukraine. Poroshenko was invited, even though Ukraine was not a member. (Prime Minister Arseniy Yatsenyuk had warned from Kiev that Ukraine would soon ask for NATO membership, which, if granted, would severely test the limits of Putin's patience.)[26] NATO took a split-level approach to Ukraine. On one level were warm-hearted invitations, reassuring words, high-level visits, and proclamations, such as the one that concluded this summit. NATO agreed that it "stands with Ukraine" in the face of Russia's "destabilizing" actions. It called on Russia "to pull back its troops" and end its "illegal" annexation of Crimea. Secretary-General Anders Fogh Rasmussen, who enjoyed nothing more, it seemed, than appearing before western TV cameras, sat next to Ukraine's Poroshenko and stated that NATO's partnership with Ukraine was "strong," and NATO was "determined to make it even stronger."[27] Behind cupped hands, officials went further, promising Poroshenko that another round of sanctions was imminent. These words were proper for the occasion but somehow sounded sanitized and scrubbed.

But, on another level, NATO seemed cool, pragmatic, and unemotional about its dealings with Ukraine. It would do its diplomatic best to de-escalate the crisis, it made clear, but it would not be sending troops or heavy weapons to Ukraine. Poroshenko knew, as did Putin, that, in the Minsk minuet, he might have to bow to Moscow and make concessions in order to reach a mutually acceptable cease-fire agreement, one that would hold off further Russian/rebel military advances. In this respect, Putin held the trump cards. Poroshenko did what he could to advance Ukraine's cause: he attended every meeting, to which he had been invited; he delivered impassioned speeches; he pledged his devotion to democracy and freedom; and he embraced every NATO member, as though each was a family member. But as an experienced politician and businessman, he had to have known there was a big difference between the words of reassurance that he was hearing and the "boots on the ground" that he needed if he cherished any hopes of prevailing in this ongoing conflict.[28] From Wales, Obama flew home, but, on September 5, Poroshenko flew back to Minsk, where he and Putin finally agreed on a cease-fire plan.[29] Poroshenko announced "final agreement," but the Kremlin quickly corrected him. There was no "final agreement," it said, but there was a loosely worded understanding signed by representatives of Russia, Ukraine, the rebels, and the Organization for Security and Cooperation in Europe (OSCE). Putin did not want to be on record as agreeing to a deal. Still, whether an agreement or just an understanding, it called for a cease-fire, a pulling back of forces, a humanitarian corridor, and an exchange of prisoners, all substantive achievements. Between the lines, there was another understanding, too. Putin and the rebel clients demanded a quid pro quo: In exchange for the cease-fire, the Donbas would obtain a "special status," to be translated in concrete terms as the rebels wished it to be. It would still be a part of Ukraine, but it would be an autonomous part, where Russian would be one of the two official languages and relations with Russia would be close and cooperative.

Prime Minister Yatsenyuk, who was always in an ideological tug-of-war with Poroshenko, read the text of the September 5 agreement, sighed deeply, and concluded that, without strong backing by the United States and the EU, Ukraine "could not manage with Russia on our own."[30] Yatsenyuk was right, of course, but Poroshenko had to be pragmatic and realistic. He understood that unless Putin was satisfied with the deal, there would not be one. For the time being, the key was maintaining the cease-fire, if at all possible. Everyone expected violations, but if the patchwork cease-fire could hold, then maybe, with additional talks, it could be extended into a "permanent cease-fire." Both sides needed a break. The war had already cost more than 2,600 killed, many more thousands wounded, and almost a million refugees displaced from the Donbas.

Putin vs. Nuland: An Always Available Irritant

Whenever Putin got a chance to attack the United States and Poroshenko's government, he seized it. On August 29, while addressing a National Youth Forum, he returned to one of his favorite themes—how the United States and Western Europe were guilty of initiating, and then supporting, the "coup" in late February that toppled Yanukovych from power. "There are no fools among us," Putin proclaimed. "We all saw the symbolic pies handed out on the Maidan. This information and political support, what does it mean?" He was referring to Victoria Nuland, a U.S. assistant secretary of state, handing out cookies in the Maidan to anti-Yanukovych demonstrators in an effort to win their allegiance. He answered his own question: "This was a case of the United States and European countries getting fully involved in a change of power, an anticonstitutional change of power carried out by force, and the part of the country that does not accept this change is being suppressed with brute military force and the use of planes, artillery, multiple launch rocket systems and tanks." He was, in fact, vastly exaggerating what happened, but once he believed something, he stubbornly clung to it. "If this is what today's European values are about, then I am more than disappointed," Putin added.[31]

Problems, Problems and More Problems

The big question in Kiev in the fall of 2014: Would the cease-fire hold, at least until the October 26 parliamentary elections in Ukraine? If it did, there was a good chance the elections could be held. Poroshenko invested time and treasure in organizing a political party he brazenly named the "Bloc of Petro Poroshenko." In the run-up to the election, his bloc was heavily favored to beat Yulia Tymoshenko's "Fatherland" and Prime Minister Yatsenyuk's "People's Front." He campaigned as a reformer. "I have enough political will," he would often affirm, "to implement the developed strategy of reforms. But I also need a majority in the Parliament." Then, after taking a deep breath, he summarized his message: "Reformist majority, not corrupt one. Pro-Ukrainian and pro-European, not pro-Soviet."[32]

He knew, as did the other presidential candidates, that Ukraine's politics were notoriously and pervasively corrupt, a state-sponsored kleptocracy governed by the president, along with a band of oligarchs devoted to the acquisition of money and power and with opaque and troubling connections to Kremlin intelligence operatives. Poroshenko tried running a campaign dedicated to reform, transparency, and the election of a pro-Western parliament.

One young politician, a former journalist now working for Poroshenko, looked skeptically at the voting system and pronounced that it was "the same as it was two years ago. Oligarchs in Ukraine did not give up after Maidan. They are still very influential players." A supporter of one local candidate laughingly added, "Before we used to change old socks for old socks. Now it's time to put on new socks."[33] And, surprisingly, the voters put on "new socks" during the October 26 election. Instead of winning handsomely, as he and everyone else had expected, Poroshenko's Bloc came in second behind Yatsenyuk's "People's Front," not by much, but enough to suggest a split between the president and his prime minister on one of the most basic problems facing the new Ukraine—how to deal with Putin's Russia. Poroshenko obviously preferred the negotiating track, though he had already shown he would fight, if necessary. Yatsenyuk, from the start, took a much harder line, never trusting the Russians to keep their word in any negotiation and believing that, with military help from the United States and NATO, Ukraine could hold its own and maintain an independent course.

The differences between the two men might have been more in appearance than reality. Both were nationalist leaders. Both distrusted Putin. Both were prepared to talk and, if need be, to fight. But Yatsenyuk took a more pugnacious, in-your-face attitude to the Russians, and that appealed to many frustrated Ukrainians who saw no end to the corruption in their society and to Russia's unchecked aggression in Crimea and in the southeastern corner of their divided country. Poroshenko, sensitive to the political winds, immediately offered Yatsenyuk the job of prime minister in a new coalition government, and Yatsenyuk accepted, in this way heading off a collision between them and giving Ukraine its best shot going forward at establishing an effective, coordinated leadership.

Poroshenko and Yatsenyuk faced two immediate problems: how to strengthen a cease-fire with the rebels, which seemed yet again to be unraveling; and how to persuade Putin to lift the lid on the sale of natural gas and oil to Ukraine—at acceptable prices. As it turned out, fortuitously, Putin was ready at this point in the crisis to reopen the spigots on the sale and delivery of natural gas and oil to Ukraine and Western Europe. It was another one of his periodic gestures, ever since the war started, to soften Russia's image in Western Europe. Also, if Putin anticipated another upsurge of fighting, which he did, he wanted to be able to show everyone that, with winter approaching, Russia was not without a heart. He was ready to negotiate, which meant that Ukraine had to pay Russia back for past shipments of gas and oil, billions of dollars' worth; if it did, then Russia would resume new shipments, beneficial to both Ukraine and Western Europe. All Ukraine had to do was attract new loans from the West. And so it did, from the EU. On its own, Ukraine had no money; it was broke. The energy deal was struck shortly after the October 26 election.[34]

On the problem of the fraying cease-fire, it seemed in early November that the gods were concocting new difficulties every day. It was not enough that both sides disliked and distrusted each other, resulting in persistent daily violations of the cease-fire. Now, they also found one more reason for a new round of warfare, and they had conflicting interpretations of the September 5 agreement on the matter of elections. The elections were to take place, the agreement said, in accordance with Ukrainian law. Kiev interpreted that to mean that Ukraine could hold a national election on October 26, which it did "legally," and then schedule local elections on December 7.

No way! objected rebel leaders. We'll hold our own elections in the Donetsk and Luhansk People's Republics on November 2, a week later. This defiant decision triggered a new round of rhetorical warfare, in advance of another upsurge in fighting. Poroshenko quickly announced that Ukraine would not recognize the results of the November 2 elections, and neither would the United States or the EU. In Western eyes, they would be "illegal" and a "clear violation" of the September 5 agreement. Russia added its voice, inevitably, to the widening dispute. Foreign Minister Sergi Lavrov gently warned Ukraine to mind its own business. If Donetsk and Luhansk wanted to vote, then that was their right. "We hope that it will be a free declaration of will," he said, "and that nobody will try to ruin it from the outside."[35]

Ukraine could bark at Donetsk and Luhansk, but it was powerless to stop the election. It had lost control over the southeastern corner of the country, which was now under the effective control of Putin's rebels. On November 2, hundreds of thousands of Ukrainians voted in Donetsk for Aleksandr Zakharchenko, a 38-year-old former electrician, and in Luhansk for Igor Plotnitsky, a 50-year-old ex-Soviet army officer and former consumer protection agency employee. Both were inexperienced, heavily favored, self-proclaimed prime ministers, and both won in an election lacking any suspense.[36] To drum up a ripple of excitement, the polling places provided food in addition to ballots. A *New*

York Times reporter noted that "gigantic piles of heads of cabbage, potatoes, carrots, beets and onions" were on sale outside at "far below market price." At other polling places, vegetables were being given away free of charge, while men with accordions and three-piece Slavic folk bands serenaded the voters—anything apparently to build up the vote count. The purpose of the November 2 election, opined one Donetsk politician, was to boost the legitimacy of the state. "By the end of the day," he said, confidently, "the Donetsk People's Republic will have a new status. The election confirms our status as a state."[37] Two days later, Zakharchenko and Plotnitsky each raised his right hand and took the oath of office as "president" of the Donetsk and the Luhansk People's Republics. Both got a promotion. Yury Ushakov, Putin's foreign policy adviser, told reporters that Russia "respected" the "will of the people," while drawing a distinction between "recognizing" and "respecting"—"recognizing" being more formal, carrying more diplomatic weight, than "respecting." "These are different words," he stressed. "The word 'respect' was chosen deliberately. We fundamentally respect the voters' expression of will."[38] The distinction meant little—Russia backed the November 2 elections and the results. And Russia did a lot more.

Over the next few days, Russia sent a column of thirty-two tanks, sixteen howitzer artillery pieces, and thirty transport trucks, loaded with troops and ammunition, across the border. NATO confirmed these reports. General Philip Breedlove, the four-star U.S. Air Force general who served both as the commander of the U.S. European Command and as NATO's supreme allied commander, stressed that the convoys included "Russian tanks, Russian artillery, Russian air defense systems, and Russian combat troops."[39] But for what purpose? Was Russia preparing to launch a major offensive, or was Russia merely protecting its rebel clients against a possible Ukrainian offensive? Par for the course, the Russians denied Breedlove's report.

On November 7, according to Kiev officials, rebels opened fire on Ukrainian positions near the Donetsk airport. Ukrainian artillery fired back, killing up to 200 rebels, suggesting a major boost in casualties, probably on both sides.[40] On November 8, AP reporters and cameramen took photos and video of three columns of more than eighty unmarked Russian military vehicles entering Ukraine. When pressed, Russian spokesmen again denied that Russia was sending arms and troops into Ukraine.[41] In Kiev, Poroshenko met urgently with his national security team and ordered reinforcements to be sent to Ukrainian military positions in the east. He went on television and told the Ukrainian people that he had not yet given up on the September 5 agreement, but if the newly reinforced rebels launched fresh attacks, Ukraine had to be ready to stop the "spread of this cancerous tumor." Russia, meantime, called for new peace talks between the rebels and the Kiev authorities, adding that, like Poroshenko, it too had not yet given up on the September 5 agreement.[42]

Neither Putin nor Poroshenko wanted to be the one who announced the death knell of the September 5 agreement, but if it was not already dead, it was well on its way to dying; and everyone knew it. So what now? Andrei Purgin, deputy prime minister of the Donetsk Republic, told reporters that the Ukrainian army had launched an "all-out war" against rebel positions.[43] Vladyslav Selesnyov, a Ukrainian military spokesman, denied the rebel charge. "We refute these allegations," he said. "We're strictly fulfilling the Minsk memorandum on a ceasefire."[44]

In Moscow, Putin met with his senior defense and security officials, focusing on "the deterioration of the situation in the Donbas due to repeated violations of the ceasefire by the armed forces of Ukraine." A Reuters reporter in Donetsk said he could see no sign of conflict in or around the separatist capital. Yet, from other sources, came reports of "heavy artillery fire" rocketing Donetsk and renewed fighting near Luhansk.

By mid-November, it was clear Putin was supplying the rebel fighters in Donetsk and Luhansk with enough weaponry and manpower to withstand any possible Ukrainian military assault. The heavy resupply might also have been intended to leave Russians in a position to contain any wild rebel plans for an offensive aimed at a military victory. Putin knew that the rebels were split between those like Zakharchenko, who were willing to follow Putin's lead, and those like commander Pavel Dremov, a hard-line, openly anti-Semitic nationalist who opposed Putin and dreamed about building a "socialist, neo-Soviet 'Cossack' republic." Dremov opposed the cease-fire, criticizing Zakharchenko and others of his ilk who, he charged, wanted only power and money. Dremov yearned for the day when he had the resources to go on the offensive, expand his land base, and create a neo-Soviet paradise.[45] Among militia leaders who reluctantly supported Poroshenko, there was an increasing restlessness about the war, which seemed inconclusive. They had hoped that the Maidan rebellion that ousted Yanukovych in February would already have produced major changes in Ukraine, but they did not see any. They denounced the continuing corruption and warned, "There'll be a military takeover." A pro-Kiev commander, Yuriy Bereza, a tall officer with a pistol strapped to his side, put a time frame on his warning: "We're going to give them [Kiev] half a year to show the country has somehow changed, that even if it's hard, there is light ahead." And if, by then, nothing has changed? a reporter asked. Bereza did not hesitate. "A coup," he threatened. [46]

As winter approached, everyone expected freezing weather and, possibly, a wider war. With the recent arrival of additional Russian arms and troops, the war had just turned another corner—that was obvious!—but everyone still had trouble reading Putin's mind. Would he be satisfied with another "frozen" victory, similar to the one he had scored in Abkhazia and South Ossetia in the 2008 Georgian War? Would he push for a land corridor to Crimea? Would he challenge NATO directly with a military feint toward the Baltics? Some Russians thought Putin was vamping, that he had no clear course in mind. Others feared he had a plan, and it was to widen the war.

CHAPTER 17

"Master of the Taiga?"

My mother is Russian. My father is Ukrainian. I have lots
of Russian friends. I like books in Russian. I speak Russian
at home. So, I am asking myself, "Who am I?"
ALEKSEY RYABCHYN, UKRAINIAN POLITICIAN

No DOUBT, VLADIMIR PUTIN represents an insurmountable problem
for Petro Poroshenko and Ukraine, but he is not their only problem. In many
ways, Ukraine is Ukraine's bigger problem. Ever since 1991, when Ukraine
proclaimed its independence from Russia, Ukrainian leaders have been struggling to lift their country out of its slothful, Soviet-manufactured rut. All of
them have failed. Leonid Kravchuk tried, then Leonid Kuchma. Then, in the
wake of the Orange Revolution, which so frightened Putin, came Viktor Yushchenko and Yulia Tymoshenko, the one-time darlings of Ukrainian politics.
Even they proved to be colossal flops. Viktor Yanukovych brought Russian
politics to Kiev, but he too came up short. Now Poroshenko leads a decidedly
pro-Western government but faces the same steep curve of challenges. Can he
succeed where all of the others before him have failed?

One huge problem for Poroshenko is that Ukraine is experiencing a severe
identity crisis, linked largely to its deep Russian roots. Can Ukraine ever truly
be independent of Russia? Or is its destiny to be tied irrevocably to Russia?
Can Ukrainian Orthodoxy truly separate itself from Russian Orthodoxy? If
Lvov is the birthplace of Ukrainian nationalism, then why don't the nationalists living in Donetsk respect it as such? Were the Cossacks the original Ukrainians, or was it the Slavs living in Kievan Rus'? When a Cossack leader struck
a secret deal with a Polish or Swedish king, his tsar kept in the dark, was he
guilty of treason, or was he engaged in a defiant act of Ukrainian patriotism?
Is Ukraine really two Ukraines: one leaning to the East, the other drawn to
the West?

Complicating this continuously unsatisfying quest for national identity is the question of borders: Just where does Ukraine begin and where does it end? Many nations are endowed with natural borders—oceans, rivers, a mountain crest. With Ukraine, over centuries, borders have shifted, depending on diplomatic deals or military conquests and defeats. Over time, Ukraine has been a part of Poland, Austria, and other countries in the West, and a part of the eastern land mass called Russia. Through these changes, a kernel of Ukraine, the land to the east and west of the Dnieper River, with Kiev its capital city, has survived, starting with the medieval kingdom known as Kievan Rus'— the first Russia—and continuing today.

So unsettled have been Ukraine's outer borders, in fact, that when Lenin and Stalin organized the Soviet republic of Ukraine in 1922, they could see no obvious, natural border between the eastern half of Ukraine and Russia. So it was left hazy: people and products wandering back and forth from Ukraine to Russia, and Russia to Ukraine, with little to no acknowledgment of the sanctity of a normal national border. Is it any wonder then that the eastern corner of Ukraine is currently the scene of a separatist rebellion?

Ukraine, the name itself, complicates the search for national identity. In Russian, the word usually means the "far edge," the "rim," the "border." But of . . . what? Of Russia. That is one reason it has been so difficult for Russians to think of Ukraine as an independent country. While many of them now do so, it has taken a long time to get used to it. The 2014–15 war has helped to accelerate the transition.

Let's turn from national borders to people's nationality. Consider the case of Aleksey Ryabchyn, a budding politician who was an economist in Donetsk. "I considered myself part of the Russian culture," he told a reporter. "My mother is Russian, my father is Ukrainian. I have lots of Russian friends. I like books in Russian. I speak Russian at home. So I am asking myself, 'Who am I?'" When Russia moved across its frequently violated border with Ukraine in early March, 2014, "the Russian part of me died," said Ryabchyn. "It was the biggest shock of my life." In a way, Putin forced Ryabchyn to decide he was a Ukrainian.[1]

Or consider Savik Shuster, one of Ukraine's most popular talk show hosts. He began his TV career in Moscow. "There was that dream to succeed in Moscow," he told a visitor. But Moscow proved to be too steep a climb, and he moved to a provincial capital, Kiev, found an audience there and learned to draw a distinction between the two Russias. "You have Pushkin's Russia," Shuster said, his voice up, "and you have Putin's Russia," his voice down. "Nobody wants to deal with Putin's Russia."[2]

In searching for Ukraine's true identity, it's instructive to think about novelist Mikhail Bulgakov, who wrote *The Master and Margarita* and *The White Guard*, among other classics in Russian literature. Bulgakov was born in Kiev in 1891. His home is now a popular museum there. With a pride felt by many Ukrainians, he is called the "Great Kiev Citizen," a writer who loved his native city but still mocked the idea of a Ukraine independent of Russia.

In *The White Guard*, Bulgakov described a family of White Russians during the Russian Revolution. The main character, a doctor named Alexei Turbin, disliked Ukrainian peasants as much as he hated the Bolsheviks, describing peasant leaders as cowardly, cruel, anti-Semitic, and treacherous. Their language, Ukrainian, he wrote, could be understood only at river docks, where "ragged men unload watermelons from barges." Gentlemen spoke and wrote in Russian.

When the immensely popular book was made into a Russian TV miniseries, it was banned in Ukraine, because it exhibited "contempt for the Ukrainian language, people, and statehood." For Bulgakov, opined Volodymyr Fedorin, a former editor of *Forbes Ukraine*, "Ukrainian independence was something between a joke and a tragedy." Bulgakov lived in two worlds: he loved Kiev, but loved Russia, it seems, even more.[3]

Ukraine's Urgent Need for Economic Reform

Each Ukrainian leader has had to cope with the vagaries of his nation's national identity crisis. Now it is Poroshenko's turn, and because there is no immediate solution, he, as a successful businessman, has chosen to tackle two other urgent problems. One is the war against the secessionist southeast corner of Ukraine; the other is economic reform. He knows the Ukrainian economy is in shambles; it is inefficient, corrupt, and clearly unable to emerge from its Slavic indolence, made worse by the pitfalls of Soviet-era stagnation. Yet, every Ukrainian leader—fearing political blowback, lacking an essential core of courage, often on the take himself—has approached the door of reform and, abruptly, stopped, as though paralyzed by the prospect of change. Now, under Poroshenko, it has what may be its last chance to initiate and implement substantial reform. As economist Anders Aslund put it bluntly: "Reform hard and fast to survive or cease to exist as a nation."[4]

For example, according to Steven Pifer of Brookings, a former U.S. ambassador to Ukraine, the per capita GDP of both Ukraine and Poland were roughly the same on the eve of independence in 1990, with Poland possibly trailing by a bit. Today, Poland's per capita GDP is more than three times larger than Ukraine's. The explanation is that Poland's leaders acted boldly and decisively. They made difficult decisions that eventually jump-started the Polish economy. It is obviously time for Ukraine to follow Poland's lead, if it wishes to break out of its economic impasse.[5]

On December 9, 2014, Prime Minister Arseniy Yatsenyuk surprised everyone by announcing a major new program of economic reform. It was almost as though he were listening to Aslund, an economist sympathetic to Ukraine's problems. Aslund has stressed that Ukraine's problems were so huge that "only a radical program of reform" had a chance of turning the economy around. Yatsenyuk, reflecting Poroshenko's priorities, promised that he would cut public spending by a staggering 10 percent, slash red tape, and reform the energy sector of the economy. He made no pledge, however, to curb the power of Ukraine's oligarchs, who effectively run the country's economy and, in many places, the government itself. That might have been too high a mountain for him to climb. Yatsenyuk knew Ukraine desperately needed an additional $15 billion loan. "It's hard for us to make ends meet ourselves," he acknowledged. But "we are not begging for money. We are not moaning. We are saying, 'we are partners.'"[6]

His minister for economic development seemed more willing to be candid. "The state is, as a matter of fact, bankrupt. So it is hugely unrealistic to expect us to offer real, not just declarative, programs of motivation."[7] Yet that was exactly what the prime minister was doing. The U.S. ambassador to Ukraine, Geoffrey Pyatt, said in early December 2014 that "business as usual" in Ukraine was a "bigger threat than Russian tanks."[8] Charitably put, Ukraine still teeters on the brink of bankruptcy.

For example, consider Ukraine's chronic need of energy. Though it has begun to receive oil and gas from West European sources, it is still dependent on Russian gas and oil, therefore inescapably subject to Russian pressure. Yet, up to now, Ukraine itself has done pitifully little to address the problem. It has been easier for a prime minister to subsidize heating and energy, throwing the economy entirely out of whack, than to take the steps necessary to right the ship of state.

The 2014 gas-oil deal between Russia and Ukraine, midwifed by the EU, depended on Ukraine paying off its huge debt to Russia, in stages, before Russia again opened its pipelines to Ukraine. But, for many reasons, including the vast uncertainties in the Ukrainian economy, Poroshenko balked at paying Ukraine's debt, and, for a time, Putin pulled the plug, stopping gas and oil deliveries to Ukraine. Looming on the immediate horizon was the 2014–15 winter. Then, on December 9, as a signal of negotiating flexibility,

Putin decided to resume deliveries. Without a long-term deal, though, Putin can again change his mind. Uncertainty is one of his trump cards.

In diplomatic and journalistic accounts of Ukraine's travails, we have tended, for the most part, to focus on Poroshenko, on the parliament (the Rada), on the militia fighting in the southeast, and on the continuing East-West struggle for power and influence in this historically neglected corner of Europe. We in the West do not know enough about Ukraine's economy, its local politics, and its warring militia commanders—some of whom apparently think they are fighting on behalf of the Nazis in World War II, while still others hold important government jobs. For example, in September 2014 one of the leaders of the neo-Nazi Azov militia was named chief of police in Kiev. Ukraine's interior minister, Arsen Avakov, a key aide to Prime Minister Yatsenyuk, instead of reining in far-right militias, has actually been providing them with tanks and armored personnel carriers. Adrian Karatnycky, who tracks Ukraine developments for the Atlantic Council, researched the rise of the right-wing militia and, after praising Poroshenko's reform efforts, concluded nevertheless that a "pattern of blatant disregard for the chain of command, lawlessness and racketeering is posing a growing threat to Ukraine's stability."[9]

But as Washington is poised to make deeper commitments to Ukraine, how much do Americans know about what is happening there? The American public is being shortchanged because news media coverage of the whole Ukraine story has been inadequate. Even if, as can be assumed, the U.S. government knows a lot more, it has chosen to share little of that with the public. The public catches some of the headlines about war and peace but often misses the more meaningful sidebar stories about politics and politicians, literature and the arts, religion and history. We are left with a shortage of data, a perfect setup for making poor, hasty decisions.

For example, how are we to read the fact that in Babi Yar, the ravine outside of Kiev where 33,000 Jews were murdered in September 1941, swastikas were recently painted on the memorial monument there? Is it important or not? And what about the anti-Semitic graffiti ("Kill the Jews" and "Heil Happy Holocaust") spray-painted on a Jewish religious school in Kharkov? Are these incidents representative of anti-Semitism again rearing its foul head in Ukraine, and if so, what does this mean? Or are these incidents so isolated and infrequent as to be judged inconsequential?[10] The American people deserve to know more about today's Ukraine before their government embraces Ukraine as an American strategic responsibility. Is this really the country Congress should now be rushing to subsidize? Shouldn't Ukraine first show signs that it is starting to manage its floundering economy, that its announced reform package is taking root, that the oligarchs have begun to think about their country's needs, not just their own—and that democracy in Ukraine is a genuine possibility?

The fact is that Ukraine is an international ward. Without a steady flow of loans from the International Monetary Fund (IMF), it would already be belly-up. But to extend a loan, the IMF understandably sets benchmarks, demanding real economic performance and an end to corruption. No performance, no loan. On March 11, 2015, the IMF decided to extend a $17.5-billion loan on the twin assumptions that Ukraine was in desperate need of the money and that it would actually show progress on its program of reform.[11] In this way, the IMF becomes the ultimate arbiter of Ukraine's fate. It ends up being responsible for keeping Ukraine from becoming a failed state. It is, for the IMF, a painful decision; for Ukraine, it is an almost impossible challenge.

No one is more sympathetic to what he calls the "new Ukraine" than financier and philanthropist George Soros. Yet, even he warned that Ukraine faces the real likelihood of sovereign default, capital flight, and a bank run. Ukrainian banks "desperately need bigger capital cushions," cautioned Soros, "if Ukraine is to avoid a full-blown banking crisis."[12] In late December 2014 a Kiev official described Ukraine's banking system as "nonfunctioning." The following month, Soros said Ukraine actually needed a $50 billion loan.[13] Is there a ceiling on how much Ukraine might need?

Soros, who has been investing in Ukraine since 1990, argued that preserving Ukraine's independence is an absolute necessity for the West—that "the collapse of Ukraine would be a tremendous loss for NATO, the European Union, and the United States."[14] Moved either by a romantic illusion of a free and democratic Ukraine or by a businessman's effort to protect an early investment, Soros has already inserted Ukraine into his basket of personal responsibilities. For him, it was no longer a question of whether Ukraine tips East or West; for him, it tips West—that battle has already been won. But, in fact, has it? From every available yardstick, that battle continues: inconclusively, on the bloody battlefield in southeastern Ukraine and, frustratingly, in presidential mansions and diplomatic chanceries around the world.

In Soros's view, Putin had "repeatedly resorted to force and he is liable to do so again unless he faces strong resistance." Soros strongly supported the idea of providing Ukraine with unlimited aid, lethal weapons, and a protective NATO umbrella. Europe was already at war, he argued, and it ought to "wake up" and help Ukraine defend itself against Russian aggression.[15]

The U.S. Responsibility for Ukraine: What Is It?

For the United States, the basic question is whether, at this point, it makes sense to adopt Ukraine as an American strategic responsibility, more than it already has. Ukraine remains an economic basket case: It is trapped in a war it cannot win, and it is struggling to find and implement a realistic formula for economic reform. A number of unethical Ukrainian politicians may feel they already have found the formula: bedazzle the West into believing that Ukraine is a vital strategic asset in a continuing East-West struggle between democracy and autocracy, between freedom and oppression, and then support this Ukraine in every way—economic, political, and military. The promised pay-off: The West wins, Russia loses, and Ukraine is saved.

Apparently, though, Congress was prepared to believe that American aid would produce a Ukrainian democracy. On one of the last days of business before the Christmas holiday in 2014, Congress unanimously passed the Ukraine Freedom Support Act. When was the last time Congress considered an issue to be so important in the foreign policy sphere that it voted unanimously for its adoption? In this case, Congress voted for tougher U.S. sanctions against Russia's energy sector. It voted also for lethal military assistance to Ukraine, going up the ladder of commitment from nonlethal to lethal. The total cost would be $510 million, $350 million earmarked for military supplies.

"Unanimous support for our bill demonstrates a firm commitment to Ukrainian sovereignty and to making sure Putin pays for his assault on freedom and security in Europe," said Tennessee Republican senator Bob Corker, the new chair of the Senate Foreign Relations Committee. Before President Obama even had a chance to sign the legislation, the Russians condemned it. Foreign Ministry spokesman Alexander Lukashevich said the legislation would "destroy cooperation," though there was very little "cooperation" between the two countries. Russia, he stressed, "won't succumb to blackmail, won't compromise its national interests and won't allow interference in its internal affairs."[16]

President Obama signed the measure into law on December 18, but said he was not yet ready to impose the additional sanctions Congress had advocated.[17] He can do so, of course, whenever he wishes, but Congress placed it in his diplomatic tool kit as a warning to Moscow of things to come. Congress has a soft spot in its heart for underdogs struggling to build a democracy while, at the same time, fighting an aggressive Russia. As one observer put it, "Russia is a wonderful enemy to have."

NATO and the Putin/Poroshenko Minuet

Putin has warned numerous times, as the crisis has unfolded, that he strenuously opposes NATO expansion, and he sees Ukraine in NATO as an absolute no-no. Indeed, Russia's current military doctrine holds that NATO expansion is the No. 1 threat to Russia's national security. Poroshenko has always understood Putin's no-NATO policy, and until he convened his new pro-Western Rada in late November 2014, it seemed that he would not push Putin on this issue. And yet he did. "Today it is clear," Poroshenko told the Rada, "that the nonalignment status of Ukraine proclaimed in 2010 couldn't guarantee our security and territorial integrity. This position has led to serious losses. That's why we've decided to return to the course of NATO integration."

On December 23, 2014, the Rada voted overwhelmingly, 303 to 8, to abandon the policy of "non-participation of Ukraine in military-political alliances." Instead, Ukraine would henceforth pursue membership in NATO. Poroshenko realized that membership was not likely in the immediate future; for now, he said, Ukraine had to "deepen cooperation with NATO in order to achieve the criteria required for membership in this organization."[18] Poroshenko might have switched positions to accommodate Yatsenyuk, his 40-year-old firebrand prime minister, who had always favored Ukrainian membership in NATO. He might even have privately informed Putin, in advance of his statement to the Rada, that he would not really press for NATO membership. It was just, "between you and me, politics." Possibly, but in any event, Poroshenko was playing with fire, and he must have known it.

Putin's spokesman, Dmitry Peskov, spelled out his boss's position on this sensitive subject in an interview with the BBC. "We would like to hear a 100 percent guarantee," he said, "that no one would think about Ukraine's joining NATO."[19] One-hundred-percent guarantees are rare in life, rarer still in global affairs. But, in Putin's Kremlin, the idea of bringing Ukraine into NATO, or moving NATO closer to the Russian border, would certainly be interpreted as a deliberate challenge to Russia's "vital national interest." As Peskov noted: "We would like to hear that NATO would discontinue to approach Russian borders, that NATO will discontinue attempts to break the balance, the balance of power. But unfortunately we fail to hear these words."[20] Peskov spoke against a backdrop of tougher talk from the Kremlin, suggesting that if there are differences of opinion among Russian insiders over Putin's Ukraine policy, and there appear to be, the hard-liners seem to be more than holding their own. Even Dmitri Medvedev, Putin's obedient prime minister, usually regarded as a liberalizing influence on policymaking, felt the need to crush the notion of a new "reset" in Russian-American relations. "Impossible," he impatiently snapped in an October 2014 interview. Western sanctions were, in his words, "stupid" and "destructive." Worse, he said Obama's annual speech a month earlier to the UN General Assembly was a direct insult to Putin and to Russia—that the president must have been suffering from a "mental aberration," or breakdown.[21] Obama had listed three "threats" topping his list of daily worries: first—ebola, second—Putin, and, third—the Islamic State. That offended Putin and dismayed his chief lieutenants, who concluded that the president might really be engaged in a policy of "regime change," meaning a policy aimed at unseating Putin.

On this matter, Foreign Minister Lavrov, who serves increasingly as Putin's chief foreign policy spokesman, was quite precise. The West, he said in November 2014, "is making clear it does not want to force Russia to change policy but wants to secure regime change." How would that be accomplished? In Lavrov's words, by adopting sanctions "that will destroy the economy and cause public protests."[22] In Putin's own words, Western sanctions were "driven by a desire to cause a split in the elite and then, perhaps, in society."[23]

Putin and his closest aides appear to live in a state of chronic fear that one day, sooner rather than later, the "people" will rise against the regime and, in a spasm of violence, overthrow it. "They would merely have to show," wrote Masha Gessen, "that the tyrant had feet of clay. . . . The tipping point in Russia" is "as unpredictable as in any tyranny."[24] History has proven that if a regime is illegitimate, based not on popular support but on an autocrat's personal power, then it can be unseated in a week, a month, a year. Putin has always worried about "bacteria," those who work within the state to undermine the state. They are traitors. "They sit inside you, these bacilli, these bacteria; they are there all the time."[25]

On February 27, 2015, Boris Nemtsov, an outspoken critic of Putin, one of "these bacilli," was gunned down on a Moscow bridge not far from the Kremlin. His murder dealt a crippling blow to Putin's already fragmented political opposition. One activist, Maxim Katz, blamed Putin. "If he ordered it, then he is guilty as the orderer," Katz wrote on Twitter. "And even if he didn't, then [he is responsible] as the inciter of hatred, hysteria, and anger among the people." Since the seizure of Crimea, Putin has stimulated a mood of rabid nationalism, describing his political opponents as "national traitors" and a "fifth column." Gleb Pavlovsky, an independent political consultant, said that "in this atmosphere, everything is possible. This is a Weimar atmosphere. There are no longer any limits."[26]

Ever since the Rose and Orange Revolutions in Georgia and Ukraine, which frightened Putin, he has tried to freeze political debate. He has spoken out repeatedly about "the tragic consequences of the wave of so-called 'color revolutions,' the turmoil in the countries that have undergone the irresponsible experiments of covert and sometimes blatant interference in their lives." He said, "We take this as a lesson and a warning, and we must do everything necessary to ensure this never happens in Russia."[27] The spontaneous, the unexpected, terrifies Putin.

Because the Ukraine crisis has been personalized as a war between an evil, irreconcilable Putin and a benign, democratic West, more than it has been as a contest of wills and interests between Russia and the West, then it could be imagined in both Washington and Moscow that the toppling of Putin would result in a radical shift in Russian policy. The simplistic—and possibly erroneous—assumption is that Putin is the bad guy in the Kremlin—remove him, and the good guys, waiting in the wings, would slide into power. Putin is far from an angel; indeed, Putinism may be one of the bleakest of modern autocracies—prompting a Russian art critic to question, bravely, if the country was "plummeting into the abyss of militarist aggression, obscurantism, and proto-fascist nationalism."[28]

Putin may be the worst of the current lot of possible Russian leaders, or he may be holding off someone even worse. Russia has always had room in its history for an Ivan the Terrible or a Stalin. Frightened by the unorthodox, Putin has sometime gone to absurd lengths. He arrested the perpetrators of the notorious "punk prayer" of the Pussy Riot trio in a Moscow church in February, 2012, but, giving full reign to his ever-expanding ego, he allowed a huge exhibition in central Moscow celebrating his sixty-second birthday. Shamelessly comparing Putin to the Greek god Hercules, it showed him wearing a toga, his biceps bulging, his chin jutting forward, as he successfully battled terrorism, sanctions, oligarchs, and the United States—while supporting the rebels in Ukraine and Assad in Syria.[29]

He has been, without doubt, the strongest Russian autocrat since Stalin, yet oddly the most vulnerable. He has said he would preside over the Kremlin until 2018, when his current six-year term expires, or maybe 2024, when the next six-year term ends, but no longer, depending, he explains, on his "mood." Not the political system, which he controls, or the will of the people, but his "mood." It may also depend on a worsening Russian economy, and his health may slip. Putin lives in a strange corner of the Kremlin where fear and hubris coexist in an awkward embrace. He conveys self-confidence, yet worries that the West is trying to "isolate" him by building an "Iron Curtain" around him. "We will not go down this path, . . . and no one will build a wall around us," he said in late November 2014.[30] An aide to German chancellor Angela Merkel, studying Putin, believes that "this political isolation hurts him. He doesn't like to be left out."

Putin runs Russia at a time of restless change in his people (thousands demonstrate in Moscow against cuts in health care, consumer goods, and jobs) and in the downward spiral of his economy, triggered by falling oil prices and continuing Western sanctions. Will his people continue to ride with Putin, or one day rise in opposition? In April 2015 the *New York Times* reported that wildcat strikes and worker layoffs, which have occurred with increasing frequency, reflect a popular unhappiness and impatience with the bad economy.[31]

Poroshenko, while he still retains power, needs to stop playing mind games with the other Ukrainian oligarchs and arrange a serious, one-on-one negotiation with Putin about Ukraine's future—realizing in advance that Putin holds the trump cards and he, Poroshenko, will have to accept the best deal he can get, no matter how distasteful that deal may be. It is in Washington's interests to encourage such a settlement. That is, if the challenge is to avoid a bigger war, reach a negotiated solution, and ready the table for the next round of talks, all the while waiting for Russia to come up with a more moderate leader willing to negotiate a generous deal with Ukraine, and for Ukraine to begin a serious program of economic and democratic reform and put an end to widespread corruption. In this context, the immediate future cannot be rightly seen in rosy hues. There are still as many questions as problems, and dangers loom on the near horizon.

What should be clear is that this is no time for diplomatic diddling or romance. It is a time for realistic, hard-headed bargaining.

Whither this Russian President?

For Putin, the question of "whither Russia?" is not uppermost in his mind. He is absorbed with the present, basically with perpetuating his own power. He believes he is the "strong leader," the "strong hand" Russians have always coveted, and the polls suggest he is right. He runs a kind of kleptocracy. A small group of ex-KGB, *siloviki*-style businessmen, all loyal to Putin, controls everything. Putin has amassed a personal portfolio reportedly valued at $40 billion, give or take a billion, but this has never been confirmed.[32] According to the global watchdog group Transparency International, Russia ranks as more corrupt than 86 percent of all other countries, fitting in between Nigeria and Comoros.[33]

Putin apparently believes that even if he acts like a tyrant, an unscrupulous rascal, a majority of Russians will still support him. Even Stalin, who was a tyrant par excellence, remains a positive memory for at least half of the Russian people. What accounts for this strange paradox? asks Harvard historian Richard Pipes. A tyrant who is admired by his people? "The great majority of Russians," Pipes explains, "have little interest in politics. They regard politicians as crooks and esteem them only to the extent that they protect them from their neighbors and foreigners. Their concerns are not national, but local, which means that the majority of them do not participate in politics in the sense in which the ancient Greeks have taught us." Pipes continues, "Thus when the Soviet Union collapsed in 1991 after nearly three-quarters of a century of unprecedented tyranny, there were neither protests nor jubilations; people simply went about their private business. The lives of the great majority of Russians are uncommonly personal, which makes them excellent friends and poor citizens."[34]

For almost 200 years, Russians, like Ukrainians, have struggled with their own identity crisis. Are we true Russians, they ask, or are we really Europeans, like the Germans or the French? Are we a blend of Slavs living a providential life on the Eurasian steppe—religious, nationalistic, setting an example of salvation for Europe and the rest of the world? In short, are we Slavophiles, or are we Westerners? The question has reverberated through Russian history. It has never really been answered. Russians have often admired the West, even on occasion desperately yearned to be like the West—and then, moments later, they could denounce the West. Foreign Minister Lavrov can, on one day, blast the United States with eye-opening invective, and then, a day later, summoned by Secretary of State John F. Kerry, rush to Rome for an urgent meeting about the civil war in Syria. Many Russians seek to be part of the West; yet they are anchored somewhere between East and West. They find themselves living in two worlds: one, their own, on the Slavic steppe; the other, while rooted in the steppe, reaching out to the West. Putin seems to stand in loose limbo between the Westerner and the Slavophile, undeniably fascinated by Western trade and technology but generally dismissive of Western ideas and ideals. Translation: For the time being, anyway, Russia will continue to live in its own world. The West can wait. East-West tensions will rise.

Though Obama has tried to "isolate" Russia, he has failed; Russia has contacts everywhere, including China, contacts that balance out America and undermine efforts to isolate it. In 2014, during the Ukraine crisis, Putin signed a $400-billion-dollar, thirty-year gas deal with the Chinese. He visited India and signed agreements there for the joint manufacturing of military helicopters and nuclear reactors. Putin has cultivated allies in the Balkans, in Hungary, Slovakia, Serbia, the Czech Republic, even Poland. Damon Wilson of the Atlantic Council raised an interesting question with the *Washington Post*'s Jackson Diehl: "The issue for many politicians will be how to survive when the Russians are back, nastier than ever . . . and the Americans are remote, available only for genuine 911 calls."[35] Like a spoiled child, Putin does not like being ignored or scolded, but, for the time being, he swims for two hours every morning, so we're told, travels the world like a Hollywood star, and runs Russia, when he finds the time, pretending all the while that he is enjoying every minute of his day.

The Kremlin Speech, the Other Bookend

One of Putin's genuine pleasures appears to be delivering a speech in the Kremlin. It does wonders for his ego. By definition, any such speech is an important event. It is televised from St. George's white marble hall in the Great Kremlin Palace. It attracts a "live" audience of roughly a thousand of his trusted followers from Russia's new political elite. They sit politely, waiting for Putin's arrival. Above, hanging from the ceiling, is a row of immense, gilt-edged chandeliers, exactly as conceived in the mid-1840s, when Nicholas I ordered Italian architects to build the palace. At the end of the hall, clearly on cue, two massive doors are slowly opened by a goose-stepping, resplendently uniformed honor guard, revealing a comparatively short Putin, wearing a business suit. He enters the hall, ignoring the guards who remain standing near each door, and walks briskly down a long red carpet to his podium. His walk, by now, is familiar to everyone. At regular intervals, he seems to swing his right shoulder down, then up. By the time he reaches the podium, his audience is silent and still.

Putin, unlike Obama, does not stop to shake hands with anyone; nor does he use a teleprompter. For someone who usually loves a good show, he comes through in this setting as all business. Flanked by state flags, he reads his speech in a conversational tone, looking down frequently, rarely smiling. When he comes to a riff, obviously crafted to spark sustained applause ("stormy" is the preferred Kremlin adjective), he pauses slightly, but then quickly goes on. When he is done, he leaves the way he came.

On December 4, 2014, he delivered his eleventh annual "state of the nation" speech in St. George's Hall. He coauthored parts of it, if we are to believe his spokesmen. On this occasion, for reasons related to Ukraine and a dramatically worsening economy, the mood was somber. No one was sure what Putin would say about these two interrelated crises.

Ever since Putin moved into the Kremlin in 2000, good fortune had smiled down on his rule, largely because oil prices skyrocketed from $28 a barrel in 1999 to a peak of $140 a barrel in 2008. When oil profits were high, the economy flourished, and the average Russian's standard of living rose accordingly. Putin benefited politically from these "big boom" years. The economy expanded by roughly 7 percent a year. Pensions were paid, on time, satisfying the old-timers. Putin boasted that "not only has Russia now made a full turnaround after years of industrial decline, it has become one of the world's ten biggest economies."[36] During most of Putin's rule, Russians have felt proud of their "rodina," their homeland. They linked their country's success to Putin's leadership. A majority of Russians were clearly prepared to sacrifice a good measure of their personal freedom, which they did under Putin's increasingly authoritarian rule, so long as he provided for their prosperity and security.

Because the reign of Putin coincided with a rising economy, his popularity shot through the roof, hitting 85 percent after the Crimea takeover in March 2014. It remained atmospherically high through the crisis-filled year, even though, by the following December, the popularity of his government had dropped to 59 percent—and there were good reasons.

Starting in June 2014, Western sanctions began to bite. For example, large Russian corporations owed Western banks nearly $650 billion.[37] To pay their debts, the corporations needed access to Western credit markets, but, because of the sanctions, they could not gain access. So how were they going to pay their debt? Another example: Oil prices nose-dived from $80 a barrel in June 2014 to $58 a barrel in December, and fell below $50 early in 2015. The value of the ruble plummeted by more than 45 percent of its value by November 2014, precipitating a panic on the Moscow stock market. During the course of 2014 businesses, investors, and others pulled more than $150 billion out of Russia, double the previous year—prompting the Kremlin to consider offering an "amnesty" to those willing to bring their money back into the country.[38] The inflation rate for 2014 was about 10 percent. For Putin, this was all catastrophically bad news.

Finally, confirming the obvious, the Kremlin conceded that Russia now faced a serious recession in 2015. Economists had earlier looked into their crystal balls and predicted that the economy would grow by 1.2 percent in 2015. Now they were glumly revising their estimates: the economy would not grow at all—it would likely drop by 0.8 percent. Other Russian economists, using data available in early 2015, projected a much more dramatic contraction of 4.5 percent, perhaps even higher, if oil prices dropped below $60/barrel, which they already had.

How would Putin deal with this abrupt turnaround? That was the question, as the suddenly beleaguered Russian leader began his report to the nation on December 4, 2014. There had been speculation in Moscow that Putin would, in this crunch, favor conservative policies rather than liberal ones. Typical for a politician in trouble, though, he ended up favoring both, coming down decisively on the conservative side in foreign affairs and half-heartedly on the liberal side in domestic ones.

Looking grim, he acknowledged upfront that 2014 had been a "difficult year," one in which Russia had "faced trials that only a mature and united nation, and a truly sovereign and strong state, can withstand." There was never a doubt in his mind that Russia was such a nation—"mature," "sovereign," and "strong." (He later called it "a year of trial.") "Russia has proved," he said, "that it can protect its compatriots [presumably in Crimea and Ukraine] and defend truth and fairness."[39]

In foreign affairs, Putin tried sounding tough. But, in this speech anyway, his words lacked their usual bite, echoing his by now familiar rant about the West, led by the United States, attempting, in the words of a *New York Times* editorial, to "dismantle, undermine, isolate, humiliate, contain and otherwise destroy Russia."[40] The United States had become Putin's unalloyed adversary, in his crosshairs in every critique. Over many years, even decades, he stressed, whenever the United States has attempted to "undermine" or "contain" Russia, it has failed abysmally, just as the Nazis had failed in World War II. Putin often evoked memories of what the Russians call the "Great Patriotic War," a brutalizing experience that left 20 million of them dead. Hitler had "set out to destroy Russia and push us back beyond the Urals," he reminded his audience. "Everyone should remember how it [WW II] ended." The Nazis were repulsed, Russia won the war.[41]

"The policy of containment was not invented yesterday," Putin went on. "It has been carried out against our country for many years, always, for decades, if not centuries. In short, whenever someone thinks that Russia has become too strong or independent, these tools are quickly put to use." The sanctions, for example, were a "nervous reaction by the U.S. and its allies to [Moscow's] stance regarding the coup d'état and other developments in Ukraine." Because Russia under Putin has become "strong and independent," the United States has sought to encircle and weaken Russia, using the Ukraine crisis as a convenient pretext. But even if there were no Ukraine crisis, Putin asserted, "they'd come up with another reason to stall Russia's growing capabilities."[42]

Nothing seemed more important to Putin than his decision to absorb Crimea into the Russian Republic. Why? Because, he explained, Vladimir the Great, who Christianized medieval Kievan Rus', was baptized in Crimea in the tenth century. It was where Russia derived its religion. "Crimea has enormous civilizational and holy meaning for Russia," Putin noted. "That's how we will see it henceforth and forever." It was a "historic event," he asserted, never to be reversed.[43] Indeed, Crimea was so crucially important to Russian civilization that, in Putin's view, it could now only be compared to the Temple Mount in Jerusalem, a sacred site in the annals of Judaism, Christianity, and Islam.

Clearly, Putin must never have read Mussolini's rapturous account of Italy's seizure of Ethiopia in 1935. "Ethiopia, from now and forever," boasted Italy's dictator, "belongs to Italy, which has become what it was during the time of Julius Caesar."[44] "Now and forever" lasted until 1941, when Emperor Haile Selassie, aided by the British, kicked the Italians out of Ethiopia. Putin's plans for Crimea, he must have hoped, had deeper roots.

When Putin turned to his domestic policy, his tone changed from one of pride and belligerence to one of caution and conciliation. Perhaps, that December morning, Putin had read the editorial in *Vedomosti*, a business newspaper that has managed to retain a limited degree of journalistic independence. "The economy is seriously ill," the editorial cried, "and the ruble rate is one of the indicators crying about the illness." The ruble's value had been dropping rapidly. The biggest problem, the editorial continued, was the Russian leadership's "inability to admit mistakes." Pointing to Putin but not using his name, *Vedomosti* declared: "Russia's leadership refuses to admit there is an illness and pushes it [the economy] into the depths."[45] Putin proposed three changes in the Russian economy designed to streamline markets, spur investment, and generate self-confidence:

—First, strike a blow against pervasive corruption by drastically reducing the number of government inspections of small and midsize businesses;

—Second, freeze the business tax rate for the next four years; and

—Third, grant full amnesty to Russians who repatriate assets they had stashed abroad. No questions asked.

Measured against the seriousness of Russia's economic woes, these changes represented, at best, a modest effort at reform, but an effort almost certain to fail. If Putin really believed that these proposed changes, by themselves, could right the Russian economy, then he was either badly advised or he was deluding himself. Or, as many Russians hoped, maybe Putin was simply trying to buy time on the slippery assumption that if he negotiated an acceptable compromise on Ukraine, the Europeans would agree to lift their sanctions on Russia by mid-2015. In this way, Putin's economic problems would ease, while Russia would still be able to retain ownership of Crimea and considerable influence in southeastern Ukraine. But was he again miscalculating Western resolve? It was just as likely that the West, seeing Putin in deep trouble at home, and enjoying the sight, would let him wallow in his self-inflicted misery, hoping that at the end of the day he would be replaced, another discarded relic in the ash can of modern Russian history.

Even as Putin voiced guarded optimism for the record, a few of his ministers intoned more realistic opinions. They viewed the chances of Western Europe lifting its sanctions against Russia in 2015 as remote, at best. Thus, Alexei Ulyukayev, Russia's minister of economic development, told a reporter for the *Vedomosti* newspaper that the Western sanctions would last "for a very long time." He added that U.S. sanctions, in particular, could be "in place for decades."[46]

What did Putin think of his December 4 speech? He did not say himself, but a good second-best would be asking Dmitri Kiselev, Putin's favorite TV anchorman. Kiselev said it reminded him of the great speeches delivered by Roosevelt, Churchill, and de Gaulle during and after the Second World War. He did not mention Stalin's speeches. After a speech in which Putin bitterly criticized the West, especially the United States, the man often called his chief propagandist could find solace only in comparing Putin, rhetorically anyway, to the giants of the Western world—but not to a single Russian leader.[47]

The December 4 Bookend

If there were bookends to the story of Putin's adventures, or misadventures, in 2014, one of them would be his speech on March 18 about the Crimean annexation, and the other would be his speech of December 4, primarily focused on the faltering economy. In March he seemed triumphant, a leader with limitless horizons. He walked on water. His eyes twinkled with mischievous pleasure. He had presided over the Olympics. He had seized Crimea, a monumental prize, and swiftly absorbed it into Russia. He then went even further, instigating a pro-Russian rebellion in southeastern Ukraine. Looking beyond his "near abroad," he traveled to China and India and meddled in the Middle East. Putin's Russia was back as a major player in global diplomacy, impossible to ignore.

But only nine months later, in December 2014, it seemed as if Putin's world had lost its vibrant colors. President Obama was quick, and delighted, to note the change. In a year-end interview with NPR's Steve Inskeep, he seemed almost to gloat about Putin's troubles. "You'll recall," he said, "that three or four months ago, everybody in Washington was convinced that President

Putin was a genius. And he had outmaneuvered all of us, and he had, you know, bullied and, you know, strategized his way into expanding Russian power. And today, you know, I'd sense that at least outside of Russia, maybe some people are thinking what Putin did wasn't so smart."[48]

While addressing the Russian people at year's end, Putin himself appeared cautious, even anxious, about Russia's immediate future. He continued, to be sure, to glory in his Crimean conquest, but now he did not frame it, as he had in March, as the opening of a new phase in Russian history—a *"Novorossiya"* plan to recapture parts of Ukraine in a new Russian empire. Neither the word nor the plan appeared in the December speech. Now Putin used Crimea solely to polish his political credentials, and move on. But to what? An economy in crisis.

For the first time, Putin acknowledged that the Western sanctions, which he had earlier disparaged as harmless pinpricks, were hurting Russia's economy—indeed, to the point where a number of Russian economists were openly worrying about a meltdown, a repeat of Russia's 1998 economic collapse, which, no one needed reminding, led a year later to Yeltsin yielding power to a then-unknown politician from St. Petersburg named Putin. Was there now another Putin lurking somewhere in Putin's future?

Putin also acknowledged that Russia's economic problems were serious, requiring urgent reform. But the reforms he proposed were so modest, compared to the challenges, that it seemed as if Putin did not truly understand the depth and breadth of the problems his country faced. Going one step further, it also seemed that he might not have grasped the possibility that the Russian elite, the people he put in power, might feel Putin was no longer the man for the job. Further still, that there was the danger that the Russian people, in a series of popular street demonstrations, might rise in opposition to Putin and Putinism and throw the country into unpredictable chaos.

All this may still happen. His days may indeed be numbered. But two weeks later, at his annual end-of-the-year news conference on December 18, 2014, fielding questions for more than three hours, on "live" TV, from an auditorium filled with 1,200 Russian and foreign reporters, Putin seemed like the Putin of old, a self-confident master of the modern means of communication. The questions ranged from the economy to the war in Ukraine, from the possibility of a "palace coup" to his pride in Russia's unbeatable bear.[49]

For the better part of a week, during which Russia's dismal economy had dominated the news, Russian TV had run a snazzy ad about Putin's 2014 leadership—the Olympics, the annexation of Crimea, the deals with China and India—closing with a reminder that the news conference would run on Thursday, December 18, 2014. In other words, Putin wanted the Russian people to tune in. Message: their leader was unafraid, proud, tough, patriotic.

Even the Russian bear played an unexpectedly central role in the news conference. It was almost as though Putin wanted to be seen as a "Russian bear," wandering through a global taiga—peaceful, self-absorbed, but, when challenged, capable of a defiant, angry response.

Using this analogy, he said that "sometimes I think that maybe it would be best if our bear just sat still. Maybe he should stop chasing pigs and boars around the taiga but start picking berries and eating honey." Who were the pigs and boars? The United States? Britain? Germany? He did not say. Putin went on, "Maybe then he will be left alone. But no, he won't be! Because someone will always try to chain him up. As soon as he's chained they will tear out his teeth and claws." By "teeth and claws," he meant, he said, "the power of nuclear deterrence."

He continued: "And then, when all the teeth and claws are torn out, the bear will be of no use at all. Perhaps they'll stuff it and that's all. So, it is not about Crimea but about us protecting our independence, our sovereignty and our right to exist. That is what we should all realize."

Putin often used the bear analogy to warn the West that Russia had only limited patience with its political and economic maneuvering. Russia would negotiate about Ukraine, but it would also fearlessly defend its interests, at home and abroad.

With regard to the Russian economy, Putin seemed to have persuaded himself that, one way or the other, it would bounce back, more quickly than many believed. "The most unfavorable foreign economic situation," he said—blaming Russia's problems on "external factors" having nothing to do with his stewardship of Russia—could last "for about two years." However, he quickly added, "it may not last that long and the situation could take a turn for the better sooner. It could improve in the first or second quarter of next year, by the middle of next year, or by its end." He was trying, with bumbling imprecision, to sound optimistic. "Further growth and a resolution of this situation are inevitable," he said. Putin even tried making a virtue of Russia's economic misery, saying that "the external conditions are forcing us to become more efficient and to shift to innovative development." Russians had a reputation for patience, Putin knew. "Two years" were for them but a blink of the eye—good times would inevitably return.

On Ukraine, Putin changed the tone of his policy but not its essence. Instead of describing the Kiev regime as a "fascist junta," as he had for most of 2014, he seemed to accept Kiev as a legitimate negotiating partner and even applauded Poroshenko's peacemaking efforts. "I still think that President Poroshenko is oriented towards settlement," he said—but only after noting that "we have been hearing statements from other officials, who advocate basically a war to the end." This seemed to be a deliberate attempt to split Kiev into two camps: one favoring Poroshenko's bid for a peaceful settlement, and the other, a band of unnamed hawks, pushing for aggressively prosecuting the war against the rebels in southeastern Ukraine. Putin concluded that "concrete actions and steps are needed" to end the fighting, but he did not detail them, nor did he say whether he believed Ukraine was capable of taking those steps.

Putin softened Russia's negotiating position without seeming to abandon his rebel allies in southeastern Ukraine. Russia was no longer pressing for "autonomy" or "federalizing the separatist territories," he said. Russia wanted Ukraine to emerge from the negotiation in one piece, which would seem to place Putin in opposition to his rebel allies, who still favored separate, autonomous republics in Donetsk and Luhansk. But actually would it? As Putin saw the problem, he could have it both ways: continue to support the rebels with "volunteers" and arms, thus retaining his influence over them, while at the same time negotiating with Poroshenko over Ukraine's future shape. So long as he was negotiating with Poroshenko while aiding the rebels, he would retain his influence on both sides of the Ukrainian civil war.

Nothing is more important to Putin than the continuing support of the Russian people. He need not worry about a "palace coup"—with a disdainful smirk, he brushed aside the question—nor about Russia's slumping economy. So long as his approval ratings stayed steady in the mid-80s, Putin felt no heat from potential competitors for political power. Indeed, none were visible on the near horizon. Although an autocrat, Putin recognized the value of popular support. "There is no other stability as solid as the support of the Russian people," he told the assembled reporters. "I don't think you have any doubts as to whether our key foreign and domestic policy initiatives benefit from such support. Why is this happening? Because people feel deep down inside that we, and I in particular, are acting in the interests of the overwhelming majority of Russians." The *Washington Post* duly reported an 85 percent approval rating for Putin.

By Dawn's Early Light

If there was even a flicker of hope that 2015 would open with some sort of a miraculous peace formula for solving the Ukraine crisis, it was quickly crushed by Western intelligence reports showing a sharp increase in Russian military supplies to the rebels in southeastern Ukraine. If in the early days of the war Russians went to great lengths to disguise their involvement in the war, now they seemed indifferent to Western overhead surveillance. Russian troops, identified again as "volunteers," openly crossed the border between Russia and Ukraine. Reporters were able to observe them taking command positions in battles around Donetsk but not do the fighting themselves. That was left for the rebels, who seemed ready to advance on Mariupol, a major port on the Black Sea, which served as a door to Crimea. By mid-January, the fighting intensified throughout the region, surprising many NATO officers who had not expected an upsurge until springtime. The cease-fire, negotiated by Putin and Poroshenko in September 2014, was clearly unraveling. Western leaders, such as Obama and Merkel, scratched their heads; they still could not figure out what Putin was up to.

The Russian economy was staggering under the weight of Western sanctions and falling oil prices, and Russian consumers were beginning to complain, but Putin seemed not to be looking or listening. He kept his focus on Ukraine. Brazenly, he deepened the Russian imprint in Ukraine, while baldly denying any involvement and accusing Washington of stirring the pot. If Putin was deliberately seeking a new confrontation, perhaps as a diversion from his economic problems, perhaps as a way of exciting a wider wave of Russian nationalism, he was close to achieving his goal. One proud Russian, Denis Gariyev, a 36-year-old St. Petersburger who had "volunteered" to fight in the Donbas, stressed that his country's policy was only a response to Western aggression. "Those who join the rebels in Luhansk and Donetsk are those who understand that this is their war, our common war against the enemies of Russia, against the expansion of the West," said Gariyev.[50] He reflected an extraordinary rise in anti-Western, and especially anti-American, sentiment in Russia since the Crimean annexation. Ninety percent of Russians now harbored negative feelings about the United States, according to the Levada Center, an independent polling operation, a big jump up from what it used to be.[51] Putin has been able to tap into this street corner anti-Americanism whenever it suits his purposes.

Washington responded in a flurry of predictable anxiety, everyone, it seemed, absorbed with the burning question of whether the United States should now begin to provide lethal arms to Ukraine. Up to this point, American military aid had been "nonlethal"—communications equipment and other items that aided Ukraine's military but did not kill anyone. The feeling was that Russia was getting away with murder, literally, and Putin had to be stopped. For the first time, senior officials, including Secretary Kerry, Defense Secretary Ashton Carter, and General Martin E. Dempsey, chairman of the Joint Chiefs of Staff, began openly to support the idea of sending American lethal weapons to Ukraine, but Obama would not yield to the building pressure, even from his closest advisers—at least not yet. He remained instinctively opposed to a deeper American military involvement in Ukraine. Yet, he found himself slipping into one, promising to protect the Baltics and increasing the flow of nonlethal aid to Ukraine. Most important, perhaps, he began, in April 2015, to send roughly 300 American military advisers to Ukraine. Maybe, at the same time, he was praying that Putin would one day change his policy.

Three think tanks—Brookings, the Atlantic Council, and the Chicago Council on Global Affairs—combined in late January 2015 to propose $3 billion in military assistance to Ukraine, their way of putting the heat on Obama to get tough with Putin. "The West needs to bolster deterrence in Ukraine," they insisted, "by raising the risks and costs to Russia of any renewed major offensive."[52] The thought that suddenly the United States might become militarily involved in Ukraine touched off a torrent of concern on both sides of the Atlantic. There had always been a deep-seated fear that one day Ukraine would somehow draw Russia and America into the war—on opposite sides. The *New York Times* worried editorially that "lethal assistance could open a dangerous new chapter in the struggle."[53] An alarmed Chancellor Merkel flatly ruled out Germany sending any military supplies to Ukraine. She would not hear of it. "I am convinced that this conflict cannot be solved militarily."[54] Merkel, joining up with French president François Hollande, then decided to give diplomacy one more chance. She was, according to a few of her aides, getting desperate. She called Putin and Poroshenko, solemnly urging both to agree to a new cease-fire, or to a new effort to strengthen the old cease-fire of September 2014, before the fresh fighting in the Donbas got totally out of hand. She began to worry that the fighting in Ukraine could spread to the Baltics and then farther west.

A rushed round of shuttle diplomacy followed. Merkel and Hollande flew to Kiev and then to Moscow, pressuring the leaders of both belligerents to return to Minsk for another go at diplomacy. Poroshenko reluctantly agreed. He could see he had few cards to play; his economy was in shambles, and his army was under-armed and under-staffed. Putin agreed, realizing he was in the catbird's seat. His rebels, freshly rearmed, were on the offensive. Before diplomacy could stop them, they would likely have captured Debaltseve, a railroad hub important for resupplying the Donbas basin. With their agreement in hand, Merkel flew to Washington for urgent meetings with Obama, and then, on February 11, 2015, to Minsk, where she and Hollande met with Putin and Poroshenko. The quartet was expanded to include the ambassador of the Organization for Security and Cooperation in Europe and the two rebel "prime ministers" of Luhansk and Donetsk.

For sixteen hours, the exhausted politicians met and negotiated not a new cease-fire but an elaboration of the old one, agreeing to an "immediate and comprehensive ceasefire *in certain areas*" (italics added) of Luhansk and Donetsk, a withdrawal of heavy weapons from the front lines by both sides, and the kind of constitutional reform that would allow greater autonomy for the Donbas region of Ukraine. Most of the time, they debated the status of Debaltseve, Poroshenko arguing that it was under Ukrainian control and should remain that way, Putin arguing that it would soon be under rebel control. Putin was right—the rebels captured it on February 23.[55] On that issue, they could reach no agreement. Merkel suggested that they formalize their agreement on all other matters, and the deal was struck.

Putin later told Russian reporters that "we have managed to agree on the main issues. Why did it take so long? I think this is due to the fact that the Kiev authorities still refuse to make direct contact with the representatives of the Donetsk and Luhansk people's republics." Hollande said, "The coming hours will be decisive." Merkel, before boarding her plane back to Berlin, summed up the negotiation by saying "big obstacles" remained but there was now a "glimmer of hope" for a meaningful cease-fire.[56] One of the obstacles was a Ukrainian report that fifty Russian tanks, forty missile systems, and forty armored vehicles had just crossed the border into rebel-held territory. Another was the common assumption that the rebels would continue fighting until they captured Debaltseve, which was exactly what happened. But then the fighting subsided and, except for a skirmish here and there, stopped. Poroshenko time and again accused the Russians and the rebels of violating the cease-fire, but unless the rebels rushed on to Mariupol, opening a land route to Crimea, Western leaders, led by Merkel, seemed prepared to look the other way. None ever thought there would be a complete cease-fire.

Putin, if he was capable of being objective about himself, could look in the mirror, pat himself on the back, and acknowledge that he had reached an enviable position on the Ukraine war. His rebels were in undisputed control of the Luhansk and Donetsk provinces, a fact confirmed now by international agreement. His adversaries in Kiev were reeling from economic calamity and military setbacks. Western leaders understood that he, Putin, was key to any resolution of the crisis. Obama seemed bewildered, and Merkel tired and cranky. Since rising to absolute power in 2000, Putin has watched a succession of world leaders bite the dust, while he remained in power. As Eugene Rumer of the Carnegie Endowment for International Peace observed, George W. Bush left the White House with two unfinished wars and the deepest recession since the Great Depression; British prime minister Tony Blair left 10 Downing Street with his reputation severely tarnished by the Iraq War; Germany's Gerhard Schroder now seemed to be in Putin's hip pocket, holding a retainer for Russia's state-controlled gas company; Italy's Silvio Berlusconi was in disgrace; Jacques Chirac of France, Jean Chretien of Canada, and Junichiro Koizumi of Japan were all out of power and fading from view. "Mr. Putin alone remains at the helm," Rumor wrote, "with domestic approval ratings above 80 percent."[57] Of course, he had one clear advantage over his contemporary rivals: He was an autocrat, operating in an authoritarian environment; the others were, for the most part, democrats, operating in an open political environment.

Novorossiya, the rebel newspaper, summed up the Minsk II negotiation in a very positive way. "Following our military victory, we have achieved a diplomatic victory in Minsk: we have become de facto independent." Putin was their negotiator, and they were in his debt but seemed not to mind. A man like Putin, the newspaper crowed, "is born only once in a thousand years. The day will come when he will also be our president."[58]

CHAPTER 18

Whither Ukraine? Whither Russia?

Putin has dug himself in, and he can't get out.
SENIOR AIDE TO CHANCELLOR MERKEL

IF *FORBES* MAGAZINE WAS RIGHT in declaring Putin, for the second year in a row, to be the "most powerful person" on Earth, and if the Carnegie Endowment for International Peace was right in describing Putin as "the most influential person" of 2014, then his decisions about Ukraine and Russia may go a long way toward determining the future of both countries.[1] Putin, a pugnacious politician with an enormous ego and thuggish ambition, has, in recent years, combined daring with guile, duplicity with audacity, to both challenge and frighten different parts of the world. Whether the issue happens to be Iranian nuclear weapons, or the "Islamic State," or Syria's uncivil war, or China, or Ukraine, Putin's Russia has played a key role either in stirring things up or in joining a multinational effort to settle or stalemate a problem. Russia has risen, as though from the ashes of the Soviet collapse in 1991, to a new prominence in global affairs. In sum, Russia is back. That was one of Putin's key goals, and he has achieved it.

In the tumultuous year of 2014, Putin went from presiding over Olympic glory to sponsoring anti-Ukrainian aggression—rarely missing a beat, violating international norms as though they were meaningless bumps in the road. He has acted like Peter the Great (some say Ivan the Terrible), with a dash of Stalin, boldness at one level, paralyzing dread at another. His Russia has not been noted for its scientific or cultural achievements but rather, in the words of a *Washington Post* editorial, for its "graft, cronyism, paranoia and resentment," and, toward the end of the year, for its dramatic economic decline.[2]

Putin, a former KBG apparatchik, has clearly calculated that if he added fear and brute force to his penchant for unpredictability, he could get his way on just about anything—and so far he just about has. Gernot Erler, Germany's special coordinator for Russia policy, who usually leans toward pro-Russian sentiments, framed Putin's policy as following "the principle of organized unpredictability."[3] The West, in response, seems able only to sanction Russia, but do little else; it issues warnings of increasing costs and isolation, but they apparently fall on deaf ears. After more than a year of frustrating diplomacy and inconclusive warfare, Ukraine, as of mid-2015, was frozen in a strategic deadlock between Russia and the West. Both sides were engaged in what sociologist Karl Deutsch would have termed a "war by proxy"—"military actions that take place on the territory, and utilize the resources of a third country, under cover of resolving an international conflict in that country."[4] Such deadlocks can be very dangerous, especially when one of the sides—in this case the Russian one—has hunkered down in a belligerent crouch.

During the G-20 summit held in mid-November 2014 in Brisbane, Australia, German chancellor Merkel—who had spent more time on the phone with Putin than she had with any other world leader, often discussing the crisis in Ukraine—thought it was time for a fresh approach. To this point, she had been getting nowhere. She decided to confront Putin alone, no aides, no interpreters. Having been reared during the cold war in the former German Democratic Republic (GDR), she spoke Russian, while Putin, as a former KGB operative in the GDR, spoke fluent German. She invited Putin to her Brisbane hotel suite and there put the basic, unanswered question to him: What do you want in Ukraine? What in the final analysis will you accept?

They spoke for four hours, but all she got were the same denials and dodges she had been hearing for months. "He radiated coldness," a Merkel aide later told Reuters. "Putin has dug himself in, and he can't get out." Merkel now expects a "prolonged conflict." "We are essentially in a waiting game," said another aide.[5] Her basic view, according to Alexander Lambsdorff, a German member of the European Parliament, was that Russia was "a traditional hegemonic power that was subdued for a while and now has re-emerged." And it has reemerged with a leader holding some odd, old-fashioned beliefs about Russia's relations with the outside world. "Putin believes that we're decadent, we're gay, we have women with beards," a German official quoted Merkel as believing. "That it's a strong Russia of real men versus the decadent West that's too pampered, too spoiled, to stand up for their beliefs if it costs them one percent of their standard of living."[6]

No one seemed more distressed by Putin's policy than Merkel, who thought she understood the Russians. She had hoped for a new positive era in East-West relations but now faced a bleeding crisis in Ukraine that was the result, she felt, of Putin's "old thinking," of his trampling on international law, of his reckless opportunism. "After the horror of the two world wars and the end of the cold war," she said during the G-20 meeting in Australia, "this calls into question the peaceful order in Europe." She meant the period following the Soviet collapse in 1991.[7]

Irritating Merkel and many other West Europeans even more has been Putin's penchant for mixing his apparently irrepressible urge to boast about all things Russian with an ego-driven need to be in everyone's line of sight. Putin spoke at the October 2014 Valdai Discussion Club meeting in Sochi, which focused on whether the global community will develop ground rules for managing world politics or whether it is a game without any rules, where everyone must fend for himself. The Russian leader, in his welcoming address, stressed how differently the West reacted to Kosovo in the 1990s and to Crimea now. His PR people, always thinking about new ways of putting Putin in the limelight, had apparently come up with a proverb, designed to make him look like an intellectual, an image he enjoyed projecting. "*Quod licet Iovi, non licet bovi*," he pronounced. It meant: "What is permissible for Jove is not permissible for an ox." He was trying to say, in artful language, that a hypocritical West believed it could get its way in Kosovo, but Russia could not in Crimea. He felt that was wrong. "We cannot agree with such an approach," he objected. "The ox may not be allowed something, but the bear will not even bother to ask permission." A bear, he added with mock humor, was "master of the taiga," suggesting that Russia, as a bear, could, with impunity, invade Crimea, Ukraine, anywhere, and emerge triumphant. No one could stand in a bear's way.[8]

When one looks back at 2014, it may be that the return of the cold war, or something close to it, will be seen as Putin's crowning accomplishment. What a shame! He could have done so much more for Russia, Ukraine—and his own legacy. But he did not—and we must ask why. It was because, in his mind, what happened in Ukraine in late February—what he described as a pro-Western "coup" that toppled Yanukovych—was an injustice that could not be allowed to stand. Ukraine, until 1991, had always been a part of Russia, its history and destiny intertwined with Russia's, he believed, and it could not now be allowed to spin out of its natural Slavic orbit and become a Western outpost, an "existential" threat, in Russia's own backyard: its "near abroad," as Moscow describes its neighborhood, its "sphere of influence," as the diplomats prefer to put it.

In Putin's twisted, rear-view image of the crisis, Ukraine had to be kept in the Slavic world. It could not be allowed to go "Western," or, at least, too

"Western." If Ukraine insisted on being independent, that was an acceptable point of view, Putin seemed to believe, but not if, at the same time, it harbored hostile intent toward Russia. Putin gambled that he could—and would—get his way. Result: In the short term, yes, he would, and has. But, in the middle to long term, it's not very likely, and the reason may lie more in his governance of Russia than anything else.

The Future Is the Past

Ukraine is the witch's cauldron, out of which have recently arisen deep concerns about Russian insecurities and Western misjudgments. When explaining his policy to a doubting world, Putin has always returned to the disintegration of the Soviet Union in 1991 as the key to understanding his Ukraine policy and much else. "We should acknowledge," he said, in April 2005, and many times since, that "the collapse of the Soviet Union was a major geopolitical disaster of the century."[9] The phrase cried out for hype, and the Associated Press willingly obliged, rephrasing it to read "the greatest geopolitical catastrophe of the 20th century," which became the preferred translation in the West. Either way, it was central to his thinking.

At the Valdai meeting in Sochi, Putin charged that the West, "the so-called winners of the cold war," exploited the "disaster"/"catastrophe" to marginalize and ignore Russia rather than engage it in a meaningful dialogue aimed at creating a new world order. "A sensible reconstruction should have been carried out," he explained, "and a system of international relations should have been adapted to the new realities."[10] Putin argues that Russia was ready then, but the West was not. As proof, it's said that Yeltsin was seriously considering joining NATO, possibly also the EU, so deep apparently was his vision of post–cold war Russia as an essentially Western nation seeking a close institutional relationship with other Western nations. But no, Putin continued, that was unfortunately not to be. "Now there has soared the risk of a string of acute conflicts with the direct or indirect involvement of major powers."[11] He meant Ukraine, more than any other problem.

This is a vision of recent history that sends Western officials, and former officials, into a form of diplomatic apoplexy. They argue persuasively that Putin picks his way through history to find support for his policy, or confirmation of his beliefs while discarding history that does not conform to his worldview. If he has concluded that the reason for the Ukraine crisis lies in a Western-contrived coup in Kiev in February 2014, then he will say so, and come to believe it, no matter what the actual facts reveal. At an Aspen

Institute luncheon in late November 2014, Nicholas Burns, a former senior State Department official and now a Harvard professor, stated, with considerable passion, that, in the late 1990s and early 2000s, the West offered Russia a full tray-load of opportunities to join in a "sensible reconstruction" of East-West relations. The West, he said, wanted Russia to become part of a "new world order," to use President George H. W. Bush's memorable phrase.[12]

But, in fact, though Russia accepted a few of these opportunities, it rejected most of the others, leaving many in the West to believe that basically Russia did not want to link arms with the West, either because it did not see its future tied to the West or because it was profoundly suspicious of Western intentions. At the moment, Putin personifies these suspicions; they undergird his policy, his grasp of history, and his decisions about Russia's national interest. If the West hopes to resolve the Ukraine crisis, and many other divisive problems, it must understand the roots of Putin's policy, no matter how rooted they may be in a false appreciation of history.

There is, for sure, a degree of personal and professional gratification in denouncing Putin, in comparing him to Hitler, in gloating about his current economic problems. But these rhetorical flourishes do not really help Russia or the West find an acceptable pathway to solving such difficult problems as Ukraine. This is especially the case when a number of statesmen, East and West, have begun to assert that Putin's understanding of the communist collapse in 1991, and the Western reaction to it, may actually be based more on fact than fancy.

For example, Mikhail Gorbachev, whose admiration for Putin could comfortably fit into a thimble, interestingly leaped to his defense in November 2014, during Berlin's twenty-fifth anniversary celebrations of the fall of the Berlin Wall. Gorbachev should know; he was president of the Soviet Union at the time. He picked up Putin's oft-repeated theme that the West ignored Russia in 1991, leaving an unfortunate vacuum of misunderstanding and confusion in later years. "Our Western partners," Gorbachev recalled, did not "take Russia's point of view and legal interests in security into consideration. They paid lip service to applauding Russia, especially during the Yeltsin years, but in deeds they didn't consider it." His prized example was NATO expansion. "They literally said, 'this is none of your business.' As a result, an abscess formed, and it burst." He meant whatever good will might have accumulated during the Yeltsin years "burst" during the Putin years. "Instead of accusing Russia of everything," Gorbachev advised, the West ought to remember the promise of the early 1990s and compare it to "what it has unfortunately turned into in recent years."[13]

A number of former American officials have come, in varying degrees, to share Gorbachev's (and Putin's) assessment of the 1991 changes in East-West relations, at the core of which was the dramatic collapse of the Soviet Union. For example, consider the opinions of Robert Gates, who served as director of the CIA before becoming secretary of defense for both Presidents George W. Bush and Barack Obama. During the cold war, he was a hard-liner; now he is in Gorbachev's corner on the 1991 controversy. "They [the Russians] believed they had a commitment that we wouldn't try and move NATO to the East," Gates told the Council on Foreign Relations. And "when we tried to move towards Georgia and Ukraine, . . . it was, if you will, a bridge too far. And particularly, when you consider Kiev as the birthplace of the Russian empire, back in the tenth century, ninth century, and when you consider that Crimea is then part of Ukraine, Russia's only warm water port, and its only naval base on the Black Sea." His summary: "I think all of those things made Ukraine especially sensitive, and I think that's why Ukraine is so sensitive for them right now. And why what's happening there is key."[14]

Gates, a student of Russian history, pointed to the traumatic upheavals in 1991 as the basic reason for Putin's (and Russia's) deep distrust of the West. "We in the West," Gates stressed, "dramatically underestimated the degree of humiliation on the part of the Russians with the collapse, not just of the Soviet Union . . . but the collapse of the Russian empire, a thousand years in the building." Putin "needs to be taken seriously when he says that he thought that the collapse of the Soviet Union was the greatest geo-strategic catastrophe of the twentieth century. I absolutely believe that he believes that. . . . He and others like him have been determined from the beginning to restore Russia as a world power, as a force to be reckoned with." One conclusion, in Gates's view, was that Putin believes he has a special responsibility to protect all Russians living in neighboring countries, even if that means crossing a national border to protect them. Putin "believes this protection of Russians who were left behind by the collapse of the Soviet Union in northern Kazakhstan, elsewhere in Central Asia, and Ukraine, and Moldova, and in the Baltic states, is a historical calling for him."[15]

Henry Kissinger, often portrayed as the patron saint of cold war diplomacy, agreed with Gates and Gorbachev and, in tsk-tsk fashion, waved a finger at the West for not understanding "the impact of these events [on Russia], starting with the negotiations about Ukraine's economic relations with the European Union and culminating in the demonstrations in Kiev. All these, and their impact, should have been the subject of a dialogue with Russia." But there was no dialogue, and therefore little understanding of Ukraine's "special significance for Russia." By trying to lasso Ukraine to the West, economically, diplomatically and politically, Kissinger said, the West ignored Russian concerns. Putin's seizure of Crimea "was not a move toward global conquest," he said. "It was not Hitler moving into Czechoslovakia"—an analogy raised by, among others, former secretary of state Hillary Rodham Clinton. It clearly had a more limited objective. Putin wanted to protect Russia from "NATO expansion." In fact, Kissinger believed, the West was as responsible as Russia for the Ukraine crisis, a position radically at odds with the conventional wisdom in Washington. [16] But Putin was so defiantly outrageous in his seizure of Crimea, and in his subsequent support for rebellion in southeastern Ukraine, that most of the Western world immediately and instinctively opposed him.

Russian aggression was compared with Hitler's before the outbreak of World War II. Obama was on the phone to Putin warning Russia would be isolated, its reputation damaged, its economy, already hurting, would be further undermined by economic sanctions then under serious consideration by the United States and the EU. When Obama offered Putin an "off-ramp," a face-saving way out of the crisis he created, it was summarily rejected. The UN Security Council met in emergency session. The focus was on the obvious fact that Russia had crossed an international border and thereby violated a set of post–World War II norms recognized by the West and presumed to have been recognized by Russia as well, though they never had been. By arbitrarily crossing an international border, Russia had, by definition, invaded another country. Russia had become the aggressor, Ukraine the victim. In the Western view, aggression could never be considered cost-free; Russia had to pay a price. That has been the firm Western position since the beginning of the crisis in March 2014.

Putin, who had been seen in Western chanceries as an unappealing character in a Slavic sideshow, was catapulted into the global spotlight, and questions naturally arose about him. Again, as earlier in his career, when he was mysteriously selected to replace Yeltsin, when he ordered the crushing of the Chechen uprising, when he quickly readjusted the Russian bureaucracy to acquire exceptional political and personal power, when he sent his army into the former Soviet republic of Georgia and seized Abkhazia and Ossetia, two of its provinces, and when, early in 2014, he grabbed Crimea, questions bubbled to the surface about Putin the man, the politician, the strategist. Just what did Putin want in Ukraine? Ultimately, on a broader canvas, what were his goals? These were the same questions Merkel asked, the same questions Putin ducked.

2014—Not a Good Year for Diplomacy

Diplomacy is not meant to travel at warp speed. It needs time for politics to work its magic, for politicians to find formulas for making or avoiding decisions, for wars to unwind. But in 2014 there was little time for diplomacy to nurture compromises. Ukraine became an instant crisis, and therefore an instant media attraction—big news in the West, and in Russia, where most journalists became propagandists for Putin's vision of the crisis. The "CNN effect" had returned, playing a big role in planting Ukraine on the front page of global affairs, forcing statesmen to focus on its inherent dangers. Radio and TV talk shows featured "Russian experts," relics of the cold war era who did their best to look into Putin's soul, just as George W. Bush had once famously tried to do. Putin became the man of the hour, his policy dissected and vivisected, and Ukraine became the story of the day. As death tolls mounted (more than 6,000 reported dead by March 2015), Russia's actions were described as "nineteenth century" in tone and spirit, dangerous and demonic; the West's response, on the other hand, as "twenty-first century," modern and pragmatic.

Poor Ukraine, Westerners Groaned. What's to Be Done?

Surely what was *not* done was for high-level policymakers to study, if only briefly, the long and intricate history of Russian-Ukrainian relations. There, in this history—ever since the tenth century, in the commerce, the wars, the literature, the intermarriages, in Vladimir the Great's conversion to Orthodox Christianity, in medieval Kievan Rus', in the Mongol invasion, devastating to both Kiev and Moscow, and its lingering legacy of absolutism, in Catherine the Great's absorption of Crimea and later Ukraine, in Stalin's creation of a Ukrainian republic—in all this history, Ukraine, as Russia's "little brother," lived in a close but uncomfortable and contentious relationship with its "big brother." One always was tied to the other, a record of intertwined interconnections, in which they shared the same religion, culture, traditions, history, even essentially the same language. When Russia won a war, Ukraine benefited, its loosely defined borders swelling. When Russia lost, Ukraine suffered—and its borders accordingly shrunk. Ukraine was almost always the battleground, mid-way, in scholar Stephen Kotkin's vision, between German power and Russian power, geography often determining loyalty.[17]

Over the centuries, Ukraine developed a split personality, locked in a nonstop war between East and West, between an inescapable linkage to Russia and an attraction to, or revulsion against, Catholic Poland or Austria. In cities such as Lvov, Ukrainians felt themselves to be Western; in cities such as Donetsk or Luhansk, they felt Russian. This split persists to this day, one reason why a division of Ukraine between east and west as a way out of the current mess falls into the realm of the possible.

Only in 1900 did a small band of Ukrainian nationalists announce the formation of an "independence" party. It got nowhere. Only between 1917 and 1921, during the wild years of the Russian Revolution, did the same nationalists flirt, albeit unsuccessfully, with the responsibilities of independence. They failed, because, ultimately, Lenin's Bolsheviks defeated them on the field of battle. Ukraine then became a "republic" in the newly formed Soviet Union, only because Lenin and Stalin decreed it would be so. For the first time, it enjoyed some of the trappings of a state, down to a figurehead foreign minister. But it lacked any real power, any real sovereignty, any real dignity. After World War II, its borders and population swelled to unprecedented levels, as Stalin, riding the crest of his military victory over the Axis powers, propelled Soviet power westward. Stalin had, as Kotkin noted, unintentionally become "Father of Ukraine."

When the Soviet Union disintegrated in 1991, Ukraine took advantage of the political chaos and proclaimed itself an independent nation, free of Moscow's control. It was for Ukraine a bold step. Its leaders, cautious to the bone, acted only after every other Soviet "republic" had already done so.

Otherwise, in its history, Ukraine had never been an independent nation. It had always been associated with Russia, either as the birthplace of the "first Russia," to quote historian Bernard Pares, or as the inspiration for the "second Russia," which originated in Moscow and spread out from there. No one, not even Putin, has argued that Ukraine does not have the right to be independent. It is independent, and it is recognized as such by much of the world. Its current president, Petro Poroshenko, has been received at the White House, and he has addressed the U.S. Congress, an honor bestowed on a minority of visiting heads of state.

And yet, to paraphrase Abraham Lincoln, there is no escaping history. For many centuries, Ukraine's fate has been enmeshed with Russia's. It always has been, and probably always will be. Ukraine cannot alter its geography. It cannot move to a better neighborhood in Western Europe. It cannot readjust its economic realities, so that *it* enjoys a gas and oil monopoly, for example, making Russia dependent on *Ukrainian* gas and oil. It cannot, at least in the immediate future, become a major nuclear power in the Slavic world. It gave up its nuclear weapons more than twenty years ago. In its edgy relationship with Russia, Ukraine is the junior partner. Therefore, any realistic solution to the current crisis must first satisfy the interests of Russia and then those of Ukraine. In sum, the first step out of the current crisis is an acceptable modus vivendi between Russia and Ukraine, an arrangement under which Russia, because it is by far the stronger of the two, gets the larger half of the loaf, Ukraine the smaller one. The West can approve, or disapprove, but if it continues to intrude into this delicate game of diplomatic shadow-boxing, then it is very likely doomed to fail.

This formula flies in the face of global etiquette and strategic concerns. Russia was the aggressor. It seems immoral, just wrong, to be asked to take Russia's interests into account—indeed, to give Russia a primary position in determining the final outcome. In Kiev, it might even border on treason to bend a knee in Moscow's direction. The Western view is that Russia must obey international law or pay a terrible price. But according to an increasing number of scholars, including Samuel Charap, a senior fellow at London's International Institute for Strategic Studies, an "unsentimental assessment" of Ukraine's current problems leads to only one inescapable conclusion: If Ukraine is to survive, not as a failed state, but as one that has enough resources to meet its bills, then it must first strike a political and economic deal with Russia, principally because Ukraine has little choice.[18] Unless the West, led by the United States, decides to underwrite Ukraine's debts and fight its wars, Ukraine inexorably will remain vulnerable to Russian pressure. And there is little reason to believe the West is willing to assume that dangerous and expensive burden at this time.

Think for a moment about the Donbas, the area of eastern Ukraine largely under rebel control as of mid-2015. It accounts for 15 percent of Ukraine's population, 16 percent of its GDP, 25 percent of its industrial output, and 27 percent of its total exports, much of that to Russia.[19] The Donbas is the heart of the runaway Donetsk and Luhansk People's Republics. If the Kiev government loses all control of the Donbas, which in many ways it already has, then it faces the realistic prospect of becoming a partitioned country, Kiev leaning for support on the West, the Donbas on Russia—a circumstance that would be nothing new in Ukrainian history. If Putin were inclined to compromise with Poroshenko, then perhaps a loose arrangement leaving Ukraine technically in one piece would still be possible. But Putin now imagines himself to be in the driver's seat in any negotiation with Poroshenko. If he comes to believe that his power base in Moscow has been weakened, and his job is in jeopardy, then he might at some point agree to a compromise. But, to this point in the crisis, even with Russia's economic problems on the rise, Putin's popularity remains high and his power base seems unassailable. The hope among some Russians that the once-vaunted oligarchs would one day rise from their comfort zones and drive Putin from power is far-fetched and, in a way, foolish—the oligarchs no longer have any power independent of Putin. They still have money, lots of it. But these days their wealth and privilege are measured by their continued loyalty to Putin. They know that if they challenge him, they will lose their power and position.

Putin can, of course, decide to strike a deal with Poroshenko. Perhaps, at some time in the near future, Russia's economic decline, which seems to grow worse by the day, may oblige him to soften his Ukraine policy and trim his support of the rebels in southeastern Ukraine. While that is possible, it is also unlikely. He would not only lose face; he would likely lose his job. Russia would again be humiliated. Putin would view a Russian rollback in Ukraine at this time as a replay of 1991. No, he is apt to conclude, not on his shift.

CHAPTER 19

A Look Back to Look Ahead

For him, there are no inviolable rules, nor universal values,
nor even cast-iron facts. . . . There are only interests.
THE ECONOMIST

SINCE RUSSIA SEIZED CRIMEA in March 2014, Western leaders have had numerous conversations with Russian president Vladimir Putin, probing for his ultimate intentions in Ukraine. What is his bottom line? They hear him, but do not understand him. Germany's Angela Merkel says Putin must be "on another planet." She is exasperated by his refusal to play by Western rules in Ukraine. Barack Obama is equally flummoxed by Putin. He keeps offering the Russian president a series of face-saving "off-ramps," believing apparently that Putin is desperately scrambling for a way out of his Ukrainian gamble, and he needs Western help. The "off-ramp" is an Obama illusion. Putin is not seeking a way out of Ukraine; on the contrary, he seems determined to keep Russian forces in Ukraine, able in this way to "freeze" its destiny. Obama, disappointed in Putin, like a teacher in an errant pupil, then dismissively refers to Russia as a "regional power." Putin has a different vision of Russia. He sees it as a global power with nuclear weapons and borders stretching across nine time zones from Poland to the Pacific.

Just as Western leaders have trouble understanding Putin, he has trouble understanding them. They speak one language of diplomacy, he another. They sincerely believe in the rule of law in international relations, even if their actions do not always conform to the law. For them bilateral and multilateral treaties, agreements, and understandings are the stuff of sensible coexistence; the integration of the many into one manageable whole is often their goal. They have tried, since the pivotal year of 1991, when the Soviet Union died and Russia was reborn, to persuade first Boris Yeltsin and then Putin to accept this basic approach to global relations, and at times the Russian presidents have bought into the idea. Or so it seemed. For a time they engaged in summitry, spoke about mutual cooperation, and negotiated important agreements.

For example, in 1994, under Yeltsin, Russia signed onto NATO's Partnership for Peace program, designed to encourage better relations between NATO and former Soviet satellites in Eastern Europe. In 1997 Russia joined the Euro-Atlantic Council, whose central purpose was that East and West come to see each other as partners, no longer as adversaries or enemies. In 2002, when Putin was president, the Russia-NATO Council was formed, in part to fight global terrorism but also to stimulate military cooperation. And in 2012, after eighteen years of stubborn negotiations, Russia was finally admitted to the World Trade Organization—but only after Russia promised to live by its rules of the road, which were drafted in Washington.

Putin has lived in two worlds: one reaching out toward the West, however tentatively, the other riveted in the East, suspicious of Western intentions and policies. These are two worlds colliding in one mind and opening an ambivalent chasm in his strategic thinking. But by the time he returned to the presidency in 2012, after four years as prime minister, he had fused his two worlds into one, and that one was unmistakably rooted in Russia, now, in his mind, fully recovered from its post-1991 woes but besieged by Western intrigue and duplicity. He spied a return to a cold war "policy of containment," and he attacked political critics as a "fifth column," as "traitors" who had to be exposed, uprooted, and destroyed.

Putin had seen the anti-Russian "color" revolutions in his own backyard, in "rose" Georgia and "orange" Ukraine, and they terrified him. Even worse, he had seen hundreds of thousands of disgruntled Russians demonstrating in Moscow and other Russian cities against him and his increasingly autocratic and kleptomaniacal system of governance. Placards emblazoned with bold calls, such as "Down with Putin" and "Russia—Without Putin," were raised to the skies. These scenes must have reminded him of the late 1980s, when, as a KGB officer in Dresden, he watched with helpless horror as the German Democratic Republic was dismantled by angry mobs, frustrated by a cruel communist dictatorship. And then, only a few years later in 1991, he again watched as his once mighty Soviet Union fell apart, his Marxist dreams disintegrating into street corner migraines, and he was determined that, if he ever had the power, Russia would never again face such chaos and dismay. "Never again" became his battle cry. Russia, for Putin, was a peaceful, trustworthy, if edgy and unpredictable bear, wandering through the taiga, but, when challenged, a bear capable of a fierce and ferocious response.

Now, as "master of the taiga," Putin shows a capacity for self-delusion that has become dangerous. He has bought into the myth that Russia is again a superpower, as it was during Soviet times—a superpower armed with nuclear weapons, natural resources, and a talented people, deserving honor and respect and a backyard sphere of influence that would include the Slavic states of Ukraine and Belarus and the Islamic states of Azerbaijan, Kazakhstan, Kyrgyzstan, and Uzbekistan—all former republics of the Soviet Union. Over this vast expanse Russia would again rule with absolute authority. This is his guiding vision, however self-delusional, and it inspires his policy and strategy. In Ukraine, we have all seen its devastating consequences.

In truth, Russia remains, in many ways, a vulnerable third world country. Its economy still relies heavily on two or three natural resources—oil, gas, and timber—the same resources Nicholas II depended upon before the Russian Revolution of 1917. The rest of its economy is rickety, corrupt, and unproductive. In 1991 it suffered major strategic setbacks, including the dissolution of the Soviet Union, the loss of its East European empire, and the end of communism as a transformational ideology. It also lost half of its population, unceremoniously reduced to roughly 145 million as fourteen of the Soviet republics peeled away. Finally, though Russians are a literate people, justifiably proud of their culture, they remain, as individuals, largely inchoate cogs in an authoritarian system that yields little to no room for creative expression. The Mongols left a legacy of political obscurantism that still dominates Kremlin thinking. When Boris Nemtsov, an anti-Putin patriot, was murdered in February 2015, the small oasis of political dissent in Moscow, which he led, shriveled to nothingness, leaving a muddy wake of fear and uncertainty.

Yet, there is reason for hope—granted, not much. Russian history has always provided examples of surprising and sudden change. The quality of *stikhinost'*, or spontaneity, has spawned totally unexpected outbursts of rebellion and revolution. Bogdan Khmelnitsky did his mischief in the 1640s—he had anger on his side but no real strategy. Emelyan Pugachev went on his wild adventure in the 1770s, ravaging the countryside, frightening the Kremlin but also with no clear strategy. The Decembrists forced their way into Russian history in 1825. No one planned it. The 1905 Revolution just happened. No one planned that either. And then, of course, there was Vladimir Lenin's 1917 revolution. All of these upheavals had profound effects on Russia, its environs, and the world. Another may yet be stirring in the dark underbrush of Russian society.

Putin, like most Russian leaders, seems to fear nothing more than spontaneous upheavals. He is convinced that only an authoritarian, ultranationalist regime can protect Russia from its enemies, internal as well as external. He believes that for now he, and he alone, can ensure Russia's future as a great and respected nation. According to polling data, which is always suspect in an authoritarian state, most Russians share his view. One example: A Moscow shopper, unhappy about Russia's slipping economy, blamed not Putin but the United States. In fact, she felt sympathy for Putin. "America is an international bandit," she charged. "Poor Putin is pushing back the best he can."[1] The West is portrayed as the enemy, Putin as the Russian hero battling the perfidious West. Evgeny Minchenko, identified as a political consultant, told a BBC reporter that "sanctions may have hurt the Russian economy. But politically they unite people against the West. Recent polls show the highest level of anti-Western feeling in recent history." Putin has encouraged this result.[2] He knows that supporting him involves hating the West.

Putin loves Russians who love him, and he plays the game of statecraft by his own guidelines. As *The Economist* noted, "for him, there are no inviolable rules, nor universal values, nor even cast-iron facts (such as who shot down the Malaysian airliner). There are only interests."[3] And because Russia's interests, as he sees them, may not conform to international rules and regulations as the West sees them, a gulf in mutual understanding has emerged between Moscow and Washington. The gulf has widened considerably during the Ukraine crisis, enough so that diplomats on both sides think they are again operating in a new cold war.

Putin, like Stalin in his time and many other autocratic leaders, has created his own history, and he shamelessly and successfully trumpets it on state media—90 percent of Russians get *most* of what they know about the world from state-run television, 55 percent get *everything* they know from state-run television. He controls state media, even a so-called "troll army" of hundreds of well-paid bloggers who work round-the-clock to flood Internet forums, social networks, and op-ed pages with articles praising Putin and raging against the depravity of the West.[4] He has also used public exhibitions to sell his version of Russian history. For instance, in the fall of 2014—an uncertain time in the Ukraine war—he allowed the Russian Military-Historical Society to sponsor what the *New York Times* called a "blockbuster show" of Russian history dating back 1,000 years. According to historian Nikita P. Sokolov, the theme, bluntly stated, was that "Russia is a besieged fortress that needs a strong commander, and anyone trying to democratize Russia and shake the power of the commander is trying to undermine this country." The connection between the "strong commander" and Putin was not lost on many of the 250,000 Russians who visited the exhibition.[5]

Putin functions with a misbegotten halo of omniscience. He approves the harassment of foreign ambassadors based in distant capitals and the assassination of political critics, whether they live in Moscow or London. He starts wars, and then pretends he is an innocent bystander. He boasts that during the early days of the Crimea crisis, he was the man in charge and at one point even considered putting Russia's nuclear weapons on alert—but then reconsidered.[6] As a former KGB officer, he engages in blatant distortions, believing, as Fiona Hill and Clifford G. Gaddy observed, that "lies are part of the coin of the intelligence operative, and facts are fungible."[7] When "little green men" occupied Crimea, Putin vigorously denied there were any Russian troops there. Months later, with a grin, he admitted, yes, there were. Now, in Ukraine, the official line stays the same: that there are no Russian troops in the war, even though Russian soldiers, returning from the front, give newspaper interviews detailing the movement of troops in and out of Ukraine. In late March 2015, a wounded 20-year-old tanker from Siberia, identified as Dorzhi Batomunkuyev, told the independent newspaper *Novaya Gazeta*, "There were lots of troop trains. Before us there were guys from special operations in Khabarovsk, from various cities, just from the east. One by one, you see? Every day."[8]

Putin has become an old-fashioned tsar posing as a modern elected president, without doubt a highly important figure on the world stage. Even his whereabouts are now big news. When he vanished from sight for ten days in early March 2015, diplomatic chanceries went into an uncharacteristic flurry of activity. Rumors ran rampant: that he was incapacitated, that he had a virulent strain of the flu, that he had a face lift, that he had flown to Switzerland for the birth of a love child, that he had had a stroke, that he had been ousted in a coup. When he was then seen on television, back in action, he quipped wryly that "things would be boring without rumors."[9] But he did not disclose where he was or what he was doing.

The Russian word *vozhd* connotes not just one who leads a nation but one who leads it with fearsome force, the way Stalin ruled over the Soviet Union in World War II. Putin is Russia's current *vozhd,* though a decidedly more challenged one in 2015 than he was in 2014. His face is still omnipresent—in the media, on placards, even on a box of chocolates. A macho close-up of Putin wearing dark glasses is featured above an audacious sales pitch: "You need balls to be a King, when all around are mere pawns." A pro-Putin youth organization, called "Network," stages rallies around the country to whip up enthusiasm for its *vozhd.* "Russia and Putin go together," proclaimed Oleg Sokolov, a "Network" leader. "We just don't see another way."[10] Putin is the inescapable image of a resurgent Russia.

Short-Term and Long-Term Strategies

So, at the end of the day, what does Putin want?

He wants first to keep his job, not just because he cannot imagine life without an autocratic grip on political power but also because he apparently has come to believe his own propaganda about being indispensable to Russia's national standing and security. Only he can protect "Mother Russia," he feels, and he clearly enjoys playing tsar and issuing pronouncements. When the Kremlin celebrated the first anniversary of its annexation of Crimea, Putin addressed the Red Square rally like a political patriarch missing only his crown of thorns. "This was not about land, of which we have no shortage as is," he proclaimed. "The issue at stake was the source of our history, our spirituality and our statehood—the things that make us a single people and a single, united nation."[11]

As important to Putin as his job, however, is his vision of Mother Russia, the restoration of its glory and the protection of its national interests. Putin, like most leaders, has short-term goals and long-term goals, sometimes pursuing both at the same time. In pursuit of his goals, he improvises, he plays games, he feints, he prods and pokes, and, when necessary, he pauses and maybe retreats. But he does have a strategy, propelled by a narrow vision of Russian history, and he pursues it with an odd mix of rigidity and occasional flexibility.

His short-term goal unfolds in waves of deceptive cease-fires and bloody violence in the southeast corner of Ukraine, a neighbor that for centuries was part of the Russian empire, and his long-term goal, which focuses on a new Yalta-type rearrangement of European power, including the dismantling of NATO, is only now beginning to unfold. The old Yalta of 1945 had Roosevelt and Churchill acquiescing to Russian control over Eastern Europe. The Western response so far has ranged from angry rhetoric to economic sanctions. However, direct military intervention has been ruled off the table, in Washington under the Obama administration and in Berlin, Paris, and London. Likewise with a coordinated Western policy aimed at "regime change" in the Kremlin, another way of saying "let's get rid of Putin." If the West knew that the Putin after this Putin would be a better, more moderate leader, then an attempt at "regime change" might make sense—on the highly questionable assumption that the West has any way of influencing regime change in Moscow. But officials fear that the next Putin may be worse than this one. And then what? Often missed in this analysis is that Putin does not operate in a bubble. He is surrounded by a close-knit clique of ultra-nationalist zealots, "Putin's friends," as they are called, any one of whom could be, from a Western perspective, worse than Putin. They have accumulated enormous wealth and power and think they are entitled to both. Democracy is not in their tool kit.

In any case, the Russians are deeply suspicious of any policy of "regime change" and insist with increasing frequency that that is, in fact, Western policy; but according to senior U.S. officials, that is not the case. Even if it were, said one former official in a position to know about current thinking in Washington, "we probably couldn't do it well enough to be effective." He added: "If there is to be regime change, it will come when the Russian people decide they have had enough of Putin and his regime."

A Curtain-Raiser in Georgia

The curtain actually rose on Putin's intervention in Ukraine in the summer of 2008, when Russian troops moved into Abkhazia and South Ossetia, two small, secessionist provinces of Georgia, a former Soviet republic in the Caucasus. Both had sought Russian protection after proclaiming their independence from Georgia, a state of affairs Georgia found outrageous. The upshot was a series of mini-wars between the two provinces and Georgia, starting in 1991. Under a 1992 international agreement, Russian "peacekeepers" were sent to South Ossetia and Abkhazia, basically to protect the two provinces from a Georgian attempt to reassert political control.[12] In 2008 Georgia broke an uneasy truce and sent troops into the provinces, in the process killing a number of the "peacekeepers." Russia reacted by launching a full-scale invasion of South Ossetia and Abkhazia, creating a major rift between Russia and the West. France, on behalf of the West, intervened diplomatically and arranged a cease-fire. Obvious to everyone was that Russia won the war and tightened its grip over the two provinces.[13]

The 2008 Russia-Georgia war was an example of Putin at the gambling table. His chips represented options, each option posing a question. He did not trust the West, but what was he to do with the West? He worried about NATO's eastward expansion, but how would he stop it? (NATO for a time even considered admitting Georgia.) He feared Georgia's pro-Western adventurism, especially its unpredictability, but how was he to control it? Though there was no real threat to Russia at the time, he decided that Russia had to be protected, and he rolled the dice and rolled in the troops, safely assuming that neither NATO nor the United States would commit its military power to stop him. They would complain, of course, but do nothing more, and Russia would get its way. Georgia's once flamboyant president, Mikhail Saakashvili, now serving oddly as Poroshenko's governor of Odessa, expressed the Western view. "This is inconceivable lawlessness and insolence," he exclaimed. "Russia has done unthinkable damage to its place in the international community." Putin saw things differently. The Georgia war had given him a superb opportunity to make his central point: that he would employ Russian military power in Georgia, or anywhere else for that matter, to protect Russia's sphere of influence and its national interests, as he interpreted them. By employing Russian power, he was saying to the West that the 1991 collapse in Russia's global standing following the dismemberment of the Soviet Union was now history. Russia must again be respected, he argued, its point of view represented and understood in a new and broader European dialogue.

But he found that was not always the case. Sometimes the Russian view was deliberately ignored. A perfect illustration concerned Kosovo, once a province of Yugoslavia and then of Serbia. Pressed by ethnic Albanians, Kosovo proclaimed its independence from Serbia on February 17, 2008.[14] One day later, suggesting the tightest possible coordination between Kosovo and the West, the United States, France, and Great Britain extended diplomatic recognition to Kosovo. In a UN Security Council debate, China abstained, but Russia—Serbia's Slavic ally—strongly objected, arguing Kosovo had no legal authority to proclaim its independence from Serbia. Russia in this case found itself baying at the moon, its lonely objection mushrooming into a diplomatic embarrassment. Serbia stood alone, while Kosovo gained widespread diplomatic support. Putin was livid with rage. Two can play this game, he decided. Six months later, Russia arbitrarily extended diplomatic recognition to South Ossetia and Abkhazia, one of only a handful of nations to take this step. If the United States could recognize Kosovo, he figured, then Russia could recognize South Ossetia and Abkhazia. In this way, the Russia-Georgia crisis over South Ossetia and Abkhazia "froze" into an example of successful Russian aggression. Moscow's control over these once-rebellious provinces would no longer be questioned. Over the years, Putin was to use Kosovo as an example of unfair and even illegal Western machinations in the global arena—all designed, he concluded, to cheat, corner, or discredit Russia, which he said he would not allow.

Ukraine, a Short-Term Goal

Ever since the Orange Revolution of 2004, Putin must have suspected that one day he would have to use Russian military power to block the pro-Western tide in Ukraine. He had hoped, for a time, that Viktor Yanukovych, his man in Kiev, would be able to do the job, but the Maidan Square demonstrations in late 2013 and early 2014 persuaded him that Yanukovych had neither the subtlety nor brutality to check the challenge. In late February 2014, when hundreds of demonstrators were killed in Maidan—which by then resembled an unruly army camp in wartime, and the battle cry from the hundreds of thousands assembled there hit a distinctly shrill anti-Russian note—Putin knew that his options were dwindling and action would soon be required. In his conspiracy-seeded imagination, he believed that the Maidan leaders, whom he considered "fascists," were CIA stooges, agents of the West purchased to do its bidding. Many were clearly anti-Russian and sympathetic to the West, but few if any were reported to be on a CIA payroll.

Early in the demonstrations, in December 2013, Putin had alerted his military command to be ready for action. When the Sochi Olympics ended in a blaze of Russian glory, he convened his generals one night and ordered the seizure of Crimea, which he had always considered rightfully Russian in any case. Then they were to organize an anti-Kiev insurrection in the pro-Russian Donbas corner of southeastern Ukraine. His imperial gamble was now to begin.

For Putin and many other Russians, Ukraine was never an independent, sovereign country. It was, in their minds, a region of Russia that happened to be called Ukraine. It was a sort of wayward cousin who lived in the attic of the Russian empire, someone to be tolerated and, if necessary, clothed and fed, but never invited to the main dining room. The Russians and the Ukrainians thought they knew one another because their histories had been so closely intertwined for centuries. Russians lived and worked in Ukraine, and Ukrainians lived and worked in Russia, the latter often feeling like country hicks, their noses pressed up against the window of Russia's presumed cultural superiority. Both read the same books, appreciated the same music, and vacationed at the same watering holes, and many intermarried. Just because Nikita Khrushchev, described as a "petty tyrant" by writer Alexander Solzhenitsyn, handed administrative control of Crimea to Ukraine in 1954 did not mean that Crimea had really been given, as a "gift," to another country. The Soviet Union was, in 1954, one country, composed of fifteen republics, including Russia and Ukraine. For this reason, among others, Putin argued, he was not really "invading" another country when he entered and later annexed Crimea in March 2014. As he put it a year later: "We in Russia always saw the Russians and Ukrainians as a single people. I still think this way now."[15] In other words, by his reckoning, he was simply righting a wrong, and he wanted the world to know there were other wrongs to be righted.

One such "wrong" was the Russian diaspora formed after the 1991 Soviet collapse. There were now tens of millions of Russians cut off from the Russian heartland, living in newly independent nations formed on the fringes of Russia. They posed both a problem and an opportunity. If Putin had read Solzhenitsyn's "The Russian Question at the End of the Twentieth Century," he would surely have agreed with the famed writer's observation that "Russia has truly fallen into a torn state: 24-million have found themselves 'abroad' without moving anywhere, by staying on the lands of their fathers and grandfathers. . . . the largest diaspora in the world by far; how dare we turn our back to it??—especially since local nationalisms . . . are everywhere suppressing and maltreating our severed compatriots."[16]

Putin, like Solzhenitsyn a Russian nationalist, sees "local nationalisms" in Crimea, Ukraine, the Baltics, the Caucasus, and "southern Siberia" (the northern rim of Kazakhstan in central Asia) "suppressing and maltreating our severed compatriots," and he has felt the need, he said, to protect them. In this context, Putin was referring to Russians and Slavs living in "near abroad" nations. By invoking the alleged plight of the Russian diaspora, he could use an emotional bond with other Russians, living in other countries and stretching back over centuries, as a political pretext for "influencing," "pressuring," or actually "invading" another country.

Putin used this rationale in Crimea and Ukraine. He could yet use it in the Baltics or Transnistria (the breakaway province of Moldova), if it suited his purposes. When Russians needed his help, he would provide it. In both Crimea and Ukraine, though, he has paid a heavy price. Crimea has proven to be an expensive ward; the rebellious Donbas, an even more expensive one. Both are overshadowed, though, by a larger strategic question: Does Putin want all of Ukraine, as many in Kiev have warned, or would he settle for just the southeast corner now under rebel control? Militarily, there is little doubt Russia could conquer all of Ukraine. His generals have boasted that in two weeks they could take Kiev. But why bother? By controlling a corner of a country already suffering from deep economic and political wounds, Putin has put himself in position to influence its destiny without excessive risk to Russia.

Putin—"Over the Top"

And yet, the fear among many Western statesmen is that Putin, flushed by military success in Ukraine but plagued by economic crisis at home, may now, as one of them put it, "go over the top." Putin is portrayed by some

Putin-watchers as a follower of Richard Nixon's "mad man theory" of warfare as a tool of modern diplomacy: *convince your enemy that, in extremis, you may resort to horrible measures, perhaps even the use of nuclear weapons, to achieve your ends. You cannot be trusted to act rationally.* There is an unanswered question about Putin: Is he mad, or pretending to be mad, or just plain *khitri*, meaning cunning, clever, street smart?

At a March 2015 meeting in Germany, Russian generals were quoted as threatening "a spectrum of responses from nuclear to non-military" if NATO were to make an effort to retake Crimea and return it to Ukraine or move forces to the Baltics.[17] Either the generals were loose cannon with looser fuses, which was unlikely, or they were specifically authorized to threaten the use of nuclear weapons. Either way, they would be acting in a way entirely consistent with Putin's aim of keeping the West on tenterhooks, never quite certain of his next step. It could come in further action in Ukraine or no action, Russia resting on its laurels of Crimea and the Donbas under its firm control; or, more alarming, it could come in a new burst of hybrid warfare in the Baltics.

If it proved to be further action in Ukraine, everyone would soon discover that Putin's rebels were armed not only with fresh weapons but also with fresh explanations of why "new battles" aimed at the "total destruction of the Ukrainian party of war"—meaning President Petro Poroshenko's pro-Western regime in Kiev—would be necessary. Aleksandr Zakharchenko and Igor Plotnitsky, the self-proclaimed prime ministers, respectively, of the People's Republics of Donetsk and Luhansk, have already claimed that "Kiev does not want peace" and the Minsk II cease-fire between them and Ukraine "has practically halted." In fact, repeated violations, on both sides, have been reported. The rebel understanding of Minsk II, according to Zakharchenko, was: "*remove all [of your] troops from here, end military activity, and we'll take all of our cities where referendums were held.*"[18] These cities would include Mariupol, a key port on the Sea of Azov, as well as Kramatorsk and Sloviansk, both held by Ukrainian troops as of mid-2015. Indirectly, the rebel leaders were stating their true objective: They want Mariupol and all of Donetsk and Luhansk provinces, a challenge to the Kiev regime that it could not possibly accept without a climactic battle against the rebels and the Russians, a battle it would almost certainly lose. And if Kiev lost the battle, Poroshenko would lose his job as president. His government would fall, and further chaos in Ukraine would ensue. Western diplomats have hinted broadly that if the Russian-backed rebels actually attacked and took Mariupol, the West would quickly provide defensive lethal weapons to Ukrainian forces, raising the temperature of the crisis and the possibility of an East-West confrontation.

Two accomplished students of Russian policy, Harvard's Graham Allison and *National Interest* editor Dimitri K. Simes, have raised the troubling question of whether Russia and the West, following the unfortunate pattern of events leading to World War I, might now be "stumbling to war."[19] That possibility seemed not to disturb Putin, at least judging by Kremlin descriptions of a Russian leader determined to pursue a policy of peace.

Or Putin could direct his attention to the more sensitive Baltic region, home for Estonia, Latvia, and Lithuania, all three now members of NATO but also, historically, a key outpost of the Russian empire since the time of Peter the Great. Here, by widening his strategic vision, he could meld his short-term goals with his longer-term strategy. A daring Russian move in or around Estonia, a Washington nightmare since the early days of the Ukraine war, would pose a potentially cataclysmic challenge to the United States and NATO. Such a move would, undoubtedly, take the form of hybrid warfare, in which Russia would not deploy troops or heavy weapons but would rely instead on cyberwar, disinformation, economic pressure, and, finally, insurrection by the ethnic Russians living there. The ethnic Russians represent 26 percent of Estonia's total population of 1.4 million.

Taavi Rõivas, Estonia's 35-year-old prime minister, the EU's youngest head of government, has been pleading for more NATO arms and troops. Some say he has been begging. He believes the current crisis "will stay with us for a long period of time. . . . This is not just bad weather, this is climate change." He sees Europe and Russia in a deadly standoff, the worst since the end of the cold war in 1991.[20] Whether or not Putin moved against Mariupol, Rõivas was convinced he would move against Estonia. In his calculations, it was only a matter of time.

Rõivas did not need a nuclear warning from Russian generals to appreciate the dangers facing his country. He recognized that the generals had also stressed that "the same conditions that existed in Ukraine and caused Russia to take action there" also existed in Estonia, Latvia, and Lithuania. Presumably, they meant that the ethnic Russians living there could rise against the established Baltic governments and take "destabilizing actions that would be even harder to trace back to Russia than those of eastern Ukraine."[21]

One could approach this Russian threat with a heavy dose of skepticism but still acknowledge that it does closely coincide with current Russian policy. According to the British newspaper *The Independent*, "Russia would hope slowly to entice those Russian populations towards Russia without giving NATO a pretext to deploy troops."[22]

Clearly intending to pressure the Baltic states into submissive compliance,

Russia has conducted military maneuvers, one after another, near their borders. Tens of thousands of Russian troops have participated in these maneuvers. If the order were given to march on Tallinn, it is estimated that it would take the Russians no more than seven hours to reach the Estonian capital. Russia has also maneuvered as far afield as Norway's Arctic Circle. In response, as a show of strength, the United States, flying a NATO flag, has sent a hundred pieces of military hardware to Estonia—namely, Abrams tanks, Bradley fighting vehicles, and Scout Humvees. It has also sent 150 troops to a temporary NATO base in Estonia, hardly enough to hold off the Russians but enough for President Obama to claim that the United States was doing something. NATO also has plans for establishing modest command centers with a spearhead force of 5,000 troops in six former Soviet satellites (Bulgaria, Poland, Rumania, and the three Baltic states)—less a serious tripwire against a Russian strike than reassurance of NATO's stated determination to protect its members. Major General John R. O'Connor of the U.S. Army, overseeing the delivery of NATO equipment, told reporters the weapons were intended to "demonstrate to President Putin and Russia that collectively we can come together."[23]

The army general said all the right things, using all the right words, but the fact remains that Estonia lives in Russia's sensitive "near-abroad," where memories of "little green men" in Crimea and the Donbas set off alarm bells in 2014, raising fears that a Russian program of hybrid warfare, if and when unleashed, could undermine the Baltic governments, just as it has already done much to undermine Ukraine's. Lithuania's President Dalia Grybauskaite dispensed with all diplomatic small talk. "The first stage of confrontation is taking place," she pronounced solemnly. "I mean, informational war, propaganda and cyber attacks. So we are already under attack."[24] To this challenge, NATO has, in fact, been slow to respond. Its deputy secretary-general, Alexander Vershbow, a former U.S. ambassador to Russia, has admitted that NATO is *"looking at how we prepare for, deter, and—if required—defend against hybrid threats"* (italics added).[25] He is saying, in his diplomatic way, that if Putin decided to open a "hybrid" attack on Estonia, NATO would not now be in position to repel it. But even if NATO were in position to repel it, would it? Could it? Would the United States, which is NATO's most powerful member, act on its own to repel a Russian attack, or would it duck behind the need first to get NATO's unanimous consent?

According to James Sheer of Britain's Chatham House, Russia's hybrid warfare is "designed to cripple a state before that state even realizes the conflict has begun."[26] Estonian journalist Olga Dragileva was quoted as saying that a

Russian media war aimed at sowing "dissatisfaction and illusions" in the Baltics was already under way. Using the language of war, Janis Karklins, director of NATO's Strategic Communications Center, spoke of Russia's "weaponization of [the] social media," as though he was talking about tanks, not the Internet's Facebook or Buzzfeed. Modern warfare now includes both tanks and websites, and Russia has spent heavily on building and developing both.[27]

But let us, for a moment, hypothesize that Estonia has been truly rattled by Russian warnings and military maneuvers, which it considers threatening to its sovereignty and territorial integrity. President Toomas Hendrik Ilves underscored his country's deep concern by asking NATO to set up a permanent base in Estonia for "a brigade" of troops, saying politely that the 150 American troops already there were "not a lot."[28] Let us further hypothesize that Estonia formally requested NATO's help, based on Article 5 of its founding charter. Estonia would have every right to expect a clear and firm NATO response. Would it get such a response? The intent of Article 5 is clear—an attack on one would be considered an attack on all. But, realistically, what could an under-staffed NATO do when so many of its members do not set aside the required 2 percent of their annual budgets for national defense? This has been a chronic problem. Every U.S. secretary of defense in recent times has repeatedly warned NATO members about this problem, but to little effect. What would the United States do? What could it do when so many Americans are tired of foreign wars and adventures?

The Baltic nations of today, independent since 1991, are not the "captive nations" of the mid-1950s. At that time, President Dwight D. Eisenhower and his secretary of state, John Foster Dulles, could promise American help in liberating the "captive nations" from Soviet control but, in fact, when challenged, do little more than mimeograph tissue-thin statements of support. Today the Baltic nations—members of NATO but still vulnerable to Russian attack—would expect NATO's assistance, but that assistance would depend ultimately on the decision of an American president to lead NATO. But would the president lead? It would depend, obviously, on party, personality, and circumstance. Putin, always the gambler, is betting the answer would be no.

The weakening and eventually the dissolution of NATO, which the Kremlin's chief propagandist, Dmitri K. Kiselev, has described as a "cancerous tumor," has been Russia's principal goal for a long time.[29] Nikita Khrushchev used to describe the Western half of Berlin as a "bone in my throat." Russians' metaphors range, apparently, between "tumors" and "bones" when describing threats to their national security. They haven't yet come up with an apt body part for Estonia, but there is no doubt that a Russian move against Estonia would kick off a new East-West confrontation. The United States and NATO would immediately condemn Russia and issue warnings and threats but not bullets and bombs. Likewise, a majority of the UN Security Council would join in the condemnation of Russian "aggression," as it did after the Crimean takeover. And after words presumably comes action: the United States would urge a unified NATO response, knowing in advance that unity was an almost impossible dream in an alliance of twenty-eight sovereign states.

Meanwhile, according to this scenario, ethnic Russians in Estonia, following a political and military pattern already familiar from Russian actions in Crimea and Ukraine, would systematically raise a rumpus in the capital city of Tallinn, attract a scuffle with Estonian police, present a hot picture of cold confrontation for the international media, and, ultimately, appeal for Russian help, which Putin would provide, although not necessarily with "little green men." The Baltics would in this way again fall under a dark Russian cloud. Everyone would understand that there was never a chance that Estonia could defeat Russia, even if Latvia and Lithuania were to throw their troops into the struggle. The military imbalance between a powerful Russia and the vulnerable Baltics would be obvious to everyone. All would depend on NATO. Would this alliance, led by the United States, take on Russia? Would Obama take on Putin?

On April 9, 2015, five Nordic nations, concerned with what they termed "aggressive Russian conduct," agreed to cooperate militarily. They decided not to wait for NATO. What was especially interesting was that Sweden and Finland, two countries usually following a neutralist foreign policy, joined Norway, Denmark and Iceland, three members of NATO, in this ad hoc anti-Russian alliance.[30] Putin, by his threats and actions, has apparently succeeded in washing away the distinctions between neutrality and a NATO commitment.

Transnistria or the Baltics?

Not only northern Europeans but also southern Europeans have worried about Putin's strategy of unpredictable aggression. In a sliver of territory, sandwiched between Moldova and Ukraine, called Transnistria, 400 Russian troops conducted intensive maneuvers in early April 2015, firing 100,000 rounds of ammunition, a noisy demonstration of Russian power and interest in a normally sleepy corner of Europe. Like Abkhazia and South Ossetia, Transnistria is a small, "frozen" slice of Moldova that has been firmly in Russian hands since 1991.[31] NATO leaders have been concerned about the possibility that the Russians might be tempted to move into Moldova, once part of the Soviet empire, in this way flanking Ukraine not just from the east but also from the west. Unknown at this time is whether Putin intends to create a new Malorossiya—a series of Russian protectorates running from the Donbas to Moldova, though this has been hinted at since the start of the Ukraine war.

Officials in Washington have spent many sleepless nights worrying about Putin's next steps—whether he is planning a move against Transnistria or the Baltics or neither. The betting is the Baltics, for one simple reason. A Russian strike against Estonia could unhinge NATO and humiliate the United States—for Putin, a major accomplishment but one that, in his judgment, would not at this time mushroom into a U.S.-Russian war. Why? Because, according to Washington calculations, a Russian attack on Estonia, while challenging and dangerous, would not now be regarded as a direct threat to American national security and therefore would not likely lead to an American counterstrike.

This, by the way, is not a new story. In 1953 the East Germans rebelled against Soviet domination, and the Russians crushed their rebellion. Washington expressed its support for the East German people but did little more than smother the Russians in harsh invective, which did not change Russian policy. In the fall of 1956, the Hungarian people rose in bitter opposition to Soviet control, and for a brief time it seemed as if Moscow was going to accept a new, noncommunist government in Hungary. But on November 4 the Kremlin suddenly rolled tanks and troops into Budapest and smashed the uprising, killing thousands and scattering several hundred thousand Hungarians to different countries. In 1968 the Czechs rose against Soviet domination. This time, without hesitation, the Russians sped tanks and troops into Prague and brutally suppressed the uprising. In every case, the United States offered strong rhetorical support to the people who rose up against Russian domination, but not once did it employ its military strength—or take any other significant action—to stop Moscow's aggression. The basic reason was that in every case Washington did not want to risk a war with Russia. It was the same with Georgia in 2008, the same with Crimea and Ukraine in 2014, and it would likely be the same with Transnistria or the Baltics if Russia intervened in either place.

Putin Squeezes the West into a Tizzy

In many of his speeches, one way or another, Putin returns to the tumultuous year of 1991, when the Soviet Union disintegrated and communism died as an inspirational force. He is obsessed with the lessons of this startling turn in Russian history. One lesson, in his mind, was that the West took advantage of Russia's weakness and confusion and, without even conferring with Yeltsin, or anyone else in the Kremlin, pushed NATO expansion to Russia's borders, even while privately assuring the Kremlin that it had no such intention. Putin and many others in Russia's ruling elite—including even Mikhail Gorbachev, no fan of Putin—concluded, according to this view of history, that rather than open a dialogue with Russia about the future shape of Eastern Europe, the West simply imposed a new post–cold war order on the region and then insisted on Moscow's compliance. Putin and his followers had little choice but to swallow their pride.

Even Ilya Ponomarev, an exiled member of the Russian Duma and fierce Putin critic, writing from his new home in San Jose, California, regretfully sided with Putin when discussing the way the West treated Russia in 1991. "At the end of the Cold War," Ponomarev said, the West "repeated the mistakes of Versailles of 1919, by imposing shock capitalism instead of integrating Russia into a stable world order."[32]

This is the vision of recent European history that Putin believes to be true, even though it is, to a large extent, an illusion. The West did, for a time, try to confer with Russian leaders, but the talks slowed to a crawl, and then stopped, when American diplomats raised the issues of human rights and democratic values under Putin's tightening autocracy; they got nowhere. Now Putin is determined to rewrite recent European history. By way of Crimea, Ukraine, and elsewhere in the region, he has been mixing conventional and hybrid warfare in an effort, so far successful, to expand Russian power and influence in Europe. In much the way Peter the Great awakened Western Europe to the rise of a new Russian empire at the beginning of the eighteenth century, so Putin has shaken Europe out of its post–cold war slumber by parading, or threatening to parade, Russian power across Eastern Europe. In this way he, like Peter, is changing the power game in Europe as well as the rules of international diplomacy. Putin has awakened Berlin, Paris, London, and—most important—Washington, to his demand for a new global dialogue, a new rearrangement of European power. An updated version of what Roosevelt, Churchill, and Stalin achieved in 1945, he would like to achieve now. By beating the drums of war, he has thrown the West into a tizzy, but he has not yet won the prize he most covets—namely, a new Yalta that would roll back NATO's eastward expansion and realign Europe's power structure. And he is not likely to win it, given the rise of a new cold war, for which he, ironically, is most responsible.

Chto Delat? Lenin Asked—"What Is to Be Done?"

On this question made famous in Russian history by writer Nikolay Cherny-shevsky, many in the West are split. Among government officials, one finds the rather simplistic view that Russia has committed aggression, which is true, and therefore Russia must now pay a price, which is not necessarily true. Economic sanctions have been applied, not once but thrice, and, together with falling energy prices, they have begun to bite, deepening the recession in Russia and spreading labor unrest. Wild-cat strikes, worker protests, and "forced" vacations—all signs of popular unhappiness with a worsening econ-omy—have been reported in the Russian hinterlands.[33] Diplomatic observ-ers of Russia's current "time of troubles," enjoying these signs of domestic discontent, are also demanding that Putin pull his forces out of Ukraine and relinquish control of Crimea. They want to see Putin discredited and humili-ated, a leader so weakened he would soon be thrown out of power. However, other observers of the Russia scene, mostly Europe-based, have adopted a more pragmatic approach to the Ukraine crisis. Instead of holding out for a pound of flesh, they are more willing to consider an economic and political accommodation with Russia, based first on a recognition that Russia is the dominant military power in Eastern Europe, that it is not going anywhere, and the West had best adjust to this obvious fact of life. The second factor is that Putin would not be likely, under just about any circumstance, to give up Crimea, which he hails as a monumental Russian victory, or to abandon his strategic position in the Donbas. In Putin's calculations, Ukraine would have to become a political and economic eunuch, a nation linked unquestionably to a Slavic world run by Russia.

Here are two clashing visions of "what's to be done?" Both are dependent, for the most part, on what happens in Ukraine in the next few years—and on how the West responds. Ukraine is likely to be the key to unveiling Rus-sia's response—and America's. The future of the crisis lies in the place where it started. Only then do Russian and American options matter. One fact, though, is undeniable: Putin has thrown a dangerous challenge before the West, and the West must now find a magic formula for ending a small war before allowing it to become a big one.

Ukraine—The Place Where It Started

If Ukraine can somehow reform its economy, which has been dangling on the edge of a precipice for decades, and its politics, which is still a stubborn example of corruption at play, it might attract enough foreign investment, diplomatic support, and institutional loans to survive for a while. Even so, Ukraine would survive only as a fragile, fractured nation, frightened by the threat of further Russian expansion and utterly dependent on foreign financial support. Ukraine collapsing into a failed state—the fear in many Western capitals—is a distinct possibility. Experts agree that it will take a long time, if ever, for Ukraine to become, for example, another Poland—an East European country, once part of the Russian empire, that has swung to the West and, in recent years, registered impressive economic and political progress. In Ukraine, many mistakenly thought that becoming another Poland was, in fact, a realistic goal. "Everyone thought Ukraine would suddenly turn into Poland," confessed Taras Yakubovsky, a mechanic, expressing a dream he once cherished. "But we've become more like Europe's Somalia."[34]

In late 2014 and early 2015, the Poroshenko regime unveiled a much-anticipated reform package, and no doubt some progress has been made. Much more is promised. But Ukraine often finds a way of disappointing its staunchest supporters. Its record of economic and political reform since the liberation year of 1991 has been consistently dismal, not just in the view of Western bankers but also in that of many Ukrainians who have battled against stiff odds to achieve even limited ends. Ukraine's future remains a murky question mark, with the western half of the country swinging toward the West, and the eastern half clinging to Russia, much the same as it has been for hundreds of years.

Poroshenko's financial and economic ministers seem to spend more time in Washington, London, and Berlin selling upbeat tales of reform than they do in Kiev putting their plans into practice. They know their paychecks depend on the flow of foreign dollars. More important, their country's entire economy depends on foreign dollars—many of its banks still hovering near default, its borrowing capacity almost totally dependent on the good will of foreign institutions. The national currency, called *hryvnia*, has depreciated by nearly 70 percent. Inflation has been running at close to 30 percent. The economy contracted by 7.5 percent in the early months of 2015, and the average monthly wage has dropped to roughly $150. In addition, a number of supermarkets in major cities have had to impose short-term rationing of flour and cooking oil to meet public demand. The traveling ministers sing a more encouraging tune, of course, itemizing for officials and think tanks in Washington how many corrupt officials have been arrested, how many banks have become more solvent, and, they claim, spirits have been running high. Their melodious message: Just keep the dollars flowing, and all will be well! Maybe, maybe not.

As important, veterans of the Maidan demonstrations have become disillusioned with the promise and performance of reform. They are losing patience with Poroshenko and his elite cadre of ministers, whom they see as part of the problem. They express anger at what they see as the continuing corruption. They demand economic progress and political accountability. They even threaten a new Maidan. Would a new Maidan be possible? Absolutely, say many experts. When? By the end of 2015 or early in 2016, they predict, a finger to the winds.

Support for the war against the pro-Russian rebels in the East has weakened, even though, ironically, Ukrainian nationalism has strengthened. Ukrainian flags flapping in the breeze are now a common sight in Kiev. For much of 2014, many young Ukrainians volunteered for military service. Their parents donated money, clothing, and even arms to the struggle. They were proud of their military. Now, the war continues, without end it seems, and casualties remain daily reminders of the human costs of the war. Victory is nowhere to be seen on the near horizon, or even the far one. The effect is that volunteering has vanished, morale is slipping, and increasingly the government has had to mount unannounced raids on factories and farms to corral recruits for what is clearly becoming an unpopular war. For example, as of late April 2015, only 15–20 percent of soldiers rotated off the battlefield returned to duty. In the eastern city of Sloviansk, of forty young men who received draft notices, only one showed up for duty.[35]

All over Ukraine, east and west, symbols of the Soviet era and the Nazi occupation during World War II dot the landscape. In early April 2015, the Kiev government passed an odd series of laws designed to erase the country's past and direct people's attention to their still-undefined future. The laws required that statues of Red Army soldiers, including many Ukrainians, and wartime monuments glorifying the Soviet victory over Nazi Germany be destroyed, but, interestingly, not the statues of Ukrainian leaders who cooperated with the Nazis. They would continue to be honored. Even before the new laws, statues of Lenin, symbols of the Soviet era, were being destroyed or besmirched. What was truly remarkable about the new laws was not that there still were pro-Soviet statues and monuments in Ukraine (Ukraine was, after all, part of the Soviet war effort against Germany), but that there were still statues and monuments honoring pro-Nazi WWII heroes in Ukraine—strongly suggesting that pro-Nazi sentiment still persists in contemporary Ukraine. Indeed, pro-Nazi Ukrainians have been elected to parliament and given important jobs. Though a number of Poroshenko's ministers and advisers have made a strenuous effort to put distance between themselves and extreme right-wing parties and politicians, they have never quite managed to do so.

The Russian Foreign Ministry promptly denounced the new laws as "betraying millions of veterans." Rebel leader Aleksandr Zakharchenko wasted no time warning that the new laws would "lead to the complete disintegration of the country," adding "it causes disgust and revulsion. It formalizes the victory of fascism."[36] He was, as always, tying the Kiev government to Ukrainian fascists who helped the Nazis during World War II.

The Poroshenko government knows from past experience that if it wanted to irritate Putin, all it had to do was raise the prospect of Ukraine joining NATO. On April 9, 2015, whether deliberately or not, the prospect surfaced once again. Oleksander Turchynov, head of Kiev's national security agency, announced a new strategic doctrine. Among its most important bullet points: Ukraine's membership in NATO was "the only reliable external guarantee" of its sovereignty and territorial integrity. Until Poroshenko was elected president in May 2014, Ukraine was officially "non-bloc," or neutral, in its foreign relations. Now, according to this new doctrine, it would, if accepted, become a member of NATO. The early 2020s was the time projected for NATO's consideration of Ukraine's admission.[37] This is by no means automatic: admission is based on a unanimous vote among current NATO members, and not all NATO members want Ukraine as a member, fearing Russian objections.

In examining options, Ukrainian public opinion must also be considered. According to a March 2015 study by the University of Maryland's Program for Public Consultation and the Kiev International Institute of Sociology, the Ukrainian people remained split on whether to turn east or west, a problem they have faced, but left unresolved, for centuries. "The conflict there does arise from a deep division among the Ukrainian people," wrote Steven Kull, the primary investigator, "on the central question of whether they should move closer to the European Union or close to Russia." The majority of the people were described as wanting to "preserve the unity of Ukraine," even while recognizing that "the cohesion" of the country remained "tenuous." They are walking on eggs.[38]

One option, though, would seem to supersede all others: Would Ukraine be better off if it were divided in two—one country with loosely patrolled borders becoming two countries with tightly controlled borders? If possible, and in theory, most Ukrainians would prefer to remain one country, incorporating the rebel-held southeast corner, currently controlled by Moscow. But if Ukraine were to remain one country, it would have to recognize that it cannot change its geography. On any map, wherever purchased, in Kiev or Moscow, Ukraine is still affixed to Russia's southwest, and, like it or not, Ukraine cannot win a war against Russia, which remains the preeminent military power in Eastern Europe. Russia cannot be ignored or wished away.

In this sense, Ukraine's future is linked to Russia's, its freedom of action likely to be strongly influenced by Moscow for many decades to come. If Ukraine succeeds, somehow, in mastering its economic and political ills, in balancing its pro-Western desires with its unavoidable geographic and historic links to Russia, then it might avoid sliding into the abyss of a failed state. But if not, its future would be dim indeed. Its future is in its hands.

Finally, Russia

The Ukrainian government is not split down the middle, but it is split into at least two camps. One is headed by Poroshenko, who is a reasonably pragmatic president, a patriot, a former oligarch prepared, if necessary and if possible, to negotiate a compromise agreement with Putin, if he can arrange acceptable terms. The other is led by his prime minister, Arseniy Yatsenyuk, a fiery young nationalist with no love for the Russians. Indeed, he has made clear in many statements that he hates them. He cannot imagine a compromise with the Russians.

Poroshenko knows that his political options are limited, shrinking by the day. He also knows that his position in Kiev has weakened since the Minsk II accords in February 2015. A number of his colleagues already smell blood—his. Poroshenko desperately needs an opening-to-China-type victory—a negotiation with Russia that holds out the possibility of a compromise agreement. A Minsk III, as some observers have put it. As chief executive, now a shaky position in Kievan politics, Poroshenko alone has the power to negotiate with Putin. If he is interested in negotiating an acceptable and realistic modus vivendi between Ukraine and Russia, then he ought to reach out now and try to organize a one-on-one summit with the Russian leader—just the two of them. They would have the opportunity to strike a deal. The option of a summit with Putin, he knows, would be tricky, controversial, and dangerous—and a sensible result very difficult to achieve. A successful negotiation would have to rest on a realistic appraisal of Russian and Ukrainian power: economic, political, military, and perceived power. An unrealistic appraisal of any of these factors would almost certainly lead to crushing disappointment—and more war.

Because Putin has the stronger hand, he would get the better of the deal. He would emerge from the negotiation, according to many experts, still in control of both Crimea and the southeast Ukrainian provinces of Donetsk and Luhansk, with the understanding that the provinces would stand as autonomous parts of a unified country. Putin would insist on a submissive regime in Kiev, one that would be pro-Russian or at least not anti-Russian. As Putin reads his history, Moscow would be entitled to such a regime, because, except for the comparatively brief period from 1991 to the present, it has always held a power position in Ukrainian affairs.

There is another reason why Putin would insist on a compliant Ukraine. Like Yeltsin before him, Putin lives with the fear that one day Russia's Muslims living in the northern Caucasus would join forces with the Muslims of central Asia—the so-called 'stans, such as Kazakhstan and Uzbekistan—and challenge Russian power in the lands traditionally dominated by Moscow. Only by keeping Ukraine in a Slavic orbit, controlled by Moscow, can the Christian Slavs have a chance of holding off the Islamic assault they fear is coming. Putin believes this concern ought to be as compelling in Kiev as it is in Moscow. In this context, Ukraine would logically have to scuttle all plans for joining NATO and return to its "non-bloc," Slavic status.

Poroshenko would emerge from this negotiation with diminished power and status, but still as president of a neutral Ukraine, able to salute the flag, walk at the head of a parade, attend summit meetings, and seek emergency funding from both Russia and the West. Still, by negotiating such a deal, he would probably lose his job, just as Khrushchev did after the Cuban missile crisis. Many would ask, how could he have caved to Putin? But, in the callous cruelty of Ukrainian politics, he might have lost his job anyway, even without a deal.

No doubt, such a negotiation would profoundly disappoint many in Kiev and the West who remain committed to punishing Russia for its annexation of Crimea and its continuing aggression in other parts of Eastern Europe. Appeasement! they would shout from the rooftops, Neville Chamberlain's bow to Hitler in 1938 very much on their minds. Why bow to Putin? they would ask. Why allow him to retain the fruits of his illegal conquests? Just as pertinent are two other questions that cut to the heart of the Ukraine crisis and frame the essential dilemma for the many participants. Do we want to punish Russia, even if that runs the risk of stumbling into a war with Russia? (Is that what we truly want?) Or would we be willing to accept a compromise agreement that ends the Ukraine conflict, one that recognizes that no Western leader has an appetite for a war with Russia? Clearly, if the choice is between a war with Russia or a compromise agreement with Russia, Western leaders would choose the compromise agreement. Most Westerners would. No one wants a war with Russia, even though Russia stands guilty before world public opinion of flagrant aggression against Ukraine. Initially, one must recall, the West did nothing of a military nature when the Russians seized Crimea and the Donbas. After a few months, it imposed economic sanctions against Russia, hoping naively the sanctions would persuade Putin to change his policy, and it dropped Russia from the G-8, an act of petulant diplomacy unlikely to have impressed Putin. From his initial moves into Crimea, Putin gambled that the West would not go to war over Ukraine and, later, the Donbas, and he won his gamble. He considered Ukraine to be a vital national interest. He acted on that basis, employing Russia's military might. The West did not flash a full stop sign, warning it too would use its military might in Ukraine, nothing like it. Now, from no regional or global institution does one hear a cry for Putin to return Crimea. Quite the contrary, his conquests have become shameful "facts on the ground." We are now in a post-appeasement phase of the Ukraine crisis.

Now, It's America's Turn

Washington's approach to the Ukraine crisis has been a mixed bag of anger and acquiescence, on- and off-ramps, pragmatism, and romance. At the beginning, most officials, politicians, think tank analysts, and scholars were in agreement that Russia had done more than violate a neighbor's borders; it had also violated the international order created after the 1991 collapse of the Soviet empire. It had to pay a price. Economic sanctions were imposed, diplomatic isolation attempted. But, as time passed, it became apparent that, though Russia was paying a price, it was not changing its policy. In fact, it always seemed on the edge of going further into the unknown, raising the possibility, according to a number of scholars, that East and West might be stumbling toward a bigger war neither side wanted. And the reason from the start was Russian aggression against Ukraine.

Was Ukraine worth a bigger war, from the West's perspective? Was Ukraine a vital national security interest of the United States? The answers have been inconclusive—and for good reason. The current situation in Ukraine presents a highly complex problem in which all options are extremely difficult and fraught with potentially serious consequences. For example, if you were a U.S. official, you would likely acknowledge, off the record, that Ukraine was not really a vital national security interest, meaning that the problem was not really of a magnitude that would compel America to go to war with Russia. You would add, however, that it *could* become a national security interest and therefore a possible threat to the United States, depending on what Russia did. For example, if Putin aggressively pushed what he sees as Russian interests in the Black Sea, or the Middle East, or the Baltics, he would be challenging NATO—especially the United States—and a military response of some kind might be required. Or if, by his example, Putin encouraged others to be foolishly reckless in a part of the world where the United States has unmistakable vital interests, supported by defense treaties, the United States might find itself obliged to take military action in defense of its interests. On the record, however, you as a government official would do your best to duck such questions.

But, if—in today's exceptionally polarized political environment—a presidential candidate were asked whether Ukraine should be considered a vital national security interest, in other words whether Ukraine was worth a war with Russia, he or she would probably have a somewhat different take. Few candidates would want to appear either too hawkish or too dovish about the Ukraine crisis, but all would want to come through as supporting the poor Ukrainians and opposing the unruly Russians. After all, the Russians were guilty of aggression. Politically, it is safe to be anti-Russian in an international climate disturbingly similar to the cold war. The upshot has been unanimous votes in Congress about providing American economic and military assistance to Ukraine (the only questions have been "when" and "how much") and the Obama administration deciding, after much deliberation, to send 298 American military advisers to Ukraine to train 900 of its national guardsmen. The Pentagon stressed the number 298, calculating apparently that 300 might sound like too many.[39]

President Obama has been extremely cautious about involving American troops in new or expanding wars, but he seems to be stepping into a potential quagmire in Eastern Europe with small, reluctant half-steps—unable apparently to stop either for political or diplomatic reasons. We should have learned from the unfortunate American experience in Vietnam and Iraq that half-steps may in time develop into larger, national commitments if the half-steps fail to achieve their intended results. Ukraine is tricky, uncertain turf. We in the United States and other Western countries don't know enough about its politics, its economy, its culture, its people, its future. It is a gigantic question mark. Yet, because of Ukraine's civil war, we stand on the cusp of major decisions about U.S.-Russian relations. As one former senior official noted: "We truly run the risk of embracing a Ukraine that does not really exist. We must be much more realistic about what we are supporting." Are we really being realistic about Ukraine?

Of course, history demonstrates that anything is possible. Ukraine may yet emerge as a functioning democracy in a generation, or two, or three, but this journey will tax the patience of a saint (and none currently rules in either East or West) and cost hundreds of billions of dollars, acceptable perhaps in a time of abundance but not now. Moreover, there is little reason to believe the money would be spent well or wisely.

In the meantime, until an acceptable solution to the Ukraine crisis can be found, it would seem to be unwise for the West, led by the United States, to drop its economic sanctions against Russia, unless dropping them would advance an acceptable solution. The United States, for its part, should adopt a clearer, more discriminating, and realistic policy toward Russia than it is currently pursuing. It should be willing to negotiate with Russia on issues of common concern—such as Iran's nuclear development, Syria's civil war and other Mideast turmoil, global terrorism, and international trade. Occasionally there are overlapping interests. We should stop personalizing East-West differences, laying all problems on Putin's shoulders, as though, if he were replaced, all of our difficulties with Russia would disappear. At the same time, we should encourage Ukraine and Russia to negotiate a realistic modus vivendi between them, aware that Russia, by virtue of its power position, is likely to get the better of the deal. Only then would it make sense to open the door to timely, responsible East-West negotiations on the future shape of Eastern Europe. War should be the very last option in the president's tool kit.

This is not the time for dangerous games of chicken with Russia, though the Ukraine crisis has spawned a number of "war games" in Washington. In one such game, the United States, frustrated by Russia's continuing aggression, sends defensive lethal arms to Ukraine, and NATO strengthens its military position in the Baltics and Poland—in hopes that such muscle-flexing will persuade Putin to change his policy. But Putin does not change his policy. In fact, he ups the ante and intensifies his hybrid war in Ukraine and, in this war game, the Baltics. Does Washington then double down and send still more arms? Many in Congress, happy to display their self-proclaimed toughness toward Putin, encourage the president to do just that. And he does. This is the moment for the big question. What happens if Putin, in response, ups the ante once more? What then? Should the United States send even more arms, possibly with even more military advisers? Or should it back off, thereby running the risk of looking weak? The war gamers must now face the real possibility that the increasing escalation will lead, by design or accident, to an unwanted war between the United States and Russia. The concluding question in this scenario: Is Ukraine worth it? Unfortunately, this war game comes up with no easy answers, because there are no easy answers.

In real life, unfortunately, the questions have been the same as in table top war games. If Washington decides to protect and defend the territorial integrity of pre-Crimea Ukraine—trying in this way to force a return to something like the status quo ante—is this decision worth the risk of a Russian-American war? Put another way, is Ukraine worth a continuing serious deterioration in East-West relations? If the answer is yes, it would be best to prepare for it, meaning the president should level with the American people about the dangers before them and redeploy American military strength around Russia, and Congress should quickly increase the defense budget—in other words, the United States should return to the "containment policy" pursued during the cold war. However, if the answer is no, if deep down, after due deliberation, the United States concludes that Ukraine is not worth the risk of war with a nuclear-armed Russia, then it must be realistic and seek a sensible path toward resolving the Ukraine crisis, taking the national interests of Russia and Ukraine, born of history and geography, into full account. It's time for a cold dash of realpolitik.

For decades, we have all heard the romantic rhetoric about building democracy in such places as Vietnam, Iraq, and Afghanistan, and we often hear such rhetoric about Ukraine. Despite its appeal, despite the major efforts of many Ukrainians to turn their country in a more positive direction, such rhetoric can be dangerous. Ukraine is not Great Britain, nor is it France, Germany, or the United States. It is an unstable, middle-sized country in Eastern Europe caught in a bloody civil war that pits it in an unwinnable contest with Russia. It has to find a way, on its own, to coexist with its stronger neighbor. It cannot count on the United States to fight its battles and guarantee its ultimate security or on the International Monetary Fund to provide endless streams of capital to fix its economy. The United States has other problems that demand its attention, directly affecting its vital national security interests, and Ukraine at the moment is not one of these. Declaring Ukraine to be such an interest would—inevitably—mean that the United States will slide into a confrontation with Russia.

Ukraine deserves its place in the sun as a truly independent nation, but it must be realistic about the journey to that goal. If Ukraine truly believes it can become a viable part of the West, able to live within its post-1991 borders, including Crimea and the Donbas, and to disregard Russian influence and power, then it is going to have a very bumpy ride.

Notes

Chapter 1

1. Lilia Shevtsova, "The Putin Doctrine: Myth, Provocation, Blackmail, or the Real Deal," *American Interest*, April 14, 2014 (www.the-american-interest.com/2014/04/14/the-putin-doctrine-myth-provocation-blackmail-or-the-real-deal/).

2. Henry A. Kissinger, "To Settle the Ukraine Crisis, Start at the End," *Washington Post*, March 5, 2014 (www.washingtonpost.com/opinions/henry-kissinger-to-settle-the-ukraine-crisis-start-at-the-end/2014/03/05/46dad868-a496-11e3-8466-d34c451760b9_story.html).

3. Angela Stent, "Why America Doesn't Understand Putin," *Washington Post*, March 14, 2014 (www.washingtonpost.com/opinions/why-america-doesnt-understand-putin/2014/03/14/81bc1cd6-a9f4-11e3-b61e-8051b8b52d06_story.html).

4. Anne Applebaum, "A Need to Contain Russia," *Washington Post*, March 20, 2014 (www.washingtonpost.com/opinions/anne-applebaum-a-need-to-contain-russia/2014/03/20/8f2991dc-b06b-11e3-9627-c65021d6d572_story.html).

5. Peter Baker, "3 Presidents and a Riddle Named Putin," *New York Times,* March 23, 2014 (www.nytimes.com/2014/03/24/world/europe/3-presidents-and-a-riddle-named-putin.html?_r=0).

6. Markian Dobczansky, ed., "The Fifteenth Anniversary of the End of the Soviet Union: Recollections and Perspectives," Occasional Paper 299, Kennan Institute, Woodrow Wilson International Center for Scholars, p. 6 (Jack F. Matlock Jr. remarks) (www.wilsoncenter.org/sites/default/files/OP299_fifteenth_anniversary_end_soviet_union_dobczansky_2008.pdf).

7. Quoted in Roger Cohen, "Russia's Weimar Syndrome," *New York Times*, May 1, 2014 (www.nytimes.com/2014/05/02/opinion/cohen-russias-weimar-syndrome.html?_r=0).

8. Angela Stent, "Putin's Ukraine Endgame and Why the West May Have a Hard Time Stopping Him," CNN, March 4, 2014 (http://edition.cnn.com/2014/03/03/opinion/stent-putin-ukraine-russia-endgame/index.html).

9. Mary Elise Sarotte, "Putin's Belligerence Today Has Its Roots in the Fall of the Berlin Wall," *Los Angeles Times*, November 8, 2014 (www.latimes.com/opinion/op-ed/la-oe-sarotte-putin-berlin-wall-20141109-story.html).

10. Thomas L. Friedman, "Foreign Affairs; Now a Word from X," *New York Times*, May 2, 1998 (www.nytimes.com/1998/05/02/opinion/foreign-affairs-now-a-word-from-x.html).

11. Francis Fukuyama, "The End of History?," *National Interest* (Summer 1989) (http://history.msu.edu/hst203/files/2011/02/Fukuyama-The-End-of-History.pdf).

12. James Atlas, "What Is Fukuyama Saying? And to Whom Is He Saying It?," *New York Times Magazine*, October 22, 1989 (www.nytimes.com/1989/10/22/magazine/what-is-fukuyama-saying-and-to-whom-is-he-saying-it.html).

13. Robert Kagan, "The End of the End of History," *New Republic*, April 23, 2008 (www.newrepublic.com/article/environment-energy/the-end-the-end-history).

Chapter 2

1. Secretary of State John Kerry, "Interview with David Gregory of NBC's Meet the Press," State Department, March 2, 2014 (www.state.gov/secretary/remarks/2014/03/222721.htm).

2. Alison Smale, "Ukraine Crisis Limits Merkel's Rapport with Putin," *New York Times*, March 12, 2014 (www.nytimes.com/2014/03/13/world/europe/on-ukraine-merkel-finds-limits-of-her-rapport-with-putin.html?_r=0).

3. "Remarks by President Obama, His Majesty King Philippe, and Prime Minister di Rupo of Belgium at Flanders Field Cemetery," Waregem, Belgium, March 26, 2014, White House Press Office, Washington.

4. President Barack Obama, "Remarks by the President in Address to European Youth," Palais des Beaux Arts, Brussels, Belgium, March 26, 2014 (www.whitehouse.gov/the-press-office/2014/03/26/remarks-president-address-european-youth).

5. Peter Baker, "Preparing for Trip to Russia, Obama Praises Putin's Protege, at Putin's Expense," *New York Times*, July 2, 2009 (www.nytimes.com/2009/07/03/world/europe/03moscow.html).

6. "Remarks by President Obama and Prime Minister Putin of Russia before Meeting," Novo Ogaryovo, Moscow, Russia, July 7, 2009 (www.whitehouse.gov/the_press_office/REMARKS-BY-PRESIDENT-OBAMA-AND-PRIME-MINISTER-PUTIN-OF-RUSSIA-BEFORE-MEETING/).

7. Tom Parfitt, "Anti-Putin Protesters March through Moscow," *The Guardian*, February 4, 2012 (www.theguardian.com/world/2012/feb/04/anti-putin-protests-moscow-russia).

8. Andrew Osborn, "Vladimir Putin Accuses Hillary Clinton of Inciting Protests," *The Telegraph*, December 8, 2011 (www.telegraph.co.uk/news/worldnews/europe/russia/8942456/Vladimir-Putin-accuses-Hillary-Clinton-of-inciting-protests.html).

9. Associated Press, "Russian Anti-Gay Bill Passes, Protesters Detained," CBS News, July 11, 2013 (www.cbsnews.com/news/russian-anti-gay-bill-passes-protesters-detained/).

10. "Russia Population 2014," *World Population Review*, October 19, 2014 (http://worldpopulationreview.com/countries/russia-population/).

11. Peter Baker and Steven Lee Myers, "Ties Fraying, Obama Drops Putin Meeting," *New York Times*, August 7, 2013 (www.nytimes.com/2013/08/08/world/europe/obama-cancels-visit-to-putin-as-snowden-adds-to-tensions.html?pagewanted=all).

12. David Rohde and Arshad Mohammed, "How America Lost Vladimir Putin," Reuters, April 18, 2014 (www.reuters.com/article/2014/04/18/us-ukraine-putin-diplomacy-special-repor-idUSBREA3H0OQ20140418).

13. Ibid.

14. President Obama, "Remarks by the President in Address to European Youth."

15. Secretary of State John Kerry, "Remarks at the Atlantic Council's 'Toward a Europe Whole and Free' Conference," State Department, April 29, 2014 (www.state.gov/secretary/remarks/2014/04/225380.htm).

Chapter 3

1. Vladimir Putin, "Address by President of the Russian Federation," March 18, 2014 (http://en.interaffairs.ru/events/501-vladimir-putin-addressed-state-duma-deputies-federation-council-members-heads-of-russian-regions-and-civil-society-representatives-in-the-kremlin.html).

2. An English-language text of Khrushchev's speech is at http://legacy.fordham.edu/halsall/mod/1956khrushchev-secret1.html.

3. Mikhail Gorbachev, *Memoirs* (New York: Doubleday, 1995), pp. 61, 62, 70–71.

4. Steven Lee Myers and Ellen Barry, "Putin Reclaims Crimea for Russia and Bitterly Denounces the West," *New York Times*, March 18, 2014 (www.nytimes.com/2014/03/19/world/europe/ukraine.html?_r=0).

5. President George Bush, "Address before a Joint Session of the Congress on the Cessation of the Persian Gulf Conflict," March 6, 1991, Presidency Project (www.presidency.ucsb.edu/ws/index.php?pid=19364&st=&st1=).

6. Michael T. Florinsky, *Russia: A History and an Interpretation*, vol. 2 (New York: Macmillan, 1955), p. 797; and Fiona Hill and Clifford G. Gaddy, *Mr. Putin* (Brookings, 2013), pp. 64–66.

7. Vladimir Putin (with Nataliya Gevorkyan, Natalya Timakova, and Andrei Kolesnikov), *First Person: An Astonishingly Frank Self-Portrait by Russia's President* (New York: Public Affairs, 2000), pp. 11–12: "In 1993 . . . I went to Israel as part of an official delegation. Mama gave me my baptismal cross to get it blessed at the Lord's Tomb. I did as she said and then put the cross around my neck. I have never taken it off since."

8. David Brooks, "Putin Can't Stop," *New York Times*, March 3, 2014 (www.nytimes.com/2014/03/04/opinion/brooks-putin-cant-stop.html?_r=0).

9. Ibid.

10. Ibid.

11. Nicholas Bachtin, "Lectures and Essays" (University of Birmingham, England, 1963), p. 43.

12. Putin, "Address by President of the Russian Federation," March 18, 2014.

13. Ibid.

14. Ibid.

15. Hill and Gaddy (2013), pp. 106–07.

16. "Donetsk Separatists Call for Russian Absorption, Troops," Radio Free Europe/Radio Liberty, May 12, 2014 (www.rferl.org/content/donetsk-separatists-ask-moscow-absorption-after-referendum/25382227.html).

17. James Paton and Aching Guo, "Russia, China Add to $400 Billion Gas Deal Accord," Bloomberg Business, November 10, 2014 (www.bloomberg.com/news/articles/2014-11-10/russia-china-add-to-400-billion-gas-deal-with-accord).

Chapter 4

1. "Ukraine 'As Close to Civil War' as Possible," May 14, 2014, Bloomberg TV (www.bloomberg.com/news/videos/b/331ab1f6-a759-47c3-820b-57e651319bc8).

2. Bernard Pares, *A History of Russia* (New York: Alfred A. Knopf, 1953)

3. Michael T. Florinsky, *Russia: A History and an Interpretation* (New York: Mac-Millan Co., 1955), pp. 1–9.

4. From "The Vikings" exhibition at the British Museum, March–June 2014.

5. Florinsky (1955), pp. 13–14.

6. "The Vikings" exhibition, British Museum, 2014.

7. Ibid.

8. Ibid.

9. Pares (1953), p. 33.

10. Pares (1953), p. 38.

Chapter 5

1. Hillary Rodham Clinton, "Hillary Clinton Reviews Henry Kissinger's 'World Order,'" *Washington Post*, September 7, 2014, p. B6 (www.washingtonpost.com/opinions/hillary-clinton-reviews-henry-kissingers-world-order/2014/09/04/b280c654-31ea-11e4-8f02-03c644b2d7d0_story.html).

2. Bernard Pares, *A History of Russia* (New York: Alfred A. Knopf, 1953), p. 56.

3. Michael T. Florinsky, *Russia: A History and an Interpretation* (New York: Mac-Millan Co., 1955), p. 63.

4. Pares (1953), p. 82–83.

5. Ibid., p. 97.

Chapter 6

1. Until recently, "Ukraine" was invariably referred to as "*the* Ukraine," because, in Slavic usage, Russians and others thought of Ukraine as a "borderland" on the "periphery" of Russia. People traveled to "*the* Ukraine." Even in the twelfth century, a monk wrote about "the Ukraina." Now, no longer a borderland but a recognized country, the "the" has been dropped.

2. Nikolai Vasilevich Gogol, *Taras Bulba* (Moscow: Foreign Languages Publishing House, no date) pp. 45–46.

3. Ibid., Introduction.

4. Bernard Pares, *A History of Russia* (New York: Alfred A. Knopf, 1953), p. 176.

5. Robert K. Massie's *Peter the Great: His Life and World* (New York: Modern Library, 2012) is a rich, readable resource.

6. For a full biography, see Robert K. Massie's *Catherine the Great: Portrait of a Woman* (New York: Random House, 2011).

7. Ibid., p. 380.

8. Ibid., p. 555.

9. Ibid., p. 557.

10. Ibid., p. 558.

11. Ibid., p. 559.

Chapter 7

1. Andrew Wilson, *The Ukrainians: Unexpected Nation* (Yale University Press, 2000), p. 88.

2. Ibid., p. 89.

3. Ibid., p. 92.

4. Serhy Yekelchyk, *Ukraine: Birth of a Modern Nation* (Oxford University Press, 2007), pp. 41–44.

5. Mikhaelo Hrushevsky, "Ukraine's Struggle for Self-Government; Leader in Nationalistic Movement Tells How Race Kept Its Individuality Under Alien Masters—He Was Not in Favor of Complete Independence Ukraine's Struggle for Self-Government," *New York Times*, February 17, 1918. Also available at http://chroniclingamerica.loc.gov/lccn/sn90061556/1918-03-30/ed-1/seq-7/.

6. Wilson (2000), p. 99.

7. Ibid., p. 83.

Chapter 8

1. Serhy Yekelchyk, *Ukraine: Birth of a Modern Nation* (Oxford University Press, 2007), p. 79.

2. Ibid., pp. 80–83.

Chapter 9

1. Stephen Kotkin, *Stalin, vol. I, Paradoxes of Power, 1878–1928* (New York: Penguin Press, 2014), p. 133.

2. Richard Pipes, *The Russian Revolution* (New York: Alfred A. Knopf, 1990), pp. 368–69.

3. Andrew Wilson, *The Ukrainians: Unexpected Nation* (Yale University Press, 2000), pp. 138–39.

4. David Pryce-Jones, *The Strange Death of the Soviet Empire* (New York: Henry Holt and Co., 1995), pp. 36–37.

5. See Serhy Yekelchyk, *Ukraine: Birth of a Modern Nation* (Oxford University Press, 2007), pp. 103–12, for a clear explanation of Stalin's economic plans.

6. Wilson (2000), pp. 144–45.

7. Stephen Kotkin, "If Stalin Had Died," *New York Review of Books*, November 6, 2004, p. 34.

8. Yekelchyk (2007), pp. 112–16.

9. William Taubman, *Khrushchev: The Man and His Era* (New York: W. W. Norton, 2003), pp. 116, 120.

Chapter 10

1. William L. Shirer, *The Rise and Fall of the Third Reich* (New York: Simon and Schuster, 1960), pp. 384–96.

2. Serhy Yekelchyk, *Ukraine: Birth of a Modern Nation* (Oxford University Press, 2007), p. 132.

3. Yekelchyk (2007), p. 133.

4. Zhores and Roy Medvedev, eds., *N. S. Khrushchev: The "Secret" Speech* (Nottingham, UK: Spokesman Books, 1976), p. 58.

5. Yekelchyk (2007) pp. 133–34; and Andrew Wilson, *The Ukrainians: Unexpected Nation* (Yale University Press, 2000), p. 132.

6. Wilson (2000), pp. 129–31.

7. In 1939, on the eve of the Soviet takeover of western Ukraine, Dontsov left Ukraine and moved to Bucharest, then Prague, Paris, Germany, and finally the United States. In 1949 he went to Montreal, where he taught Ukrainian literature at the French-language Université de Montreal.

8. Wilson (2000), pp. 131–34.

9. Ibid, p. 132.

10. Nikita Khruschev, *Khrushchev Remembers* (New York: Little Brown, 1970), pp. 180–81.

11. George Bush and Brent Scowcroft, *A World Transformed* (New York: Alfred A. Knopf, 1998), p. 516.

12. Yevgeny Yevtushenko, *Selected Poems* (New York: E. P. Dutton, 1962), p. 82.

13. Yekelchyk (2007), p. 149.

14. Khrushchev (1970), p. 140.

15. Ibid.

16. Ivan L. Rudnytsky, *Essays in Modern Ukrainian History,* ed. Peter L. Rudnytsky (Canadian Institute of Ukrainian Studies Press, 1987), p. 467.

17. Rudnytsky (1987), p. 463.

18. Roman Szporluk, "Mapping Ukraine: From Identity Space to Decision Space," (Self-published, Naples, Italy, September 16–18, 2008), p. 11.

Chapter 11

1. See, for example, Vitali Shevchenko, "'Little Green Men' or 'Russian Invaders,'" BBC News, March 11, 2014 (www.bbc.com/news/world-europe-26532154).

2. Andre de Nesnera, "Khrushchev's Son: Giving Crimea Back to Russia Not an Option," Voice of America, March 6, 2014 (www.voanews.com/content/khrushchevs-son-giving-crimea-back-to-russia-not-an-option/1865752.html).

3. "USSR's Nikita Khrushchev Gave Crimea Away to Ukraine in Only 15 Minutes," *Pravda*, February 19, 2009 (http://english.pravda.ru/history/19-02-2009/107129-ussr_crimea_ukraine-0/).

4. Ibid.

5. Conference on Security and Cooperation in Europe, Final Act, Helsinki, August 1975 (www.osce.org/mc/39501?download=true).

6. U.S. Nuclear Regulatory Commission, "Backgrounder on Chernobyl Nuclear Power Plant Accident," May 2013 (www.nrc.gov/reading-rm/doc-collections/fact-sheets/chernobyl-bg.html).

7. Serhy Yekelchyk, *Ukraine: Birth of a Modern Nation* (Oxford University Press, 2007), p. 180.

8. Jack F. Matlock Jr., *Autopsy on an Empire: The American Ambassador's Account of the Collapse of the Soviet Union* (New York: Random House, 1995), p. 230.

9. Ibid.

10. Rokas M. Tracevskis, "January 13, 1991: The Day That Changed the World," *Baltic Times*, January 21, 2010 (http://www.baltictimes.com/news/articles/24215/).

11. Serhii Plokhy, *The Last Empire: The Final Days of the Soviet Union* (New York: Basic Books, 2014), pp. 59–61.

12. David Pryce-Jones, *The Strange Death of the Soviet Empire* (New York: Metropolitan Books, 1995), p. 389.

13. Yekelchyk (2007), p. 186.

14. Ibid.

Chapter 12

1. David Pryce-Jones, *The Strange Death of the Soviet Empire* (New York: Metropolitan Books, 1995), p. 400.

2. "All-Union Referendum on 'Preservation of Renovated Union,'" March 17, 1991, Yeltsin Presidential Library (www.prlib.ru/en-us/history/pages/item. aspx?itemid=462).

3. Gennady Burbulis, with Michele A. Berdy, "Meltdown," *Foreign Policy*, June 20, 2011.

4. Mikhail Gorbachev, *Memoirs* (New York: Doubleday, 1995), pp. 626–32.

5. Serhii Plokhy, *The Last Empire: The Final Days of the Soviet Union* (New York: Basic Books, 2014), p. 101.

6. This account of the U.S. response to the coup is based on George Bush and Brent Scowcroft, *A World Transformed* (New York: Alfred A. Knopf, 1998), p. 524; and Jack F. Matlock Jr., *Autopsy on an Empire: The American Ambassador's Account of the Collapse of the Soviet Union* (New York: Random House, 1995), pp. 587–91.

7. President George Bush, "Statement on the Attempted Coup in the Soviet Union," August 1991, the Presidency Project (www.presidency.ucsb.edu/ws/index. php?pid=19913&st=&st1=).

8. Bush and Scowcroft (1998), p. 515.

9. Ibid., p. 527.

10. Masha Gessen, *The Man without a Face: The Unlikely Rise of Vladimir Putin* (New York: Riverhead Books, 2012), pp. 116–18.

11. Andrew Wilson, *The Ukrainians: Unexpected Nation* (Yale University Press, 2000), p. 166.

12. Pryce-Jones, *The Strange Death of the Soviet Empire* (1995), p. 403.

13. Mary Mycio and Carey Goldberg, "The Ukraine Proclaims Its Independence," *Los Angeles Times*, August 25, 1991 (http://articles.latimes.com/1991-08-25/news/ mn-2029_1_ukraine-proclaims).

14. Francis X. Clines, "Ukrainian Voters Crowd the Polls to Create Nation," *New York Times*, December 2, 1991, p. A10 (www.nytimes.com/1991/12/02/world/ ukrainian-voters-crowd-the-polls-to-create-nation.html).

15. Chrystyna Lalpychak, "Independence," *Ukrainian Weekly*, December 8, 1991.

16. Clines, "Ukrainian Voters Crowd the Polls to Create Nation."

17. Plokhy (2014), p. 294.

18. Ibid., p. 295

19. Alexander Solzhenitsyn, "How We Must Rebuild Russia," *Komsomolskaya Pravda*, September 18, 1990.

20. Book Q&As with Deborah Kalb, May 13, 2014 (http://deborahkalbbooks. blogspot.com/2014/05/q-with-professor-serhii-plokhy.html).

21. Plokhy (2014).

22. Ibid., p. 304.

23. Ibid.

24. Tatyana Tolstaya, *Pushkin's Children: Writings on Russia and Russians* (New York: Houghton Mifflin Company, 2012), p. 151.

25. "Agreement on the Creation of the Commonwealth of Independent States," December 8, 1991.

26. Plokhy (2014), p. 315.

27. Ibid.

28. Ibid., p. 316.

Chapter 13

1. Andrew Wilson, *The Ukrainians: Unexpected Nation* (Yale University Press, 2000), p. 207.

2. Ibid., pp. 211–14.

3. Ibid.

4. Serhy Yekelchyk, *Ukraine: Birth of a Modern Nation* (Oxford University Press, 2007), p. 193–94.

5. Serhii Plokhy, *The Last Empire: The Final Days of the Soviet Union* (New York: Basic Books, 2014), p. 290.

6. Ibid.

7. Laurence Lewis, "Ukraine Crisis: What Does the Budapest Memorandum Obligate the U.S. to Do?," *Daily Kos*, March 4, 2014 (www.dailykos.com/story/2014/03/04/1282010/-Ukraine-crisis-What-does-the-Budapest-Memorandum-obligate-the-U-S-to-do).

8. Jon Sawyer, "Ukraine's Straits Put Rosy Glow on Old USSR," *St. Louis Post Dispatch*, March 6, 1994, p. 6.

9. Yekelchyk (2007), p. 198.

10. Fiona Hill and Pamela Jewett, "Back in the USSR: Russia's Intervention in the Internal Affairs of the Former Soviet Republics and the Implication for United States Policy toward Russia," Occasional Paper, Strengthening Democratic Institutions Project, Belfer Center for Science and International Affairs, Harvard Kennedy School, January 1994 (http://belfercenter.ksg.harvard.edu/files/Back%20in%20the%20USSR%201994.pdf)

11. Zbigniew Brzezinski, "The Premature Partnership," *Foreign Affairs* 73, no. 2 (1994): 80.

12. Michael Specter, "Setting Past Aside, Russia and Ukraine Sign Friendship Treaty," *New York Times*, June 1, 1997 (www.nytimes.com/1997/06/01/world/setting-past-aside-russia-and-ukraine-sign-friendship-treaty.html).

13. Ibid.

14. Katya Soldak, "Out of Prison in California, Former Prime Minister Lazarenko Is Not in a Rush to Go to Ukraine," *Forbes*, November 2, 2012 (www.forbes.com/sites/katyasoldak/2012/11/02/ukraines-prison-prone-prime-ministers/).

15. Wilson (2000), pp. 195–96.

16. Mark Kramer, "Ukraine, Russia, and US Policy," Program on New Approaches to Russian Security Policy Memo 191, Harvard University, April 2001 (www.ponarseurasia.org/sites/default/files/policy-memos-pdf/pm_0191.pdf).

17. Yekelchyk (2007), p. 209.

18. Ibid., p. 212.

19. Ibid., p. 213.

20. Ibid., pp. 216–25.

21. Steve Rosenberg, "Ukraine Crisis: Is the Noose around Putin Tightening?" BBC News, Europe, September 5, 2014 (www.bbc.com/news/world-europe-29076189).

22. Viktor Yushchenko, "Ukraine's Future Is in the EU," Address by President of Ukraine, European Parliament, February 23, 2005, CEPS Neighborhood Watch, Issue 1, February 2005 (www.ceps.eu/files/old/NW/NWatch1.pdf).

23. Taras Kuzio, "Analysis: Yuschchenko's Visit to U.S. Heralds return to 'Golden Era,'" Eurasia Daily Monitor, April 4, 2005 (www.ukrweekly.com/old/archive/2005/150505.shtml).

24. United States Senate Republican Policy Committee, "Promoting a Robust U.S.-Ukraine Agenda: Securing the Orange Revolution in Ukraine," March 31, 2005 (www.leader.viitorul.org/public/615/en/mar3105robustukrainedf.pdf).

25. "Ukrainian President Yushchenko's Address before Joint Session of U.S. Congress," April 6, 2005 (www.president.gov.ua/en/news/164.html).

26. Jean-Christophe Peuch, "Ukraine: Regional Leaders Set Up Community of Democratic Choice," Radio Free Europe/Radio Liberty, December 2, 2005 (www.rferl.org/content/article/1063461.html).

27. Yekelchyk (2007), p. 221.

28. "Ukraine: Presidential Election, 17 January and 7 February 2010," Office for Democratic Institutions and Human Rights, Organization for Security and Cooperation in Europe, April 28, 2010, p. 32 (www.osce.org/odihr/elections/ukraine/67844?download=true).

Chapter 14

1. Dmitri Vlahos and Peter Leonard, "Ukraine's Facebook Revolution, 1 Year Later," Associated Press, November 21, 2014 (http://news.yahoo.com/ukraines-facebook-revolution-1-later-162725498.html).

2. "УВАГА! Збір сьогодні на Майдані Незалежності о 22:30 !!! (+відео)," [Bulletin: Gather Today at Maidan Squate at 10:30 p.m.], November 23, 2013 (http://blogs.korrespondent.net/blog/pro_users/3289622-uvaha-zbir-sohodni-na-maidani-nezalezhnosti-o-2230-video).

3. Richard Balmforth, "Mass Rallies in Ukraine against Government U-Turn on EU," Reuters, November 24, 2013 (http://uk.reuters.com/article/2013/11/24/uk-ukraine-eu-idUKBRE9AN0C920131124).

4. "Police Violently Break Up Independence Square Protests at 4 a.m. Today; Many Injuries Reported (videos and updates)," *Kyiv Post*, November 30, 2013 (www. kyivpost.com/content/ukraine/reports-police-forcefully-break-up-protest-site-on-maidan-nezalezhnosti-this-morning-332674.html).

5. David Stern, "Analysis," BBC News, December 2, 2013 (www.bbc.com/news/world-europe-25192792).

6. David M. Herszenhorn, "Amid Unrest, Ukrainian President Defends Refusal to Sign Accords," *New York Times*, December 2, 2013 (http://mobile.nytimes.com/2013/12/03/world/europe/ukraine-unrest.html).

7. David M. Herszenhorn and Andrew E. Kramer, "Police Push into Kiev Square as Crisis Grows," *New York Times*, December 10, 2013, p. 1 (www.nytimes.com/2013/12/11/world/europe/ukrainian-security-forces-confront-protesters-in-Kiev-square.html?pagewanted=all&_r=0).

8. "Russia and Ukraine Leaders Seek Partnership Treaty," BBC News, December 6, 2013 (www.bbc.com/news/world-europe-25267130).

9. Darina Markchak and Katya Gorchinskaya, "Russia Gives Ukraine Cheap Gas, $15 Billion in Loans," *Kyiv Post*, December 17, 2013 (www.kyivpost.com/content/ukraine/russia-gives-ukraine-cheap-gas-15-billion-in-loans-333852.html).

10. Shaun Walker, "Vladimir Putin Offers Ukraine Financial Incentives to Stick With Russia," *The Guardian*, December 18, 2013 (www.theguardian.com/world/2013/dec/17/ukraine-russia-leaders-talks-kremlin-loan-deal).

11. Sergei L. Loiko, "Ukraine Announces $15-Billion Russian Loan," *Los Angeles Times*, December 17, 2013, p. 1 (http://articles.latimes.com/2013/dec/17/world/la-fg-ukraine-russia-20131218).

12. Adam Taylor, "'Novorossiya,' The Latest Historical Concept to Worry about in Ukraine," *Washington Post*, April 18, 2014 (www.washingtonpost.com/blogs/worldviews/wp/2014/04/18/understanding-novorossiya-the-latest-historical-concept-to-get-worried-about-in-ukraine/); text of broadcast at "Direct Line with Vladimir Putin," President of Russia, April 17 2014 (http://eng.kremlin.ru/transcripts/7034).

13. "Russian Historians Preparing Textbooks on 'Novorossiya,'" Euromaidan Press, August 30, 2014 (http://euromaidanpress.com/2014/08/30/russian-historians-preparing-textbooks-on-novorossiya/).

14. Tom Parfitt, "Putin Reveals the Moment He Gave the Secret Order for Russia's Annexation of Crimea," *The Telegraph*, March 9, 2015 (www.telegraph.co.uk), and Neil MacFarquhar, "Putin Contradicts Claims on Annexation of Crimea," *New York Times*, March 9, 2015 (www.nytimes.com/2015/03/10/world/europe/putin-contrary-to-earlier-assertions-suggests-planning-to-seize-crimea-started-in-early-2014.html?ref=topics&_r=0).

15. Maxim Trudolybov, "Putin's Evolution," *New York Times*, February 2, 2015 (www.nytimes.com/2015/02/03/opinion/maxim-trudolyubov-putins-evolution.html).

16. Masha Gessen, *The Man without a Face* (New York: Riverhead Books, 2012), pp. 68–69.

17. "Direct Line with Vladimir Putin," April 17 2014.

18. Russia-EU Summit, Brussels, Belgium, January 28, 2014 (http://eng.kremlin. ru/transcripts/6575).

19. Andrew E. Kramer, "Russia Defers Aid to Ukraine, and Unrest Persists," *New York Times*, January 29, 2014, p. A8 (www.nytimes.com/2014/01/30/world/europe/ ukraine-protests.html).

20. Alexei Anishchuk and Justyna Pawlak, "Russia Says Will Honour $15 Billion Loan Pledge to Ukraine," Reuters, January 28, 2014 (http://uk.reuters.com/ article/2014/01/28/uk-eu-russia-idUKBREA0R0FM20140128).

21. Andrew Higgins, "With President's Departure, Ukraine Looks toward a Murky Future," *New York Times*, February 22, 2014, p. A15 (www.nytimes.com/2014/02/23/ world/europe/with-presidents-departure-ukraine-looks-toward-a-murky-future.html).

22. "Meeting of the Valdai Discussion Club," Sochi, Russia, October 24, 2014 (http://eng.kremlin.ru/transcripts/23137).

23. "Ukrainian Leader, Opposition Reach Deal to End Crisis," Agence France-Presse, February 21, 2014.

24. "Meeting of the Valdai Discussion Club," October 24, 2014.

25. Higgins, "With President's Departure, Ukraine Looks toward a Murky Future."

26. Yuras Karmanau and Jim Heintz, "Ukraine: Parliament Chief Takes Presidential Power," Associated Press, February 23, 2014 (http://news.yahoo.com/ukraine-parliament-chief-takes-presidential-power-105847930.html).

27. Neil MacFarquhar, "Putin Says He Weighed Nuclear Alert over Crimea," *New York Times*, March 16, 2015 (www.nytimes.com/2015/03/16/world/europe/putin-says-he-weighed-nuclear-alert-over-crimea.html).

28. "Obama on the World, with Thomas Friedman" *New York Times*, August 8, 2014 (www.nytimes.com/2014/08/09/opinion/president-obama-thomas-l-friedman-iraq-and-world-affairs.html).

29. Sergey Rogov, "From Bad to Worse," *Harvard Gazette*, October 23, 2014, p. 1 (http://news.harvard.edu/gazette/story/2014/10/from-bad-to-worse/).

30. "Obama on the World, with Thomas Friedman."

31. Ibid.

32. Fiona Hill and Clifford G. Gaddy, *Mr. Putin: Operative in the Kremlin*, 2nd ed. (Brookings, 2015), p. 388.

33. "Obama on the World, with Thomas Friedman."

Chapter 15

1. Helene Cooper and Steven Erlanger, "Military Cuts Render NATO Less Formidable," *New York Times*, March 26, 2014, p. A12 (www.nytimes.com/2014/03/27/world/ europe/military-cuts-render-nato-less-formidable-as-deterrent-to-russia.html).

2. Tim Sullivan and Vladimir Isachenkov, "Russian Troops Seize Crimea," Associated Press, March 1, 2014 (www.bigstory.ap.org/article/crimean-leader-claims-control-military-police).

3. BBC News, "Russian Parliament Approves Troop Deployment in Ukraine," March 1, 2014 (www.bbc.com/news/world-europe-26400035).

4. "Readout of President Obama's Call with President Putin," White House, Office of the Press Secretary, March 1, 2014 (www.whitehouse.gov/the-press-office/2014/03/01/readout-president-obama-s-call-president-putin).

5. Neil MacFarquhar, "Putin Contradicts Claims on Annexation of Crimea," *New York Times*, March 9, 2015 (www.nytimes.com/2015/03/10/world/europe/putin-contrary-to-earlier-assertions-suggests-planning-to-seize-crimea-started-in-early-2014.html?ref=topics&_r=0).

6. Karen DeYoung, "Obama Speaks with Putin by Phone, Calls on Russia to Pull Forces Back to Crimea Bases," *Washington Post*, March 1, 2014 (www.washingtonpost.com/world/national-security/us-and-allies-try-to-decide-on-response-to-ukraine-crisis/2014/03/01/463d1922-a174-11e3-b8d8-94577ff66b28_story.html).

7. BBC News, "Russian Parliament Approves Troop Deployment in Ukraine," March 1, 2014.

8. "Statement Attributable to the Spokesperson for the Secretary-General on Ukraine," United Nations, March 2, 2014 (www.un.org/sg/statements/index.asp?nid=7492).

9. Masha Lipman, "Putin's Crisis Spreads," *New Yorker*, March 8, 2014 (www.newyorker.com/news/news-desk/putins-crisis-spreads).

10. Ben Watson, "Dempsey Reassures NATO Allies on Ukraine," *Defense One*, March 7, 2014 (www.defenseone.com/threats/2014/03/dempsey-reassures-nato-allies-ukraine/80125/?oref=d-interstitial-continue).

11. "Vladimir Putin Answered journalists' Questions on the Situation in Ukraine," President of Russia, March 4, 2014 (http://eng.kremlin.ru/transcripts/6763).

12. "President Putin's Fiction: 10 False Claims about Ukraine," U.S. State Department, March 5, 2014 (www.state.gov/r/pa/prs/ps/2014/03/222988.htm).

13. Robert Mackey, "Russia's Defense Minister Calls Evidence of Troop Presence in Crimea 'Complete Nonsense,'" *New York Times*, March 5, 2014 (http://thelede.blogs.nytimes.com/2014/03/05/russias-defense-minister-calls-evidence-of-troop-presence-in-crimea-complete-nonsense/?_r=0).

14. "Putin Acknowledges Russian Military Servicemen Were in Crimea," RT News, April 17, 2015 (http://rt.com/news/crimea-defense-russian-soldiers-108/).

15. David M. Herszenhorn, "Crimea Votes to Secede from Ukraine as Russian Troops Keep Watch," *New York Times*, March 16, 2014, p. A8 (www.nytimes.com/2014/03/17/world/europe/crimea-ukraine-secession-vote-referendum.html).

16. Ibid.

17. Ibid.

18. "Readout of the President's Call with President Putin," White House, Office of the

Press Secretary, March 16, 2014 (www.whitehouse.gov/the-press-office/2014/03/16/readout-president-s-call-president-putin).

19. "FACT SHEET: Ukraine-Related Sanctions," White House, Office of the Press Secretary, March 16 2014 (www.whitehouse.gov/the-press-office/2014/03/17/fact-sheet-ukraine-related-sanctions).

20. "From Senior State Department Official: Readout of Secretary Kerry's Call with Foreign Minister Lavrov," Embassy of the United States, Kiev, Ukraine, March 16, 2014 (https://ukraine.usembassy.gov/statements/kerrylavrov-03162014.html).

21. Neil MacFarquhar, "Euphoric Russia Turns Thoughts to Ukraine," *New York Times*, June 14, 2014, p. A10 (www.nytimes.com/2014/06/15/world/europe/after-annexing-crimea-euphoric-russia-turns-thoughts-to-ukraine.html).

22. Eurasia.net, "Kiev Making Gains in Religious Dimension of the Ukrainian-Russian Conflict," *Moscow Times,* January 15, 2015 (www.themoscowtimes.com/article.php?id=514436).

23. Amanda Cochran, "Obama Calls on Putin to Move Troops from Ukraine Border," CBS News, March 28, 2014 (www.cbsnews.com/news/obama-calls-on-vladimir-putin-to-move-russian-troops-from-ukraine/).

24. Yuras Karmanau, "In Ukraine's East, Mayor Held Hostage by Insurgent," Associated Press, April 22, 2014 (www.bigstory.ap.org/article/ukraines-east-mayor-held-hostage-insurgent).

25. "Ukraine Says Donetsk 'Anti-terror Operation' Under Way," BBC News, April 16, 2014 (www.bbc.com/news/world-europe-27035196).

26. Miran Jelenek and Maria Tsvetkova, "Dozens Killed in Ukraine Fighting and Fire; OSCE Monitors Freed," Reuters, May 3, 2014 (www.reuters.com/article/2014/05/03/us-ukraine-crisis-idUSBREA400LI20140503).

27. "Press Statements and Replies to Journalists' Questions," President of Russia, May 7, 2014 (http://eng.kremlin.ru/transcripts/7143).

28. "Ukraine Dismisses Putin's Move to De-escalate Tensions as 'Hot Air,'" Euronews, May 8, 2014 (www.euronews.com/2014/05/08/ukraine-dismisses-putin-s-move-to-de-escalate-tensions-as-hot-air).

29. Elizabeth Piper, "Ukraine Ready for Talks with the East, Not with 'Terrorists,'" Reuters, May 8, 2014 (http://uk.reuters.com/article/2014/05/08/uk-ukraine-crisis-talks-idUKKBN0DO08T20140508).

30. "Putin Says Eastern Ukraine Referendum Be Postponed," *The Guardian*, May 8, 2014 (www.theguardian.com/world/2014/may/07/ukraine-crisis-putin-referendum-autonomy-postponed?view=mobile#opt-in-message).

31. BBC News, Europe, "Petro Poroshenko Claims Ukraine Presidency," May 25, 2014 (www.bbc.com/news/world-europe-27569057).

32. Shaun Walker, "Ukraine Says It Controls Donetsk Airport after Fighting Leaves Dozens Dead," *The Guardian*, May 27, 2014 (www.theguardian.com/world/2014/may/27/ukraine-rebel-30-dead-donetsk-airport-air-strikes).

33. Nick Paton Walsh and Laura Smith-Spark, "Ukrainian Military Helicopter

Shot down; 14 Dead, President Says," CNN News, May 29, 2014 (www.cnn.com/2014/05/29/world/europe/ukraine-crisis/).

34. "Allies Enhance NATO Air-Policing Duties in Baltic States, Poland, Romania," North Atlantic Treaty Organization, April 29, 2014 (www.nato.int/cps/en/natolive/news_109354.htm).

35. President Richard Nixon, "Address to the Nation on the Situation in Southeast Asia, April 30, 1970," American Presidency Project (www.presidency.ucsb.edu/ws/index.php?pid=2490&st=&st1=).

36. "Putin Meets Obama, Poroshenko on D-Day Event Sidelines," VOA News, June 6, 2014 (www.voanews.com/content/putin-merkel-meet-on-ukraine-crisis/1930938.html).

37. Ibid.

38. Ibid.

39. "Ukraine Crisis: Russia Condemns Attack on Kiev Embassy," BBC News, June 14, 2014 (www.bbc.com/news/world-europe-27853698).

40. Daniel Sanford, "Ukraine's President Petro Poroshenko Declares Ceasefire," BBC News, June 20, 2014 (www.bbc.com/news/world-europe-27948335).

41. Shaun Walker and Alec Luhn, "Putin Removes Threat of Military Interventions after Ukraine Ceasefire," *The Guardian*, June 25, 2014 (www.theguardian.com/world/2014/jun/24/ukraine-crisis-putin-russia-military-intervention-ceasefire).

42. Laura Smith-Spark, Ben Brumfield, and Mick Krever, "Ukraine Signs EU Deal That Sparked Months of Upheaval; Extends Ceasefire," CNN News, June 27, 2014 (www.cnn.com/2014/06/27/world/europe/ukraine-crisis/index.html).

43. Alan Cullison and James Marson, "Ukraine Suspends Truce, Renews Attacks," *Wall Street Journal*, June 30, 2014 (www.wsj.com/articles/ukraine-fighting-as-cease-fire-due-to-end-1404129631).

44. Shaun Walker, "Ukrainian President Hails Breakthrough as Slavyanks Seized from Separatists," *The Guardian*, July 6, 2014 (www.theguardian.com/world/2014/jul/06/ukraine-forces-seize-slavyansk).

45. "Ukraine Military Plane Shot down as Fighting Rages," BBC News, July 14, 2014 (www.bbc.com/news/world-europe-28299334).

46. Ivan Nechepurenko, "Exerts Say Russian Role in Downed Ukrainian Aircraft Doubtful," *Moscow Times*, July 16, 2014 (www.themoscowtimes.com/news/article/no-evidence-tying-russia-to-downed-ukrainian-aircraft/503588.html).

Chapter 16

1. Shaun Walker and others, "Malaysia Airlines Flight MH17 Crashes in East Ukraine," *The Guardian*, July 17, 2014 (www.theguardian.com/world/2014/jul/17/malaysia-airlines-plane-crash-east-ukraine).

2. Peter Baker, Michael R. Gordon, and Mark Mazzetti, "U.S. Sees Evidence of Russian Links to Jet's Downing," *New York Times*, July 18, 2014 (www.nytimes.com/2014/07/19/world/europe/malaysia-airlines-plane-ukraine.html?_r=0).

3. Alec Luhn, "Three Pro-Russia Rebel Leaders at the Centre of Suspicions over Downed MH17," *The Guardian*, July 20, 2014 (www.theguardian.com/world/2014/jul/20/three-pro-russia-rebel-leaders-suspects-over-downed-mh17).

4. "Vladimir Putin: Ukraine Bears Responsibility for Crash of Malaysian Airliner," Associated Press, July 17, 2014 (http://politi.co/1jUU8W8).

5. "Background Conference Call on Ukraine," White House, Office of the Press Secretary, July 29, 2014 (www.whitehouse.gov/the-press-office/2014/07/29/background-conference-call-ukraine).

6. Leon Aron, "Putin Is Courting the Home Crowd," *Los Angeles Times*, July 29, 2014 (www.latimes.com/opinion/op-ed/la-oe-aron-putin-ukraine-russia-20140730-story.html).

7. Neil MacFarquhar, "A Russian Convoy Carrying Aid Is Dogged by Suspicion," *New York Times*, August 12, 2014, p. A6 (www.nytimes.com/2014/08/13/world/europe/russian-convoy-leaves-moscow-for-ukraine-bearing-aid.html).

8. Andrew Roth, "A Separatist Militia in Ukraine with Russian Fighters Holds a Key," *New York Times*, June 4, 2014 (www.nytimes.com/2014/06/05/world/europe/in-ukraine-separatist-militia-with-russian-fighters-holds-a-key.html?_r=0).

9. Andrew E. Kramer, "Separatist Cadre Hopes for a Reprise in Ukraine," *New York Times*, August 3, 2014 (http://www.nytimes.com/2014/08/04/world/europe/separatist-pro-russian-leadership-in-eastern-ukraine-with-a-goal-of-establishing-government.html?_r=0).

10. Anna Nemstova, "Putin's Number One Gunman in Ukraine Warns Him Defeat Possible," *Daily Beast*, July 25, 2014 (www.thedailybeast.com/articles/2014/07/25/putin-s-number-one-gunman-in-ukraine-warns-him-of-possible-defeat.html).

11. Andrew Kramer, "Putin Trumpets Economic Strength, but Advisers Seem Less Certain," *New York Times*, October 2, 2014, p. A4 (www.nytimes.com/2014/10/03/world/europe/putin-russia-economy.html?_r=0).

12. Ben Hoyle, "Russia 'Two Years from Meltdown' as Economic Distress Grows," *The Times*, November 29, 2014 (www.theaustralian.com.au/news/world/russia-two-years-from-meltdown-as-economic-distress-grows/story-e6frg6so-1227138724839).

13. Henry Meyer, Irina Reznik, and Ilya Arkhipov, "Russian Billionaires in 'Horror' as Putin Risks Isolation," Bloomberg News, July 21, 2014 (www.bloomberg.com/news/articles/2014-07-20/russian-billionaires-in-horror-as-putin-risks-isolation).

14. "A Wounded Economy," *The Economist*, November 22, 2014 (www.economist.com/news/leaders/21633813-it-closer-crisis-west-or-vladimir-putin-realise-wounded-economy).

15. Delphine d'Amora, "Putin Strikes Back against Sanctions with Food Import Bans," *Moscow Times*, August 6, 2014 (www.themoscowtimes.com/article.php?id=504675).

16. Evgenia Pismennaya and Irina Reznik, "Putin Said to Stun Advisers by Backing Corruption Crackdown," Bloomberg News, November 19, 2014 (www.

bloomberg.com/news/articles/2014-11-18/putin-said-to-back-crackdown-on-corruption-as-sanctions-bite).

17. "BBC Team under Attack in Southern Russia," BBC News, September 18, 2014 (http://www.bbc.com/news/world-europe-29249642).

18. Neil MacFarquhar and Michael R. Gordon, "Ukraine Leader Says 'Huge Load of Arms' Pour in from Russia," *New York Times*, August 28. 2014 (www.nytimes.com/2014/08/29/world/europe/ukraine-conflict.html?_r=0).

19. Ivo Daalder and others, "Preserving Ukraine's Independence, Resisting Russian Aggression: What the United States and NATO Must Do," Atlantic Council, Brookings, Chicago Council on Global Affairs, February 2015 (www.thechicagocouncil.org/sites/default/files/UkraineReport_February2015_FINAL.pdf).

20. "Ukraine crisis: Poroshenko Says 'Roadmap' to Ceasefire with Russia Possible," Reuters, August 26, 2014 (www.cbc.ca/news/world/ukraine-crisis-poroshenko-says-roadmap-to-ceasefire-with-russia-possible-1.2746851).

21. "Ukraine Crisis: Troops Abandon Lugansk Airport after Clashes," BBC News, September 1, 2014 (www.bbc.com/news/world-europe-29009516).

22. "NATO Rapid Response Force: Plan to Boost Europe Presence," BBC News, September 1, 2014 (www.bbc.com/news/world-europe-29016170).

23. "Russia 'to Alter Military Strategy towards NATO,'" BBC News, September 2, 2014 (www.bbc.com/news/world-europe-29026623).

24. "Press Briefing by Press Secretary Josh Earnst," White House, Office of the Press Secretary, September 2, 2014 (www.whitehouse.gov/the-press-office/2014/09/02/press-briefing-press-secretary-josh-earnest-922014).

25. "Nato Summit: Alliance 'Stands with Ukraine,'" BBC News, September 4, 2014 (www.bbc.com/news/world-europe-29056870).

26. "Ukraine to Seek NATO Membership, Says PM Yatsenyuk," BBC News, August 29, 2104 (www.bbc.com/news/world-europe-28978699).

27. "Opening Remarks by NATO Secretary General Anders Fogh Rasmussen at the Meeting of the NATO-Ukraine Commission at the Level of Heads of State and Government during the NATO Summit Held in Newport," NATO, September 4, 2104 (www.nato.int/cps/en/natohq/opinions_112482.htm).

28. "Nato Summit: Alliance 'Stands with Ukraine.'"

29. "Ukraine and Pro-Russia Rebels Sign Ceasefire Deal," BBC News, September 5, 2014 (www.bbc.com/news/world-europe-29082574).

30. "Poroshenko, Putin Agree Ukraine Truce Holding," Radio Free Europe/Radio Liberty, September 6, 2014 (www.rferl.org/content/article/26569719.html).

31. "Seliger 2014 National Youth Forum," President of Russia, August 29, 2014 (http://eng.kremlin.ru/transcripts/22864).

32. David M. Herszenhorn, "Parliamentary Elections Show Political Turmoil is Continuing in Ukraine," *New York Times*, October 25, 2014, p. A13 (www.nytimes.com/2014/10/26/world/europe/parliamentary-elections-show-political-turmoil-is-continuing-in-ukraine-.html?_r=0)/.

33. Ibid.

34. "Poroshenko: EU Leaders Press Putin on Rebel Votes," Radio Free Europe/Radio Liberty, October 31, 2014 (www.rferl.org/content/ukraine-russia-eu-elections/26667998.html).

35. Andrew E. Kramer, "Rebel-Backed Elections to Cement Status Quo in Ukraine," *New York Times*, November 2, 2014 (www.nytimes.com/2014/11/03/world/europe/rebel-backed-elections-in-eastern-ukraine.html?_r=0).

36. Thomas Grove and Richard Balmforth, "Ukraine Crisis Deepens after Rebel Vote in East," Reuters, November 3, 2014 (www.reuters.com/article/2014/11/03/us-ukraine-crisis-rebel-election-idUSKBN0IL3AP20141103).

37. Ibid.

38. "Kyiv Says 200 Rebels Killed, Russian Tanks, Troops Cross over Border," Radio Free Europe/Radio Liberty, November 7, 2014 (www.rferl.org/content/ukraine-russia-border-crossed-military/26679428.html).

39. "Ukraine Crisis: Russian Troops Crossed Border, Nato says," BBC News, November 12, 2014 (www.bbc.co.uk/news/world-europe-30025138).

40. "Kyiv Says 200 Rebels Killed, Russian Tanks, Troops Cross over Border," Radio Free Europe/Radio Liberty, November 7, 2014 (www.rferl.org/content/ukraine-russia-border-crossed-military/26679428.html).

41. "Large Military Convoys Seen in Eastern Ukraine," Radio Free Europe/Radio Liberty, November 8, 2014 (www.rferl.org/content/ukraine-large-rebel-military-convoy/26681070.html).

42. "Ukraine Crisis: Tanks 'Cross Border' from Russia," BBC News, November 7, 2014 (http://www.bbc.co.uk/news/world-europe-29952505).

43. Neil MacFarquhar, "Ukraine Accuses Russia of Sending Tanks across Border," *New York Times*, November 7, 2014 (www.nytimes.com/2014/11/08/world/europe/ukraine-accuses-russia-of-sending-tanks-and-troops-across-border.html?_r=0).

44. "Putin Discusses 'Deterioration' in East Ukraine, Kiev Denies Fresh Offensive," Reuters, November 6, 2014 (www.reuters.com/article/2014/11/06/us-ukraine-crisis-military-idUSKBN0IQ1RJ20141106).

45. Oliver Carroll, "Welcome to the Cossack People's Republic of Stakhanov," *Politico*, November 2, 2014 (www.politico.com/magazine/story/2014/11/welcome-to-the-cossack-peoples-republic-of-stakhanov-112420.html#.VRa4qUvl-sZ).

46. Sebastian Smith, "Ukraine Soldiers to Government: We're Coming for You Next," Agence France-Presse, October 31, 2014 (http://news.yahoo.com/ukraine-soldiers-government-were-coming-next-155843129.html).

Chapter 17

1. Neil MacFarquhar, "Conflict Uncovers a Ukrainian Identity Crisis over Deep Russian Roots," *New York Times*, October 18, 2014 (www.nytimes.com/2014/10/19/world/europe/conflict-uncovers-a-ukrainian-identity-crisis-over-deep-russian-roots-.html).

2. Ibid.

3. Ibid.

4. Anders Aslund, *Ukraine, What Went Wrong and How to Fix It* (Washington: Peterson Institute for International Economics Press, 2015), p. xi.

5. Steven Pifer, "Taking Stock in Ukraine," *American Interest*, October 28, 2014 (www.the-american-interest.com/2014/10/28/taking-stock-in-ukraine/).

6. Peter Spiegel and Roman Olearchyk," IMF Warns Ukraine Bailout at Risk of Collapse," *Financial Times*, December 10, 2014.

7. "Ukraine's New Minister of Economic Development Says Ukraine Is Bankrupt," TASS, December 10, 2014.

8. Christian Caryl, "The Other War in Ukraine," *Foreign Policy*, December 11, 2014 (http://foreignpolicy.com/2014/12/11/the-other-war-in-ukraine/).

9. Adrian Karatnycky, "Ukraine's Rising Warlords," *Washington Post*, December 31, 2014, p. A13 (www.washingtonpost.com/opinions/the-rise-of-warlords-threatens-ukraines-recovery/2014/12/30/a23b2d36-8f7b-11e4-a412-4b735edc7175_story.html).

10. Cynthia Blank, "Swastikas Painted on Babi Yar Monument in Kiev," Reuters, November 17, 2014. Also see "Swastikas Painted on Babi Yar Memorial, Jewish School," Jewish Telegraph Agency, November 17, 2014 (www.jta.org/2014/11/17/news-opinion/world/swastikas-painted-on-babi-yar-memorial-jewish-school.).

11. "Statement by IMF Managing Director Christine Lagarde on Ukraine," International Monetary Fund, March 11, 2015 (www.imf.org/external/np/sec/pr/2015/pr15105.htm).

12. George Soros, "Wake Up, Europe," *New York Review of Books*, November 20, 2014, p. 6 (www.nybooks.com/articles/archives/2014/nov/20/wake-up-europe/).

13. "Soros Urges Giving Ukraine $50 Billion of Aid to Foil Russia," Reuters, January 8, 2015 (www.reuters.com/article/2015/01/08/us-ukraine-crisis-soros-idUSKBN0KH0NQ20150108).

14. George Soros, "Wake Up, Europe."

15. Ibid.

16. Indira Lakshmanan, "Congress Passes Tougher Russia Sanctions," *Bloomberg Businessweek*, December 12, 2014 (www.bloomberg.com/politics/articles/2014-12-12/congress-passes-tougher-russia-sanctions-but-gives-obama-leeway).

17. "Statement by the President on the Ukraine Freedom Support Act," White House, Office of the Press Secretary, December 28, 2014 (www.whitehouse.gov/the-press-office/2014/12/18/statement-president-ukraine-freedom-support-act).

18. David M. Herszenhorn, "Ukraine Vote Takes Nation a Step Closer to NATO," *New York Times*, December 23, 2014 (www.nytimes.com/2014/12/24/world/europe/ukraine-parliament-nato-vote.html).

19. Ibid.

20. David M. Herszenhorn, "A Tilt toward NATO in Ukraine as Parliament Meets," *New York Times*, November 28, 2014, p. A14 (www.nytimes.com/2014/11/28/world/europe/a-tilt-toward-nato-in-ukraine-as-parliament-meets.html?partner=rss&emc=rss&_r=0).

21. Geoff Cutmore and Antonia Matthews, "Russia-US Relations Reset 'Impossible': PM Medvedev," CNBC, October 15, 2014 (www.cnbc.com/id/102086463#.).

22. Polina Devitt, "Lavrov Accuses West of Seeking 'Regime Change' in Russia," Reuters, November 22, 2014 (www.reuters.com/article/2014/11/22/us-ukraine-crisis-idUSKCN0J609G20141122).

23. Lynn Berry, "Vladimir Putin Says He Won't Be Russia's President for Life," Associated Press, November 23, 2014 (www.cbc.ca/news/world/vladimir-putin-says-he-won-t-be-russia-s-president-for-life-1.2846199).

24. Masha Gessen, *The Man without a Face,* (New York: Riverhead Books, 2012), p. 262.

25. Berry, "Vladimir Putin Says He Won't Be Russia's President for Life."

26. Julia Joffe, "After Boris Nemtsov's Assassination, 'There Are No longer Limits,'" *New York Times Magazine,* February 28, 2015 (www.nytimes.com/2015/02/28/magazine/after-boris-nemtsovs-assassination-there-are-no-longer-any-limits.html).

27. "Security Council meeting," President of Russia, November 20, 2014 (http://eng.kremlin.ru/transcripts/23268).

28. Serge Schmemann, "Once Again, Art in Russia Carries Moral and Political Overtones," *New York Times,* July 11, 2014 (www.nytimes.com/2014/07/11/opinion/once-again-art-in-russia-carries-moral-and-political-overtones.html).

29. Katie Zavadski, "Putin's Birthday Present Is a Hercules-Themed Art Show about How Manly and Amazing He Is," *New York Magazine,* Daily Intelligencer, October 6, 2014 (http://nymag.com/daily/intelligencer/2014/10/putin-birthday-present-hercules-art-show.html).

30. Gabriela Baczynska, "Putin Says Russia Not Isolated over Ukraine, Blames West for Frosty Ties," Reuters, November 23, 2014 (www.reuters.com/article/2014/11/23/us-russia-putin-idUSKCN0J709320141123).

31. Andrew E. Kramer, "Unpaid Russian Workers Unite in Protest against Putin," *New York Times,* April 21, 2015 (www.nytimes.com/2015/04/22/world/europe/russian-workers-take-aim-at-putin-as-economy-exacts-its-toll.html?ref=topics&_r=0).

32. Gessen (2012), p. 254.

33. "Corruption Perceptions Index 2014," Transparency International (www.transparency.org/cpi2014/results).

34. Richard Pipes, "The Cleverness of Joseph Stalin," *New York Review of Books,* November 20, 2014, p. 37.

35. Jackson Diehl, "Eastern Europeans Are Bowing to Putin's Power," *Washington Post,* October 13, 2014 (www.washingtonpost.com/opinions/jackson-diehl-eastern-europeans-are-bowing-to-putins-power/2014/10/12/2adbf4c2-4fd0-11e4-babe-e91da079cb8a_story.html).

36. Andrew C. Kuchins, "Will Economy be Putin's Downfall?," CNN Opinion, December 7, 2014 (http://edition.cnn.com/2014/12/07/opinion/kuchins-putin-economy-problems/index.html).

37. Dmitry Zhdannikov and Vladimir Soldatkin, "Kremlin Corp Debt Weighs in West's Standoff with Russia," Reuters, March 11, 2014 (www.reuters.com/article/2014/03/11/ukraine-crisis-russia-debt-idUSL6N0M72U720140311).

38. Andrey Biryuko and Anna Andrianova, "Russia Sets Terms for Capital Amnesty to 'Correct Past Mistakes,'" Bloomberg News, March 26, 2015 (www.bloomberg.com/news/articles/2015-03-26/russia-sets-terms-for-capital-amnesty-to-correct-past-mistakes-).

39. "Presidential Address to the Federal Assembly," President of Russia, December 4, 2014 (http://eng.kremlin.ru/transcripts/23341).

40. "The Winter of Mr. Putin's Discontent," *New York Times*, December 5, 2014 (www.nytimes.com/2014/12/05/opinion/the-winter-of-mr-putins-discontent.html?_r=0).

41. Michael Birnbaum, "In Kremlin Speech, Putin Rails at West, Tries to Bolster Economy as Recession Looms," *Washington Post*, December 4, 2014 (www.washingtonpost.com/world/europe/in-kremlin-economy-speech-putin-rails-at-west-tries-to-avert-russia-recession/2014/12/04/f940afe8-79b4-11e4-8241-8cc0a3670239_story.html).

42. "Presidential Address to the Federal Assembly."

43. Ibid.

44. "Putin's People," *The Economist*, December 13, 2014 (www.economist.com/news/europe/21636047-president-remains-popular-his-ukrainian-adventure-could-change-faster-many).

45. Neil MacFarquhar and Andrew E. Kramer, "With Russia on Brink of Recession, Putin Faces 'New Reality,'" *New York Times*, December 3, 2014, p. A6 (www.nytimes.com/2014/12/03/business/russia-forecasts-a-recession-in-2015-signaling-a-toll-from-sanctions-and-oil-prices.html?_r=0).

46. Katya Golubkova, "Western Sanctions May Last for Decades: Russian Minister Tells Newspaper," Reuters, December 18, 2014 (www.reuters.com/article/2014/12/18/us-russia-crisis-sanctions-idUSKBN0JW0GN20141218).

47. "Putin's People," *The Economist*, December 13, 2014.

48. "Transcript of President Obama's Full NPR Interview," NPR, December 29, 2014 (www.npr.org/2014/12/29/372485968/transcript-president-obamas-full-npr-interview).

49. "News conference of Vladimir Putin," President of Russia, December 18, 2014 (http://eng.kremlin.ru/transcripts/23406).

50. Marina Koreneva, "Patriotism, Adventure Lure Russian Volunteers to Ukraine Conflict," Agence France-Presse, March 6, 2015 (www.digitaljournal.com/news/world/patriotism-adventure-lure-russian-volunteers-to-ukraine-conflict/article/427643).

51. Michael Birnbaum, "Russia's Anti-American Fever Goes beyond the Soviet Era's," *Washington Post*, March 8, 2015 (www.washingtonpost.com/world/europe/russias-anti-us-sentiment-now-is-even-worse-than-it-was-in-soviet-union/2015/03/08/b7d534c4-c357-11e4-a188-8e4971d37a8d_story.html).

52. Ivo Daalder and others, "Preserving Ukraine's Independence, Resisting Russian Aggression: What the United States and NATO Must Do," Atlantic Council, Brookings Institution, Chicago Council on Global Affairs, February 2015, p. 1 (www.thechicagocouncil.org/sites/default/files/UkraineReport_February2015_FINAL.pdf).

53. "Mr. Putin Resumes His War in Ukraine," *New York Times* editorial, February 2, 2015, p. 18 (www.nytimes.com/2015/02/02/opinion/mr-putin-resumes-his-war-in-ukraine.html?ref=opinion&_r=0).

54. Alison Smale, "German Chancellor Rules out Weapons Aid to Ukraine," *New York Times*, February 2, 2015, p. A9 (www.nytimes.com/2015/02/03/world/german-chancellor-rules-out-weapons-aid-to-ukraine.html?_r=0).

55. Andrew E. Kramer, "Ukraine Rebels Celebrate Their Taking of Debaltseve," *New York Times*, February 23, 2015 (www.nytimes.com/2015/02/24/world/europe/ukraine-rebels-celebrate-victory-at-strategic-city-with-a-festive-rally.html).

56. "Cease-Fire Deal Offers 'Glimmer of Hope' after Ukraine Peace Talks," Reuters, February 12, 2015 (www.themoscowtimes.com/news/article/agreement-reached-after-overnight-peace-talks-in-minsk/515808.html).

57. Eugene Rumer, "From Inside Putin's Parallel Universe," *Financial Times*, December 22, 2014 (http://carnegieendowment.org/2014/12/22/from-inside-putin-s-parallel-universe-crisis-looks-bright/hxsr).

58. Christian Neef, "The Isolation of Donetsk: A Visit to Europe's Absurd New Border," Spiegel Online International, March 9, 2015 (www.spiegel.de/international/europe/ukraine-ceasefire-leaves-donetsk-isolated-a-1022234.html).

Chapter 18

1. "The World's Most Powerful People," *Forbes* 2014 Ranking (www.forbes.com/profile/vladimir-putin/); and "What Our Experts Think about the World," Carnegie Endowment for International Peace, November 2014 (http://carnegieendowment.org/specialprojects/YearInCrisis2014/index.cfm/?fa=survey).

2. "Mr. Putin Amplifies His Anti-Western Propaganda," *Washington Post* editorial, November 13, 2014 (www.washingtonpost.com/opinions/mr-putin-amplifies-his-anti-western-propaganda/2014/11/13/9e628b9c-69f5-11e4-b053-65cea7903f2e_story.html).

3. "Putin's Reach: Merkel Concerned about Russian Influence in the Balkans," Spiegel Online International, November 17, 2014 (www.spiegel.de/international/europe/germany-worried-about-russian-influence-in-the-balkans-a-1003427.html).

4. Karl W. Deutsch, "External Involvement in Internal War," in Harry Eckstein, ed., *Internal War, Problems and Approaches* (New York: Free Press of Glencoe, 1964).

5. Noah Barkin and Andreas Rinke, "Merkel Hits Diplomatic Dead-End with Putin," Reuters, November 25, 2014 (www.reuters.com/article/2014/11/25/us-ukraine-crisis-germany-insight-idUSKCN0J91EN20141125).

6. George Packer, "The Quiet German," *The New Yorker*, December 1, 2014 (www.newyorker.com/magazine/2014/12/01/quiet-german).

7. Barkin and Rinke, "Merkel Hits Diplomatic Dead-End with Putin."

8. "Meeting of the Valdai Discussion Club," October 24, 2014 (http://eng.kremlin.ru/transcripts/23137).

9. "Address to the Federal Assembly," President of Russia, April 25, 2005 (http://archive.kremlin.ru/eng/speeches/2005/04/25/2031_type70029type82912_87086.shtml).

10. "Putin: New Serious Conflicts Involving World Powers Possible," TASS, October 24, 2014 (http://tass.ru/en/russia/756311).

11. Ibid.

12. "Dialogue on the Crisis with Russia," Aspen Institute, November 21, 2014 (www.aspeninstitute.org/video/dialogue-crisis-russia).

13. Maxim Korshunov, "Mikhail Gorbachev: I Am against All Walls," Russia Beyond the Headlines, October 16, 2014 (http://rbth.com/international/2014/10/16/mikhail_gorbachev_i_am_against_all_walls_40673.html).

14. "Russian and Chinese Assertiveness Poses New Foreign Policy Challenges: A Conversation with Robert M. Gates," Council on Foreign Relations, May 21, 2014 (www.cfr.org/defense-and-security/russian-chinese-assertiveness-poses-new-foreign-policy-challenges/p35645).

15. Ibid.

16. "Do We Achieve World Order through Chaos or Insight?," Interview with Henry Kissinger, Spiegel Online International, November 13, 2014 (www.spiegel.de/international/world/interview-with-henry-kissinger-on-state-of-global-politics-a-1002073-druck.html).

17. Stephen Kotkin and Strobe Talbott, "Putin and Russian Power in the World: The Stalin Legacy," Brookings Institution discussion, December 1, 2014 (audio at www.brookings.edu/events/2014/12/01-putin-and-russian-power-stalin).

18. Samuel Charap, "Is a Stable Agreement Possible between Russia and Ukraine?," International Institute for Strategic Studies, November 1, 2014 (www.iiss.org/en/expert%20commentary/blogsections/2014-051a/november-dcf3/is-a-stable-agreement-possible-between-russia-and-ukraine-415c).

19. Ibid.

Chapter 19

1. Andrew E. Kramer, "Russian Consumers Reflect the Pinch of Economic Sanctions," *New York Times*, April 10, 2015, p. B1 (www.nytimes.com/2015/04/10/business/international/in-moscow-economic-sanctions-rattle-malls.html?_r=0).

2. Bridget Kendall, "Russians Reel from Economic Crisis," BBC News, April 13, 2015 (www.bbc.com/news/world-europe-32220335).

3. "Putin's War on the West," *The Economist*, February 14, 2015 (www.economist.com/news/leaders/21643189-ukraine-suffers-it-time-recognise-gravity-russian-threatand-counter).

4. Shaun Walker, "Salutin' Putin: Inside a Russian Troll House," *The Guardian*, April 2, 2015 (www.theguardian.com/world/2015/apr/02/putin-kremlin-inside-russian-troll-house).

5. Neil MacFarquhar and Sophia Kishkovsky, "Russian History Receives a Makeover That Starts with Ivan the Terrible," *New York Times*, March 31, 2015, p. A4 (www.nytimes.com/2015/03/31/world/europe/russian-museum-seeks-a-warmer-adjective-for-ivan-the-terrible.html?_r=0).

6. "Ukraine Conflict: Putin 'Was Ready for Nuclear Alert,'" BBC News, March 15, 2015 (www.bbc.com/news/world-europe-31899680).

7. Fiona Hill and Clifford G. Gaddy, *Mr. Putin: Operative in the Kremlin*, 2nd ed. (Brookings, 2015), p. 391.

8. Anna Smolchenko, "Putin's Mystery Military Award Points to Ukraine Involvement," Agence France-Presse, March 27, 2015 (http://news.yahoo.com/putins-mystery-military-award-points-ukraine-involvement-212125679.html).

9. Andrew E. Kramer, "Putin Returns after Curious Absence and Shrugs off Rumors," *New York Times*, March 16, 2015 (www.nytimes.com/2015/03/17/world/europe/vladimir-putin-rumors.html?_r=0).

10. Sarah Rainsford, "Brand Putin: Russia's President Still in Fashion 15 Years On," BBC News, March 27, 2015 (www.bbc.com/news/world-europe-32076836).

11. David M. Herszenhorn, "A Year after Seizing Crimea, Putin Celebrates as Ukraine Seethes," *New York Times*, March 19, 2015, p. A9 (www.nytimes.com/2015/03/19/world/europe/a-year-after-seizing-crimea-putin-celebrates-as-ukraine-seethes.html?_r=0).

12. "Agreement on Principles of Settlement of the Georgian-Ossetian Conflict," Sochi, Russia, June 24, 1992 (http://peacemaker.un.org/sites/peacemaker.un.org/files/GE%20RU_920624_AgreemenOnPrinciplesOfSettlementGeorgianOssetianConflict.pdf).

13. Charles King, "The Five-Day War: Managing Moscow after the Georgia Crisis," *Foreign Affairs*, November-December 2008 (www.foreignaffairs.com/articles/64602/charles-king/the-five-day-war).

14. Dan Bilefsky, "Kosovo Declares Independence From Serbia," *New York Times*, February 18, 2008 (www.nytimes.com/2008/02/18/world/europe/18kosovo.html?pagewanted=all&_r=0).

15. David M. Herszenhorn, "A Year after Seizing Crimea, Putin Celebrates as Ukraine Seethes," *New York Times*, March 19, 2015, p. A9.

16. David T. Koyzis, "Solzhenitsyn on Russia and Ukraine," *First Things*, March 28, 2014 (www.firstthings.com/blogs/firstthoughts/2014/03/solzhenitsyn-on-russia-and-ukraine).

17. Ian Johnston, "Russia Threatens to Use 'Nuclear Force' over Crimea and the Baltic States," *The Independent*, April 2, 2015 (www.independent.co.uk/news/

world/europe/russia-threatens-to-use-nuclear-force-over-crimea-and-the-baltic-states-10150565.html).

18. Herszenhorn, "A Year after Seizing Crimea, Putin Celebrates as Ukraine Seethes."

19. Graham Alison and Dimitri K. Simes, "Russia and America: Stumbling to War," *National Interest*, April 20, 2015 (http://nationalinterest.org/feature/russia-america-stumbling-war-12662).

20. Stuart Garlick and Mary Sibierski, "Estonians Vote under Shadow of Resurgent Russia," Agence France-Presse, March 2, 2015 (https://sg.news.yahoo.com/nerves-over-russia-overshadow-estonian-election-050254844.html).

21. Ian Johnston, "Russia Threatens to Use 'Nuclear Force' over Crimea and the Baltic States," *The Independent*, April 2, 2015.

22. Ibid.

23. "US Sends Heavy Armour to Baltic States to 'Deter' Russia," Agence France-Presse, March 9, 2015 (http://news.yahoo.com/us-sends-heavy-armour-baltic-states-deter-russia-132033780.html).

24. Mike Collier and Mary Sibierski, "NATO Allies Come to Grips with Russia's 'Hybrid Warfare,'" Agence France-Presse, March 18, 2015 (www.france24.com/en/20150318-nato-allies-come-grips-with-russias-hybrid-warfare/).

25. "ESDP and NATO: Better Cooperation in View of the New Security Challenges," speech by Alexander Vershbow, Riga, Latvia, March 5, 2015 (www.nato.int/cps/en/natohq/opinions_117919.htm).

26. Collier and Sibierski, "NATO Allies Come to Grips with Russia's 'Hybrid Warfare.'"

27. Ibid.

28. David Blair, "Sitting Near a Nuclear Tripwire, Estonia's President Urges Nato to Send Troops to Defend His Country," *The Telegraph,* April 11, 2015 (www.president.ee/en/media/interviews/11263-qsitting-near-a-nuclear-tripwire-estonias-president-urges-nato-to-send-troops-to-defend-his-countryq-the-telegraph/index.html).

29. Andrew Higgins, "Norway Reverts to Cold War Mode as Russian Air Patrols Spike," *New York Times*, April 2, 2015, p. A1 (www.nytimes.com/2015/04/02/world/europe/a-newly-assertive-russia-jolts-norways-air-defenses-into-action.html?_r=0).

30. Sveinung Berg Bentzrod, "Russian Aggression: Nordic States Extend Their Military Cooperation," *Aftenposten*, April 9, 2015 (http://www.aftenposten.no/nyheter/uriks/Russian-aggression-Nordic-states-extend-their-military-cooperation-7975109.html).

31. "Russia's Next Target," *Wall Street Journal*, April 9, 2015.

32. Ilya Ponomarev, "In Exile, but Ready to Save Russia," *New York Times*, April 16, 2015 (www.nytimes.com/2015/04/16/opinion/in-exile-but-ready-to-save-russia.html?_r=0).

33. Andrew E. Kramer, "Unpaid Russian Workers Unite in Protest Against Putin," *New York Times*, April 21, 2015 (www.nytimes.com/2015/04/22/world/

europe/russian-workers-take-aim-at-putin-as-economy-exacts-its-toll.html?
ref=topics&_r=0).

34. Alessandra Prentice, "War and Poverty Bring Doubt to Heartland of Ukraine's
Pro-Europe Revolt," Reuters, April 10, 2015 (www.reuters.com/article/2015/04/10/
us-ukraine-crisis-west-idUSKBN0N112E20150410).

35. Karoun Demirjian, "Ukraine's Military Mobilization Undermined by Draft
Dodgers," *Washington Post*, April 26, 2015 (http://www.washingtonpost.com/world/
europe/ukraines-military-mobilization-undermined-by-draft-dodgers/2015/04/25/
fc3a5818-d236-11e4-8b1e-274d670aa9c9_story.html).

36. Claire Rosenberg and Oleksandr Savochenko, "Russia Lashes Out at Law to
Erase Ukraine's Soviet Past," Agence France-Presse, April 10, 2015.

37. "Ukraine Sets Sights on Joining NATO," Reuters, April 9, 2015 (www.reuters.
com/article/2015/04/09/us-ukraine-crisis-nato-membership-idUSKBN0N01OW
20150409).

38. Steven Kull, "The Ukrainian People on the Current Crisis," Program for Public
Consultation and Kiev International Institute of Sociology, March 9, 2015 (www.
public-consultation.org/studies/Ukraine_0315.pdf).

39. Andrew Roth, "U.S. Army Trainers Arrive in Ukraine," *New York Times*, April
17, 2015 (www.nytimes.com/2015/04/18/world/europe/us-army-trainers-arrive-in-
ukraine.html?_r=0).

Index

Slovakia, 7, 84, 200
Slovenia, 7
Sloviansk, 164, 171
Snowden, Edward, 14
Sobchak, Anatoly, 107
Sochi Olympics (2014), 144–46, 231
Socialist Party (Austria), 73
Social media, 236
Sokolov, Nikita P., 226
Sokolov, Oleg, 227
Solana, Javier, 131
Solovyov, Vladimir, 22
Solzhenitsyn, Alexander, 111, 231–32
Soros, George, 193
South Ossetia, 134, 146, 160, 229–30
Soviet Union: education system in, 24;
    fall of, 4, 6, 107–15; rise of, 75–77; in
    World War II, 81–89. *See also* Russia;
    specific leaders
Spain, 6
Stalin, Josef, 77–80; and birth of
    Ukraine, 189, 220; on drought in
    Ukraine, 90; and Lenin, 73; and
    Marxism, 73–74; and nationalism in
    Ukraine, 76; and Orthodox faith, 23;
    public opinion on, 199; on Ukraine
    as independent nation after World
    War II, 90; and World War II, 82
State Department (U.S.), 161
Strelkov, Igor, 176
Sudetenland, 81
Suvorov, Aleksandr, 56, 57, 60
Suzdal, 34, 36
Svyatoslav I (Kievan prince), 30, 31
Sweden, 48, 49–50, 57
Syria, 17–18
Szporluk, Roman, 86, 89

Tajikistan, 110
Talbott, Strobe, 9
"Tale of Bygone Years" (Nestor), 32
Taras Bulba (Gogol), 45–46, 63
Tarasiuk, Borys, 133
Terek, 54
Terrorism, 3–4, 13, 224

Three Sisters (Chekhov), 118
Totalitarianism, 8–9
Transcarpathia, 69, 75, 81
Transcaucasian Federation, 114
Transnistria, 1, 232, 237–38
Transparency International, 198
Treaty of Kuchuk Kainarji (1774), 54,
    56, 57
Treaty of Nerchinsk (1689), 52
Treaty of Riga (1921), 72
Trudolyubov, Maxim, 147
Tsars, 40, 43–60. *See also specific tsars*
Tulip Revolution (Kyrgyzstan), 134
Turchynov, Oleksandr, 153–54, 158, 165,
    243
Turkey: and NATO, 6, 16; Poland's alli-
    ance with, 54; Russia's conflicts with,
    56–58
Tver, 40
Tyagnibok, Oleg, 144
Tymoshenko, Semen, 82
Tymoshenko, Yulia: election campaign
    of, 182; governance of, 188; and
    Maidan protests, 153; reforms of,
    135–39; rise to power, 125–27, 128

Ukraine: anticommunist demon-
    strations in, 100; birth of, 67–72;
    and Bolshevik Revolution, 68–72;
    borders of, 189; and Catherine the
    Great, 53–55; cease-fire in, 179–82;
    civil war in, 163–67; and cold war,
    90–101; Crimea transferred to,
    91–94, 119–20; culture in, 76–77,
    118; diplomacy in, 219; drought in,
    76, 90–91; economic reforms needed
    in, 122, 184, 190–93, 241; educa-
    tion system in, 65; elections in, 27,
    109, 123, 130–32, 167–68, 182–85;
    famine in, 78–79; future of, 223–50;
    gerontocracy in, 96–99; identity
    crisis in, 188, 219–20; independence
    movement in, 99–101; independence
    of, 116–39; long-term strategies
    for, 228–29; Maidan Revolution in,